MW00989242

OSPREY
PUBLISHING

BRITISH BATTLE TANKS

BRITISH-MADE TANKS OF WORLD WAR II

DAVID FLETCHER

First published in Great Britain in 2017 by Osprey Publishing,
PO Box 883, Oxford, OX1 9PL, UK
1385 Broadway, 5th Floor, New York, NY 10018, USA
E-mail: info@ospreypublishing.com
Osprey Publishing, part of Bloomsbury Publishing Plc

Some of the material in this book has been previously published by Osprey Publishing as: New Vanguard 8 *Matilda Infantry Tank 1938–45* by David Fletcher; New Vanguard 14 *Crusader and Covenanter Cruiser Tanks 1939–45* by David Fletcher; New Vanguard 136 *Churchill Crocodile Flamethrower* by David Fletcher; New Vanguard 104 *Cromwell Cruiser Tank 1942–50* by David Fletcher and Richard Harley; and New Vanguard 233 *Valentine Infantry Tank 1938–45* by Bruce Oliver Newsome Ph.D Artwork is by Peter Sarson, Tony Bryan and Henry Morshead © Osprey Publishing. All photographs are © The Tank Museum, Bovington

A CIP catalogue record for this book is available from the British Library.

ISBN: 978 1 4728 2003 7
PDF e-book ISBN: 978 1 4728 2004 4
ePub e-book ISBN: 978 1 4728 2149 2
XML ISBN: 978 1 4728 2150 8

Index by Zoe Ross
Typeset in Adobe Garamond and Swiss 721
Originated by PDQ Media, Bungay, UK
Printed in China through World Print Ltd.

17 18 19 20 21 10 9 8 7 6 5 4 3 2 1

Front cover: © The Tank Museum, Bovington
Back cover: © The Tank Museum, Bovington

Osprey Publishing supports the Woodland Trust, the UK's leading woodland conservation charity. Between 2014 and 2018 our donations are being spent on their Centenary Woods project in the UK.

To find out more about our authors and books visit **www.ospreypublishing.com**. Here you will find extracts, author interviews, details of forthcoming events and the option to sign up for our newsletter.

CONTENTS

INTRODUCTION

There was still a lot of uncertainty about the tank and its role on the battlefield when World War II broke out on 3 September 1939. There were those who believed that what had been demonstrated by the Mechanised Force in 1927 and the various Brigade exercises carried out subsequently was the way forward – that the Army needed more numerous and more mobile tanks to defeat the enemy. Others thought the Germans would create strong defensive positions, and saw a need for more and stronger infantry tanks, while a third element, thinking in World War I terms, visualised a new Western Front for which only massive heavily armoured assault tanks were the answer.

They could not all be right. In May 1940 the Germans showed Britain how armoured warfare was going to be fought. Although it was the infantry tanks that were initially favoured, in fact the cruiser tank was the real answer. Those Britain had built and were still building, however, were under-powered, unreliable, poorly armoured and feebly armed.

This mixture of tanks, along with some other British-designed armour and a few oddities, is what this volume concerns itself with. Even those backing big assault tanks had their moment, with the A20 and TOG prototypes. In fact it was not until American tanks filled the ranks of the British Army[1], and Britain's own cruisers gradually became more reliable, that it was able to gain the upper hand. Even British infantry tanks became more trustworthy. This was largely due to industrial power, as Britain slowly learned to trust the manufacturer to produce the kind of tanks it needed, and not rely upon the ponderous methods and poor decisions of the official Department of Tank Design.

By the end of the war Britain had shown that, apart from the ridiculous Tortoise, its tanks had the measure of the opposition. Germany was building ever-bigger and heavier tanks in ever-decreasing numbers, which were formidable on a one-to-one basis but could not be everywhere at once. The inferior Allied tanks had the advantage not only of numbers, but also of their increasingly cunning crews.

1 A companion to this book, *British Battle Tanks: US-built tanks of World War II,* will be published in 2018

VICKERS-ARMSTRONGS L1E3

Since it was not completed for testing until 1939 L1E3 really counts as a World War II tank. It was ordered by the War Office but Sir Noel Birch, once Master General of the Ordnance, but now a director of Vickers-Armstrongs, was very anxious to generate more interest in amphibious tanks and may well have used some of his old Army contacts to secure the order. There is no evidence to suggest that the British Army needed such a tank, or indeed were very interested in it (except the statement in the Mechanization Experimental Establishment's (MEE) report that the General Staff had asked for 100, having abandoned the idea of acquiring ordinary light tanks with attachable floats).

Although, in terms of suspension and its engine L1E3 was an inter-war light tank it had a number of modern features, including drum wheels: that is, ordinary light tank wheels of disc pattern but hollow to increase flotation. Later it had spoked wheels on the front bogie and only one return roller on each side instead of two in its original form. It was powered by a Meadows model ESTB engine rated at 88hp driving through a Vickers five-speed and reverse gearbox. But unlike the earlier Vickers-Carden-Loyd amphibious tank it featured two propellers instead of one. Each propeller was driven by a separate shaft driven off the tank's final drive.

As with some of the earlier tanks each propeller was encased within a shroud, creating what is known in marine terminology as a Kort nozzle which is most effective on slow moving vessels where propeller diameter is limited and manoeuvrability vital, such as a tugboat for instance. To effect steering each propeller moves within its shroud. L1E3 had a narrow armoured hull with room inside for a crew of two, a driver and turret gunner. The narrow hull was surrounded by a series of flotation chambers, filled with kapok and originally encased in alloy covers although this was later replaced by steel. The tank was thus inherently amphibious although it experienced the usual difficulty in getting out of the water when it encountered reeds or thick mud. The tank was tested and then duly set aside for the duration of the war but then for some reason tested again before being relegated to the Tank Museum. As a fighting tank it was of no use at all and as an amphibian it was very limited.

L1E3, the Vickers-Armstrongs amphibious tank as newly built. You can just make out the starboard propeller drive, starting from behind the drive sprocket, passing behind the two return rollers, and ending in the cowled propeller at the rear. There is rope and an anchor behind the turret. Notice also the top of a periscope above the turret and the 'Caution Unarmoured' triangle on the side.

CHAPTER 1
MATILDA INFANTRY TANK

DEVELOPMENTAL HISTORY

In 1929 the Chief of the Imperial General Staff announced a broad review of establishments and organisation within the British Army, prompted by recent progress in mechanisation. He proposed to start with the infantry and two brigades were designated for experimental purposes, each supported by a light tank battalion, equipped for the time being with the tiny Carden-Loyd Mark VI Machine Gun Carriers, although such vehicles were entirely unsuited to the task. Exercises soon indicated that the infantry would expect their tanks to make the first break into enemy defensive positions, which implied a slow moving tank, well armoured to absorb heavy punishment.

By 1934 thoughts were turning towards a tank designed specifically for the purpose; an Infantry, or 'I' tank. The Inspector, Royal Tank Corps, Major-General P.C.S. Hobart, detailed the alternatives; an inconspicuous tank, moderately well armoured and equipped with a machine gun, available in large numbers to swamp the enemy defences; or a larger type, mounting a cannon and armoured sufficiently to be proof against field artillery. The final decision rested with the Master-General of the Ordnance, General Sir Hugh Elles, the Tank Corps Commander in France during World War I. Influenced by his own experience, Elles strongly favoured the concept of Infantry tanks and, constrained by a peacetime economy, he gave priority to the smaller type.

A11 MATILDA

In October 1935 Sir John Carden, head of tank design for Vickers-Armstrongs Ltd., attended a meeting at the War Office with Colonel M. A. Studd, Assistant Director of Mechanisation. Sir John left with a draft proposal under the codename 'Matilda' for a small, two-man tank, armed with a single machine gun. Studd made two significant provisos. The design was to be ready within six months, and above all the new tank was to be cheap. It would bear the General Staff specification number A11.

Since the project could hardly be described as technically challenging the prototype, designated A11E1 (WD (War Department) No.T1724), was ready for

A11E1, the prototype of the Infantry Tank Mark I. Looking first at the suspension, notice how the return roller brackets share the same mounting as the main suspension units, the low setting of the drive sprocket and toothed front idler wheels. The front hull plate and the strong panels that support the idlers may also be seen while the open driver's hatch shows how it obstructs the gun. It also has no periscope mounting.

testing by the Mechanisation Experimental Establishment (MEE) in September 1936. It was not an imposing machine. The low, narrow hull was surmounted by a tiny cast steel turret containing a single Vickers machine gun. The commander's head and shoulders almost filled the turret space, while the driver was located ahead of him in an equally cramped compartment with an overhead hatch which, when opened up, effectively blocked the turret and fouled the gun. The engine, a 70hp Ford V8, was situated behind the turret under a sloping rear deck. It was linked to a Fordson four-speed gearbox and Vickers light tank-type clutch-and-brake steering assembly driving the rear sprockets. The suspension, which was derived from the Dragon Medium Mark IV artillery tractor, consisted of two stations per side, each of which comprised four pairs of rollers acting against quarter elliptical springs from a central support that included a return roller. The tank also featured toothed idlers and medium-pitch manganese steel tracks. Both these, and the suspension units, were totally exposed. Although the prototype was only constructed of mild steel it was built to a commendable 60mm standard at the front, and indeed relied on the rigidity of its thick plate for structural integrity, there being no internal frame to support the

HMH788 (T3433) was the first production A11. This front view shows the new arrangement of the front hull plate and the typical Vickers track adjusting mechanism. Other features to observe are the driver's narrow vision slit and periscope, in his hatch. On the turret one can see two mountings for the smoke dischargers and notice the lack of the prominent lip seen on the prototype.

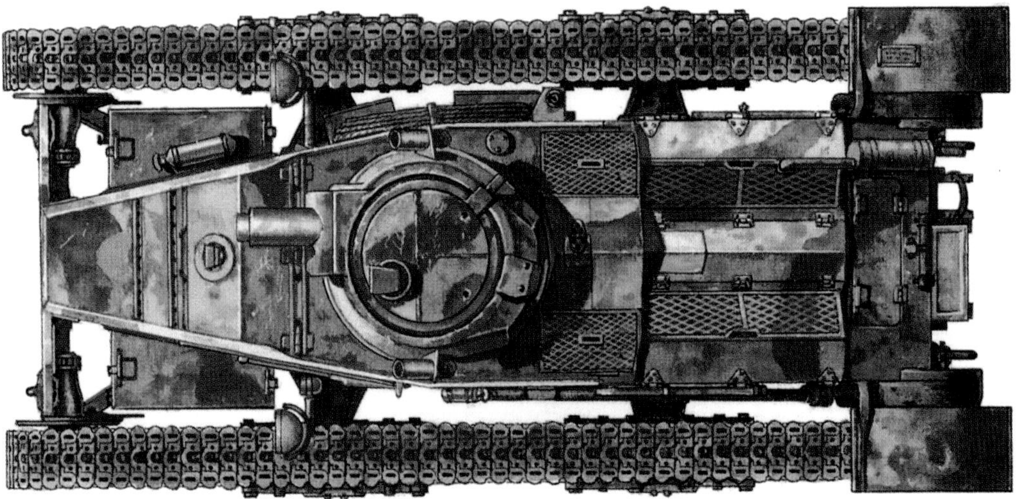

DERWENT
4
HMH
793

A11, INFANTRY TANK MARK I DERWENT, 4th Battalion, Royal Tank Regiment, 1st Army Tank Brigade, BEF; France, 1940

In accordance with War Office instructions this tank is painted in khaki green with a disruptive pattern of dark green. Twelve-inch square white markings on all surfaces were adopted as the British recognition sign and the palette shaped patch of greenish-yellow colour in front of the driver's visor is a gas-sensitive paint which changes hue in the presence of poison gas.

The white figure '4' on a red square was the unit identification while the white bar across the top indicates that the brigade was operating as corps troops; in this case 1st Corps. Since the figure was the same for both battalions they can best be distinguished by the vehicle's name, the initial letter of which matched its order in the alphabet. The 4th Battalion, however, also used the traditional Chinese Eye inherited from 6th Battalion, Tank Corps in 1919. Other markings on this tank are the War Department (WD) number, T3438, and the civil registration plate HMH793 drawn, as were most pre-war British military vehicles, on groups issued to Middlesex County Council.

Derwent was from the first batch of A11s to be built. It was the tank selected by the Germans for complete evaluation, which resulted in its destruction. (Art by Peter Sarson, © Osprey Publishing)

armour. The tank weighed close to 11 tons – about the same as a Vickers Medium, yet MEE always referred to it as a Heavy Infantry Tank – and had a top speed of around 8mph, which was deemed sufficient to keep pace with infantry.

Early trials revealed the usual crop of faults, the worst of which was a constant failure of track pins. This was cured in April 1937 when the rear suspension unit on each side was lowered, which in effect raised the height of the drive sprocket by 5in. Similarly, since they wore badly, the two rear sets of rubber-tyred road rollers on each side were replaced by all-steel ones. Complaints were also received about the driver's vision arrangements and turret hatch, but these matters were held over for improvement in the production machines, although in fact little was done until the second batch appeared.

The most significant difference between the prototype and production machines involved the turret, which lost its prominent lip and now featured a two-segment hatch. These tanks had idlers without teeth and return rollers that were not linked directly to the suspension brackets while the tracks were located further away from the hull than on the prototype. Those from the first batch had headlamps mounted

Another view of T3433 with the engine covers lifted. The Ford engine almost fills the space but ahead of it one can see the radiator and fan which separate the engine from the crew compartment. The catch on the left, and the cable leading to it, show how the covers are secured. They can only be released from inside the tank.

high on the hull, just ahead of the turret. The remaining 79 had them fitted lower down, near the nose, due to changes required when the mine plough was adopted, as explained later. Most A11s also had two stowage lockers, arranged pannier fashion either side of the nose.

Although there is no doubt that these little tanks were designed to be used against specific objectives in large numbers, for in practice they were little more than mechanised infantry machine guns, they were never ordered in quantity. A contract for 60 was placed with Vickers-Armstrongs at the end of April 1938, and a repeat order for the same number just ten days later – about enough to equip two battalions. This was not due to excessive penny-pinching but a change in policy, and the final order to Vickers for the Infantry Tank Mark I, placed in January 1939, only amounted to 19 machines. The reason was that, with war now inevitable, it had been decided to produce a cannon-armed Infantry tank after all, and create up to six army tank battalions to operate them. The new tank was to be known as the Matilda Senior.

A12 MATILDA

The first proposal for an enlarged Infantry tank dates from September 1936, although the emphasis at that time was on greater power and speed with a three-man crew rather than better protection, or even firepower. There followed three months of haggling over design priorities, which invariably stumbled over the problem of a suitable engine, and the search for a contractor, before the former was settled under GS Specification A12, and the latter in the form of the Vulcan Foundry at Newton-le-Willows, Cheshire.

A requirement for two A12 tanks, at £30,000, was included in the 1937 Army Estimates. Although, in the early stages, an armament of two co-axial machine guns was proposed, this was quickly abandoned in favour of a 2-pdr anti-tank gun and co-axial Vickers machine gun in a three-man turret. In view of the tank's proposed role there were some who would have preferred to see it mounting a weapon capable of firing high explosive (HE) rounds. But the official argument was that these tanks were there to protect the infantry from enemy tanks, and at that time the 2-pdr was the best anti-tank gun in the world.

A12E1, the first Matilda prototype, during trials. Measuring instruments are connected up on the rear deck but with no provision for external stowage the tank looks very stark. Stains on the lower hull plates show how the mud chutes work but compare the arrangement of these with those on a production tank.

The problem of providing a suitably powerful engine was resolved by using two. The same solution had been adopted in the case of the Medium A Whippet tank of 1917, and once again the chosen power unit was from a London bus. But in this instance the selected engine was a diesel, an AEC straight-six water-cooled unit delivering a maximum 87bhp at 2,000rpm. Two of these engines were located side by side in the rear half of the tank, driving into an enclosed spur gear housing at the forward end of the engines which concentrated their power into a single output shaft that passed down between them into a six-speed, Wilson epicyclic, pre-selector gearbox, operated by compressed air from a Reavell two-stage compressor. The output shafts from the gearbox passed through Rackham cam-operated steering clutches into final reduction gears which connected with the rear drive sprockets. Cooling fans were mounted above the gearbox but driven independently by each engine's crankshaft, while the radiators, which could be swung upwards to give access, were directly above the fans. The use of twin engines was never a satisfactory compromise; it effectively doubled maintenance time and resulted in uneven wear to drive components unless both engines were perfectly balanced. The only saving grace being that if one engine failed the tank could just about limp along on the other, the redundant engine having been permanently declutched from within the fighting compartment.

The suspension adopted for A12 was known as the Japanese type. It was a highly interdependent system of bellcranks and horizontal coil springs first developed by Vickers-Armstrongs for the Medium C tank sold to Japan in 1928. It had been tested extensively on a British Medium loaned to the Vulcan Foundry during the design stage and proved very efficient where high speeds were not required. The tracks, at least on the prototypes, were of the single-piece stamping type with a deep H shaped indentation in each shoe, as developed for the Medium Mark III tank. The prototypes, and some early production tanks had track return rollers, but later examples used skid rails, which were much simpler to produce.

Despite earlier indifference it was armour protection that became one of the most significant factors in the A12 design. The hull front was an impressive 78mm and even the thinnest plates were 20mm, which was more than double that of a Vickers Medium. In fact the tank was capable of withstanding any known anti-tank gun and most other forms of artillery of its day. Structurally it was a mixture of rolled plates and castings with more than enough integral strength to offset the need for a frame. But since it was believed that the hull would take considerable punishment at top speed across country the upper and lower hull plates were rebated into the sides to reduce stress on the securing bolts.

Among the more interesting features was the nose, which contained the driver's compartment. Like A11 there was no provision for a front hull machine gun and gunner. On the instructions of the Assistant Director of Mechanisation this section was modelled on the imported Christie cruiser tank then being tested by MEE, yet the gaps that this shape would create between the nose and track frames were filled by triangular shaped tool lockers with top mounted, louvred lids. The complex shape of this nose piece was the main cause of bottlenecks in Matilda production. While the casting was suitably thick where it mattered it was also far too thick in areas where this was not important, creating an obvious weight penalty. It therefore proved necessary to grind away a good deal of this excess armour from the inside, a time consuming task which could only be undertaken with a great deal of care by suitably skilled craftsmen. The suspension, in marked contrast to A11, was totally enclosed,

INFANTRY TANK A12, MATILDA MARK I GAMECOCK, 7th Battalion, Royal Tank Regiment, 1st Army Tank Brigade, BEF; France 1940

This tank also sports the khaki green and dark green disruptive camouflage scheme and the white identification squares peculiar to the BEF, however the Matildas of 7th RTR seem rarely to have carried unit identification plates, if at all. Thus the only other markings are the WD and registration numbers plus the name, painted somewhat unusually across the back. This tank was photographed after capture and is thus known to be one which had the modified suspension and trench-crossing tail skid attachment. (Art by Peter Sarson, © Osprey Publishing)

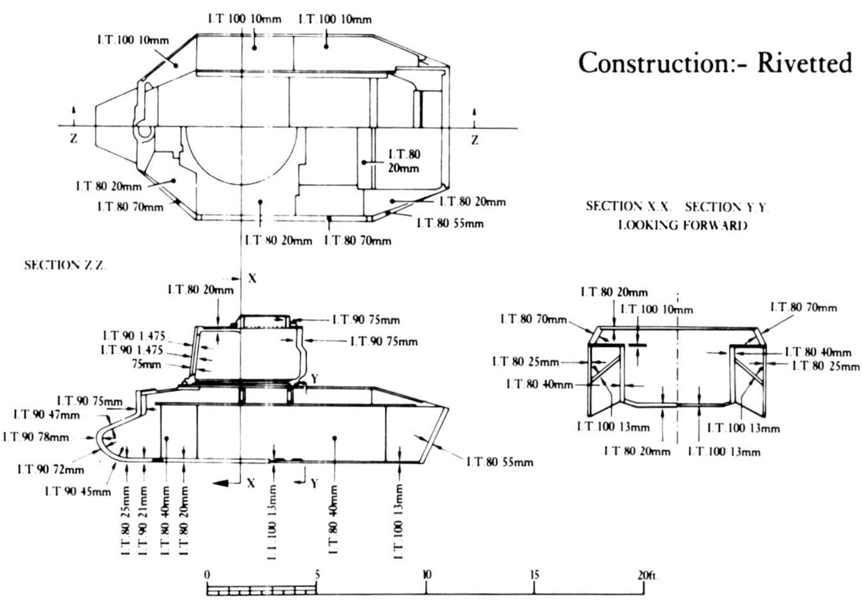

An official diagram showing the Matilda's armour thickness on all surfaces, mostly in metric, along with the izod test value of the plate.

not only at the top but with deep side skirts containing mud chutes and complex hinged inspection panels.

The turret was a casting, with separately bolted top panels containing a drum shaped commander's cupola at the left, with a small loader's hatch alongside it. The loader was also the wireless operator for the No. 11 set (originally) housed in the back

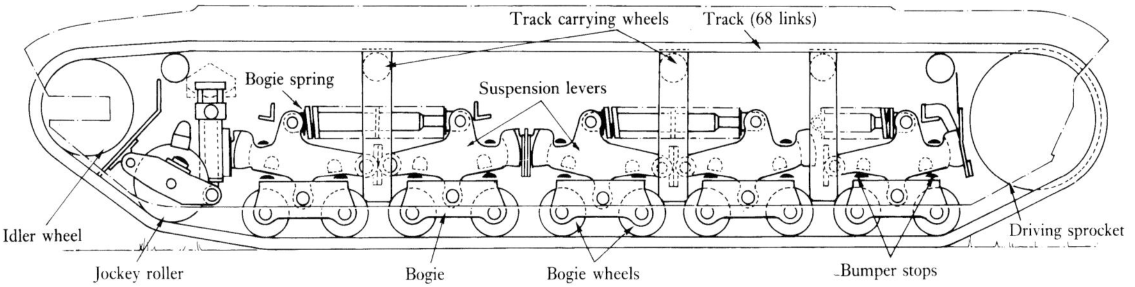

The suspension adopted for Matilda consisted of two double, and one single, horizontally sprung bogies and the larger diameter, vertically sprung jockey wheel at the front. This diagram, from an early handbook, shows five return rollers (identified as track carrying wheels) which were later replaced by skid rails.

of the turret. The gunner was installed ahead of the commander, serving the 2-pdr quick-firing (QF) gun and co-axial water cooled Vickers .303 machine gun. A pair of 4in smoke dischargers were mounted on the offside of the turret. Because the turret was a good deal heavier than anything which had gone before it was supplied with a hydraulic power-traverse system, but since firing on the move was now the accepted British method of tank warfare the gun was elevated and depressed by shoulder action of the gunner. This meant that the weapon had to be well balanced, which in turn required that a good deal of the breech end, behind the trunnions, was inside the turret.

FROM PROTOTYPE TO PRODUCTION

A12E1 (T3431) the first Matilda Senior prototype, arrived at MEE in April 1938. Following an initial 1,000-mile trial its performance was described as extremely satisfactory, apart from those cooling problems endemic to all new tanks. It managed a top speed of 15mph, with plenty of power in hand and the only adverse comment concerned the tracks, which now had a bar tread added to each link that tore up the road surface. The way was now open for production to commence.

An initial order for 140 units was placed with the Vulcan Foundry in June 1938, followed in August by a contract for 40 from Ruston & Hornsby Ltd. of Lincoln. Then, as the threat of war became stark reality, other firms were drawn into the programme; John Fowler & Co. of Leeds, the North British Locomotive Company of Glasgow, Harland & Wolff in Belfast and the London, Midland and Scottish Railway Company at their Horwich works. Vulcans remained as production parents to the group. Total production ran to about 2,890, including 20 completed in mild steel as training tanks. Unfortunately construction, even on this modest scale, was allowed to run on for far too long. Fowlers, who had experienced all kinds of delays and production problems, accepted what is believed to be the last order for 75 Matilda tanks in March 1942, which was not filled until sometime in 1943 when such tanks were manifestly obsolete. In August 1940, when the British tank situation was at its most desperate, one Matilda was shipped to the United States for evaluation, with a view to having the type built over there. This was never done, but it had one most interesting side effect. L.E. Carr, of the British Tank Mission in the USA, designed a power pack for it which featured a pair of General Motors two-stroke diesels, and this arrangement was later adopted for some American medium tanks, notably the M4A2 Sherman.

1940: FAILURE IN FRANCE

The War Establishment of an Army Tank Battalion in 1940 called for 50 Infantry tanks; three companies of 16 each and two with battalion headquarters. It also included seven light tanks for liaison and eight tracked carriers for transporting relief personnel. Clearly by this time it was hoped that all such battalions would have A12 Matildas (or possibly Valentines) because the establishment also showed a strength of 50 2-pdr guns. Reality was unable to match this. The two such battalions in France with the BEF in 1940, when the Germans struck, only mustered 23 A12 Matildas out of 100 Infantry tanks, all of these with 7th Royal Tank Regiment. The rest, including all of 4th RTR's tanks, were A11s. They had clearly come to the wrong kind of war.

Matilda production line. From this angle the painfully small turret ring diameter is obvious. The turretless tanks still wait to have lids fitted to their hull toolboxes either side of the nose. At least two different patterns of track are visible.

Tanks Dreadnought and Dolphin receiving considerable attention from 4th RTR crewmen in a farmyard at Acq, before the battle of Arras. Both tanks have their turrets reversed so that the open hatches can be seen. Dreadnought's turret displays the Chinese Eye motif while on Dolphin one of its smoke dischargers is discernible.

When the fighting in the West began the Germans simply did not oblige with the static defensive positions that Infantry tanks had been designed to assault. Rather they exploited mobility over a wide front and the Matildas wore themselves out trying to stem the flood. When they did make contact with the Germans near Arras on 21 May they proved invulnerable to German 37mm anti-tank guns. They were mostly knocked out by artillery fire, the exposed tracks of the A11s proving vulnerable. On the credit side these smaller Infantry tanks certainly had the edge on reliability over their bigger sisters. Some A11s, mainly section leaders' tanks, had been equipped with the bigger .5 Vickers machine guns, which could prove rather a handful for the commander. In addition they now had two 4in smoke dischargers on the turret and a No. 11 wireless set located up against the engine bulkhead below and behind the turret. In order to tune this the commander had to leave his seat in the turret and lie almost full length on the floor.

Apart from some engine trouble the worst failings of the A12 Matildas in France were their tracks. Once the indentations had packed with mud they became virtually smooth and unable to grip on soft ground or the pavé setts of French roads. Two

An early production Matilda Mark I, as yet unarmed, posed on a bank during trials. Concentrating on the turret one can see the commander's cupola and loader's hatches open, the sighting vane ahead of the cupola and the bracket for the wireless aerial which enables it to be folded down.

INFANTRY TANK MARK II, MATILDA MARK III, GRIFFIN, No. 4 Independent Troop, Malta Tank Squadron, Royal Tank Regiment, 1942

The tank detachment on Malta adopted a curious camouflage scheme dictated by local conditions. Much of the island being exposed and bare the most common feature was the stone walling that lined the roads and surrounded the fields, so the vehicles were painted to blend in with this. Other markings were entirely absent except for individual tank names which they seem to have retained from their previous service. Thus Griffin, and possibly its crew, was ex-7th RTR. At least three Matildas are known to have served on Malta.

A variety of tanks passed through the hands of the Independent Troop including Light Mark VI, A9 and A13 Cruisers and some Valentines. (Art by Peter Sarson, © Osprey Publishing)

modifications were noted on some A12s. One resulted from trench-crossing trials held at Tilford near Aldershot in September 1939. These had shown that a 6ft trench, newly made in soft sand, was too much for an A12. Being tail heavy it tended to drop its rear end into the trench and then found it impossible to crawl out. The staff at MEE therefore devised a tail skid which fitted to the rear of the tank, between the tracks. It took the form of a steel box, flat on top but curved at the base, extending nearly 3ft from the back of the tank. Further trials at Farnborough proved that this worked on a 6ft trench but was defeated by one 7ft wide. There was talk of making an even larger skid, 3ft 9in long, but no further reports can be traced. The other modification concerned the suspension. There was some fear that the ground clearance of A12 was too low, so the pitch of the suspension was altered to lower the track bogies by 6in. This had the effect of raising the tank by the same amount, although it left the bogies exposed. It also placed excessive strain on the suspension bellcranks which were now working at an unnatural angle and more prone to breaking. Like the tail skid this modification was seen on some tanks in France, but rarely afterwards.

Every single Infantry tank with 1st Army Tank Brigade was left in France when the Allies evacuated. All that remained in Britain was the third regiment of the brigade, 8th RTR, which was equipped with A11s and A12s on roughly a two to one ratio. For some time this was the only complete tank regiment in the south of England available to resist an invasion.

MATILDA MARK II

In the immediate aftermath of the disaster in France there was no time to make sober evaluations. At least one senior officer did point out that if the Germans were going to wage war like this British tanks would soon be needing much bigger guns, but with invasion expected hourly the demand was for tanks of any kind to re-equip the army, so Matilda construction continued. It was still not very rapid. Before it could get into its stride the War Office was demanding changes in design, although these played havoc with production schedules. The first concerned the secondary armament. Just about the time when Matildas were entering production the War Office decided that it would standardise on a British version of the Czech ZB air-cooled machine gun, the .303 Besa, instead of the old water-cooled Vickers, in all of its armoured vehicles. This meant a modification to the Matilda turret design, not only where the co-axial gun passed through the mantlet, but also near the lip where an outlet, intended to discharge vapour from the water-cooled gun, was now eliminated. When the Vickers gun was removed the electrically driven pump that maintained its water supply went with it, and the circuit was modified to provide for an extractor fan in the turret roof. In this form the tank became the Infantry Tank Mark IIA, or Matilda Mark II.

MATILDA MARK III

No sooner had this matter been resolved than a search began for an alternative power unit. Both Fowlers and Perkins came forward with proposals but in the end a 7 litre Leyland diesel was selected which delivered 95bhp. While the manufacturers worked at producing right and left handed versions of this engine the Vulcan Foundry set about modifying the second prototype, A12E2 (T3432) to receive them. This tank was also fitted, experimentally, with a complete Wilson gearbox and steering system, for which the designation Mark IIB was coined to signify a version of Matilda with the full Wilson transmission, although it was never used since the project was not pursued (the gearbox is preserved at the Tank Museum, Bovington). This tank also served as a test bed for the Freeborn automatic transmission system. Once the Leyland engines had been accepted contractors were ordered to fit them into future models, to be designated Infantry Tank Mark IIA*, or Matilda Mark III.

A Matilda Mark I from the first production batch built at Vulcan Foundry showing the suspension modified to improve ground clearance. The strange device at the rear offside appears to have been designed to slice through barbed wire.

Matildas Glanton and Gloucester of 7th RTR, burnt out and abandoned in a wood after the Arras battle. Glanton has one of the louvres over its petrol tank opened to facilitate destruction. The louvred lids to the front stowage lockers caused an unforeseen problem. Items in them could be set alight under fire and the resulting heat and smoke prevented the crew from operating efficiently.

THE MARK IIICS, IV, IVCS & V

During the early stages of Matilda development it had been agreed that the turret should be made capable of mounting a 3in howitzer, as an alternative to the 2-pdr, but this weapon was only required to fire smoke rounds as cover for the gun tanks so it could hardly be regarded as a major adjunct to the assault. The Leyland engined A12 was the first to be supplied in this form and was classified as Matilda Mark IIICS, for Close Support.

As the tanks saw increased service other problems were identified. One of the worst seems to have been the three point mounting for the engines, which were twisting in relation to their adjacent components, so the next modification to be introduced was a rigid engine mounting. The opportunity was also taken to improve the position of oil and air lines, and to increase fuel capacity.

Tanks produced to this specification were classified Mark IV or IVCS as appropriate. There is a homely little passage in the vehicle handbook which tells a crew member, who might want to know whether his Matilda is a Mark III or Mark IV, to lift an air inlet louvre and peer at the nearest fuel tank; if it has an evacuation pump fitted then it is a Mark IV. The final improvement involved mounting a Westinghouse air servo directly on top of the transmission to improve gear changing, in place of the Clayton Dewandre type built into the linkage on earlier models. This seemingly modest change earned the designation Matilda Mark V; there was no Mark VCS.

Since, with the exception of the co-axial weapon on the Mark I, all Matildas look more or less alike it is almost impossible to identify them accurately from the front. From the back those with Leyland engines can be distinguished by exhaust pipes running down both sides of the engine deck; those equipped with AEC engines only display an exhaust pipe on the left side, since the other emerges from the bottom of the hull, although on all models the pipes ended in a pair of silencers mounted across the back of the hull, beneath the overhanging rear deck. From the Mark III onwards the No. 19 wireless set was fitted and from the Mark IV the turret signalling lamp eliminated, but the latter can only be seen if it is elevated and the two aerials which indicate the No.19 set are not always readily visible.

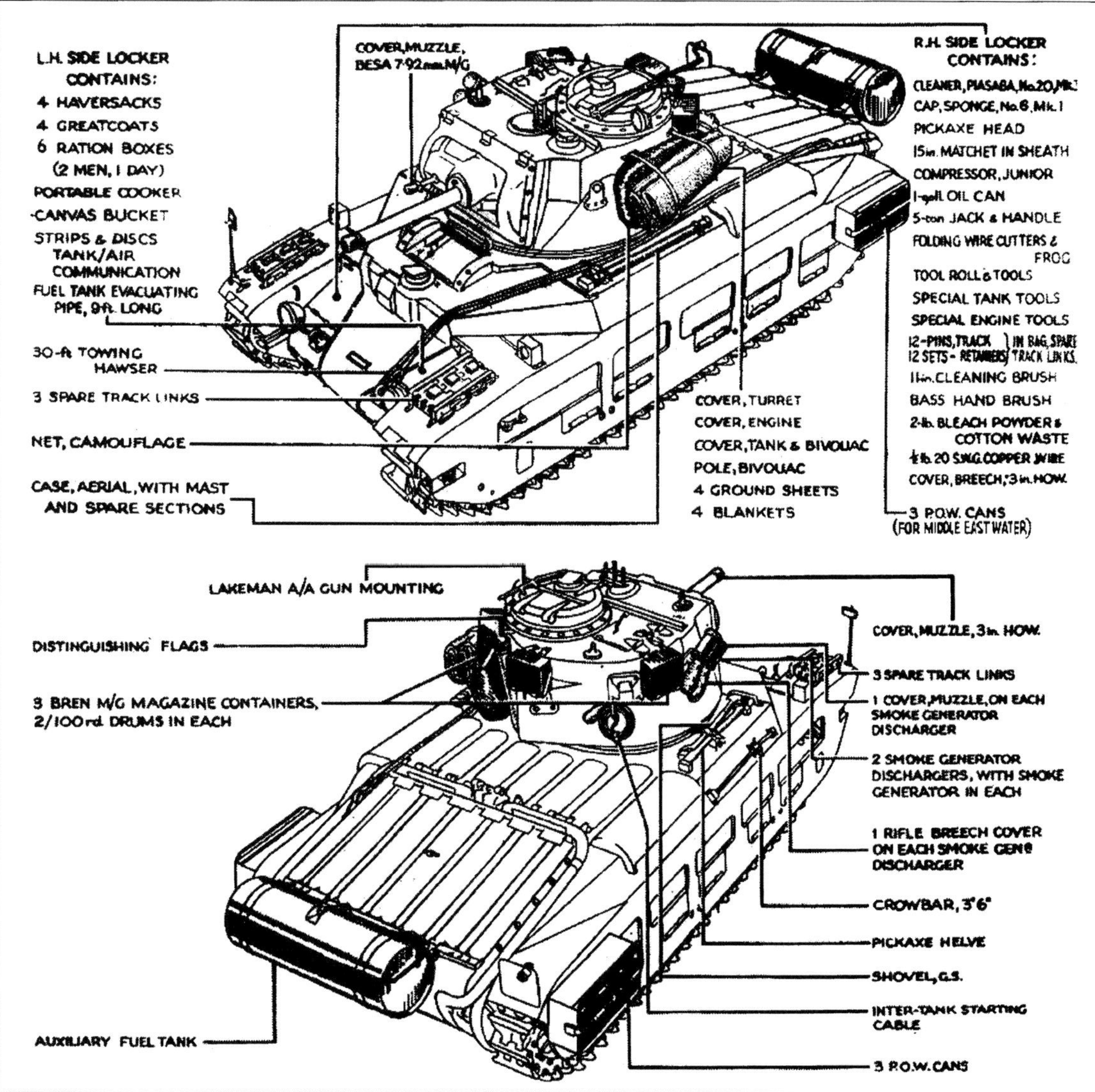

Stowage diagrams for a Matilda Mark IVCS tank. Notice the special Petrol, Oil, Water can racks fitted on each side to tanks in the Middle East, the auxiliary fuel tank and containers on the turret for Bren magazines when the machine gun is mounted for anti-aircraft defence. Oddly the artwork shows a low profile cupola but only one visible exhaust pipe.

Tracks were changed, for a heavy box section, spudded type which was as useless in the desert as the smooth ones had been in France, but this could be applied to any mark. Later production models had more obvious external hinges on the suspension inspection panels, but this is no infallible guide, and the otherwise foolproof technique of relying on the WD number is rendered futile by the production changes. A contract card dated as early as 11 June 1938, for 140 machines, was subsequently annotated Matilda I, II & III without giving any indication as to how many of each were actually produced, let alone what their respective WD numbers were, and many of the subsequent cards are equally ambiguous.

Once the worst threat of invasion was over, and the tank supply situation somewhat relieved, opportunity was taken to give some of the older Matildas a thorough overhaul. The firm selected was MG Cars at Abingdon, Oxfordshire, and from one photograph taken there it seems highly probable that in many, if not all cases, new pairs of Leyland diesels were installed in place of the AECs. This makes identification of Marks extremely difficult and to a degree renders it almost pointless.

A clear overhead view of a Matilda Mark I. On the turret notice again the sighting vane, close to the gunner's periscope and, on the other side of the turret the cast outlet for steam from the Vickers gun. On the rear of the hull the single top exhaust pipe shows up well while at the front notice that the driver's hatch is closed while the visor in front of it is open. Alongside the visor is the driver's periscope.

LATER MODIFICATIONS

The size of the Matilda's turret was kept as small as possible in order to save weight. Coupled with the need to balance the gun, already explained, this meant that it was quite impossible to think of upgunning the tank, even though by 1942 this was highly desirable. The only alternative would be to fit a larger turret, and although there is photographic evidence to prove that this was done, no documents of any kind have been found to explain it. The tank is seen with a 6-pdr turret of the type fitted to the A24/A27 series cruisers tanks, and an ugly combination it makes. But the turret ring on A27 was 57in in diameter, while that of A12 was only 54in. It would have been a drastic measure, though by no means impossible, to enlarge the Matilda's turret ring. It is more likely that a larger ring was superimposed onto the hull. Photographic evidence seems to support this. Yet the Churchill Mark III carried a similar 6-pdr turret on a 54in turret ring and this might have been a better solution. Following experience in France there was a somewhat irrational reaction against turret cupolas, and many late production Matildas, including most of those supplied to Australia, appeared with a low profile commander's hatch.

OPERATIONAL HISTORY

The spiritual home of the A12 Matilda, more by accident than design, was the Libyan Desert, indeed at one time it was known as the 'Queen of the Desert' and although this title has stuck it is not always easy to justify. Events in France have already been mentioned, and this theatre was the graveyard of the little A11. None of the 90 or so with the BEF came back to Britain. It seems that no one was particularly sorry to lose

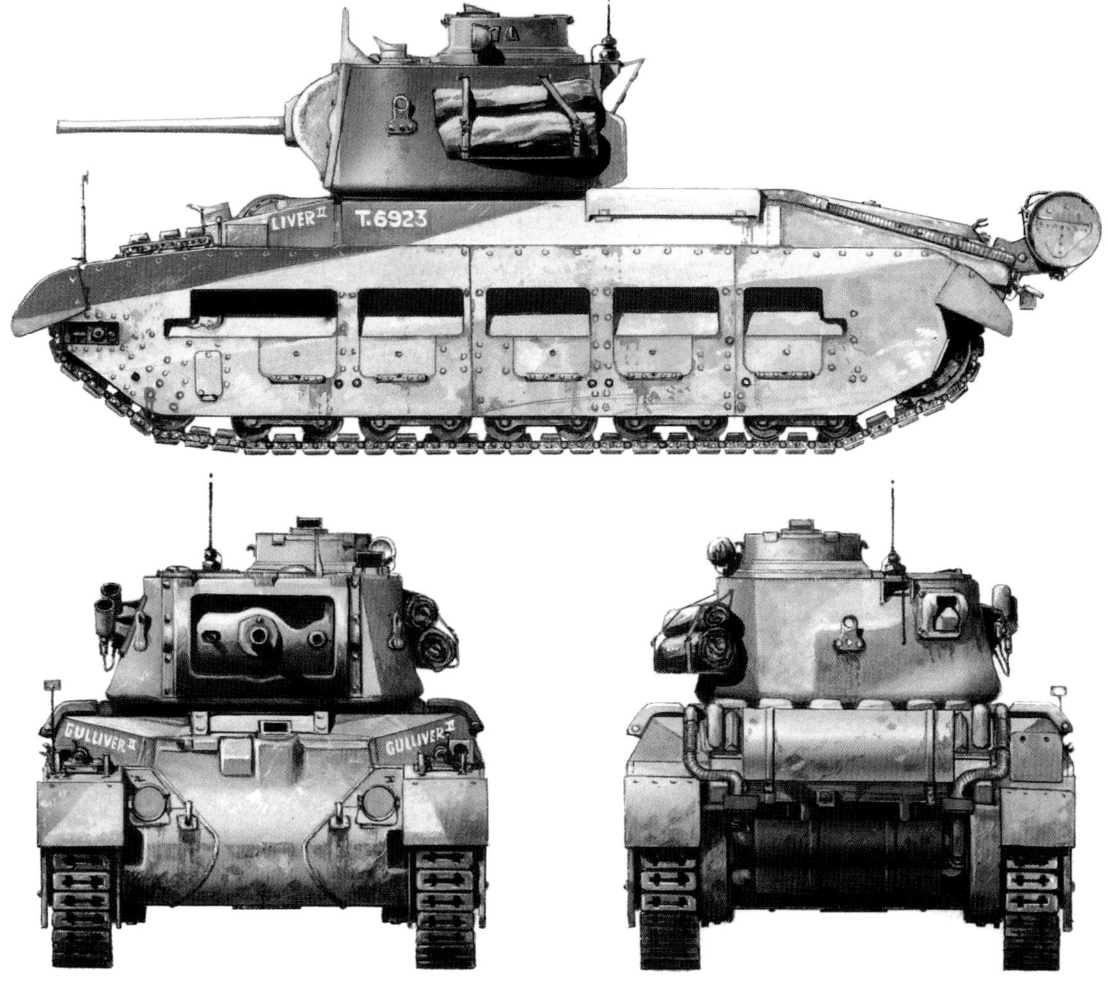

INFANTRY TANK MARK II, MATILDA MARK III, Gulliver II, 7th Royal Tank Regiment; Libya, 1941

Gulliver II of 7th RTR exhibits one of the most interesting, and controversial camouflage schemes ever applied to British tanks. Based on naval ideas originally adopted in World War I its purpose was to disguise the outline of the tank, and thus deceive enemy gunners, rather than blend it into the background. Two shades of grey, probably drawn from Royal Navy stores, are applied over the base light sand colour. There was nothing random about the design, it was worked out with mathematical accuracy and, as may be seen by half closing the eyes, had a remarkable ability to apparently alter the shape of the tank. This effect was later spoiled to some extent by the application of large white/red/white identification panels painted on the hull and turret sides of many tanks.

As in France 7th RTR seem to have been averse to using any other markings on their Matildas beyond the obligatory WD number and individual tank name. (Art by Peter Sarson, © Osprey Publishing)

them. Even the few still in Britain were phased out of service as soon as something better was available. Yet there were nowhere near enough tanks left to resist the anticipated invasion, and in a desperate attempt to improve mobility some armoured regiments and army tank battalions (among them 4th RTR now re-equipped with A12 Matildas) were permanently attached to special trains, held in readiness at strategic junctions in eastern and southeast England, ready to be hurried to a threatened area should the need arise. This led to a series of trials in which Matildas and other tanks were seen climbing on and off railway wagons over all kinds of improvised ramps.

The photograph that gives the game away. Horace of 8th RTR in the MG works at Abingdon with an empty engine bay. The two AEC units, which presumably have been removed, stand on trestles. To the left a brand new Leyland set waits to go in, as does the transmission unit at bottom right.

Largely for historical reasons the army tank brigades that operated Infantry tanks were formed from battalions of the Royal Tank Regiment. Perhaps they were not reckoned to suit the dashing image of the cavalry. But in an emergency dignity must take a back seat and at least two cavalry regiments, 16th/5th and 17th/21st Lancers both in 6th Armoured Division, numbered some Matildas among their Valentines while on home defence duties in 1940–41. In company with the four yeomanry regiments that formed 20th and 26th Armoured Brigades they normally ran two A12s with each squadron headquarters to provide close support fire and the advantage of three-man turrets. Even so they do not seem to have liked them, complaining of frequent breakdowns and weakness in the Rackham steering clutches after continual use on winding country roads. In North Africa it was a different story.

NORTH AFRICA

The first Matilda battalion to arrive in Egypt was the indefatigable 7th RTR under Lt.Col. R. M. Jerram. After two months of acclimatisation the unit took part in various successful actions with 4th Indian Division which confronted the Italians, after their timid advance into Egypt, and threw them back on their nearest coastal stronghold of Bardia. It was during General Wavell's reconnaissance in force against Marshall Graziani's army, which began on 9 December 1940 under the tactical control of General O'Connor, that the Matildas earned their regal title. The 2-pdr outclassed any Italian tank gun, the armour proved secure against virtually every Italian weapon and wear on the steering clutches became almost unknown. For one thing there was no need to turn the tank so often on desert terrain and for another the lateral motion of steering was far easier on Libyan sand than European mud.

Despite the early successes Bardia was considered to be a much tougher proposition. It was protected by an impressive anti-tank ditch and, during training with 6th Australian Division, 7th RTR created a replica of the ditch at Halfaya and developed means to tackle it. The simplest revived a First World War technique, the fascine. Unfortunately the Matilda was not designed to handle such a contraption in the normal way, by launching it over the nose, so it was slung from the side. This required the tank first to turn itself broadside on to the ditch in order to drop the thing before lining up to cross it. A more sophisticated solution was a long, wedge-shaped ramp with runways spaced to coincide with the tank's tracks. It was supported on a pair of short tracked bogies and pushed ahead of the tank until it filled the ditch, whereupon the tank detached itself and drove across. Another local modification seen on one Matilda was a simple variation of the rolled carpet device, held on a pair of extended arms in front of the tank. It was unwound by the tracks while passing over barbed wire entanglements to form a path for wheeled vehicles and infantry. The regiment was reduced to just 22 tanks at this time, yet only one of these was permanently written off in the battle. When the assault on Tobruk was launched some three weeks later 7th RTR was down to about squadron strength, but the Matildas played their part well although the majority were on their last legs.

Now, while the cruiser tanks of 7th Armoured Division headed west to inflict an overwhelming defeat on the Italian forces in North Africa, the surviving Matildas were carried east to RAOC workshops in Alexandria for a welcome refit. The kind of war that was developing in the desert was not one that suited slow Infantry tanks, and although the Matildas would continue to serve when the front stabilised they simply did not have the mobility to cope with the rapid, fluid style of warfare practised by the Afrikakorps.

THE ROLE OF THE MATILDA

Writing for his memoirs (edited by Sir Basil Liddell Hart as *The Rommel Papers*) after the Battle of Sollum in the summer of 1941, Field Marshal Rommel noted that the British employed large numbers of Matildas which, on account of their thick armour, were impervious to most German anti-tank guns. He was, however, puzzled by their armament, explaining that the gun was too small and its range too short; he went on: 'They were only supplied with solid, armour-piercing shell. It would be interesting to know why the Mark II was called an Infantry tank when it had no HE ammunition with which to engage the opposing infantry. It was also… far too slow. In fact, its only real use was in a straight punch to smash a hole in a concentration of material'. Rommel was not alone in this opinion, General Wavell made similar comments and so, no doubt, did many of his tank crews, although their views generally went unrecorded.

The upgunned Matilda. A late production hull modified to accept an A24 style 6-pdr gun turret, showing how the hull has been built up to take a larger diameter turret ring.

INFANTRY TANK MARK IIA*, MATILDA MARK III, 7th Royal Tank Regiment, Western Desert, 1941

Original specifications, issued in 1939, described an authorised shade of aluminium (silver) paint for all interior surfaces on British tanks but then qualified this by explaining that any similar shade was acceptable and, indeed, any other suitable colour if no silver paint was obtainable. It would seem that there was no authorised colour for mechanical components and these were fitted as supplied by the manufacturer, usually in natural metal finish. That portion of the gun tube inside the turret was finished in the external colour, with a natural metal breech block, but it may not have been repainted in sand before the first major overhaul. Ready-use ammunition was stowed in and around the turret basket with the reserve stock easily accessible in the adjacent hull sponsons. However it should be noted that no ammunition was stowed above turret ring level. The standard anti-tank round was a solid steel projectile with tracer in the base, painted black with a white and red banded nose cap. The earlier armour piercing shell proved faulty and was discontinued, while tanks never carried the pathetic high-explosive shell. An armour piercing capped, ballistic capped (APCBC) appeared too late for Matildas serving in the desert. (Art by Peter Sarson, © Osprey Publishing)

Specifications

Crew: Four
Combat weight: 26,924kg
Power-to-weight ratio: 7.2hp/ton (Imperial)
Overall length: 6.019m
Width: 2.59m
Height: 2.515m (high cupola)
Engines: Two Leyland Type E148 & E149 straight six cylinder water cooled diesels, each 95bhp at 2,000rpm.
Transmission: Wilson six-speed pre-selector gearbox and Rackham steering clutches
Fuel capacity: 181.8 litres plus 163.6 litres in auxiliary tank
Max speed: 24km/h.
Max. range: 80km (on internal tanks).
Fuel consumption: 2.2 litres/km
Fording depth: 1m (with fording flaps closed)
Armament: Ordnance Quick-Firing 2-pdr (40mm) Mark IX (52 calibre), co-axial Besa 7.92mm air-cooled machine-gun
Ammunition: AP solid (1kg)
Muzzle velocity: 853m/sec
Max. effective range: 1,828.8m
Ammunition stowage: 93 rounds
Gun depression/elevation: + 20°/–20°

Key

1. Besa 7.92mm machine gun
2. Gunner's sight
3. OQF 2-pdr Mark IX gun (40mm)
4. Gunner's shoulder piece
5. Commander's cupola
6. Cupola lid segment
7. Loader's hatch
8. Loader's seat
9. Commander's periscope
10. Lakeman anti-aircraft mounting
11. Bren gun drum magazine
12. Turret spotlight
13. Bren .303 in. machine gun
14. Aerial
15. Rear number plate
16. Spare Bren magazine bin
17. Right hand radiator
18. Auxiliary fuel tank
19. Left hand exhaust pipe
20. Left hand fuel tank
21. Three water cans
22. Left hand oil cooler
23. Mud chute
24. Signal flag stowage tube
25. Wireless set
26. Wireless valve box
27. Suspension spring
28. Commander's seat
29. Suspension bogie unit
30. Suspension lever
31. Compass binnacle
32. Gun recoil shield
33. Centre ammunition stowage rack
34. 2-pdr ammunition bin
35. Suspension inspection flap
36. Gunner's seat
37. Sidelight
38. Turret traverse gearbox
39. Smoke canister
40. Track tension adjuster
41. Driver's seat
42. Steering levers
43. Change speed lever
44. Throttle pedal
45. Towing/lifting ring
46. Headlamp
47. Driving mirror
48. Spare track stowage rack
49. Front stowage locker
50. Battery
51. Sidelight protectors
52. Driver's hatch control
53. Driver's hatch
54. Shovel

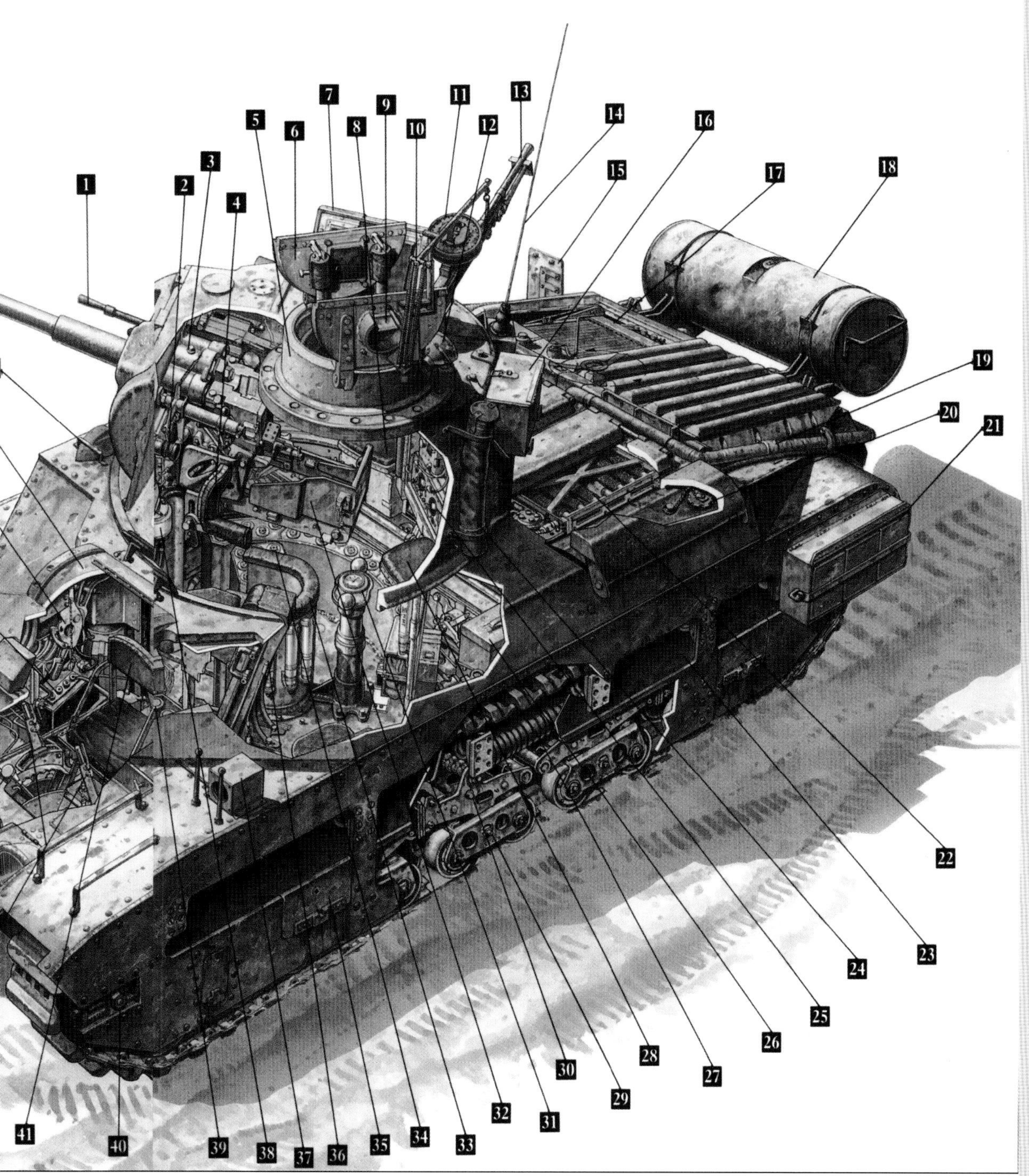
1
2
3
4
5
6
7
8
9
10
11
12
13
14
15
16
17
18
19
20
21
22
23
24
25
26
27
28
29
30
31
32
33
34
35
36
37
38
39
40
41

ABOVE Huddersfield of 8th RTR climbing onto a flat wagon over an improvised ramp of sleepers during trials at Aldershot station. The tank is finished in the early two-tone camouflage scheme and also exhibits the strange, blocked-in style of squadron markings seen on some Matildas of 1st Army Tank Brigade.

ABOVE LEFT A detailed view of the turret of a Matilda Close Support tank of 6th Armoured Division photographed during a review at Lakenheath, Suffolk. The corporal is demonstrating a Bren gun on a Lakeman mounting from the commander's cupola while the two wireless aerials suggest that the tank carries a No. 19 set.

The British view, as already explained, was that Infantry tanks should have an adequate anti-tank weapon with which to protect their infantry from enemy tanks, and in its day the 2-pdr was unmatched. But it was not provided with a high explosive round, and even if one was available its explosive content would hardly have been worth considering. Thus, when confronted with some of the Italian frontier forts, the Matildas found they could make no impression upon them with their guns and had to enter via the closed door, like a battering ram. Likewise the Italian artillery, which always proved a tenacious opponent, could usually only be dealt with by very close action, and this increased the risk to the tank, for a large HE shell at point-blank range could be most destructive. Yet the real villain of the piece was undoubtedly the German anti-tank artillery. Used in conjunction with tanks in pursuance of Rommel's policy of concentrating firepower, it proved a very difficult target for a solid, 40mm round, fired from a moving tank. The German 50mm Pak 38 could penetrate the front of a Matilda using Composite Rigid shot and when they started using 88mm anti-aircraft guns against tanks it was clear that the Matilda had at last met its match.

Nevertheless the number of Matildas in the Middle East continued to grow. The 7th RTR, bolstered by the arrival of the 4th, took an important part in 'Operation Battleaxe' in June 1941, using tanks that had been rushed out to Egypt ostensibly for 1st Army Tank Brigade, the personnel of which was then at sea. Thus when that brigade was issued with tanks in September its senior regiment, 8th RTR, was provided with Valentines while 42nd and 44th RTR remained in Matildas. Elements of all these Matilda regiments took part in the 'Crusader' battles that resulted in the relief of Tobruk in December. By the following summer the conflict had moved westwards to the Gazala line, which was about as deep into the desert as the Matildas ever went, but their numbers were much reduced. The renewed German offensive resulted in some very bitter fighting and by the time it was over, in June 1942 when Tobruk was retaken, hardly any Matildas remained fit for action. Four close support Matildas served with the Valentines of 23rd Armoured Brigade during the suicidal attack on Ruweisat Ridge at the end of July and the lone survivor could claim to be the last Matilda gun tank to see active service with the British Army during World War II.

ERITREA

'B' Squadron, 4th RTR, equipped with 16 Matildas, was shipped direct from England to Port Sudan to spearhead the British attack against the Italians in Eritrea. Here, in terrain that was hardly suitable for tanks at all, this tiny force exercised a degree of influence out of all proportion to its size. In four months, during which nearly all the Matildas were maintained in running order by their squadron fitters and the LAD without recourse to any spare parts, since none were supplied, the tanks covered many hundreds of miles on their tracks and helped to defeat a much superior force.

Not a summary field punishment, but another of Major Lakeman's inventions; a hoist for extricating injured crewmen, seen here attached to the cupola of a Matilda.

THE MEDITERRANEAN

Matildas were also turning up in other parts of the Mediterranean. Nine tanks from 7th RTR went to Crete in May 1941, only to be lost when German forces took the island. Matildas also joined the small tank detachment on Malta, where they adopted the distinctive camouflage scheme and made themselves generally useful without actually being called upon to fight.

THE CREW

The desert battles have been more than adequately described elsewhere, but the experiences of the men who crewed the tanks in action is another story. Loneliest of all was the driver, isolated in the nose of the tank. Either side of his seat he had the steering brake levers, which also acted as a parking brake, and between his knees the gear selector lever. This acted in a single line, like the selector on an automatic car, and offered reverse, neutral, emergency low and five forward gears as it was moved away from the driver. The preselector system that was a feature of the Wilson gearbox allowed the driver to move the lever into position for the next gear he would require and then activate it, as necessary, by dipping the clutch pedal. The clutch pedal was replaced on the Matilda V by a foot-operated control pedal which peformed the same function. To the right of this pedal was the accelerator. Compared with most

A posed but effective picture of an RTR Matilda under camouflage nets in the desert with all four crew members at work. The louvred lids of the tool lockers can be seen in the open position and the tracks are of the original pattern with extra bars welded on. The purpose of the two square patches on the nose has never been adequately explained.

A poor but interesting picture of a 7th RTR Matilda carrying a large fascine during trials at Halfaya. Notice that to save weight, and presumably because ordinary timber is scarce in the desert, the fascine is a fabricated crib type.

contemporary vehicles the instrumentation available to a Matilda driver was quite comprehensive. There were enough dials, lights and switches to occupy three panels on the first three marks, reduced to two on the Marks IV and V.

The driver's hatch was a curved, rolling hood, operated by a pair of levers, or screw device on later Marks. When it was open he could raise his seat and drive head out. Closed down the seat was lowered and the driver observed either through a protected vision block directly to his front or a periscope just to the left of it. Although the hood was his normal exit the driver could also use an escape hatch beneath his seat but one suspects that this was a last resort. If his hood was jammed the driver was far more likely to try to escape through the fighting compartment. But to do this it was important to have the turret traversed right, otherwise he was trapped. Thus it was crucial that, upon evacuating the tank the gunner left the traverse control switch turned to the right so that, by starting the tank's engines, the driver could move the turret himself. Even so it was equally important, if the crew returned to the tank, to reset the switch before the engines were started, otherwise injury or damage could result. The starting up procedure involved declutching both engines by handwheels in the fighting compartment; for very cold conditions Matildas Mark IV and V were provided with ether carburettors which were charged from an Ethalet capsule through a device in the engine bulkhead.

Inside the turret the commander's position was beneath the rotating cupola over to the left side. When the tank was closed down he occupied a small seat and observed through a protected vision device in the wall of the cupola, or a periscope set in one of the cupola flaps. In practice, particularly in the desert, these hatches were rarely closed, even in action; commanders chose the riskier course of working with their heads outside the turret, which improved the view, ventilation and chances of escape for the entire crew. In tanks equipped with the earlier No.11 wireless set, a switchboard gave the commander the choice of talking on the air or instructing his crew through their own headsets, although this communication worked in one direction only. When tanks were fitted with the No.19 set, two-way communication was possible with the crew and, over the air, the commander could converse with other tanks in the vicinity or, over longer distances, with his squadron or regimental HQ.

Ahead of him the gunner occupied a small, folding seat. In the firing position he leant forwards, his left hand gripping the handle of the power traverse or manual

The Matilda pushing ditch-crossing ramps for the attack on Bardia. The bogie wheels and tracks are of the Universal Carrier type.

traversing gear as required and his right grasping the firing handle with his thumb hovering over the safety catch. The shoulder piece of the elevating gear was tucked firmly into his right shoulder and his forehead pressed against the brow pad while he concentrated on the sighting telescope. This had 1.9 times magnification and was graduated separately for the main armament or machine gun, but with a narrow field of view. Thus it was normally the commander's duty to select the target and direct the gunner onto it by reference to a vane sight just in front of the cupola. This somewhat crude device was also employed when the tank was firing from a hull, or turret down position. The gunner also had a rotating Vickers tank periscope in the turret roof.

In action the loader balanced himself on the opposite side of the turret, using his right hand to steady himself and loading with his left, a 2-pdr round being quite small and light enough to be held and loaded single handed. As soon as the gun was loaded he tapped the gunner on the arm and immediately took up another round. The semi-automatic action of the gun threw out the empty case and left the breech

ABOVE LEFT The original carpet device on a Matilda being demonstrated on a barbed wire entanglement.

ABOVE A very uncommon sight. This Matilda has been fitted with a Sunshade device to disguise it as a lorry. A light framework has been created to resemble a cab at the front and the skirting plate has been painted to give the effect of a chassis and wheels.

A wrecked Matilda photographed at Tobruk in December 1941. The hull front has been penetrated twice at its thickest point and again with even greater effect around the driver's visor. The offside tool locker has been torn open while the entire turret has been dislodged. Surely such damage could only be attributed to an 88mm gun.

open ready for the next round. The loader was also responsible for firing the two smoke dischargers which were activated by bicycle brake levers and Bowden cables. There was a small, rectangular hatch in the turret roof above the loader's station, but his only other means of observing the outside world when closed down was through a protected vision device in the turret wall behind him.

FOREIGN SERVICE

Since it was in all respects a Vickers-Armstrongs design the little Infantry Tank Mark I was, theoretically, available for export sales under existing British rules. Such evidence as there is suggests that only one was ever sold, although the company records do not appear to confirm this. But it seems that in June 1939 a sample tank was purchased by the Polish Government and shipped out through Liverpool in August. Presumably it was intended for evaluation but in the event, to judge from a surviving photograph, it was used in action following the German invasion and duly knocked out, to the extent of having its turret dislodged.

GERMANY

German records claim that 97 of these tanks were captured in France, at least two of which were examined at the Kummersdorf testing ground. One, 4th RTR's Derwent, was pulled apart for a thorough examination but the type was considered underarmed and underpowered so if they were used at all by the Wehrmacht it could only have been on internal security duties.

The A12 Matilda would have been a much more valuable prize but the handful captured in France were not much use. Some, at least, were supplied to the High Seas Training Command based at Terneuzen on the Scheldt estuary. This unit converted at least one Matilda, nicknamed Oswald, into a self-propelled mount for a 50mm gun

In German hands the Matilda was known as the Infanterie Panzer Mk II 748(e). This is the example nicknamed Oswald converted to mount the 50mm tank gun, seen here on a training exercise at Terneuzen.

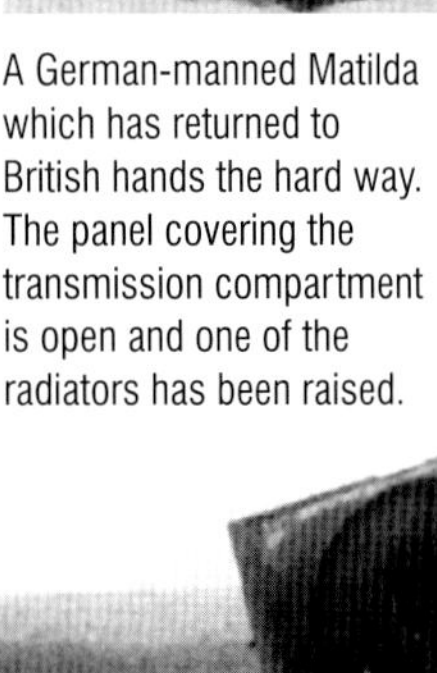

A German-manned Matilda which has returned to British hands the hard way. The panel covering the transmission compartment is open and one of the radiators has been raised.

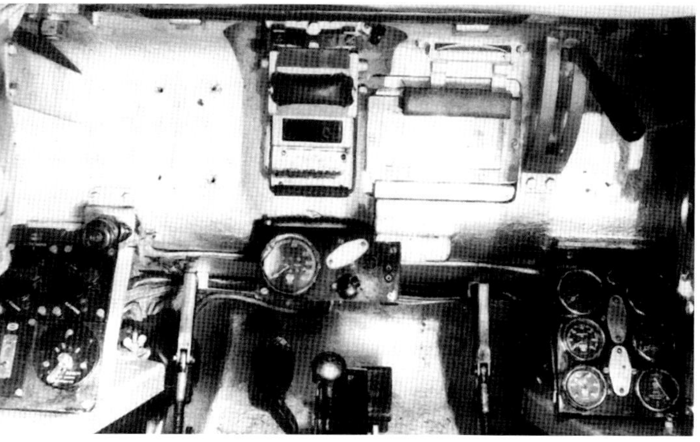

and, to add insult to injury, used others during trials for the proposed invasion of Britain. Some of those captured by the Afrika Korps were used against their former owners but, bearing in mind Rommel's comments, recorded earlier, they could hardly have been considered acceptable due to their poor mobility and in some cases their turrets were dismounted for use in fixed defences. Among those captured from the Red Army on the Eastern Front, some were converted by the Germans into extemporised artillery tractors by removing the turret.

ABOVE LEFT The driver's compartment in the Matilda tank tested in thc US. The controls, which are described in the text, include the steering levers, central speed selector and two foot pedals. All around are the switches and instruments on their various panels while above one can see the driver's direct vision block, with the lever which controls its cover on the right and the periscope to the left.

ABOVE Looking down into the cupola of the same tank, a Matilda Mark II, one can see the open hatches and the small pistons that support them, the periscope with the armoured lip that protects its head and the brow pad on the left which covers the vision block in the cupola wall. The handgrip control that moves the armoured shutter for this can also be seen, next to the knob that adjusts the spotlight. Laying on the commander's folding seat is his headset and microphone.

THE SOVIET UNION

Just over 1,000 Matildas were shipped to Russia, although some 250 were lost en route. Again their low speed and poor steering characteristics would have told against them where the battle raged over wide areas, but in winter conditions these problems were exacerbated by a tendency to clog up the suspension with snow or mud which became trapped behind the armoured skirting panels.

CANADA

Commonwealth users of the Matilda, although not falling into the category of 'foreign' in the normal sense, still warrant independent coverage. First among them, but not often recognised, were the Canadians, whose 1st Army Tank Brigade was training on Matildas in Britain in the summer of 1941 before moving on to Churchills. This may have marked the start of their disillusion with British tanks which lasted until they adopted Shermans in 1943.

NEW ZEALAND

New Zealand also received 33 Matildas, all of the Mark IVCS type. They had been ordered in 1942 when plans were being prepared for the creation of a tank brigade. This was to be based primarily on Valentines but since there was no close support version of this tank the Matildas, which also had the advantage of three-man turrets, were to be issued on the basis of six per battalion. In the event they were never used. Priorities changed with the entry of Japan into the war and a year later the brigade was broken up. One battalion was prepared for active service in the Pacific but to avoid supply difficulties the variety of tanks had to be kept to a minimum. For close support duties 18 Valentines were adapted to mount the 3in howitzers from the Matildas and, since these were now redundant, all 33 of them were handed over to the Australians in 1944.

An Australian Matilda CS tank of 2/9th Armoured Regiment on Tarakan Island in May 1945. Spare track and panels of perforated trackway have been fitted to supplement protection and the rear decks are cluttered up with additional stowage. An officer, standing between the hoops of the jettison fuel tank mounting, is directing fire using the tank's telephone handset.

AUSTRALIA

Often, when comparisons are made between British and German tanks of World War II, examples such as the PzKpfw IV are pointed to as having been in service before the war began yet still remaining suitable for front line service when it ended. It is claimed that no similar British example can be found. In the normal sense this is quite true. The PzKpfw IV had what military designers call stretch potential, meaning that it could be adapted in various respects to keep pace with developments and still hold its own. Yet the Matilda, which was at least designed before the war, could also be found fighting valiantly when the second great Axis surrender took place in August 1945, three months after VE Day had terminated the activities of the PzKpfw IVs. The reason in this case was not stretch potential, that was patently impossible; rather it was due to the Australian Army, which not only maintained and fought a temperamental, obsolete tank long after it should have been retired, but also used it in a campaign where its greatest virtue, thick armour, was still a highly significant factor.

Australia is believed to have acquired 409 Matildas from Britain and New Zealand between 1942 and 1944 and there would appear to be no truth in the legend that they were worn out veterans of the desert campaign. Indeed all but a handful seem to have been late production vehicles with the low profile cupola and therefore, presumably, the Leyland engines, so there seems little doubt that they were supplied direct from Britain.

In addition to the specialised versions recorded later the Australians introduced a number of more general modifications. One was a semblance of turret ring protection, a feature sadly absent from most British tanks. On the Matilda narrow panels of armour were arranged around the front and sides of the turret ring. Some tanks delivered from Britain already had this feature in the form of bolted-on panels, but the Australians preferred to weld theirs in place. Another addition, probably designed to prevent tenacious undergrowth from working its way in between the tracks and track guards in thick jungle, was a heavy cast shield fitted over each track at the front. On active service many crews took the traditional step of improving protection by hanging extra lengths of spare track around the front and sides of the hull, while expanded metal trackway panels were fitted at the back to prevent the Japanese from attaching sticky bombs or other adhesive demolition devices to the hull. In its final development this took the form of wire mesh panels on a steel frame covering the entire engine deck.

Although the Australian Government had raised a substantial armoured force in anticipation of contributing to the desert war this was rapidly slimmed down after 1943 when their primary commitment centred on the Pacific and what was believed to be very much an infantry war. Early experiences with M3 Stuarts did nothing to dispel this and it was only when the Matildas of 1st Army Tank Battalion landed at Milne Bay, New Guinea in August 1943 that the correct tank for this kind of warfare was discovered. Not that it was armoured warfare as any other Allied unit would have understood it, but it worked admirably. The 4th Australian Armoured Brigade, which comprised 1st Army Tank Battalion (later 1st Armoured Regiment), 2/4th and 2/9th Armoured Regiments rarely operated at more than squadron strength. Beyond the assistance of the Armoured Squadron (Special Equipment) – which prefered to be known by its old title 2/1st Armoured Reconnaissance Squadron – with their Circus Equipment, the 4th ARB had none of the usual appurtenances of an armoured brigade. This was because it relied heavily for these on the infantry to which its squadrons were attached.

By VJ Day detached squadrons from the brigade were operating in various locations on New Guinea, on Bougainville, Tarakan and Labuan Islands and North Borneo. They were often fighting at troop level on roads that were no better than jungle tracks, bisected by fast flowing rivers and liable to degenerate into swamps without warning. The enemy remained largely unseen and the tanks were often subjected to point blank fire from artillery up to 150mm-calibre which the Matildas mostly withstood, unless they were hit on their tracks. Probably for the first time since they entered service those Matildas equipped with the 3in close support howitzers now proved more popular than the 2-pdr variety since they could make an impression on Japanese bunkers.

Experience of these conditions led to further local modifications. First among these was improvised waterproofing which was essential for river crossings and the continual beach landings, for in this campaign smaller types of landing craft proved

Matildas in Canadian Army service in Britain. Only turret squadron markings are carried and the censor has even obliterated the WD numbers.

more useful for tactical moves than tank transporters. The two exhaust silencers, situated across the rear of the hull between the tracks, also proved vulnerable and a shortage of exhaust pipe elbows to repair them resulted in experiments which transferred them onto the back of the hull, each side of the engine decks. Finally an infantry telephone set was added to the rear of the hull which allowed the troops to communicate with the tank when it was closed down under fire. This reflects the increasing reliance that the Australian infantry began to place on their tanks once they had proved what they could do, even in the most incredible locations. At the same time it was soon discovered that the Japanese evinced considerable reluctance to face the tanks and often quit otherwise defensible positions once they heard the Matildas approaching.

Thus it was that these old war horses remained on active service right up to the end, even into the nuclear age. As if that was not surprising enough a few Matildas served with the Citizen Military Forces in Australia until about 1955.

VARIANTS

Towards the end of World War I the British Army invested a lot of time and effort in the development of specialised armour; that is tanks adapted to undertake subsidiary roles on the battlefield, most of which were tasks normally carried out by the Royal Engineers. Between the wars this interest lapsed; nothing of any note was done until as late as 1937 and even then only in a modest way.

MINE CLEARING

As a first step consideration was given to means of defeating mines, which were regarded as a particular threat to tanks, and the agricultural engineers, John Fowler & Co., of Leeds, patented a coulter plough device which was designed to lift mines and turn them aside without setting them off. Following trials on a Mark IV Dragon the equipment was fitted to the prototype tank A11E1. It consisted of a girder frame, pivoted to the sides of the tank, which carried sets of blades and rollers ahead of each track. When it was not unearthing mines the contraption had to be raised clear of the ground, for which purpose a power take-off gearbox was mounted on the rear of the hull, directly above the transmission. Chains from the frame ran over pulleys on this attachment and, when raised, the plough was held above the driver's line of sight.

The original Fowler roller device attached to a Matilda in Egypt. The rollers are of the open, spoked pattern with what appear to be studs on the outer surface.

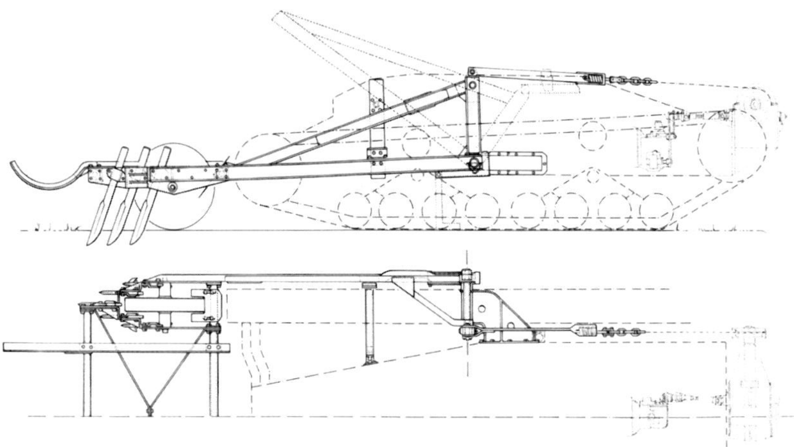

Drawings taken from the original patent documents show the Fowler Coulter Plough minesweeping device as fitted to A11E1. In addition to the tines and rollers one can see the lifting apparatus at the back and the gearbox take-off that operated it. The broken lines show where it was held in the lifted position.

Following trials, and all manner of modifications including the addition of wire cutters, the plough device was ordered for fitting to production versions of the Infantry Tank Mark I. Production of the first 60 tanks then being under way it proved impossible to make the alterations essential to accept the plough, but they were incorporated into the design of the remaining 79. By the end of January 1940, 14 ploughs had been delivered, of which 12 were with the battalions in France, but trials revealed that the equipment would not work effectively in rough or frozen ground and it was never employed. In any case the opportunity never arose.

Plans to fit a similar device to the A12 Matilda were defeated by the complications of installing a power take-off on a more sophisticated gearbox so other options were considered. The Anti-Tank Mine Committee, which appears to have been both poacher and gamekeeper, was impressed by a French device that employed six large steel discs. Although deemed unsuitable as it stood a British version was created and fitted to a Matilda, but it proved too cumbersome for operational use. Rollers of a different sort had already been designed by Fowlers for British cruiser tanks and these were readily modified to suit Matilda, first with spoked rollers and ultimately as the Anti-Mine Roller Attachment (AMRA) with an enclosed drum type.

The Fowler Coulter Plough device fitted to A11E1. The equipment is in the raised or travelling position, and it is also fitted with the tubular steel wire cutters.

An otherwise unrecorded Matilda modification from the time of the Bardia operation. A truncated anti-mine roller frame supports large ploughshares ahead of each track and the whole assembly is piloted by a pair of lorry wheels.

A Matilda with AMRA Mark IA featuring the drum pattern rollers and with a Carrot demolition device mounted at the front, shown alongside a Churchill III during trials in Britain.

The AMRA consisted of a frame, located on brackets attached to the tank's side plates, which was supported on four broad rollers, arranged ahead of the tracks. Since a roller would be destroyed when it detonated a mine the system had its limitations and could only be used to detect their presence. Once the minefield was located it had to be cleared by hand, unless some other means could be found. One school of thought favoured sympathetic detonation, and the Obstacle Assault Centre carried out trials with a device codenamed 'Carrot'. It came in three sizes; the largest contained 600lb of explosive, the second a 75lb shaped charge and the third a modest 25lb. The two larger varieties were carried on mine roller attachments which were automatically detached in the middle of a minefield, or against an obstacle, and detonated by remote control, hopefully taking all the mines out at the same time. Of 140 AMRAs supplied for Matilda, 100 were earmarked for modernisation while the rest were put aside for Carrot trials. The smallest, Light Carrot, which a Matilda or Churchill could carry on its nose, was simply designed to be pressed up against an obstacle and detonated, without harming the tank.

MATILDA SCORPION MARK I FLAIL TANK

Elements of 6th, 42nd and 44th Royal Tank Regiments operated Matilda Scorpion flail tanks at second Alamein, albeit with limited success. Most crews appear to have discarded the access panel on the side of the auxiliary engine housing, presumably in an effort to reduce the operating temperature of the Ford V8. The drive shaft, connecting this engine with the flail rotor, can be seen passing through the boom girders. Viewed from this side of the tank the flails would be turning in a clockwise direction. Also visible are the tall station-keeping indicators at the back, which were often all that could be seen of the tank in action. None of these tanks appear to have been camouflage painted at this stage and the only marking visible is the WD number, in black, on the side of the flail motor box and across the rear of the hull. (Art by Peter Sarson, © Osprey Publishing)

THE MATILDA SCORPION

A far more effective method of destroying mines was the tank-mounted flail. Again it had been considered before the war, but the system ultimately adopted derived from the work of the South African engineer Abraham du Toit. Having gained some recognition in the desert he was sent to Britain to develop his invention but unofficial experiments continued in Libya under Captain Norman Berry RAOC. Once the value of his work had been appreciated, in the late summer of 1942, some Matilda tanks were collected for conversion since by now they were virtually obsolete as fighting tanks. Known as Matilda Scorpions they were modified at a Base Workshop in Egypt. Each Scorpion was fitted with lattice girder arms extending forwards on each side of the tank, with a

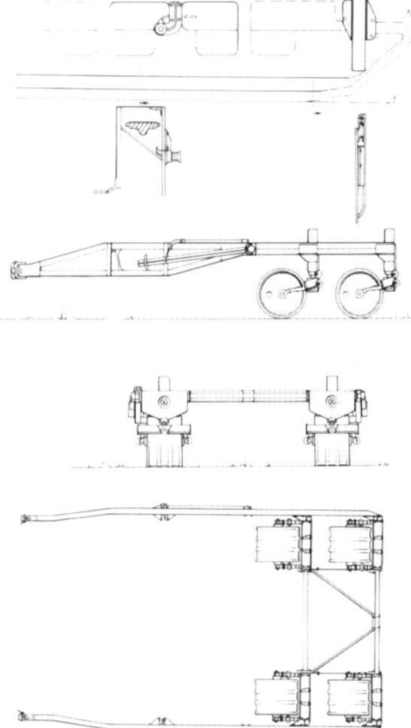

A diagram from the Anti-Mine Roller Attachment handbook showing the equipment and the brackets which attach it to the tank. The assembly pivots on the rear bearing and is free to slide within the front bracket.

A Matilda Scorpion II flail tank showing the modified girder arrangement. Viewed from this side one can see the Crusader type air-filter inboard of the engine housing and the wedge-shaped fitting at the back. In this version the flail operator formed part of the turret crew.

rotating drum mounted between their outer ends from which hung the cable and chain flails. Power for the flail was provided by a Ford V8 engine, complete with its own drivetrain and cooling system, installed in a large box hanging from the right side of the tank. This box also housed the flail operator in supreme discomfort. Twenty-four of these devices were available for the Battle of Alamein in October 1942, where they enjoyed some modest success, but there was plenty of room for improvement.

By the time the Eighth Army had reached Tunisia, early in 1943, a Matilda Scorpion Mark II had evolved, in which the flail operator worked from inside the

The Matilda modified to demonstrate the flying Bangalore torpedo equipment. The explosive tube rests in crutches on the side. To fire it is elevated from the bracket at the back and launched by remote control from within the tank. The spiked collar near the leading end causes it to catch in a barbed wire entanglement before detonating.

tank itself, but both models suffered badly from overheating of the flail engine. Mark II Scorpions were used during operations against the Mareth Line defences but by now the Matilda was being regarded as too slow for the work; not that the actual flailing could be done any faster but because there were not enough of them to do all the mine clearing required, and they were not fast enough to move quickly from one job to another.

THE MATILDA BARON

Meanwhile in Britain, du Toit, working in conjunction with AEC Ltd., continued to develop his ideas. Again the Matilda served as the basis but the codename selected here was 'Baron'. The prototype, designated Mark I, which used a Chrysler engine with chain and sprocket drive to the flail, was redeveloped as the Mark II which employed a Bedford engine and shaft drive. In both forms this prototype retained its 2-pdr turret and had the flail engine housed on the right side. The production version was a major development. The turret was replaced by a fixed superstructure and two Bedford engines were used, slung on each side of the tank. The object was to supply more power since it had now been decided to extend the scope of the Baron so that, in addition to flailing, it could chop its way through barbed wire and even excavate earthworks by lowering its rotor, which was formed from cross girders rather than a drum. This version appeared first as the Matilda Baron Mark III and, in slightly improved form, as the Mark IIIA, 60 of which were built by Curran Brothers of Cardiff and issued for training and demonstrations, although they never saw active service.

OPPOSITE The original Matilda Baron flail, probably in its second guise, showing the open style rotor in the raised position and the complicated system of linked chains adopted for the Baron.

THE CANAL DEFENCE LIGHT (CDL)

The history of the device known as the Canal Defence Light (CDL) is too involved to be included here but it is important for its associations with the Matilda tank. Indeed it was the Matilda that was first selected for conversion to this role and which, at one time, equipped four out of the five Royal Armoured Corps regiments trained to operate it. To convert the tank, the original turret was replaced by a special pattern

MATILDA BARON MARK IIIA FLAIL TANK, 'B' Squadron, 43rd Royal Tank Regiment

Matilda Barons used for training in Britain were finished in the khaki brown shade from late 1942 until 1944. Again there is no evidence of unit or squadron markings being applied although the WD number, in white, was painted on the flail motor housings, repeated on the flail boom girders, on the back of the hull and across the front of the crew compartment.

Three features worth noting are the hydraulic cylinder, multi-jointed flail rotor drive shaft and the flail motor exhaust and silencer emerging from beneath the housing. Viewed from this side the flails would rotate in an anti-clockwise direction. (Art by Peter Sarson, © Osprey Publishing)

built to a 65mm armour standard, which contained a carbon arc lamp that projected an eight million candle-power beam. Using mirrors the beam was directed through a vertical slit in the turret front, protected by a moving shutter which reduced the risk from small-arms fire and caused the light to flicker. Half of the turret, on the left, was partitioned off and occupied by the operator who controlled the light, replaced burnt out carbons and used the tank's only armament, a Besa machine gun, if required. The driver, the only other crew member, doubled as the wireless operator.

The entire CDL project was regarded as highly secret and in Britain trials were conducted in a secluded part of the Lake District. As an adjunct to night attacks the CDL tanks would line up, about 100 yards apart, and cause their beams to intercept some 300 yards from the base line, creating triangles of darkness in which attacking troops could operate. Defenders would be dazzled and, firing blind, could only inflict casualties by chance, whereas the attackers had a clear view of their objectives. Two Army Tank Brigades (1st and 35th) were converted to this role between 1941 and 1944 and from the latter 42nd Royal Tank Regiment was despatched to Egypt as the basis for a brigade to be formed out there. A CDL regiment was planned on the basis of 42 searchlight tanks and 19 gun tanks, the latter to serve as troop and squadron leader's tanks plus four, probably of the close support type, with regimental headquarters. A system was therefore devised by which gun tanks could be converted instantly to the CDL role and vice versa. The scheme involved a 5-ton capacity crane attachment that could be mounted on any Matilda enabling it to swap over turrets as required. The only other task then being to fit an extra generator, belt driven from a pulley on the drive shaft. Matilda CDL tanks were also fitted with a low visibility, monoslot headlamp on each track guard, almost a CDL in miniature, for ordinary night driving.

As a subject for CDL conversion a Matilda had the advantages of being available in quantity, well armoured and reasonably reliable. Against this it was slow, had to run its main engines in order to drive the generator when the light was being used

MATILDA CANAL DEFENCE LIGHT AND MATILDA CRANE TANK, 49th Royal Tank Regiment, 35th Tank Brigade

In this picture a Matilda fitted with a portable crane attachment is in the process of converting a 2-pdr gun tank into a CDL. The crane has lifted the special armoured turret onto a Matilda chassis, having first removed the tank's original 2-pdr turret. This gives some idea of the speed and ease with which this conversion could be carried out

Both tanks are painted in khaki brown with disruptive areas of very dark brown. Markings on the nearest vehicle include the brown and dark green diabolo device of 35th Tank Brigade. Notice the special low-visibility monoslot headlamps ahead of the original side lamps on each track guard. (Art by Peter Sarson, © Osprey Publishing)

and, with only a two-man crew, was a bit of a handful to operate. By 1943 it was also rather outdated and was duly replaced in the surviving CDL regiments by M3 Lee and Grant tanks.

OTHER VARIANTS

Apart from those minor modifications covered in the previous section there were one or two experimental versions of Matilda developed in Britain which deserve a mention. 'Black Prince' was the codename given to a radio-controlled prototype which appeared in 1941. It was based on A12E2 with the full Wilson transmission which could be activated by remote control. The experiment had a variety of aims. One was to create a mobile target tank, which was abandoned on the grounds of extravagance. Another was to use the tank as a means of drawing enemy fire to reveal locations of hidden anti-tank guns and it was also considered as a crewless tank for sacrificial, demolition missions. An order for 60 was cancelled once it was realised that all the tanks would have to have their transmissions modified since the Rackham clutches were not suitable for remote activation. Another Matilda was adapted to carry a single length of Bangalore torpedo, in crutches, on the nearside skirting plate. This could be elevated when required and then fired into barbed wire entanglements to cut a path for infantry. A project that harked back to World War I had a Matilda pushing a long section of Inglis portable bridge, on dumb caterpillar tracks, which it could propel across a gap under fire and then drive over into action.

The Matilda Restive being used to demonstrate the launching procedure for an Inglis bridge on tracks. The main alteration to the tank involved fitting a massive bracket to the nose. Notice how the rear number plate has been repainted to show the WD number.

AUSTRALIAN VARIANTS

The Australian Army developed its own range of modified Matildas under the collective title of Circus Equipment, designed in response to the requirements of jungle warfare.

Tank bulldozers

The first of these was a tank bulldozer, using a Britstand full-width blade manufactured by the British Standard Machinery Co., of Sydney. It came in two forms; the No.1 Mark I used cables to raise and lower the blade while the No.3 Mark I used hydraulics, activated by a Hydreco oil pump driven by chain and sprocket from the propellor shaft. The former type was used by 2/1 Australian Armoured Brigade Reconnaissance Squadron during the landings on Labuan and Balikapan in August 1945, but with no apparent success. The extra weight of the blade and pushpoles kept the nose of the tank down, causing the blade to dig in. The tank driver was unable to see what he was doing while bulldozing and, even with the Rackham clutches in perfect condition, it was very difficult to steer. The second version was supplied as a field fitting kit at the end of the war, but even this caused problems due to poor manufacturing standards. Most of the shortcomings already encountered with the first model were repeated in the second. The original idea had been to use the dozer tanks to remove obstacles under fire, fill in craters in roads or, as a last resort, bury occupied Japanese bunkers, while the tanks were capable of jettisoning their blades and acting as conventional tanks if necessary.

OPPOSITE An Australian Matilda with the second type of bulldozer blade, hydraulically operated. An armoured cover is fitted over the hydraulic cylinder on each side. This is one of the relatively few Matildas to be seen in Australia with the tall cupola.

The Frog

The Australian flamethrower version of Matilda was known as the 'Frog'. The projector was mounted in place of the main armament, within a tube designed to resemble the 3in howitzer, and the co-axial Besa machine gun was retained. In order to avoid the complication of feeding flame fuel through a rotary junction at the turret base the main fuel and compressed air propellant tanks were located within the turret. This left it cramped for the remaining crew member after the redundant gunner and loader had been omitted. Eighty gallons of a thickened flame fuel called Geletrol were stored in this internal tank with a further 100 gallons in an external

A Matilda Frog flamethrower blazing away at maximum range with considerable effect. Despite what was, in fact, a fairly complicated conversion the tank appears to be almost unaltered from the outside.

EXPERIMENTAL MATILDA HEDGEHOG ROCKET FIRING TANK, 4th Australian Armoured Brigade, Queensland, 1945

The 'Projector' (Hedgehog No.1 Mark I) tank is shown with the launcher box elevated, in the process of firing a barrage of rockets at a demonstration. The Matilda is finished in the Australian dark jungle green but retains the original fording height markings and displays its British WD number in large white digits, without the initial letter T. (Art by Peter Sarson, © Osprey Publishing)

jettison tank at the back, 30 gallons in tanks which replaced the tool lockers on either side of the nose and another 32 gallons shared between four small tanks in the sides of the hull. It was hardly an ideal arrangement and the system for replenishing the main tank from the reserves was complicated but essential. The Frog fired out to a range of about 90 yards and used ten gallons in every burst. When they were used on Borneo the flamethrowers proved very effective against Japanese positions, although it was considered a nuisance that, with the existing pressure feed system, there was a 30 second pause between bursts for the pressure to build up again. Not surprisingly it seems that the front and side reserve tanks were never filled when the Frogs went into action, and even the jettison tank could prove vulnerable in thick jungle conditions. An improved Matilda flamethrower codenamed 'Murray' employed cordite as a propellant. This not only speeded up the rate of fire but allowed more space in the turret, which now had an increased flame fuel capacity of 130 gallons, although this appeared too late to be used in action during the war.

The Projector

The last Australian Matilda conversion was certainly the most ambitious, and probably the most spectacular in effect although it was never employed operationally. This was the 'Projector', Hedgehog No.1 Mark I. It stemmed from an original scheme to launch an anti-submarine depth charge from a tank against enemy bunkers, but was modified to fire a battery of smaller projectiles. The conversion involved fitting a seven chambered launcher box to the back of the tank, above the engine louvres. It was pivoted at the rear and raised or lowered by hydraulics adapted from the Logan turret traverse apparatus from an American M3 Medium tank. In the travelling position the launcher, which was protected by an armoured shield, lay flat within a low, three-sided superstructure. To fire it was elevated to 45 degrees and aimed by pointing the tank.

The projectiles, which were also naval anti-submarine weapons, each weighed 63lb but were modified to accept a percussion fuse. Range was between 200–300 yards, depending on the propellant used, and firing was initiated electrically. Bombs 1, 2, 3, 4, 6 and 7 were fired with the turret at 12 o'clock but it had to be traversed to 1 o'clock when round No. 5 was fired to spare the wireless aerial. Results of trials carried out at Southport, Queensland, in May 1945 suggest that as a bunker busting weapon the Hedgehog would have been impressive. Accuracy was stated to be adequate for all practical purposes and the commander of 4th Australian Brigade commented: 'The conduct of the trial left nothing to be desired and was carried out to my entire satisfaction'.

CHAPTER 2

THE A13 CRUISER TANK

A VISIT TO RUSSIA

In 1936 Major General A.P. Wavell headed a party to attend the autumn manoeuvres of the Red Army. The party included personnel from the Royal Air Force and the Army, in particular Lieutenant-Colonel Giffard le Quesne Martel, the Deputy Director of Mechanisation, who was very impressed with what he saw. As Martel pointed out in his report the Russians used their light medium tank, the impressive BT-series fast tank, for the same purpose that Britain was using light tanks. The Russians regarded light tanks as reconnaissance vehicles and appreciated the need for a cruiser tank to fulfil the exploitation role.

This obviously appealed to Martel, as did the tanks which paraded in their thousands and put up an impressive performance on what Martel knew was their Christie suspension. His first impulse was to acquire one from the Russians in order to investigate the suspension, but this proved to be impossible; the War Office in

A BT-5 Model 1933 tank, at that time the most up-to-date Christie cruiser in Soviet service.

London was not about to purchase a Russian tank, no matter how good it appeared to be. But Martel was advised by Lieutenant-Colonel J.S. Crawford, the Assistant Director of Mechanisation (Wheeled Vehicles) to go directly to Christie in the United States. Martel was not in a position to do this himself and since he believed the War Office would take too long over what he considered to be an urgent matter he approached the industrialist Lord Nuffield, head of the Morris Motors group of companies, to ask if he would be willing to contact Christie on the government's behalf. It was an inspired move. Christie could be awkward, but Nuffield (William Morris) was equally tough, and independent enough to deal with him.

THE A13 PROTOTYPES

The War Office was expected to meet the cost of acquiring and shipping the tank, although for the sake of speed the arrangements were negotiated by Lord Nuffield's group. The Christie tank supplied to Great Britain is quoted as being Christie's M1931, the prototype of the T3-series Medium tank.

The Morris Company began the process by making a transatlantic telephone call, quite a pantomime in itself in those days, and as a result a tank was taken to New York for shipment to the UK. But here a snag arose. It appears that Christie had mortgaged the tank in order to raise funds and it was necessary for the War Office to repay the mortgage before it was released. This may be the origin of the claim that the tank was already impounded by the US Government authorities from whom it had to be released. Quite why Christie should not pay this off himself, or at least deduct this payment from the overall cost of the tank is not clear, but typically Christie. The figure quoted, £10,420 18s 4d, which included British Customs Duties and what are described as 'other expenses', is included among the documents attached to the ledger entry in the Mechanisation Experimental Establishment (MEE) at Farnborough, to which the tank was delivered on 17 November 1936.

Legend had it that the tank was shipped described as a 'Convertible Truck Tractor' to get around the US Government's prohibition of the export of war materials while other components were shipped separately, marked 'Grapefruit'. What these other components comprised is not clear except that it did not include a turret, as legend insists, because M1931 did not normally have a turret and it would have been no use to the British anyway. The tank appears to have featured chain final drive for running on wheels, as many Christie-built tanks did.

OPPOSITE BT-series tanks such as Martel would have seen, moving across country.

A13E1, the original Christie prototype imported by Lord Nuffield. Close examination of this photograph suggests that it is not the original M1931 prototype the British thought they were getting but one of the ex-US Army T3 tanks, without its turret. The air cleaners were a later British addition.

However it has been suggested that rather than the prototype M1931, the tank actually sent was one of the production tanks of the T3 series, and detailed examination of photographs seems to confirm this. The US Army had decided to replace the T3 in about 1934, and it seems that one at least was returned to Christie. Although it seems odd that this survivor, suitably repaired, should be sent over to Britain, it appears that this was all that was available. Whether the sum charged included reimbursement to the US Army is not clear. The tank that came to Britain appears to have been put together hastily in 1936, but without a turret.

On arrival at MEE the tank was given the British War Department number T2086, the road registration number BMX841 and the General Staff specification A13E1, in addition to MEE's own experimental number 958. The staff at MEE found that as supplied the tank had no air filters, so a set was provided since their main task was to test and report on performance. In this they were well gratified, as the tank proved to have a stirring performance on level ground with excellent hill climbing qualities, although when the engine backfired it blew off the air filters. Being a nine-ton tank powered by a 350hp petrol V12 water-cooled Liberty aircraft engine, it had an impressive power-to-weight ratio. They were also very impressed with the gearbox which, although basic and conventional in most respects, had been arranged with gear ratios to suit the engine and, of course, the lively suspension system – without which all the other advantages would be minimal. After all, it was for the suspension that the tank had been acquired in the first place.

MEE was not expected to comment upon armour plate thickness or the fighting compartment, although the former was only 13mm thick in order to keep the weight down, while the turret ring was so small that it would not even accept the turret from a British Light Tank, never mind anything heavier. Following trials the tank was sent to Morris Commercial Cars Ltd in Birmingham where the staff prepared to take it apart. Lord Nuffield had already agreed to buy the patent rights to the suspension system from Christie and had decided that his firm should undertake development of the tank.

Christie called it his M1938 although today it is regarded as M1937; photographed at Farnborough. Negotiations over its long-term stay in Britain broke down, and in any case Nuffield Mechanization & Aero said they knew all they wanted to know about Christie suspension from the M1931 so Christie took it back to America via France.

In fact, now that he was entering tank production in a big way, and aware that war with Germany was pending, in 1937 Nuffield formed a new company, Mechanization and Aero Ltd, also based in Birmingham, that would produce tanks and aircraft. However it is worth remarking that, deriving from firms that produced medium-weight commercial vehicles and private cars, Mechanization & Aero was not steeped in the traditions of heavy engineering, which may have told against it at least at the outset.

A13E2, the first Christie cruiser to be built in England, was a striking machine. It had many features new to British tanks and also retained enough original Christie features to betray its origins, although these were not all obvious from the outside.

First of course it was necessary to widen and lengthen the hull – only by a matter of inches, but sufficient, with the turret, to add at least two tons to the overall weight. The main reason for this was to provide a turret ring of sufficient diameter to accommodate a three-man turret based on the design first adopted for the A7 series medium tanks and, of course, the A9 and A10 cruiser tanks. The turret, which featured a large, drum-shaped cupola, mounted a 40mm (2-pdr) gun and a co-axial Vickers machine gun in addition to having an extension at the rear for a radio set.

The front of the hull was squared off, rather than having the sharp, pointed nose typical of a Christie tank. This was done because the Mechanization Board was not keen on another Christie feature, the option to run as a wheeled as well as a tracked vehicle. The pointed nose on the Christie tank was essential to provide clearance for the moveable front wheels to steer when the tank was not running on tracks. However, it also meant that the British designers did not need to adopt the sloping front plate which appears to be one of the better features of the original Christie design. Instead the hull front of A13E2, and all the tanks that followed it, was not only square, but stepped in the traditional style. There was a plan, indeed almost a requirement, to install a machine-gun mounting in the front of the hull. It was a feature of most British tanks at this time and normally increased the crew to five. And it could have been done, if the driver's cab was moved across to one side. However the Nuffield design placed the cab, a square, protruding metal box, dead centre at the front of the hull leaving no room for a machine-gun position.

The Christie parentage was obvious from outside by the arrangement of the wheels, the toothless drive sprocket at the back, and by the Christie-style tracks. These tracks were 10in-square plates, dry-pin jointed, which slapped their way violently around the idler wheel at the front, and used their large central guide horns on every second link to engage with rollers set into the spokes of the drive sprocket which, for that reason, did not need conventional teeth. There was concern about these track plates. Nothing had been seen like them in Britain since World War I and the effect they had on other components of the suspension of a high-speed tank was very marked. Lord Nuffield himself is said to have expressed doubts about them but an attempt by Morris-Commercial to reduce the size of the track links to a 5in pitch, with modified drive sprocket, did not work either.

Inside the tank, at least abaft the fighting compartment, Christie features dominated. The Liberty engine was reworked by Nuffield's company to produce 411bhp at 2,000rpm, and was linked to a constant mesh four-speed gearbox with clutch and brake steering in the final drive – a tough and simple arrangement. It is worth noting at this point that Christie, unlike most American tank designers, opted for rear sprocket drive. Most other American tanks featured a rear engine layout with gearbox and final drive at the front, a practice they pursued for most of World War

A13E3, now fitted with British-type tracks and toothed drive sprocket. The box on the side of the turret, if it is not a ballast weight, probably contains an anti-aircraft machine gun and mounting bracket. Notice also the lever-operated aerial mounting on the back of the turret.

II. In Britain a rear engine and final drive to rear sprockets was the norm, except on Light Tanks, so in that sense the A13 series conformed to normal British practice.

A13E3, which appeared in February 1938, was much the same as A13E2 except in respect of track and sprockets. Clearly the Christie-style tracks and sprockets were deemed unsuitable for use on British tanks, for the new tank featured conventional toothed sprockets at the back matched to a much shorter pitched track, albeit of a new and original design. Hitherto many of the more recent British tanks, notably the Light Tanks, had featured very short pitch, dry-pin tracks of malleable cast iron, suited to their higher speeds and vigorous cross-country performance; however, the two new cruiser tanks, A9 and A10, were equipped with longer pitch tracks connected by double pins but lubricated to give better movement. Lubricated tracks, it turned out, did not work; they leaked and attracted sand and grit, so Nuffield's company came up with an entirely new design, again with double pins but unlubricated this time and of relatively short pitch, which set the pattern for production versions of the A13 tank.

In January 1938 Christie himself arrived in Britain with a new tank which he had christened M1938. In fact it is believed to have been an earlier prototype, M1932, rebuilt. However it was quite a striking rebuild and was essentially a new tank. Christie's motives for offering this new tank to Britain, uninvited, may be put down either to desperation or, more likely, his normal habit of wanting to give his customers the benefit of his latest thinking, on the understanding that any previous tank purchased was obsolete. M1938 was a lower, more streamlined design with sharply angled main suspension springs, encased but highly visible on each side. The front of the hull was full width, in addition to being well sloped, and it does not look as if the wheel and track option was included in the design. The tank was also fitted with shorter pitch tracks, 5in rather than 10in, which suggests that Christie was aware of the requirements of his customers.

Again the tank did not feature a turret or any evidence of a weapon mounting and as such was recorded as incomplete by the staff at MEE. However Christie met with a minor disaster at the outset; his engineer and driver, Leo Anderson, did not realise that the gearbox had lost all its oil so it seized solid after going a few miles and Christie had to tour the area to find a firm able to supply replacement gears. Since it was Christie's own tank, and his latest product, he was not eager that potential customers should look at it too closely. They would know that it was powered by a

Curtiss D12 aero engine, rated at 670bhp at 2,600rpm, and despite Christie's limitations on their examination of the tank, they could still learn a lot just by looking at it.

Once repaired the tank was given further tests, but driven exclusively by Anderson. At one point it achieved 64.3mph over the Flying Quarter Mile, running slightly downhill, and Christie was so delighted by this that he requested Colonel Martel to confirm it in writing on a sales brochure for the tank. Martel believed that the British were duty-bound to purchase the tank although MEE and Nuffield's stated that they knew all they needed to know about Christie suspension from the earlier tank. Christie had also arranged that a party from France should come over to Farnborough and inspect the tank, perhaps with a view to interesting French engineers in the Christie system. But before that could happen a party from the US Embassy in London turned up and reminded Christie that under United States law he was forbidden to sell war materials abroad, and he was instructed to take the tank down to Southampton and ship it home.

However according to a reliable French book Christie actually took the tank to France and it was demonstrated at Vincennes in March 1938. The demonstration at Vincennes was very brief, either because Christie had been visited again by men from the US Embassy in Paris, or because he had reasons of his own. But although the French were clearly impressed by the Christie design they had no immediate use for it, so the tank was returned to the United States. In April 1939 a tank with Christie-type suspension was designed by Joseph Molinié of the AMX company, but Molinié was more interested in how the British had adapted the Christie running gear to a chassis of their own design, and incorporated this into what he proposed as his AMX 40. It was to feature French technology with a cast armoured hull with a thickness at the front equivalent to 60mm thick vertical armour, with space for a crew of three and powered by an Aster six-cylinder diesel engine. In the event it was never built. The French, apparently, were also impressed by the A13 cruiser and wanted to buy some but were discouraged by the cost; although this is very difficult to substantiate, it remains an intriguing 'might have been'.

T4386 (HMC738), the first production model of the A13 Cruiser in its original form, but without the smoke dischargers fitted to the bracket on the side of the turret. Notice the box above the driver's cab, for collecting spent cartridge cases from the machine gun.

ABOVE A13 Cruiser tanks, still without their guns, are sent out of the factory for proving trials on the wasteland outside.

ABOVE RIGHT A Cruiser Mark IV, viewed from the front carrying its full armament. An armoured shield has been fitted over the mantlet which may be an early 14mm version.

TANK PRODUCTION

The first order for A13 tanks was placed with Nuffield Mechanization & Aero to contract number T5114, dated 22 January 1938.The order was for 65 tanks Cruiser Mark III, with WD numbers T4385 to T4449. This would almost certainly be the first order to be placed with the Nuffield Mechanization & Aero plant in Birmingham. It was in fact the only order for Mark III Cruisers to be built. Deliveries began in April 1939 and were completed in December.

Four more orders were placed for a total of 240 A13 Mk II tanks (Cruiser Mk IV), all with Mechanization & Aero at Birmingham. They were contract numbers T6552, T7854, T9714 and T9590. But these only add to the confusion. T6552, for example, very specifically states that 64 would be completed as Mark II (Cruiser Mk IV) and 31 as Mark IIA (Cruiser Mk IVA). T7854, on the other hand, equally specifically states that all 80 tanks on that order were to be completed as Mark II (Cruiser Mk IV). Yet T9714, for 35 tanks, also specifically states Mark II (Cruiser Mk IV) and yet there is reason to believe that some, if not all of these tanks were completed as Mark IIA (Cruiser Mk IVA) and there is photographic evidence to support this. Finally the contract card for T9590, covering just 30 tanks, states quite categorically that this entire batch was ordered and completed as Mark IIA (Cruiser Mk IVA). And just to add to the confusion, note that these tanks could be described either as A13 Mark II or IIA, or as Cruiser tanks Mark IV and IVA.

The next order is certainly the most controversial and the only one for these tanks not placed with the Nuffield Organisation. A contract (number T6551) was placed on 26 January 1939 with the London, Midland & Scottish (LMS) Railway Company, and according to some records only 31 out of the 65 ordered were built. However another source claims that while 30 tanks are recorded as having been built by the LMS Railway Company at Crewe, the balance of 35 were ordered from the Horwich works in March 1939. Horwich had been the workshops of the Lancashire & Yorkshire Railway Company until it amalgamated with the London & North Western Railway in March 1921 and then shortly afterwards, on 1 January 1923, these companies

An A13 under construction at the Nuffield Mechanization & Aero factory in Birmingham. It is the start of the process showing the lower hull plate with tubular stiffeners and the base of the turret in place.

were grouped into the LMS. Horwich was also building A12 Matilda tanks at this time and the railway workshops at Crewe and Derby undertook machining and the sub-assembly of parts for the A13. Another source explains that only 31 tanks were completed out of an order for 65 that was placed with the LMS at Horwich. It is all rather confusing and may have something to do with the belief that not all heavy engineering firms had the ability to build tanks at the outset.

TOP Nuffield Liberty V12 petrol engines being assembled. An old design but a clear favourite with Lord Nuffield, at 340hp it was probably adequate for the A13.

ABOVE The A13 production line at Mechanization & Aero, making Mark IV or IVA Cruisers.

The full range of WD numbers was T7030 to T7094 and delivery was commenced in August 1939 and completed in February 1940. According to all sources, including the original contract card, they were all of the Cruiser Mark IVA type. If the figure of 31 is correct then one would expect the upper WD number figure to be T7060 but this cannot be confirmed. However suggestions that A13 Cruiser tanks were also built by Leyland Motors and English Electric are incorrect, as is the suggestion that the Cruiser Mark IVA had a Wilson gearbox. As far as it is possible to tell, based upon surviving vehicle handbooks, all of these tanks had simple clutch and brake steering.

Thus it is difficult, if not impossible, to tell how many tanks were completed as Mark IVA rather than Mark IV. Based on the information contained in the contract cards, the best we can say is that at least 97 tanks were completed as Mark IIA (Cruiser Mark IVA), leaving the balance of 143 tanks as Mark II (Cruiser Mark IV), but these are untrustworthy figures, only to be used as a rough guide.

So what were these different Mark numbers and what did they mean? The first batch, known variously as A13 Mark I, or Cruiser Mark III, were essentially copies of the prototype A13E3, built to a 14mm armour standard, with plain-sided turrets. A13 Mark II, or Cruiser Mark IV, were built to a 30mm armour standard which increased the weight by about one ton. This increase in armour thickness was a General Staff specification, theoretically applicable to all Cruiser tanks, so only the first 65 A13s slipped through the net, and then not by very much. On the A13 Mark II (Cruiser Mk IV) 30mm thick armour was to be applied around the front of the hull and to the gun mounting, while the turret itself was up-armoured by the addition of extra plates on the sides and rear but spaced away from the armour of the original

TOP Here they are assembling turrets. Notice the cupolas being put together in the foreground. Once again they are for Mark IV or IVA Cruisers, but notice how the angled turret armour is spaced.

ABOVE Now a turret is being lowered into place on a hull, using an overhead crane.

turret. This spaced armour gave the turret a more-or-less diamond-shaped frontal aspect, since the lower panels were undercut and inward sloping. Later on in the war this process of adding spaced armour was devised in order to defeat the penetrating power of hand-held weapons firing hollow-charges, but the reason given for adopting it at this stage sounds altogether more ingenious. The theory was that when a solid shot anti-tank round was fired at a tank the first layer of armour it encountered and penetrated deflected it slightly from its original course so that, when it struck the next layer, it was less likely to penetrate. Whether this worked in practice is another matter, although it was stated that the air gap between the inner and outer layers of armour had to be greater than the overall length of the projectile fired at it. It is questionable whether it would protect against anything but an anti-tank rifle round, and even if it worked with the German 37mm round of 1940 it certainly would not protect against the 50mm German round encountered later in the desert. One might ask whether if it was so effective, it was not more widely used, even on other parts of the tank.

Some of the A13 Mark I tanks were also fitted with this spaced armour around the turret although nothing could be done to improve the frontal armour. This effectively brought them up to Mark II (Cruiser Mk IV) standard, at least as far as the turret was concerned. The extra armour makes them difficult to tell apart from the Mark II, although it can be done, provided one can see the front of the turret.

The A13 Mark IIA, or Cruiser Mark IVA , was identical to the Mark II except for a change in the co-axial armament. In place of the .303 water-cooled Vickers gun fitted to Mark I and Mark II tanks the Marks IIA mounted a 7.92mm calibre air-cooled Besa machine gun alongside the main 2-pdr weapon. This seems to have resulted in a change to the design of the mantlet to accept the new weapon although the variety of mantlet shapes seen on A13 series tanks is very confusing at the best of times. Some tanks are even seen with a large, fixed armoured shield covering the front of the turret and these are believed to be tanks, more likely Mark II than Mark IIA, still fitted with the original 14mm gun mounting – as indeed some were when the decree to change to 30mm came into force.

It is said that one of the first acts of the British Purchasing Commission in the United States was to attempt to place orders for A13 Cruisers with American

manufacturers, possibly on the grounds that, being a Christie cruiser, it would give them a reasonably familiar tank to build. In the event nothing came of this, nor any of the other projects mooted to build British tanks in the United States. It seems that with the fall of France, the Americans reckoned that it was only a matter of time before Britain fell too, leaving them with British-style tanks on their hands. Since this was not acceptable all such orders were rejected. Instead the Americans were quite happy to supply American-designed tanks to the British, on the grounds that if the deal fell through the tanks would still be useful.

Finally it should be pointed out here that none of the tanks listed above were ever supplied with the close support weapon, the 3.7in howitzer, that was fitted to some examples of the A9 and A10 cruiser tanks. It would have been entirely feasible but it was never done. It may well be that the earlier cruisers were deemed more than adequate for this role, working in conjunction with the A13 type but this is another thing that is never adequately explained.

ABOVE A tank at the head of the production line is nearly complete except for the gun mounting which is 'free issue' authorised by the War Office. It is the nature of the co-axial machine gun that gives the tank its identity.

ABOVE LEFT 2-pdr guns being fitted into their mantlets. The co-axial machine guns have yet to be fitted, but the square hole suggests the 7.92mm Besa air-cooled weapon of the Cruiser Mark IVA.

Here we see the two tanks stirring up the dust. Note that the tanks are numbered but still do not carry weapons. T15218 was part of a contract for 80 tanks, contract number T7854 dated 1 December 1939.

A16E1, a precise side view showing the tank without any armament fitted but otherwise complete, even down to the cupola and sighting vane on top of the turret and the aerial mounting on the back. At the front of the hull can be seen the nearside machine-gun turret, designed to mount a Besa gun that was never fitted.

A16E1

While design work was going ahead on A13, it was being touted as a Light Medium, or later a Light Cruiser tank, largely due to its thin armour. It was envisaged as a reconnaissance vehicle for the cavalry. The main striking power of the cavalry was to be embodied in the Heavy Cruiser, or Battle Cruiser tanks, of which a number of experimental prototypes were being considered. Out of these two were ordered: the A14[2] from the London, Midland & Scottish Railway and A16, in effect a scaled-up A13 from the Nuffield Organisation. A16 was mechanically the same as A13, although its Liberty engine was improved to deliver 414bhp and it was fitted with the prototype Merritt-Maybach transmission, designed by Dr Henry Merritt of David Brown Tractors, which in Britain was later developed into the Merritt-Brown transmission. (In modified though unacknowledged form, it was also fitted to the German Tiger tank.) At one stage there were even plans to fit the British tank with a French Cotal electro-magnetic transmission and a sample unit was acquired, but never fitted.

A16 was also to have a 30mm armour basis, giving it a weight of 21.75 tons, and be armed with a 2-pdr gun and co-axial machine-gun in the main turret with extra machine-guns in two subsidiary turrets. On account of its greater size it now featured five road wheel stations per side. In December 1937, at a meeting presided over by Lord Gort, the new Chief of the Imperial General Staff, it was decided 'that a prototype of both A14 and A16 should be prepared, and if satisfactory the necessary jigs made, so that one or the other could be put into production as soon as War broke out'. This sounds like a way of avoiding making a critical decision and probably deferring production until it was too late. In the event A14 and A16 only ever saw the light of day as unarmed prototypes, neither entering production. With the up-armouring of A13 to 30mm basis and the adoption of A10 as the interim Heavy Cruiser tank a true Heavy Cruiser was considered unnecessary. Looked at from another angle, one cannot help thinking that if A16 (or A14 come to that) had been armed with a more powerful gun then the need for it would be unanswerable, but since it was only ever to be armed with the 2-pdr, just like A13, production seemed to be rather pointless.

2 See *British Battle Tanks: World War I to 1939* (Osprey Publishing, 2016)

WITH 1ST ARMOURED DIVISION IN FRANCE

The first deployment of A13 tanks, Marks I, II and IIA, was with British 1st Armoured Division which went to France towards the end of May 1940. It consisted of the 2nd Armoured Brigade comprising the Queen's Bays, the 9th Lancers and 10th Hussars, and 3rd Armoured Brigade which comprised 2nd, 3rd and 5th Royal Tank Regiments. However 3rd Royal Tank Regiment was detached at the last minute and sent to Calais. According to one authoritative source the cruiser tank complement of the Bays consisted of 22 A13 tanks and seven A9 and A10 tanks and this may be taken as typical.

In the original scheme the 2nd Armoured Brigade, the Cavalry brigade, was classified as a Light Brigade equipped exclusively with Light Tanks, while 3rd Armoured Brigade, the RTR brigade, operated the Cruiser tanks. However, before they left England a change was made so that each regiment was issued with both type of tank, on a basis of roughly three cruisers to two light tanks. It is also said that when they left Britain many of the cruiser tanks were incomplete, lacking wireless sets, gun sights and even guns in some cases, although these were sent out with the tanks to be installed on arrival.

In the original plan all regiments of 1st Armoured Division would on landing in France make for Pacy-sur-Eure, a tank training area where they would complete their training on the new tanks and prepare for the forthcoming action. However in the event the German advance proved to be far more vigorous than had been anticipated so each regiment was hurried straight to the front when it arrived. This was roughly on the line of the river Somme and any ambition to push further east and hopefully link up with the British Expeditionary Force had to be shelved. In any case by this time the BEF was being crowded back against the Channel coast and ended up at Dunkirk from which there was only one escape route. 1st Armoured Division had, however, established a depot at Le Mans, the famous motor racing circuit. In the meantime they found themselves confronting the combined Panzer divisions of the German Army, already the successful veterans of the campaign in Poland and the

BELOW An A13 Cruiser Mark III photographed in France. Sergeant Ron Huggins of 10th Hussars is resting nonchalantly on the left.

BOTTOM LEFT Cruiser Mark III tanks, knocked out and captured by the Germans. It looks like the suspension has collapsed on the nearest vehicle and the rubber tyres are missing yet there is no sign of fire.

TOP Damaged and abandoned, this Cruiser Mark III waits in a cornfield until its new owners are ready to visit it. The turret marking shows it to be an A Squadron tank, probably from the Queen's Bays or 2nd Royal Tank Regiment.

ABOVE A Cruiser Mark IV or IVA of C Squadron, 5th Royal Tank Regiment scuttling down a partially blocked French road.

recent fighting in France. Gallantry was no substitute for experience. Before long, regiments were reduced to the size of squadrons, and in the case of the two Royal Tank Regiments one squadron was formed from the remains of both of them. The 10th Hussars even found time to despatch a trainload of tanks to Le Mans, where it was hoped they could be repaired, including one A13 tank which had lost its turret, but the train appears to have been captured by the Germans who, having halted on the Somme, were now advancing westwards. 3rd Armoured Brigade, advancing towards the Somme on the 27th, discovered that German forces were already across the river and moving west.

Although they were involved in a number of minor actions the overpowering strength of the advancing Germans and the imminent collapse of French opposition meant that the British regiments were continually on the back foot and retreating as they fought. In the end, while the French surrendered, 2nd Armoured Brigade, or what was left of it, headed for Brest. The remains of 3rd Armoured Brigade headed for Cherbourg with Rommel and his 7th Panzer Division hot on its tail. Shedding tanks as it went, through mechanical breakdown or simply running out of fuel, 3rd Armoured Brigade, under the command of Brigadier J.T. Crocker, finally arrived in Cherbourg with 14 A13 Cruisers still in running condition. Some of these were hastily loaded into ships but with the Germans less than a day behind much of the transport had to be left behind. In the end seven cruiser tanks and six light tanks were shipped home.

Meanwhile 3rd Royal Tank Regiment arrived in Calais which with Boulogne and Dunkirk were vital replenishment ports for the British Expeditionary Force. They arrived on 22 May, only to find that the dockside cranes were out of action, British dock workers exhausted, and the ship loaded with 7,000 gallons of fuel which had to be unloaded before they could get at the tanks. The plan was that the tank regiment and 30th Infantry Brigade would form a mobile striking force to bolster the defence of Boulogne and menace the flanks of the advancing Germans, although it became clear at once that the Germans planned to invest Calais and eliminate the threat. To begin with the regiment faced considerable problems simply getting their tanks ashore. Most of the tanks' weapons had been clogged up with mineral jelly to prevent corrosion, and this had to be cleaned off before they could be used. A patrol of the

A Cruiser Mark IV of A Squadron, 3rd Royal Tank Regiment, captured in Calais. The external mantlet shield may be an indication that it is a Mark III Modified, with added protection for the front of the turret.

first light tanks available was sent to St Omer; it managed to get there and return, but the Germans were swiftly moving into the area. When later on 23 May a substantial part of the regiment was sent in the same direction, it ran into serious opposition, and was forced to pull back into Calais. A patrol of one A13 and three light tanks, all that remained of B Squadron, was then ordered to move eastwards to Gravelines, which it did, even passing through a large German formation on the way who seem to have taken them for friendly troops.

Still in Calais, and unable to get any feedback from the patrol – their radios did not work – the officer commanding 3rd RTR, Lieutenant-Colonel R.C. Keller, decided to break out with his remaining tanks by driving along the beach to Gravelines, which they did. Meanwhile 10th Panzer Division ultimately captured Calais on 26 May. The captured A13 tanks were something of a windfall for the Germans. They may not have regarded them as quite up to the standard of their tanks but they were good enough and they ended up with quite a few of them. The majority were issued to 18th and 19th

An unidentified Cruiser Mark IV lying abandoned and still burning at the side of a road in France.

Two A13s, either Mark IV or IVA belonging to 2nd Royal Tank Regiment, photographed on the dockside at Cherbourg. What the gunless A12 Matilda on the right is doing there is not known.

A Cruiser Mark IV or IVA is carried by a Scammell 20-ton transporter through Le Neubourg in the midst of refugee traffic.

A Cruiser Mark IV in the background, behind a camouflaged Daimler Dingo Scout Car, probably during the retreat.

Panzer Divisions which operated on the Russian Front. Spares were obtained by cannibalisation but since track wear looked like becoming a fundamental problem many of the tanks were reworked to be fitted with tracks of the Panzer II pattern and drive sprockets to match. The tanks were also fitted with additional stowage boxes and tracks, and in this form they were classified by the Germans as PzKpfw Mk IV 744(e). How long they lasted in German service is not clear.

Apparently when elements of 2nd Armoured Brigade were leaving Brest, the French 342 CACC were just landing there, having returned from Norway. Having lost all their Hotchkiss tanks in Norway they duly took over some of the abandoned British tanks, including some (at least one) A13 Cruiser. But they were obliged to give them up on 18 June 1940 when the French government capitulated.

THE WESTERN DESERT

The spiritual home of the A13 Cruisers, where they did some of their best work, was undoubtedly the Western Desert. In 1940 to 1941, they seem to have served with at least ten regiments out there including 1st, 2nd, 3rd ,5th and 6th Royal Tank Regiments, 7th Hussars and 8th Hussars plus of course the Queen's Bays, 9th Lancers and 10th Hussars who had previously been in France. These regiments sometimes moved from one division to another as occasion demanded and it is not possible to say how many A13 tanks – or of exactly what type – each regiment had, although photographic evidence suggests that the Mark IVA type dominated. Clearly not all of these regiments could have been fully equipped with A13 cruisers, as there were simply not enough of them, but the numbers would have been made up by A9 and A10 cruisers and of course light tanks.

There was a high rate of attrition due to battle damage and breakdowns, to the point where some units were pulled out of the line. For example after the battle of Bardia, in January 1941, 6th RTR was instructed to hand over its remaining tanks to 1st and 2nd RTR and to return to Egypt where it would eventually be re-equipped.

A13s, taking advantage of their speed, were in the van during the attack on the retreating Italians at Beda Fomm in February 1941. In the retreat across Cyrenaica, following Rommel's first attack in April 1941, 3rd Armoured Brigade was reduced to 12 A13s, 18 light tanks and 26 captured Italian M13s – and that was a brigade, not a single regiment. By the end of 1941 most of the early cruiser tanks were worn out and due to be replaced by tanks of the next generation, notably the A15 Crusader. However even up to the last the surviving cruisers saw action, during the battles of Sidi Rezegh in November 1941, which turned into an enormous armoured melee. At least one A13 was photographed in Greece, presumably serving with 3rd Royal Tank Regiment, and was duly abandoned in the end.

TOP The 'sunshade' style lorry disguise in mint condition on an A13 in the Middle East. Even two of the road wheels have been painted black to make it look like a four-wheeler at first glance. The idea was that sunshade could be quickly removed before going into action, but it was rather flimsy and did not last very long.

ABOVE An A13 Cruiser with its sunshade attachment starting to fall to pieces, on the back of a Mack EXBX tank transporter. Why a 'lorry' should need to be carried on a transporter is not mentioned.

TOP Since the A13 had long gone by the time British forces reached Tunisia, this very posed photo must have been taken in a more fertile part of Libya. The tank, a Cruiser Mark IVA, looks newly painted, and the long-range fuel tank on the side is unusual.

ABOVE LEFT Damage from an anti-tank mine could cripple a Christie Cruiser. This tank's track is broken, some of the tinwork torn off and individual road wheels fallen well away from their usual positions.

ABOVE RIGHT A Cruiser Mark IVA under a fixed camouflage structure, probably in the Tobruk perimeter. The tank appears to mount a captured MG34 as its turret machine gun.

An early A13 on Salisbury Plain at Perham Down Camp, while the camp was still being bulit. The tank is in service with 5th Royal Tank Regiment and looks brand new.

DEFENDING THE HOMELAND

Even before the fighting in France had started, during the period of hostilities called the 'Phoney War', A13 Cruiser tanks were beginning to come off the production lines and be issued to regiments of the new Royal Armoured Corps. 5th Royal Tank Regiment at Perham Down on Salisbury Plain was a case in point.

While the fighting in France was still going on tanks continued to be delivered, some to regiments based at home, and these tanks were never sent to France. Although seven cruiser tanks had been brought back from France the rest had to be left behind, and many of those that had not been destroyed in action entered German Army service. The new A13 had revealed a number of faults under service conditions in close country, notably with a clutch that overheated, steering brakes that failed, and even the starter solenoid on the engine often refused to function. But the tracks were the main cause for concern, failing to grip on wet ground, coming off repeatedly or breaking when the track pins fell out, and if they broke at speed the track was likely to flail about, ripping off the light metal trackguards and doing other damage. The tracks were also thought to be too narrow, a fault common to all the cruiser tanks, which resulted in higher ground pressure than was thought necessary. Such faults became less obvious in the desert, where sand made steering easier and was not as necessary as it was in France, but in any case crews were learning to anticipate trouble and correct it in time.

For regiments at home it was initially a question of waiting for new tanks to be delivered. Until then most regiments survived on a selection of old vehicles and modified private cars. The threat of invasion was also anticipated almost hourly. Since it was not known where this might take place, tank regiments were held back at central locations ready to be rushed by rail to the threatened area, which meant that practice in boarding trains, a lengthy and time-consuming process, became a vital activity. This however mostly involved infantry tanks.

A mixture of cruiser tanks, A9 and A13, advancing over flat country.

Here tanks of 1st Armoured Division are proceeding through a village while the locals appear to be unconcerned. One small boy, however, is watching.

Here a recovery operation is in progress, the tank on the left having got itself bogged down. They are all Mark IVA, but notice that the two tanks on the right each have different mantlets.

Crews on an exercise climb back into their tanks. Notice that the driver's job is not that easy.

A Cruiser Mark VIA with an RTR crew in the turret heads a line of tanks moving along a country road. It is fully armed except for its smoke bomb dischargers, which are absent from the bracket on the turret side.

As this threat gradually faded away, the regiments at home increased in strength and settled down to long periods of training that involved driving around the countryside, although legal restrictions on where they could go, in a country that was relying more and more upon its agriculture, inhibited cross-country driving in certain areas. In the south of England regions such as the New Forest in Hampshire or Salisbury Plain were popular although they were not really large enough for wide sweeping operations, let alone live-firing. Further north it got easier, such as in the Yorkshire Moors or the Peak District, although here the rugged terrain imposed its own limitations.

Then, as the risk of invasion receded and the armed forces expanded, even making good the losses from the evacuation of France, larger and more wide-ranging exercises were held, culminating in the massive Exercise Bumper in September 1941, when the Manoeuvre Act was invoked so that tanks from various regiments could proceed more-or-less anywhere. However by this time the A13 was reaching the end of its usefulness. Regiments were now being equipped with Covenanters and Crusaders and although some of the older cruisers lingered on, they were now yesterday's tank and a new generation was rolling off the production lines.

CHAPTER 3

CRUSADER AND COVENANTER CRUISER TANKS

DESIGN & DEVELOPMENT

The design of any new tank is affected by a number of factors, usually inter-related, and none of them simple. Even when the design is apparently settled other influences can come into play which will alter the concept still further – the final result is often far removed from the original drawings. Such is the case with the Covenanter and Crusader.

THE A13 COVENANTER

Developed as a lighter, cheaper alternative to the A16, the A13 Mark III, or Cruiser Mark V, became better known as the Covenanter. But it is important to stress that, despite sharing the GS designation A13 with the original Christie cruisers, the new tank was, strictly speaking, part of the heavy cruiser programme.

The official specification called for an armament of one 2-pdr (40mm) gun and at least one machine gun, Christie suspension, epicyclic steering and an armour standard of 30mm. This last factor deserves some explanation. What it meant, in simple terms, was that all vertical surfaces of hull and turret armour should be no less than 30mm thick. But it was accepted that surfaces which were not vertical need not be so thick since an angled plate of thinner material could offer protection equal to that of 30mm plate at the vertical. There are many qualifying factors but the basic principle holds good and, in the case of the Covenanter, it was adopted with such enthusiasm that there was hardly a vertical plate to be seen. Height, therefore, became a key factor in the design and this dictated two other features. In the first the coil springs of the suspension, instead of acting vertically on trailing arms, as in the original Christie system, were raked back dramatically and attached to bell cranks which formed forward extensions of the suspension arms. Secondly it was decided to employ a low profile engine. Henry Meadows Ltd of Wolverhampton was commissioned to produce a horizontally opposed, 12-cylinder petrol engine rated at

The original Covenanter prototype, T1795, with all-welded hull and full Wilson transmission. It was subsequently used to test the Merritt-Brown transmission and ended its days as a recovery hulk.

not less than 300hp. It would be linked to the full Wilson transmission, a combined gear box and steering system, originally specified for A16. Finally it was decided that the tank's armour would be welded instead of riveted, a new departure in British tank construction which was regarded with suspicion in many quarters. Thus, on the eve of war, Britain was about to produce a revolutionary new tank.

From this point matters started to degenerate. The proposed design was placed before the General Staff who, while approving the layout, requested an increase in armour standard to the extent that the front of both hull and turret should be equivalent to a 40mm basis. The Tank Board accepted, but estimated that the increase in weight would bring it to the upper limit of what the suspension was designed to carry, and no move was made to strengthen the suspension. Detail design now went ahead; Henry Meadows naturally for the engine, Nuffield Mechanization & Aero for the turret and the London, Midland & Scottish (LMS) Railway Company for the hull. Detail drawings were approved and finance agreed for 100 tanks, to be built by the LMS, on 17 April 1939. It is worth noting that, up to this time, no prototype existed. With war imminent, the tanks were ordered off the drawing board. The authorities believed that faults could be ironed out with the two pilot models and any modifications incorporated into production tanks. They were wrong.

The original Crusader, T3646, viewed from the rear. The air cleaners are mounted midway along the track guards and here the sunshine roof is seen in the open position.

TANK A13 MARK III, CRUISER MARK V, Covenanter 2nd prototype

The second Covenanter prototype shown as it first appeared from the LMS works at Crewe. In keeping with traditional railway practice it was finished in 'photographic grey' with white rims to the wheels. Also shown is the coat of arms of the London, Midland and Scottish Railway Company. (Art by Peter Sarson, © Osprey Publishing)

Covenanters under construction, revealing the double thickness hull sides and cross tubes which braced the floor. The various compartments may easily be identified and a hatch has already been fitted above the transmission section at the back.

An overhead view of a Covenanter I. The turret hatch is open and extra stowage boxes are fitted, including a long one on the right for a Bren LMG.

TANK A15, CRUISER MARK VI, prototype

The first Crusader prototype received no such treatment. It went down to the Mechanization Experimental Establishment at Farnborough, probably in the Standard Camouflage Colour No. 2, described as khaki brown, which was then becoming the predominant colour for military vehicles in Britain. Its only adornment was the War Department number T3646, painted in a rather more exotic style than normal, on a background that may have been the earlier khaki green No. 3 shade. The small red triangle on the turret warns that the tank is constructed from unarmoured plate. (Art by Peter Sarson, © Osprey Publishing)

One feature which attracted much interest and caution was the proposed layout of the cooling system. The Meadows engine was certainly low enough, but what it lacked in height it more than made up for in width, to the extent that there was no room for radiators in, or close to, the engine compartment. For this reason it was decided to locate them at the front, to the left of the driver's cab. This unusual arrangement caused such concern that a mock up system was built and tested under simulated conditions at Woolwich. By September 1939 the English Electric Company and Leyland Motors had joined the production programme and another 250 tanks were on order. A month later and the LMS, who were already constructing the first prototype, began to express doubts as to the wisdom of welding tank hulls, adding for good measure that they could forsee a shortage of skilled welders. Their recommendation that the tank should be riveted was accepted, and the associated increase in weight was estimated at some 2cwts.

To make welding easier composite armour (ie, two layers of plate) was employed. The inner plate was high quality steel and the outer homogeneous armour, the idea being that the inner layer would accept the weld without destroying the quality of the armour itself. When it was agreed to rivet instead extra frame members had to be provided to attach the plate to, but the use of composite armour was retained. Before production began two more important changes had to be incorporated in the design. The first concerned the road wheels. On earlier A13 series cruisers these had been made of aluminium to save weight, but as the war progressed this material – much in demand for aircraft production – was replaced by pressed steel, increasing the weight of the tank still further. Fears were then expressed that the complex Wilson transmission and steering system would not be available in time to match tank production. It was agreed to substitute the original Meadows four-speed crash gearbox used in the A13 with Wilson epicyclic steering units mounted on each side. There was another consequence of this change. In the original layout provision had

A Crusader is hoisted by an overhead crane at the Nuffield factory in Birmingham. It provides an excellent view of the suspension in the fully extended position, the short pitch tracks and double drive sprockets.

been made for a large fan to ventilate the transmission compartment. Production models would only accept a smaller one which was not so effective. The original pilot model Covenanter left the LMS workshops at Crewe for the MEE at Farnborough on 21 May 1940. Preliminary trials, with an ungoverned engine, indicated a top speed of 37mph and proved that with a tank weighing 16 tons the suspension was quite satisfactory. After 1,000 miles MEE was also able to report that the all-welded hull showed no signs of structural weakness. In October 1940 this tank was moved to the works of Thompson and Taylor at Brooklands in Surrey where an experimental Merritt-Brown transmission was installed. The plan was to fit this system to later production Covenanters but in the event this was never done. The second pilot model arrived at Farnborough in September 1940, but reports indicate that cooling was far less effective than on the first machine.

Soon after the design of Covenanter had been agreed, early in 1939, the Ministry of Supply approached Nuffield Mechanization & Aero with a view to having them join the production programme. It is indicative of the influence Lord Nuffield wielded that, when he refused, his objections were accepted and an alternative design sanctioned. Nuffield reasoned that it would be better for his firm to work on an improved version of the original A13 than to adopt an entirely new design and, as things turned out, it was as well that he did. Ordered under General Staff specification A15 it was designated Cruiser Mark VI and later, more famously, as the Crusader.

CRUSADER PROTOTYPE

Although outwardly similar to the Covenanter the new design was based around a modified version of the 27-litre Nuffield Liberty V12 petrol engine rated at 340hp at 1,500rpm. A similar engine had been used in the earlier Nuffield-built A13 Cruisers and, like those tanks, this first Crusader featured a compressed air starting system as an alternative to the usual method. But it is never mentioned in any subsequent description of the tank, and may have been abandoned. The space to the left of the driver was to be occupied by a subsidiary turret containing an extra Besa machine gun, but the main turret design was common to both tanks. Armour was to be to 40mm standard at the front and 30mm elsewhere while the contract specified that the weight should not exceed 18 tons, the limit for standard army bridging. Although the tracks on any vehicle help to spread the weight, and reduce ground pressure, the size and number of wheels bearing on the track also have an effect. In the case of A15 it was agreed to install another suspension station on each side in order to absorb some of the extra weight. In an effort to keep things as simple as possible Nuffield's hoped to employ clutch and brake steering. However, they were overruled and the system fitted to Covenanter was demanded instead, but using the A13-type constant mesh gearbox. Indeed it was agreed that, as far as possible, the two tanks should share common components. Despite its later start the prototype Crusader arrived at MEE, Farnborough, on 9 April 1940, a full six weeks before the first Covenanter. It was criticised for poor cooling, which is normal for most new tanks, and the authorities also disliked the tiller steering arrangement which was claimed to cause the condition known as reverse steering, where a tank turns the opposite way to that desired. Levers were adopted for production Crusaders although Covenanters continued to use a form of tiller bar. In November 1940 the tank went down to Lulworth in Dorset for gunnery trials and there, under normal circumstances, its career might have ended. But it was back in the spotlight again in 1941, for a very important reason. Among new schemes in the pipeline was one by Rolls-Royce to produce a tank powerplant from their famous V12 Merlin aero engine, which was installed in the Supermarine Spifire and many other types of British combat aircraft. The prototype Crusader was sent to Rolls-Royce to be fitted with one of these engines, now officially known as the Meteor.

Before leaving the prototypes two additional matters should be mentioned. Among the features incorporated in the Covenanter design was a pneumatic system for activating the steering epicyclics and brakes. In Crusader it was proposed to use a hydraulic system. When this proved troublesome the Arens air operated equipment from Covenanter was adopted, but in both tanks this resulted in a violent steering action which proved dangerous on roads. Extra valves were incorporated to give more gentle control. In both tanks the driver was housed beneath a box-shaped armoured cover and the prototypes featured an extra Besa machine gun, operated by the driver, in the right hand side of the cab. In practice this proved unworkable. The breech end of the gun and ammunition took up valuable space in an already tightly confined area and, when it was fired, the resulting fumes made conditions unbearable and potentially dangerous. In production tanks the mounting was replaced by a simple revolver port which the driver could use in an emergency as a last resort.

TECHNICAL ANALYSIS

Most published sources give the impression that the Crusader was an improved version of Covenanter, or at least a subsequent development, but they were of course exact contemporaries. Contracts for both models were issued at the same time, and in each case without the benefit of prototype testing. Inevitably, detail improvements on both models were subject to the vagaries of production, and may appear to be indiscriminate.

The form and structure of the hull on both tanks has already been described, except for the fact that on the sides it was formed from two spaced panels with the suspension units sandwiched in between. As with most British tanks the idler wheel was at the front, adjusted by a cam action to tension the track. The twin sets of 32in diameter road wheels were dish-shaped in pressed steel with perforated solid tyres. On some early models the wheel centres were covered by blank discs but this was later dispensed with. On both tanks the first and last wheel stations were fitted with

Three Covenanters during early trials. Many turret details have yet to be fitted. Notice the two different styles of mantlet and the variations in cooling louvre layout.

Newton shock absorbers. At the rear the tanks were driven by double drive sprockets each with 20 teeth. The tracks were of short pitch with centre guide horn in malleable cast iron, dry pin connected in the multi-hinge fashion favoured by Christie.

The driver's head cover was a small, bevelled box on the right side of the hull. It had a double flap lid and a small hinged door at the front, containing a glass visor block and armoured cover; to its right was the revolver port, operated by a quick acting lever. All tanks had a narrow vision slit on the right side of the cab but, for some reason, only the Covenanter Mark II also had one on the left.

Alongside the cab, on the Covenanter, were four cast armoured covers which protected the slots through which the radiators vented. The two radiators were cooled by a suction fan driven off the turret traverse motor. On the Crusader this area was occupied by a small, drum shaped turret containing a single Besa machine gun in a mounting which also contained a telescopic sight. It was hand traversed over an arc of 150 degrees and fitted with a hinged lid, just large enough for a man to wriggle through.

The main turret was common to both tanks. Its distinctive shape not only reduced height but, according to one advocate, increased elbow room. Commander's cupolas were temporarily out of favour at this time so the rear section of the roof formed one large hatch which lifted up and folded backwards on parallel link arms while the weight was balanced by torsion bars. The handbook lays great stress on ensuring that the hatch is firmly secured in the open position otherwise it was liable to swing shut of its own accord. The mantlet, on early examples, was a semi-internal casting of complex shape set in the vertical front plate, but an uparmoured type was later introduced: a distinctive, bulbous shaped casting with three vertical slits in it. That on the left contained the sighting telescope, the large centre one the 2-pdr gun (or 3in howitzer in close support tanks) and the right slot a Besa machine gun. To the right of this again, but independent of the mantlet, was the mounting for a 2in bomb

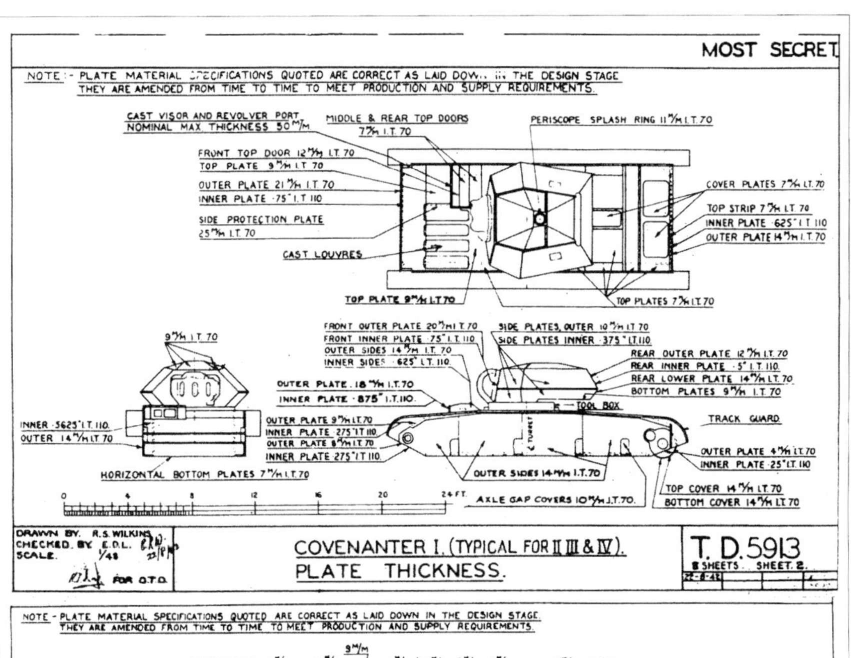

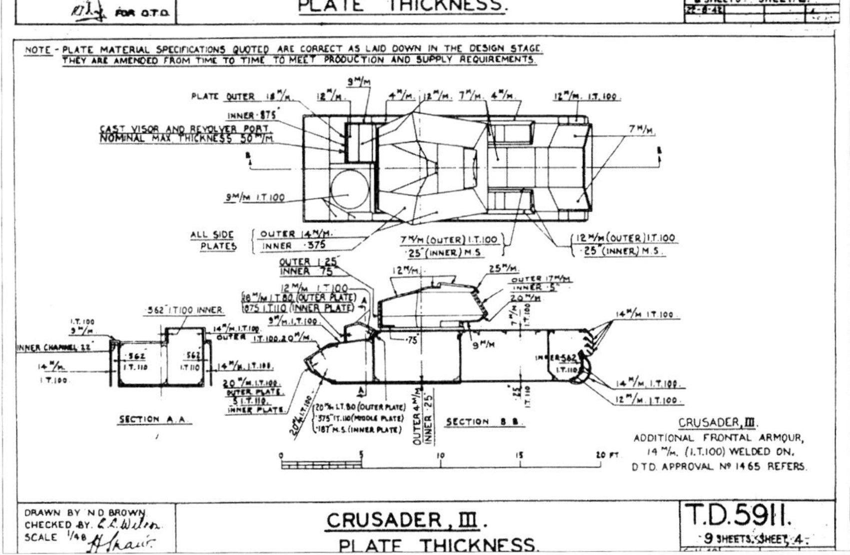

Comparative armour profiles for a Covenanter I and Crusader III. These diagrams have been reduced from the original 1/48th scale.

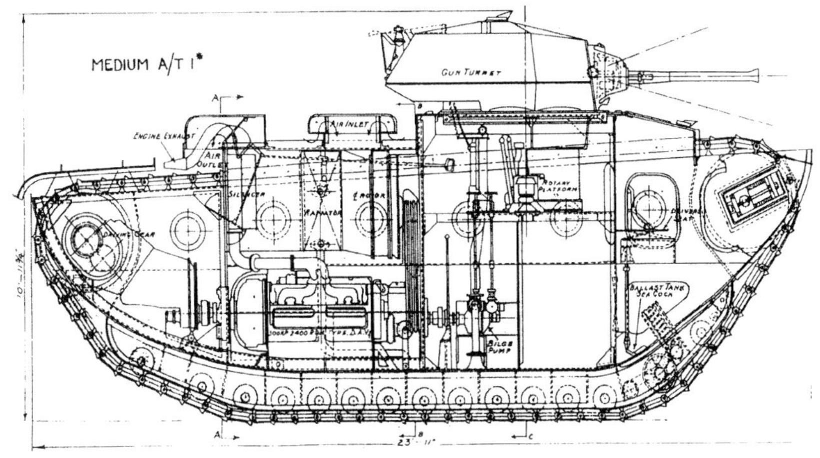

The anatomy of A/T1* showing the amazing amount of space available within the hull. Hollow sponsons filled the area inside the tracks on each side to provide additional floatation.

A Crusader I in the Middle East. It features an early form of dust guards and a rare appearance, on this type of tank, of the angular camouflage. Notice the auxiliary turret and that significant feature on the main turret, the raised lip to the gunner's vision slit, which identifies a Mark I.

thrower used to launch smoke canisters. There were two rotating periscopes in the turret roof, one for the commander and another for the loader, while the gunner had a vision slit in the front plate, on the left side. There were two aerial mounting points although only one was used when the old No. 9 set was carried. Two small, hinged flaps, which covered Triplex glass lookout blocks, were fitted on the turret sides with a spotlight bracket on the left and a small hole in the back, covered by a plug, through which the gun barrel could be withdrawn when it was changed. Some early turrets, certainly those fitted to Covenanters, had a built-in drinking water tank at the back, filled from outside. Proving more trouble than it was worth, the tank was replaced in later models by a rack of water containers stowed in the fighting compartment. In service both Covenanters and Crusaders often carried stowage lockers on the rear of the turret and other containers at the sides while many tanks were provided with a portable Lakeman mount for a Bren light machine gun, used by the commander in the antiaircraft role, which could be stowed in a long box on the right side.

ENGINE AND FUEL SYSTEMS

The Meadows model DAV engine in Covenanter was a horizontally opposed, overhead valve flat-12, with a bore of 115mm and a stroke of 130mm giving a capacity of 16,204cc. At a governed 2,400rpm it delivered 300hp, giving the tank a top road speed of 31mph. It was linked through a Borg and Beck twin plate clutch to the Meadows four-speed and reverse crash gearbox which had Wilson two-speed epicyclics bolted to its output shafts. From these drive passed through brake drums to the final drive reduction and track sprockets. Three fuel tanks were located inside the engine compartment, one on each side and another beneath the engine. Armoured panels covering the engine and transmission compartments were in 7mm plate. Twin concertina air filters were mounted crosswise on the engine decks while the silencers were located lengthwise on the track guards.

The engine fitted to Crusader was a type known originally as the United States Standard 12-cylinder Aviation Engine, christened the Liberty when it appeared during World War I. As the Nuffield Liberty Mark III it was a 45-degree V12 with a bore of 127mm and stroke of 177.8mm giving a capacity of 27,040cc. At a governed 1,500rpm it delivered 340hp which gave the tank a top speed of 27.5mph. Its main drawback, as a tank engine, was the method of construction by which the individual cast iron cylinders were bolted together. The effect of this is noted later. Behind the engine a multi-plate clutch carried the drive into a Nuffield four-speed and reverse, constant mesh gearbox to Wilson steering units and final drive as in Covenanter. Fuel tanks were located either side of the engine with the radiators fitted vertically inboard of them, drawing air through louvres on the engine decks. Two cooling fans were

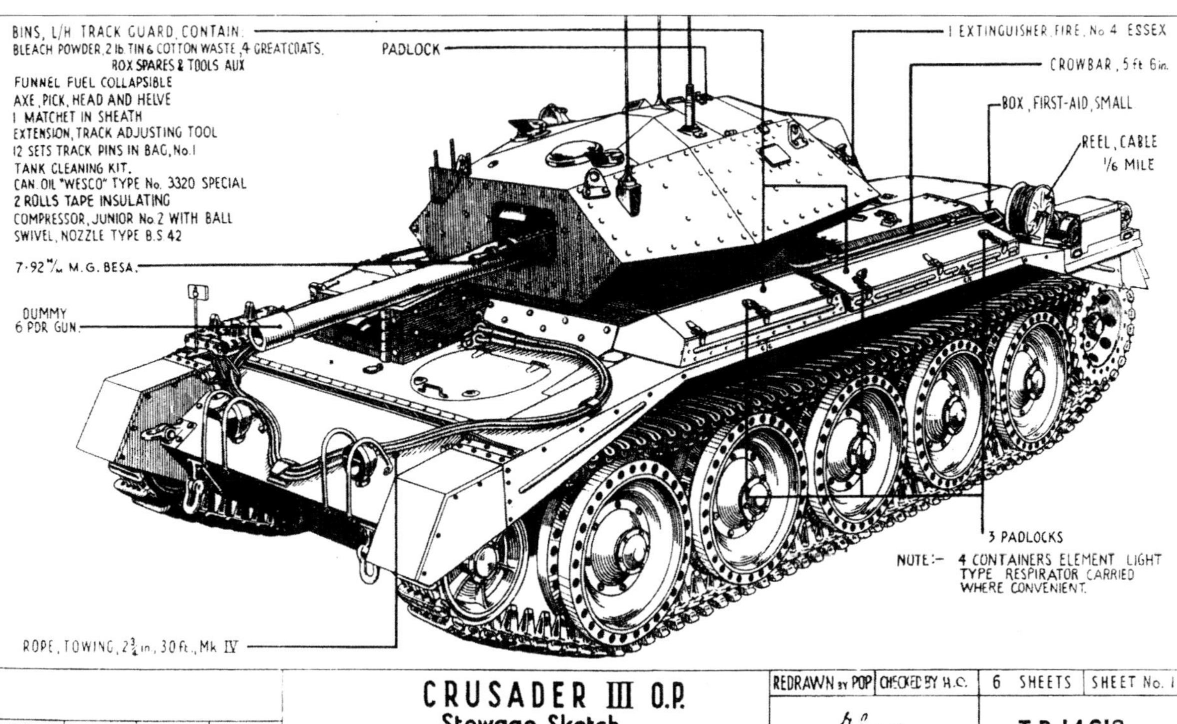

A stowage diagram for the Crusader III OP (Observation Post) tank showing the dummy gun, aerial array and extra cable reels for remote operation of the radios.

fitted into the rear engine bulkhead, driven by exposed double roller chains from the crankshaft and geared to turn at double the normal engine speed. In the desert, especially, this caused endless trouble and on later models a form of shaft drive was introduced. The exhaust pipes were entirely hidden on Crusader. From the manifold on each side of the engine they snaked over the transmission and ended inside the rear hull louvres. On early Crusaders concertina-type air cleaners were mounted on the track guards at the rear but these were soon replaced by an oil bath-type.

On both tanks an engine driven pump provided compressed air for the steering and braking systems while hydraulics were used for the turret power traverse. In keeping with contemporary British practice, which regarded firing on the move as the correct procedure for tank versus tank fighting, the gun was elevated manually by the gunner. Before the introduction of the No. 19 wireless set, which incorporated an intercom, crew communication was one way only, from the tank commander, through Tannoy speakers at all crew stations.

EARLY PRODUCTION MODELS

Obviously, when production machines followed so closely on the prototypes, a lot of work remained to be done before they were perfected. A report on one such trial throws an interesting light on contemporary attitudes. The tank in question was T15297, one of the first English Electric-built Covenanters which arrived at Wool station en route for the Gunnery School at Lulworth. The date was 2 January 1941, the weather cold and snowy, but the Experimental Officer in charge of the trial noted that it, and another Covenanter bound for the Driving and Maintenance School at Bovington, had not been sheeted over for the trip. Besides the obvious protection such cover would provide from the weather it seems amazing that a brand new tank,

T23203

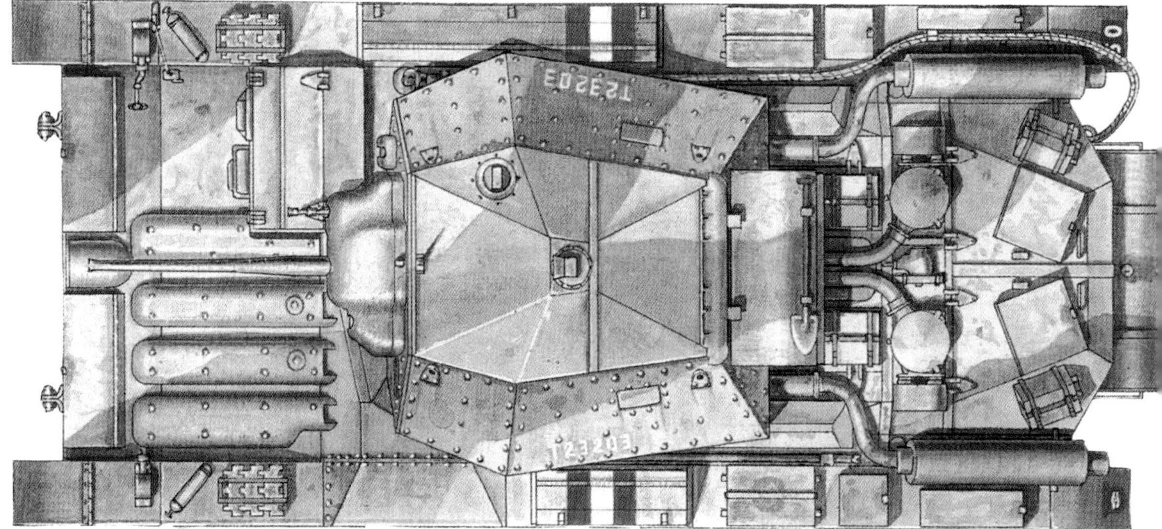
T23203
T23203

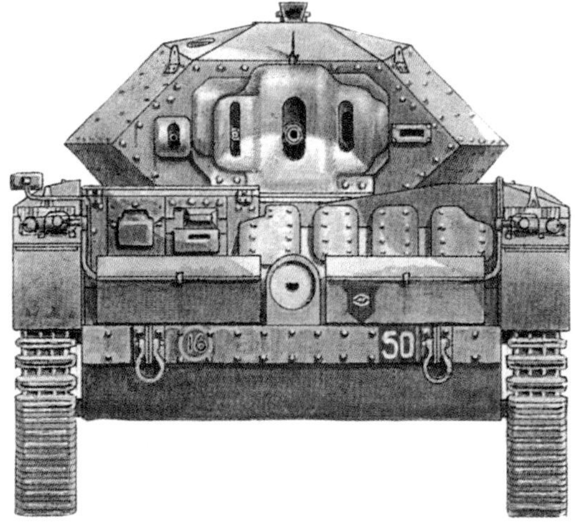
16
50

(LEFT) COVENANTER MARK III, HQ Guards Armoured Brigade, Guards Armoured Division

A Covenanter Mark III of Headquarters, 5th Guards Armoured Brigade, Guards Armoured Division. It displays the divisional sign of the Ever Open Eye, derived from the Guards Division sign of the Great War but reputedly restyled by the artist Rex Whistler, who served with the 2nd Battalion, Welsh Guards. Also shown is the unit identification number, bridge classification disc and red/white/red identification marking. The tank is finished in khaki brown with disruptive patches of very dark brown but the underside of the 2-pdr barrel and lower mantlet are painted white to reduce the effect of shadow. Compare the plan view of this tank with the overhead photograph of a Covenanter I shown earlier and notice the different arrangement of air cleaner and exhausts that distinguished this model. (Art by Peter Sarson, © Osprey Publishing)

CRUSADER MARK I, 3RD RTR, 8th Armoured Brigade, 10th Armoured Division

The brigades in 10th Armoured Division were changing at the time of the battle of Alam Halfa in 1942 so it is unlikely that tanks would have all their markings applied at this time. We show the fox's mask device of 10th Armoured Division. This Crusader is shown in a camouflage scheme designed to complement the Sunshade disguise. Notice how two of the road wheels are finished in a darker shade so that, from a distance with Sunshade fitted, the tank would look like a six-wheel lorry. (Art by Peter Sarson, © Osprey Publishing)

not yet off the Secret List, should travel openly from Staffordshire to Dorset for all to see. Even so what concerned the recipients was the fact that they were unable to start the tank because the batteries were flat and there were no instructions sent with it – the first Covenanter they had seen – to guide them. Most of the tools and equipment which the tank would normally have were also missing. Evidently Lulworth got it going in the end because they reported that, as a gun platform, the tank was excellent; as good as the Crusader they had tested earlier. But Lulworth complained that the diameter of the turret floor was much smaller than the turret ring which caused the gunner to sit in a very uncomfortable position and the commander to run the risk of getting his legs trapped when the turret rotated. Also criticised was the variety of Triplex vision devices fitted to the tank (most of which were of different sizes), and the general problems of accessibility, remarking that maintenance was both difficult and tedious. Fears were expressed about the risk of damage to the air system, it being pointed out that one fractured pipe would cripple the tank, a weakness shared by the Crusader. Despite reports of inefficient cooling there were no problems as long as the

the tank was driven carefully, although in war this was obviously an unrealistic restriction. In any case Lulworth in winter is not Egypt in summer. Finally, the external shape was judged excellent: from a distance the tank looked much smaller than it actually was. But on the subject of armour Lulworth were cautious about the 40mm basis and felt that top armour was much too thin, a view influenced by reports of air attacks on tanks.

VARIANTS

COVENANTER MARKS I, II, III & IV

Covenanter production ran to four marks, with a Close Support (CS) version of each. Late editions of the *Covenanter Instruction Book* emphasise that all models of the tank arc adequately cooled for temperate climates while later ones will be improved for use in the tropics. Other evidence suggests that this was a rather hollow claim. Photographs of the tanks in Britain reveal a bewildering variety of covers for the radiator louvres, suggesting that attempts to cure the problem were continuing. Many of the original tanks were modified in service workshops with a multi-tube oil cooler mounted on the radiator. Tanks thus reworked were designated Covenanter II. The next model, Covenanter III, was a new construction. It had oil coolers either side of the engine, a modified clutch linkage and a change in the pattern of radiator cooling louvres. But this version is most easily recognised by changes to the engine deck. New, pot shaped air cleaners were located inboard at the rear while the exhaust silencers were situated on the ends of the track guards, evacuating to the back. The final production model, the Covenanter IV, was a new build to Mark II standard but with the clutch modifications and other features typical of the Mark III.

A typical turret on a stand. The cone headed bolts, which secure the outer turret plates, were designed to deflect bullets. The sunshine roof is in the half open position and the mantlet is of the original type. The large protruberance on this side is the original aerial base mounting.

CRUSADER MARKS II & III

The Cruiser Mark VIA, or Crusader II, was introduced during production as an up-armoured version of the original model. Most of the changes affected the hull and turret front with thicker outer plates being applied. On the nose of the tank the increase, from the Mark I, was 6mm. On the turret front it was 10mm while the turret top and side plates were increased in proportion by about 3mm or 4mm. The change did not specifically involve removal of the auxiliary turret which may, or may not have been seen on either type. The surest way of identifying a Crusader II from a Mark I is to study the turret front. On the latter the small gunner's lookout, to the left of the mantlet, is surrounded by a coaming that stands proud from the armour. On the Mark II it is virtually flush. Also on the Mark II the lower corners of the front turret plate are slightly bevelled since the extra thickness would otherwise cause them to foul the auxiliary turret and driver's hood. In 1942 a further increase in protection was sanctioned which resulted in pre-cut panels of 14mm plate being welded to the nose,

Looking down on a Crusader III which bears the markings of the Gunnery School, Lulworth. The turret hatches are open and one may see the new periscopes, round ventilator cowl and the hole for the smoke bomb thrower.

front glacis plate and other frontal surfaces. Although authorised for the Mark II this improvement was mainly seen on the final model, Crusader III.

The need to up-gun existing British tanks, in order to match German progress, had been appreciated in some circles as early as 1940. A suitable weapon was already available – the 57mm 6-pdr. The problem was finding a tank to put it in. While new machines were being designed, schemes were investigated to improve three existing types, one of which was the Crusader. An attempt to fit a Churchill turret was rejected at an early stage but progress then got bogged down because official opinion regarded the project as unworkable. Thus it was September 1941 before a mock-up installation was unveiled by the Ministry of Supply. When this was inspected by engineers from Nuffield's they considered it a poor job and, six weeks later, had their own version ready for gunnery trials. In fact what they had done was to modify the original turret to accept the bigger gun, rather than design a new one, and although it worked it was not the ideal solution.

The new turret was slightly longer, and somewhat higher than the original version but it retained the same basic shape. It was built to a 50mm armour standard. The front plate was vertical, with a rectangular opening for the gun and an internal mantlet. The new mounting had the coaxial Besa machine gun on its left while the smoke discharger was altered to fire through a hole in the turret roof. The single turret hatch was replaced by a pair which opened outwards from the centre. One flap included a periscope for the commander and two more were provided further forward, along with a power operated extractor fan to deal with fumes created by the machine gun. The small flaps on each side were relieved of their Triplex blocks and now functioned as revolver ports.

Firing trials soon proved that the new arrangement worked and production of what became known as the Crusader III was authorised in December 1941, with the first examples being delivered the following summer. But the modification imposed a particular burden on the crew. Not only was it now essential to remove the auxiliary

A Covenanter bursts out of a smoke screen, looking the very essence of power and aggression, its 2-pdr gun aimed directly at the camera. Photographs such as this, released for publication, gave this handsome tank some unwarranted publicity.

turret and gunner to provide stowage space for the new ammunition but one of the main turret crew had to go as well. This meant that the tank's commander also acted as loader, while the gunner doubled up as wireless operator. What had begun as a five-man tank now only carried three, and this reduction placed considerable extra strain on all of them.

THE CREW

The driver's cab on both Covenanter and Crusader was more or less the same, although there were detail differences. Covenanter used horizontal tiller bars for steering where Crusader used levers. Gearbox layouts were different while the accelerator pedal on Covenanter was between the clutch and brake pedals but over to the right on Crusader. Each tank had a different form of revolver port and, on Crusader only, a compass binnacle was provided for the driver, within easy reach just ahead of the gear lever.

On early Crusaders the auxiliary machine gunner sat in supreme discomfort on a tiny saddle which went round with the turret. Besa ammunition boxes were stowed in front of him and he operated the traversing handle with his left hand. When closed down his view was limited to what could be seen through the sighting telescope. In the desert, particularly, conditions were so bad that many Crusaders which had the extra turret went into action without the gunner anyway.

A Covenanter of 'B' Squadron, 13th/18th Hussars, 9th Armoured Division is attacked by infantry during an exercise. The yellow crosses on the tank indicate that it was taking the part of an enemy vehicle.

In those tanks with the 2-pdr turret the commander sat at the back, within easy reach of the wireless set but always aware of the risk of having his head knocked off by the unstable hatch. Ahead of him, to the left, sat the gunner. In action gunners generally preferred to stand, so that they could aim the main gun more accurately, and bring all their body weight to

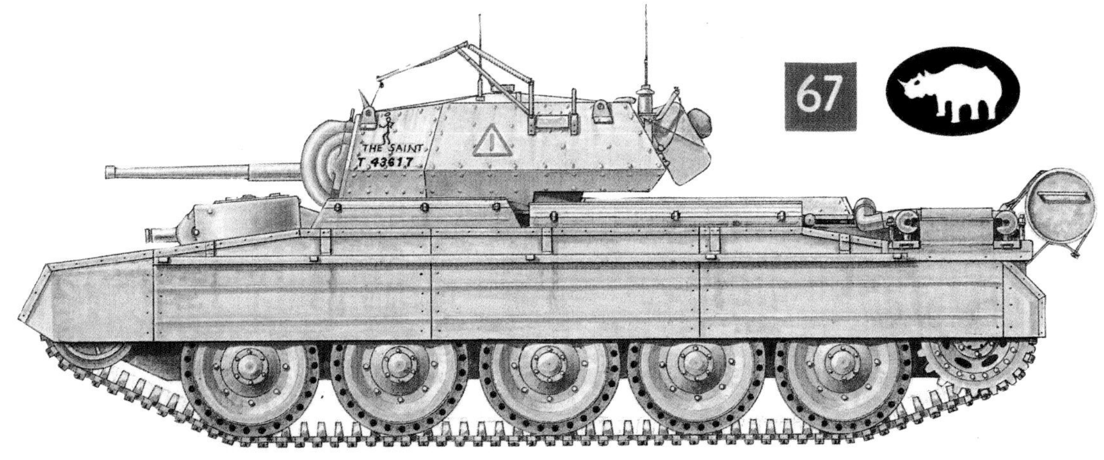

CRUSADER MARK II, THE SAINT, A Squadron, 10th Royal Hussars, 2nd Armoured Brigade, 1st Armoured Division

Crusader II of 10th Royal Hussars, 2nd Armoured Brigade, 1st Armoured Division. It is finished in a plain coat of sand colour, described by some users as light stone. It sports the divisional sign of a white rhino and the unit identification number of the junior regiment in the brigade on a red square, indicating the first brigade in the division. The 'A' Squadron triangle is in blue. The Saint was commanded by Sergeant Ron Huggins. (Art by Peter Sarson, © Osprey Publishing)

bear on the elevating arm. Across from him the loader sat on top of an ammunition bin. He was also responsible for loading and firing the smoke discharger. Tanks armed with the 2-pdr carried about 130 rounds of ammunition while the close support version carried 65 rounds of 3in smoke and high explosive.

On the 6-pdr Crusader the gunner was located on the left of the turret with the loader/commander on the right. The size of the turret turntable had been increased to give the loader more room to handle the larger rounds, of which stowage was provided for 73. Approximate productions figures give 17,765 as the main total for Covenanter while a minimum of 5,700 is suggested for Crusader.

OPERATIONAL HISTORY

Production of both Covenanter and Crusader ran more or less parallel. Deliveries began in the summer of 1941, but from this point their fates differed greatly. Trials had already proved that Covenanter, with its suspect cooling system, was only suitable for employment in temperate climes. As they came off the production lines Covenanters were issued to the regiments of 1st Armoured Division, which had managed with a motley collection of machines after losing almost all of their tanks in France a year earlier. In 1941 a British armoured division consisted of two armoured brigades, in this case the 2nd and 22nd. Each comprised three armoured regiments so there was a requirement for at least 300 tanks. The division left for Egypt later in the year and the Covenanters were transferred to 9th Armoured Division. Its six regiments formed 27th and 28th Armoured Brigades. Destined to remain in Britain as a training division 9th Armoured, with its Panda's head symbol, became a familiar sight in various parts of the country. The public were treated to media eulogies about fast and powerful cruiser tanks that the unfortunate Covenanter never deserved.

COVENANTER DEFICIENCIES

Accounts of Covenanter in service are not abundant and what there is has a uniformly critical tone. The 4th/7th Dragoon Guards received theirs in April 1941. At first the unit described them as a 'veritable deluxe model' but, having previously been in the Light Tank Mark VI, anything would seem better. They later complained of persistent mechanical failure and also remarked that the narrow tracks gave the tank an unacceptably high ground pressure, something not generally held against it. The 13th/18th Hussars were at Thetford when they received their Covenanters in August 1941. A month later the regiment took part in the five-day Exercise 'Bumper' which ranged across the English midlands, the Manoeuvre Act allowing them to go more or less where they liked. This regiment subsequently transferred from the 9th into the new 79th Armoured Division, still with their Covenanters and some Crusaders for a time, before being converted into a DD regiment. The 15th/19th Hussars claim, in their history, that the Covenanter was only produced for home defence. This sounds like a retrospective explanation, invented by an embarrassed civil servant, when it finally became clear that the tank would never be fit for active service. The tank had numerous teething troubles, each new fault requiring yet another modification. This kept the Royal Electrical and Mechanical Engineers (REME) fitters busy and consequently the tank crews were constantly having to keep up with developments.

There is an argument – probably based on the principle of making the best of a bad job – for providing training regiments with unreliable tanks. The theory is that they present personnel with a greater challenge and result in better trained crews, but for many of those involved it must have been a difficult philosophy to appreciate. No little skill and persistence was required to keep such tanks running, but when they were going well it was worth it for the Covenanter had a remarkable turn of speed. However, despite continued improvements it soon became clear that it would be a long time before the Covenanter could be described as battleworthy. The Guards Armoured Division, created in June 1941, was equipped with Covenanters in 1942. In the autumn of that year armoured divisions in Britain were reorganised to feature just one armoured brigade of three regiments; from 1943 an armoured reconnaissance regiment was added. By this time, particularly in the Guards, the Covenanter was gaining in reliablity and earning respect for its speed, low silhouette and dashing appearance. But even this could not disguise the fact that it was now completely out of date. The Covenanter could not be up-gunned nor up-armoured since any increase

August 1942 and two Covenanters of Brigade Headquarters, 5th Guards Armoured Brigade, Guards Armoured Division, demonstrate the correct way to investigate an occupied village: Stockton in Wiltshire. The next stage should be to investigate the Carriers Arms.

A Covenanter on trial in the desert. Poor though it is this picture is the only one to show the pattern of sandshields produced for this tank and the Crusader-type turret stowage bin which carried the camouflage net.

A close support Crusader, mounting the 3in howitzer, shown in a typical disruptive camouflage scheme. The tank alongside seems to sport another pattern altogether. These schemes were seen on tanks of the Royal Gloucestershire Hussars.

in weight would have overwhelmed the suspension. Its last chance for fame had gone. Later in 1943 the Covenanter was declared obsolete and orders issued that all surviving gun tanks should be scrapped.

In the meantime a handful of Covenanters had been shipped out to the Middle East for desert trials. Whether it was a case of wishful thinking or desperation is not clear, but the result can hardly have been in doubt.

When 1st Polish Armoured Division was formed in Britain it, too, received some Covenanters. Pending the formation of their armoured division many Polish troops were serving as crews on armoured trains operating in the south and east of England. Some, based in Kent, also acquired a few tanks in 1942, mostly Covenanters with some Valentines, which were intended to operate in conjunction with the trains, but not travel on them. On the night of 31 May 1942 a Covenanter attached to Armoured Train 'H', based in the Canterbury area, was destroyed by a bomb during a German raid on the city; probably the only tank of this type to be knocked out directly by enemy action.

CRUSADER DEFICIENCIES IN NORTH AFRICA

When the Crusader first entered production there were no such doubts about its reliability. By May 1941 enough were available to equip one regiment and they were hastily shipped out to the Middle East and issued to 6th Royal Tank Regiment, who employed them during the attempt to relieve Tobruk, Operation Battleaxe, in June.

CRUSADER MARK III, 2nd Lothian & Border Horse, 26th Armoured Bde, 6th Armoured Division

Crusader III of the 2nd Lothian and Border Horse, 26th Armoured Brigade, 6th Armoured Division in Tunisia. Like most tanks shipped direct from the UK for the 'Torch' landings this one is painted in a bronze green shade. It is silver inside. Markings include the divisional sign of a mailed fist, squadron symbol with troop number inside and the white/red/white recognition sign. This brigade did not use the normal unit identification system at this time and the method they did employ, of different coloured flashes, is not well enough documented to be shown here. Tanks could be supported by a Tecalemit, two-wheeled Rotatrailer containing extra ammunition and a fuel pump in its body, and up to 60 gallons of petrol in each of its drum shaped wheels. (Art by Peter Sarson, © Osprey Publishing)

Specifications

Crew: Three
Combat weight: 19,812kg
Power-to-weight ratio: 20.2bhp/ton (Imp)
Overall length: 5.98m
Width: 2.64m
Height: 2.24m
Engine: Nuffield Liberty Mark III/IV V12, watercooled, 340bhp at 1,500rpm
Transmission: Nuffield constant mesh four-speed gearbox and Wilson dual regenerative epicyclic steering, air operated
Fuel capacity: 500 litres plus 136 litres in auxiliary tank
Max. speed: 43km/h
Max. range: 177km on main tank
Fuel consumption: 2.8 litres/km
Fording depth: .96m
Armament: 6-pdr 7cwt. QF Mark III (57mm); co-axial 7.92mm Besa aircooled machine gun
Ammunition: AP. APC. APCBC. HE
Muzzle velocity: 853m/sec
Max. effective range: 1,830m
Ammunition stowage: 65 rounds
Gun depression/elevation: +20/–12.5 degrees

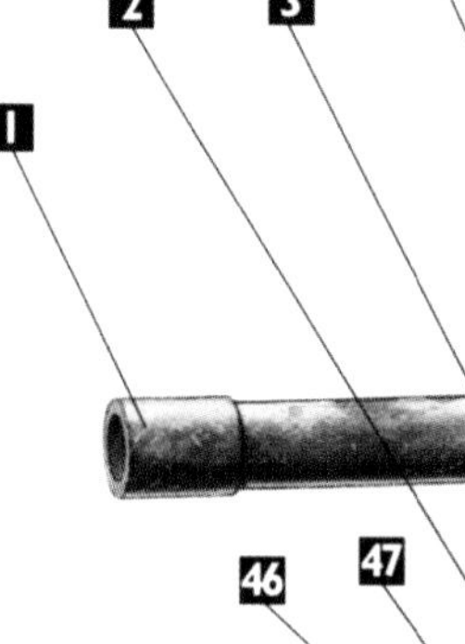

Key

1. 6-pdr 7cwt (57mm) gun
2. Steering control and lever R/H
3. Pyrene fire extinguisher
4. Replacement visor prisms
5. Driver's side lookout
6. Windscreen panels
7. 7.92mm Besa co-axial machine gun
8. Commander's vane sight
9. Driver's seat
10. 2in bombthrower
11. Gunner's periscope
12. Etched lubrication chart
13. Besa ammunition
14. Turret spotlamp
15. Signal cartridges
16. Commander's periscope
17. Signals satchel
18. Turret hatch L/H
19. No. 19 wireless set
20. Turret stowage bin
21. Auxiliary fuel tank
22. Crowbar
23. Air cleaner L/H
24. Drive sprocket
25. Bren gun magazines
26. Bren .303 light machine gun
27. Thompson sub-machine gun magazines
28. First aid box
29. Suspension spring
30. Thompson sub-machine gun
31. Road wheel
32. Suspension arm
33. Gunner's shoulder pad
34. Gunner's seat
35. Turret traverse gear
36. Idler wheel
37. 6-pdr ammunition stowage
38. Gear lever
39. Ignition control
40. Compass binnacle
41. Clutch pedal
42. Brake pedal
43. Headlamp
44. Track adjuster socket
45. Driver's mirror
46. Spare track link stowage
47. Ignition switches

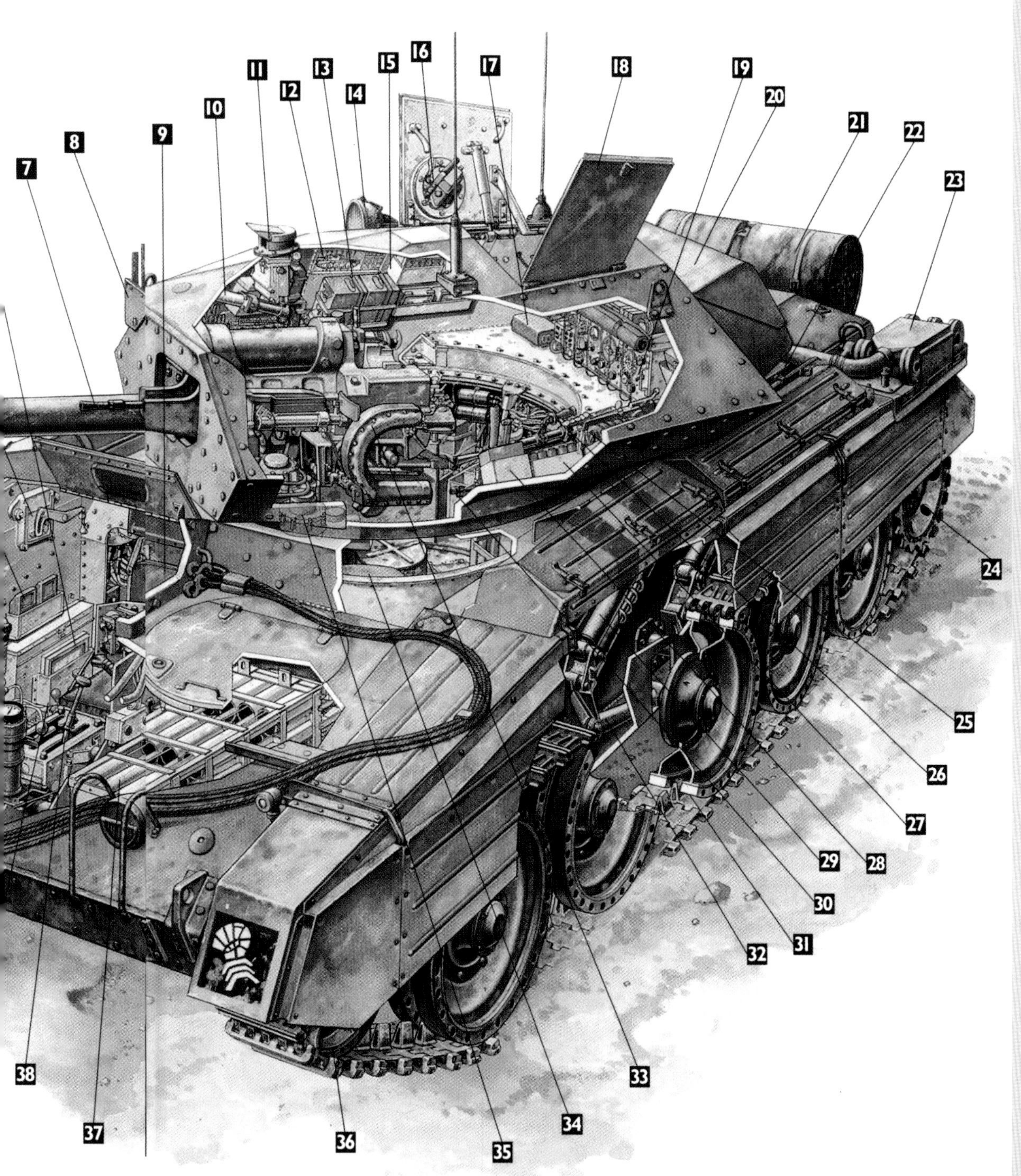
7
8
9
10
11
12
13
14
15
16
17
18
19
20
21
22
23
24
25
26
27
28
29
30
31
32
33
34
35
36
37
38

Later 22nd Armoured Brigade arrived, fully equipped with Crusaders, and they went into action in November in the aptly named Operation 'Crusader'.

There is no doubt that the Germans learned to respect the new tank for its speed, and if imitation is the sincerest form of flattery the Italians went one better, basing the appearance of their Sahariano medium tank, outwardly at least, on the Crusader. Yet it was equally clear to British crews that their tanks were under-gunned compared with German equivalents and extremely vulnerable to enemy anti-tank guns. It was not just the result of strike and penetration; when hit, most British tanks tended to burst into flames at once, which horrified their crews. Popular opinion ascribed this to hits on petrol tanks, conveniently forgetting that German tanks used the same fuel, but a British team proved where the real trouble lay. A lengthy examination of knocked out Crusaders and firing at battle damaged tanks fully stowed for the purpose revealed that the real culprit was cordite in ammunition, stowed in unprotected racks, which ignited immediately when struck with hot fragments of metal. Crews remained sceptical and it is noticeable that those with battle experience tended to use the auxiliary fuel tank at the back as a container for extra water if they could get away with it.

The chances are that even this degree of vulnerability would have been accepted if the Crusader had at least proved reliable. That it did not was due to a variety of factors. Shipping was the first problem. Tanks were driven around the docks with no water in the cooling system, which damaged the plumbing, and poor preparation meant that sea air and spray got inside and corroded components, notably alloy castings. All of this had to be made good by base workshops in Alexandria before tanks could be issued. There was an inevitable delay waiting for spares and the majority of Crusaders required many man hours of work that could not easily be spared when large numbers of damaged tanks were coming back from the battlefield. Yet that was only the beginning. After a few months of active service complaints began to pour in. As mentioned earlier the Liberty engine was assembled from separate sets of cylinders, instead of having a single block. Under stress, in a fast moving cross-country vehicle, the engine would tend to work apart, fracturing oil galleries and causing leaks. Then there was the cooling system. Sand, working its way inevitably into the water, wore away the white metal components of the water pump and caused it to leak. At the same time the exposed chain-driven fans suffered from excessive wear . If there is one place you can do without cooling problems it is the desert.

Wrecked Crusaders litter the desert. The Mark II in the foreground has lost its auxiliary turret in an explosion and fire that has buckled the front plates and burnt all the rubber off the nearside roadwheels.

A Crusader II of the RTR, perched on a sand ridge. The crew have added a rail to the sand shields from which they will hang some of their kit in service and attach the bivouac at night.

PERFORMANCE IN ACTION

User opinion is, once again, invariably negative but does contain some interesting comments. The Queen's Bays record that when they left the United Kingdom for Egypt in 1941 their tanks followed in separate ships. Once out of workshops the tanks were sprayed 'desert yellow'; when issued 'A' and 'B' Squadrons had Crusaders while 'C' had M3 Stuarts. The Crusader was regarded as more comfortable than the American tank and easier to fight and command, but on the march they considered themselves lucky not to lose six Crusaders each day to mechanical problems while the Stuarts just trundled on and on. At Msus, early in 1942, 2nd Armoured Brigade received such a mauling that they only had enough tanks between them to form one weak regiment. At Gazala they were re-equipped and the Bays were dismayed to receive many battle worn Crusaders, with all their tools missing and shot holes plugged. These were later replaced by tanks which had been renovated at base workshops. The 9th Lancers, also in 2nd Armoured Brigade, describe the desert colour in interior decorator's terms as Light Stone. The unit states that 2-pdr shot bounced off Panzer IIIs and the Germans regarded it with contempt, while their 50mm rounds would go straight through a Crusader. At Gazala, in the summer of 1942, the regiment received its first Sunshade device. This was a framework of tubular steel with canvas stretched over it which, when placed over the tank made it look like a lorry, at least from a distance. The thing was attached in two halves which, according to the 9th Lancers' historian 'in theory was dropped off by the commander pulling a quick release cord above his head. In practice it fell off all the time, except when it was required to do so'. The Royal Gloucester Hussars agree exactly.

The third regiment in 2nd Armoured Brigade was 10th Hussars. They were particularly scathing about the performance of the 2-pdr gun, claiming that 500 yards was the maximum effective range against a Panzer III which, with its 50mm gun, was effective at 1,000 yards or more. But the regiment disregarded the armour piercing performance of the short 75mm gun on the Panzer IV. The Sherwood Rangers, who refer to their Sunshade disguise as a Sun Bonnet recall 'it was a miracle if a Crusader engine functioned for 36 hours without some strange and terrible trouble developing'.

The Staffordshire Yeomanry, in August 1942, report having 'A' and 'B' Squadron in Grants while 'C' had Crusaders and, according to them, the British tank could pass over soft ground in which the American mediums would bog down. Their history contains an interesting chart showing how a regimental group formed up for a desert

This Crusader not only has a camouflage net and packs slung from the side rail it is also disguised as a lorry with a version of the 'Sunshade' device.

move. 'C' Squadron led the way with three troops abreast, followed by squadron headquarters and the forward observation officer's OP tank. They were followed by a Royal Engineers detachment and the reserve tank troop. Next came regimental headquarters with three columns in their wake. On the left was the infantry company, on the right the anti-tank battery and in the centre a Royal Horse Artillery battery. Each column was preceded by its command vehicles with a spare OP tank. The flanks were covered by 'B' squadron on the left and 'A' squadron on the right. Each squadron arranged its troops in diamond formation with its headquarters at the centre. Behind this combat phalanx came the two transport echelons.

Another chart shows how the regimental group took up close leaguer for the night. 'A' Squadron took the right flank, its tanks in line ahead with their guns pointing outwards to front, sides and rear. Regimental headquarters formed line inside them. 'C' Squadron, on the left flank were a mirror image while the next line inboard of them was 'B' Squadron with all its tanks parked gun forward, except the very last one which had its turret reversed. The anti-tank battery covered the rear with portee vehicles while the RHA battery and infantry motor company formed four inner lines.

On the subject of Crusaders the Wiltshire Yeomanry claim that most of the trouble they experienced was with water pump failures. In October 1943 their 'A' Squadron had Shermans, 'B' Crusaders and 'C' Grants. An excellent account of Crusaders in action can be found in the 9th Lancer's history. The regiment, in 2nd Armoured Brigade, 1st Armoured Division, employed Crusaders in 'A' Squadron and the action took place during the retreat to El Alamein:

> On the 16th, 'A' squadron, on the left, rang up to say that there were some suspicious-looking vehicles in front, and could these be attacked? The Colonel gave permission and the remainder of the regiment then witnessed as nice a bit of tank handling as ever was seen.
>
> Twelve graceful, putty-coloured cruisers were standing in a semi-circle, their guns pointing inquiringly towards the west where a column of dust rose on the still air. Behind them stood in line the close-support tanks of squadron headquarters. Suddenly all four fired, their guns elevated high and the shells making an are of smoke trail in the sky, and there was a puff of blue smoke behind each tank as their engines were started. The 3-in. guns were firing smoke as hard as they could be loaded and after the fourth salvo the line began to move, slowly at first until, gathering speed, each tank was throwing up a plume of sand. The squadron disappeared in a cloud of dust. The watchers saw no more, but from the bank of dust could be heard the slam of tank guns and the rapid hammer of Besas. For ten minutes the curtain remained drawn and then 'A' Squadron came slowly back through the clearing smoke.
>
> The Colonel's cruiser nosed its way over to them and stopped as each tank swung around to face west again.

In the extended pursuit that followed the battle of Alamein, Crusaders made some remarkably long journeys. A team of engineers from Nuffield's had been flown out to the desert and shipping practice had improved, while the crews themselves learned to anticipate and remedy problems before they became disasters. Unfortunately it was

In Britain, by way of contrast, the lorry disguise, seen here on a Crusader III, was known as a 'Houseboat'.

Two crew members of a Crusader III belonging to 26th Armoured Brigade, 6th Armoured Division (believed to be 17th/21st Lancers) indulge in some studied nonchalance for the camera in the Tunisian hills. The bivouac is rigged at the side. These tanks were painted green but the significance of the symbol on the turret side is not clear.

too late. The Crusader had earned such a bad reputation for reliability, especially when compared with the mass of American tanks now arriving in theatre, that no crew could visualise it as anything but second rate and everyone was anxious to get into Shermans as soon as possible.

IMPROVED ARMAMENT

Crusaders armed with the 6-pdr gun had started to arrive in the Middle East during that summer and, although the Germans had also improved the firepower of their tanks, they were heartily welcomed. Now, in terms of weapon performance at least, some Crusaders were equal to the majority of enemy tanks except the new long-barrelled Panzer IVs and, of course, the anti-tank guns. When 6th Armoured Division arrived in Tunisia as part of 1st Army in November 1942, its armoured regiments were equipped with a mixture of Crusaders and Valentines. The 16th/5th Lancers state that each of their squadrons had two troops of Crusaders and two of Valentines. The 17th/21st Lancers had six 6-pdr Crusaders to each squadron and two Crusader close support tanks with each squadron headquarters. These they describe as invaluable, having a range of 3,000 yards firing smoke or high explosive. This is the only regiment to record the use of Rotatrailers. These unsprung two-wheeled contraptions contained extra supplies of fuel and ammunition. The idea was that the tanks would tow them up to the point of action and then drop them off by remote control. In practice they leaked, bounced and turned over regularly until they were

abandoned as a nuisance.

By this time, like the Covenanter, Crusader had been declared obsolete. Before they left for Italy, all British regiments had handed in their Crusaders and moved into Shermans. Many of the best surviving Crusaders are said to have been passed on to the Free French forces that remained in North Africa.

Back in Britain Crusader production soon reached the scale at which home regiments could be equipped. General Hobart's 11th Armoured Division was one of the main users, although many other regiments operated for a while with a mixture of Covenanters and Crusaders as they were available. When the 6-pdr tanks started to enter service the 11th found that they were hard work for troop leaders who already had enough to do in a two-man turret. An extra 2-pdr Crusader was therefore introduced into each troop for the benefit of these officers.

The sample Crusader Mark I (T15630) supplied to Australia takes part in a recruiting parade in Melbourne. It was evaluated at Puckapunyal where it is now displayed in the RAAC Museum.

In June 1941 the 9th Australian Divisional Cavalry Regiment arrived in Egypt from Syria. It was rapidly equipped with a mixture of M3 Stuart tanks, Universal Carriers and Mark II Crusaders. It was the only Australian armoured unit to operate in the Western Hemisphere but it took part in the fighting around El Alamein before being withdrawn in preparation for its return to Australia. In August 1941 a single Crusader I, number T15630 from an early Nuffield contract, was landed in Melbourne in response to a request for a tank placed with the War Office in London. The tank seems to have been acquired as a sample at a time when Australia was working on the design of its own tank. A comparison between the turrets of Crusader and the Australian Cruiser reveals a basic similarity in shape, even though the turret of the AC1 was cast and therefore less angular.

TRIALS IN THE USA

A Crusader had also been sent to the United States. Under the command of a Corporal Dixey it arrived at Aberdeen Proving Ground, Maryland, in October 1941. In April 1942 it was loaned to the Westinghouse Company for installation of their gyro-stabiliser (which implies that it must have been fitted with geared elevation) and was then taken down to Fort Knox in Kentucky. After the eviction of British troops from mainland Europe, with the loss of a vast number of tanks, America was seen as the ideal place from which to order replacements. Examples of Crusader and Matilda were shipped across the Atlantic but, before any contracts could be agreed, Washington decided that American plants should only build American tanks and the project was dropped. But this prohibition did not extend to components and factories in the United States supplied many parts for Crusaders and other British types.

To the left, a close-up view of a Crusader II command tank in the desert. The dummy gun has been fitted with a sleeve to make it look more like a 6-pdr

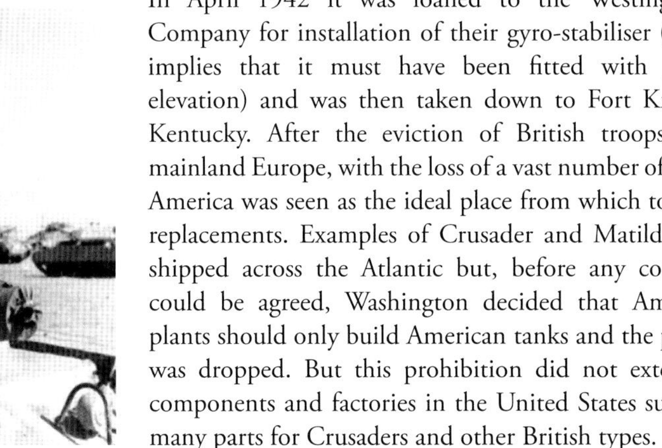

VARIANTS

COMMAND 'OP' VEHICLES

HM King George VI examines a Crusader III OP tank of 11th Armoured Division in Britain. This tank has received the final up-armouring package and the extra panels can be seen on the sloping front plate and the panel with 'Buq-Buq' painted on it.

Among special purpose variants of Covenanter and Crusader the least obvious, on purpose, were the OP (Observation Post) and Command tanks. They had to mix with the fighting tanks in action, so it was in their interests to stand out as little as possible. OP tanks were issued to Royal Artillery batteries and carried Forward Observation Officers into the front line where they could call up rapid and effective support from the guns. The fighting space was cleared of all main armament ammunition stowage, and the gun was replaced by a convincing dummy which did not intrude into the turret space. Working surfaces were installed front and back along with two No .19 and one No. 18 wireless sets. These tanks retained their turret machine guns and the smoke bomb discharger while external stowage was adapted to carry reels of signal cable so that the No. 19 sets could be operated by remote control some distance from the tank. There were OP versions of Covenanters Mark II and IV and the slightly roomier Crusader III. Each Royal Horse Artillery and field battery in an armoured division had two OP tanks; other field and medium gun batteries were issued with one. Command tanks, which were generally issued at regimental level, had similar internal arrangements but with two No. 19 sets only, one netted to the regiment, the other to brigade. They appeared on Covenanter II and Crusader II. The observant could recognise these key vehicles by their extra wireless aerials and, if one got close enough, by the silencer for the auxiliary generator. This was a single-cylinder 'Chore Horse' stowed on the turret floor of a Covenanter; in a Crusader it could be a 'Chore Horse' or 'Tiny Tim' located in the front turret space.

RECOVERY VEHICLES

During the desert war one aspect of the Afrika Korps' technique made a considerable impression upon the British. This was their ability to recover derelict tanks from the battlefield, even while the fighting was going on. In the summer of 1942 a Recovery Committee, established by the War Office, recommended the adoption of armoured recovery vehicles (ARVs). As existing tanks were the obvious basis for such vehicles it was agreed to develop ARV versions of all current types, which included Covenanter and Crusader.

Experimental conversions were undertaken at Arborfield but, of the four types converted, an official publication describes the Covenanter as unreliable and the Crusader as hopeless. All prototypes were classed as ARV Mark I and conformed to similar specifications. The vehicles were turretless and came equipped with various items of recovery equipment, welding and cutting gear, a 5-ton portable jib which could be erected at the front and a LMG mounting which fitted into the crew compartment when required for ground or air defence. The ARV had a crew of three and the turret ring aperture was plated over, with a large hatch for access. It was

CRUSADER MARK II COMMAND TANK TAURUS, HQ 11th Armoured Division

Crusader II Command Tank Taurus of headquarters 11th Armoured Division in Britain. It has additional armour at the front and both sides of the driver's cab. The name is painted boldly on the turret while the identification colours are seen on the front and sides. The name reflects the charging bull symbol of this division which was selected by its commander, Sir Percy Hobart. The white '40' on a black square applies to tanks of divisional headquarters. (Art by Peter Sarson, © Osprey Publishing)

hoped to supply these vehicles with winches but nothing suitable was available at the time and they relied upon a direct pull to remove damaged tanks that could not move under their own power. There seems little doubt that there was never more than one each of the Covenanter and Crusader ARV Mark I and no illustration of the former has yet been located.

MINE CLEARING

For minefield clearance the AMRA (Anti Mine Roller Attachment) was available for both tanks. The AMRAs were virtually identical and differed only where they were attached to their respective tank. The AMRA Mark IC, evolved for Covenanter, had two-piece brackets while the Mark 1D used on Crusader had a more substantial external frame. The device itself, which weighed just under 1.5 tons, consisted of four heavy duty sprung rollers, suspended from a frame ahead of the tracks, which detonated mines and were usually destroyed in the process. If the tank needed to

A Covenanter with AMRA negotiates a scissors bridge during a demonstration. It does not look easy.

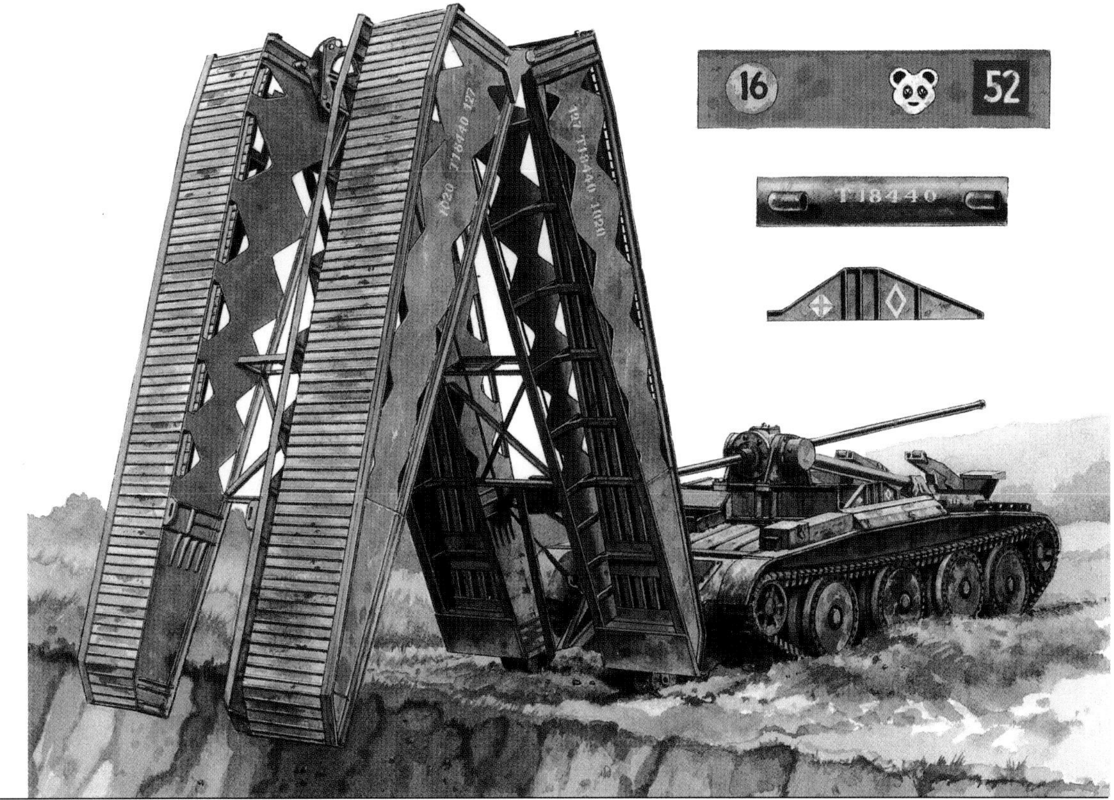

COVENANTER BRIDGELAYER, 13/18TH HUSSARS, 22nd Armoured Brigade, 9th Armoured Division

Covenanter Bridgelayer of 13th/18th Hussars, 22nd Armoured Brigade, 9th Armoured Division in Britain. The colour scheme is khaki brown and the yellow cross indicates that it is taking the part of an enemy vehicle in an exercise. The white 52 on a red square indicates the second armoured regiment in the senior brigade while the white diamond shows that it is attached to regimental headquarters. Notice that the tank's number is repeated on each segment of the bridge. (Art by Peter Sarson, © Osprey Publishing)

detach itself from the device on the battlefield an electrically fired fuse would break the connection. On sand the rollers were heavy enough to detonate the average anti-tank mine, but on harder ground, or where the mines were buried deep, the weight of the rollers had to be increased. This was done by removing a cap and half filling each roller with whatever was available, earth, sand, rubble or water. Tanks dedicated to this role carried the mounting brackets permanently, but the roller attachment itself was carried in a lorry until required. Attempts to have the tank tow it at other times were dropped, due to handling difficulties.

BRIDGE LAYING

When the Experimental Bridging Establishment invented a form of portable scissors bridge for tanks the first production model was developed on a Covenanter hull. Orders for 54 were placed with the Southern Railway workshops at Eastleigh and 30 more with another contractor, all of which were converted from new gun tanks, supplied turretless direct from the manufacturer. The bridge, known as the 30ft No. 1, was actually 34ft long but opened out to cover a 30ft gap and had a load bearing capacity of 24 tons. The laying and recovering action was entirely automatic, powered by a screw thread device driven off the tank's engine and controlled by the

TOP The prototype Covenanter bridgelayer at Christchurch, showing the launching apparatus in the open position with the weight bearing rollers on the ground.

ABOVE How to move a Covenanter bridgelayer by rail. Two Rectank wagons are required and the crew watch anxiously as the bowler hatted inspector, with his little ruler, makes sure that it is just so.

driver. Bridgelayers were issued on the scale of three per armoured brigade headquarters. They carried a crew of two and had no fixed defensive armament whatever. In 1944 a light alloy version of the bridge was developed, capable of handling 30 tons, but by then the only Covenanter bridgelayers left in service were with the Australian and New Zealand forces and it is not clear whether they received the new bridge or not. No bridgelaying version of the Crusader was ever developed.

AMPHIBIOUS MODELS

The alternative to a bridge, for wider water obstacles, was floatation. This was applied to the Crusader and took the form of a pair of large, flat decked pontoons which were locked onto the hull at each side. This was very much a manual exercise although a portable lifting device, known as the Atherton Jib, was fitted to the tank's turret to assist the operation. Once afloat the tank was propelled by special blades, attached to the track links, which acted as paddles.

No similar device is recorded for the Covenanter although this tank formed the basis of the only fully amphibious tank developed in Britain during the war. Known as the Medium Tank A/T 1, it consisted of a Covenanter turret superimposed upon a hull of enormous depth with the Meadows flat 12 engine situated deep within its bowels. Some 24ft long, 13ft wide and a massive 11ft tall it looked unwieldy on dry land but seems to have performed well enough in the water. Built by Braithwaites of Newport in South Wales it was of rivetted construction with all joints caulked to make them waterproof and a maximum armour thickness of 40mm. Weight was around 31 tons. The original model, which had no suspension at all, was replaced by A/T 1*, probably a rebuild, which featured a sprung jockey roller at the front. This was followed by A/T 1** which had Churchill type coil spring suspension on all but the first and last two rollers; it was apparently rebuilt as A/T 1*** about which little is known. Of the former two the following details are recorded. A/T1* employed the standard gearbox and Wilson steering system of Covenanter while A/T1** was fitted with the Sinclair Synchro-Self-Shifting (SSS) system which was designed to give a much smoother changing sequence. Whichever gearbox was used it was provided with an auxiliary box giving high and low ratio. The former, which gave a theoretical land speed of 20mph, was only intended for use afloat, when the tank would make about 5mph. On land, especially across country, only the lower range was used to avoid damage, and that gave it a top speed of about 10mph. A fluid coupling was also built into the transmission of both tanks to avoid any serious shock to the drive train when a tank first touched down during a swim ashore. At sea the tanks had a considerable draught of 5ft 6in but a modest freeboard, to deck level, of 15in. The crew numbered five; driver, three-man turret crew and what was described, in true nautical parlance, as an extra hand who shared the front compartment. It was his duty, no doubt, to operate the sea cocks on the ballast tank. This was located low down in the bow and its purpose was to aid traction on landing. As the amphibious tank neared the beach, water was admitted to the ballast tank so that the nose of the machine descended and helped to press the tracks down once they bit into the sand. Cross country trials were conducted at Chobham in Surrey with sea trials taking place off Barry Island in South Wales. The testing authorities were critical of the engine location, reporting that it was very difficult to work on. This is hardly surprising. In addition to being low down at the stern of the tank it was enclosed within an engine room, closed off by a pair of steel doors in a bulkhead. Crusaders were also fitted with deep wading gear for ship to shore landings over open beaches, although none ever took part in such landings apart from some special models such as anti-aircraft tanks and gun tractors.

As already noted the demise of the Crusader as a front line gun tank coincided roughly with its ultimate acceptance as a reliable machine in the mechanical sense. Since large stocks were still available the type was chosen as the basis for a group of self-propelled (SP) guns created to provide anti-aircraft protection for mobile formations.

ANTI-AIRCRAFT MODEL

In September 1941 it was decided to develop a tank mounting for the 40mm Bofors anti-aircraft gun for the Royal Artillery. It was agreed that there could never be more than limited protection for the crew and at first it was hoped to include a predictor on the vehicle. The prototype, which appeared on an early Crusader hull (T44381), featured a complex shield which was later increased in height by panels of plywood to represent more armour. When it was tested at MEE in March 1943 the turret structure proved too weak to remain rigid on cross country trials. The Department of Tank Design sought to correct the problem on a second tank (T124559) in July 1943, which had a modified turret. They complained bitterly in the process about having to undertake remedial work on something designed elsewhere; by Morris Motors. The number of turret rollers was increased and they wished to cut down the

The floating Crusader launches itself off the beach at Hayling Island. It has a deep wading cowl over the cooling louvres and the engine air intakes have been extended and raised.

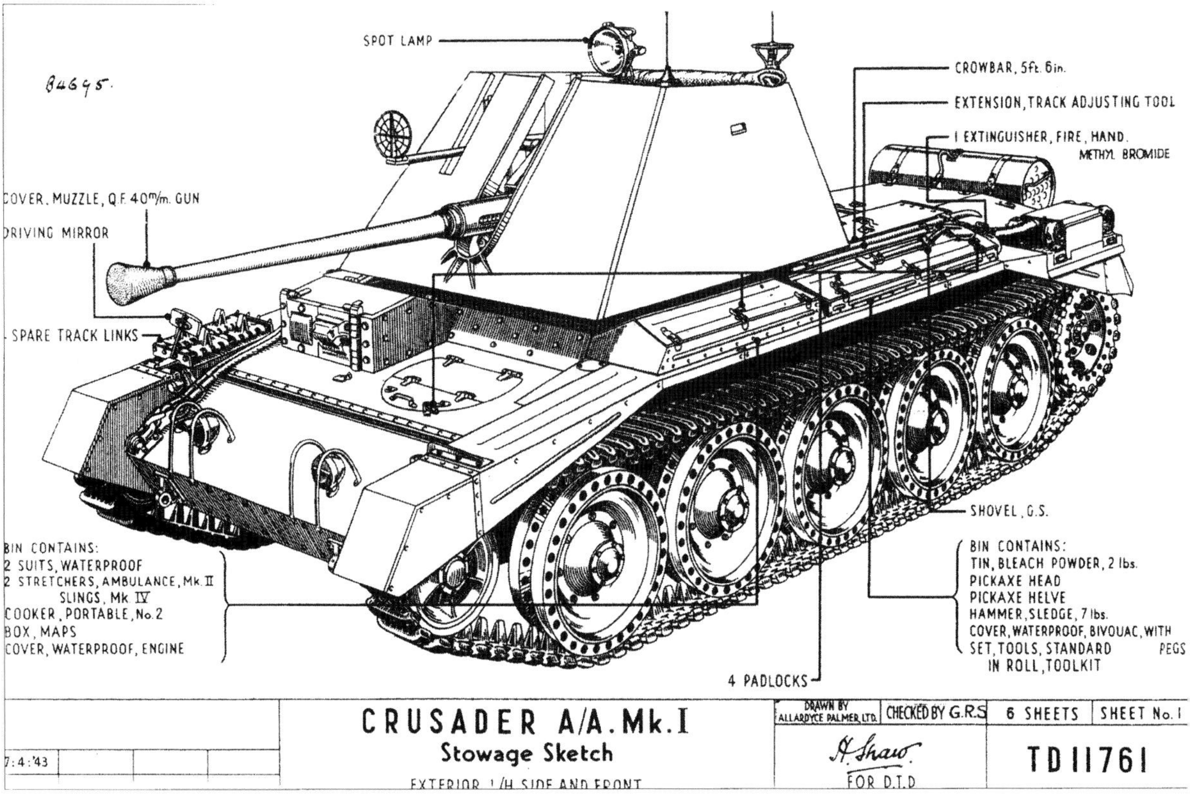

84645.

SPOT LAMP

CROWBAR, 5ft. 6in.

EXTENSION, TRACK ADJUSTING TOOL

1 EXTINGUISHER, FIRE, HAND. METHYL BROMIDE

COVER. MUZZLE, Q.F. 40m/m. GUN

DRIVING MIRROR

SPARE TRACK LINKS

SHOVEL, G.S.

BIN CONTAINS:
2 SUITS, WATERPROOF
2 STRETCHERS, AMBULANCE, Mk. II
SLINGS, Mk. IV
COOKER, PORTABLE, No. 2
BOX, MAPS
COVER, WATERPROOF, ENGINE

BIN CONTAINS:
TIN, BLEACH POWDER, 2 lbs.
PICKAXE HEAD
PICKAXE HELVE
HAMMER, SLEDGE, 7 lbs.
COVER, WATERPROOF, BIVOUAC, WITH PEGS
SET, TOOLS, STANDARD IN ROLL, TOOLKIT

4 PADLOCKS

CRUSADER A/A. Mk. I
Stowage Sketch
EXTERIOR L/H SIDE AND FRONT

7:4:'43

DRAWN BY ALLARDYCE PALMER LTD. | CHECKED BY G.R.S. | 6 SHEETS | SHEET No. 1

A. Shaw FOR D.T.D

TD 11761

ABOVE The Crusader A.A.I from a stowage diagram. The canvas cover for the turret is shown rolled up, as it would be when the weapon was in action.

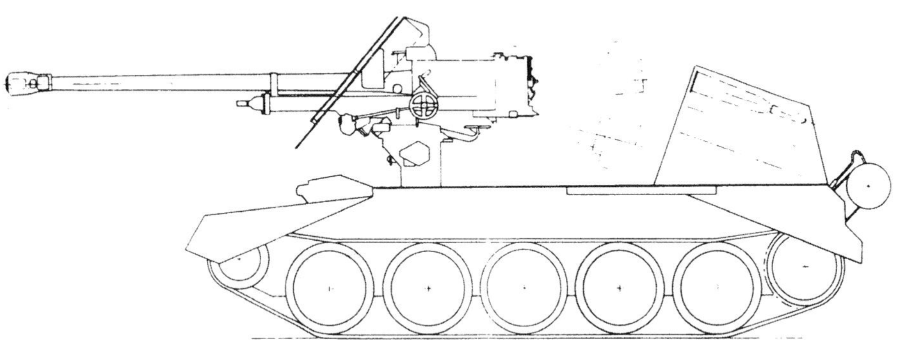

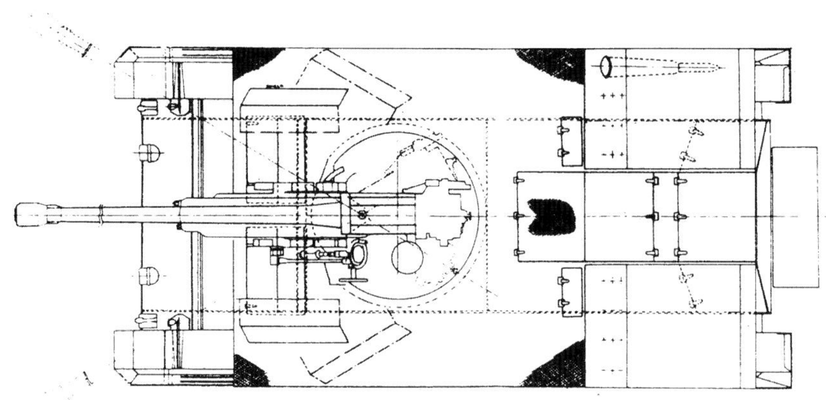

Design sketches for the Anti-Tank Crusader showing the 17-pdr gun mounting, shield and ammunition stowage. Elevation and traverse limits are also indicated.

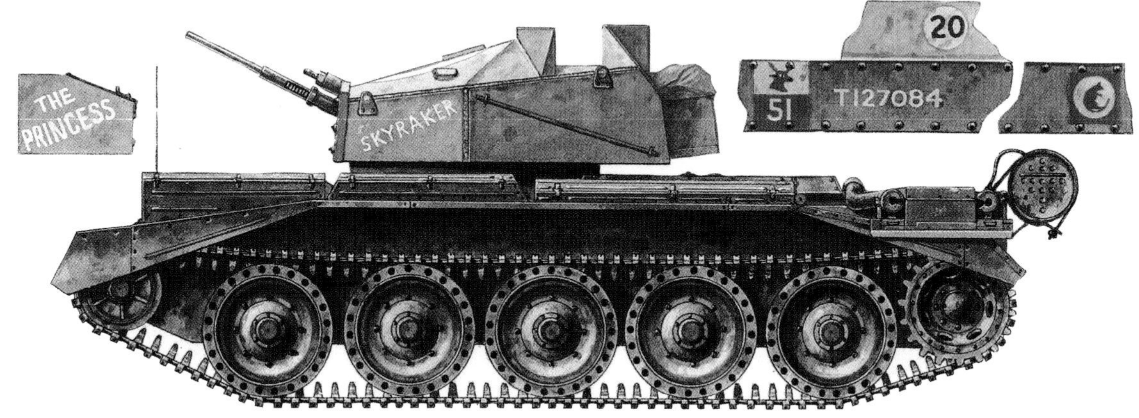

CRUSADER MARK III A.A. III, SKYRAKER OR THE PRINCESS, 1st RTR, 22nd Armoured Brigade, 7th Armoured Division.

A Crusader III A.A. III anti-aircraft tank of 1st Royal Tank Regiment, 22nd Armoured Brigade, 7th Armoured Division, in June 1944. Notice the front mounted wireless aerial and extra stowage box on the nearside trackguard. The use of two names on one tank is unusual but the circled white star was used by all Allied forces in France at this time. (Art by Peter Sarson, © Osprey Publishing)

height of the turret armour to save weight, but it never appears to have been very satisfactory. The production model, or Crusader III A.A. I, as its name implies, appeared on the Mark III hull. The gun shield was a much simplified, four-sided affair with a waterproof canvas cover for the top. The mounting was located directly above the tank's original turret ring. Traverse and elevation were controlled by a joystick, using a hydraulic system powered by an Enfield 250 cc twin-cylinder engine. In addition to the driver the tank had a gun layer and loader, who occupied the turret. The former was also tank commander while the loader operated the No. 19 set located just in front of him. Trials revealed that the Bofors mounting was not as effective as had been hoped. Of course, being associated with the Royal Artillery it was not intended that the gun should be fired on the move, hence the importance of having an auxiliary engine. Difficulty was experienced in tracking low-flying aircraft and on anything but level ground the weapon was unable to traverse at all. Even so contracts exist for at least 215 machines.

T15834, with the deep wading cowling, makes its way, head first for some reason, onto an LCT (2) on a remarkably calm day.

CRUSADER III (A.A. MK. II)

Meanwhile the Royal Armoured Corps was also studying the subject. Light anti-aircraft tanks, mounting multiple machine guns, already existed but they were cramped and unpopular on account of their limited range.

The use of tank-busting aircraft demanded a swifter response and a preference was now expressed for twin 20mm weapons such as the Oerlikon. The guns had a rate of fire of 450 rounds per minute and a muzzle velocity of 2,725ft/sec. They fired high explosive, incendiary and practice rounds, with or without tracer

AT/1* thrashes its way through the water off Barry Island. The driver's hatch is almost obliterated by spray so he relied a lot on the turret crew for guidance.

The Crusader III A.A. Mk II appeared from Morris Motors in the summer of 1943, the pilot model being issued for testing in June. The weapons were housed in a low, multi-sided turret, built from single layer armour, which certainly looked more suited to the hull than the Bofors had done. The tank had a crew of four; a driver, two loaders and a gunner who also acted as tank commander and wireless operator. The tank carried 600 rounds of ammunition, some of it in 60-round magazines, but these were so bulky they had to be reloaded by hand inside the turret. Power Mountings Ltd devised the high speed traverse and elevating gear but it appears that, even in experienced hands, the turret was liable to overrun the target due to inertia so the maximum traversing speed was limited to 10deg/sec, although it could turn faster. Space was at a premium and all crew members except the driver were extremely uncomfortable. Urgently undertaken, the resultant redesign was the Crusader III A.A.III which had an improved turret with better protection for the gunner, in the form of a raised coaming. His task was made less onerous by repositioning the wireless to the left of the driver, who now became the operator. For some reason, so far unexplained, the armament was supplemented with a Vickers K .303 machine gun in an armoured jacket. Unlike the Bofors version hydraulic power for the turret was taken from the tank's own engine. Since the Crusader A.A. II/III was intended for the support of armoured formations it would usually be mobile and having the main engine running was not regarded as a problem. But those who imagined these tanks were intended to move and shoot at the same time were corrected in a note, inserted into the original trials report by Colonel Messenger: 'A.A. tanks cannot fire on the move, there is no point in it'. It does not appear to have been very effective even when stationary. Trials with a tank using a camera gun – against a Hurricane on Wareham Common and a Jeep with a can on top at Chertsey – proved how difficult it was to accurately track a fast moving target and, once again, the turret only worked effectively on level ground. Records suggest that some 600 were built, although it is not possible to differentiate between Marks II and III from the available documents. It is easier with photographs for, even if the turret top is obscured, the position of the wireless aerials on a Mark II, either side of the commander's position, distinguishes it from a Mark III where they are mounted on the front upper hull plate. The headquarters of an armoured division, in 1944, included two anti-aircraft tanks, as did the HQ of an armoured brigade. The headquarters of an armoured regiment, at the same time, was entitled to six. The majority of those photographed in North

West Europe after D-Day seem to be of the Mark III type, with the extra Vickers gun, but the need for their services was kept to a minimum by the RAF and they were soon withdrawn. Even so the Crusader A.A.II/III is still shown on Establishment Tables for 1945, after which they disappear for good.

ANTI-TANK 'SP' VARIATIONS

Sometime before June 1944 the Royal Artillery developed a second type of Crusader anti-aircraft tank, although very little is recorded about it and photographs are few. The mounting, which could also be found on trailers and lorries, contained three 20mm Oerlikons on parallel linkage, one above the other. The gunner sat within a small armoured housing behind the guns but the turret was otherwise totally exposed. The loaders were simply stationed nearby, since in keeping with RA practice the weapon was intended for static operation to protect gun positions. This in turn suggests that an auxiliary power unit was used, rather than the main engine, and it is not beyond the bounds of possibility that these were converted from redundant Bofors tanks. A Royal Artillery report on D-Day states that the triple 20mm performed well on the Normandy beaches, but this is the only official comment so far discovered and there is no record of a proper title for this model.

When, in the face of German experience, the British started to examine the potential of self-propelled anti-tank guns in the summer of 1942, the Crusader was one of the first to be considered. The Churchill was rejected because it was too unreliable and at this stage the Valentine does not appear to have been considered. However the Crusader was capable of handling the load, it had an adequate power to weight ratio and was available in sufficient numbers, but it was required in a hurry, and therein lay the trouble. The worst feature of the design was the gun mounting. As there was no time to modify the gun a recoil of 42in had to be accepted, and in order to obtain suitable elevation the gun had to be mounted much higher than was ideal; indeed the trunnions were located some 7ft 6in. above the ground. This in turn, on account of topweight, meant that protection would be limited to a frontal shield which meant that the crew would be dangerously exposed. Ready use ammunition was to be stowed in armoured bins at the rear. The conversion was regarded as straightforward enough to suit a railway workshop but it was never adopted.

Apart from an Argentinian conversion mentioned later, the only other SP gun version of Crusader was a post-war modification to one tank which enabled it to mount the 5.5in medium gun. The exact circumstances of the conversion are not known, but it was probably no more than a test rig, built in connection with the

A Crusader A.A.I coming ashore from an LCT (4) during Exercise Fabius, the D-Day rehearsal, in May 1944. It is towing another Bofors gun on a wheeled carriage and affording a dry landing for its crew and a party of infantry.

ABOVE LEFT The prototype Crusader A.A.I with the Bofors gun trained horizontal at 8 o'clock. Notice the plywood extensions to the original armour.

ABOVE RIGHT One of the strange triple Oerlikon A.A. Crusaders in Normandy. The tank is well dug in and the crew even have their own shelter and ammunition stock at the front.

FV300 programme. The gun was mounted in an open well at the front, facing back over the engine deck. The nose of the tank now became effectively the firing platform while the driver was moved back to a position on the offside, right up against the engine bulkhead. His view to the front was almost totally obscured by the gun itself. No doubt to protect them from blast damage the air cleaners were relocated almost amidships on each track guard.

OTHER VARIANTS

Experience in Tunisia indicated that the new 17-pdr anti-tank gun was proving quite a handful to the average four-wheel drive tractor and thoughts turned to the advantages of full or half-tracked tractors. The result of these deliberations was the Crusader Gun Tractor Mark I. Trials with six gun tanks in Britain proved that the Crusader was powerful enough for the work and a prototype tractor was built, followed by an unrecorded number of production machines. The conversion was quite drastic. The entire tank, forward of the engine bulkhead, was rebuilt to house a driver, commander and six-man gun detachment in an open topped compartment protected by 14mm of armour. Ammunition was stowed in lockers on the rear trackguards and in boxes within the crew area. A spare gun wheel was mounted over the transmission compartment. Drum shaped air cleaners were fitted, well forward on the engine decks and a connection from the steering brake airline was used to activate trailer brakes on the gun. User opinion was very favourable although a request was made for a front mounted towing hook to make gun positioning easier. But it was soon discovered that the high cross country speed of the tractor – which was governed to 27mph – was punishing the guns. Fully stowed, a Gun Tractor weighed no less than a Crusader tank but it was always a very lively machine. Used in Europe from D-Day onwards some of the tractors were appropriated by battery commanders as highly mobile recce-cum-battery command vehicles and the only criticism was their vulnerability to mortars.

A rear view of a Crusader A.A.II with the turret traversed left and Oerlikons at partial elevation. Notice the armoured cover for the commander's hatch, the wireless aerial alongside and the sight mounting, linked to the guns, which rises out of slots in the roof.

A Covenanter was used, during the early stages of development for what became known as the Armoured Vehicle Royal Engineers (AVRE), as a trial mounting for the Petard spigot mortar. But the only other connection with this branch of the service was a Crusader bulldozer tank developed by MG Motors of Abingdon. The tank

CRUSADER MARK III GUN TRACTOR, B Troop, 1st Battery, unidentified anti-tank regiment of an armoured division

Crusader gun tractor of the Anti-Tank regiment, Royal Artillery, of an Armoured Division. It is shown standing by to support its 17-pdr anti-tank gun in action. Working in reverse order, '77' in white, on the red and blue square, indicates the anti-tank regiment of an armoured division in 1944. Each battery, of which there were three in the regiment, consisted of three troops and of these 'A' Troop was always self-propelled, 'B' and 'C' being towed, but all having 17-pdr guns. The battery could be identified by the position of the red square within the blue on the tactical sign and in this case the 3rd battery is indicated. Finally, the gun within the troop is shown by the white letter and number on the tactical sign. Thus we have the first gun in 'A' troop of the third battery. Only this tactical sign was repeated on the gun shield. It should be added that these markings are somewhat speculative; it has not proved possible to confirm which batteries employed Crusader tractors. Note: the divisional insignia has purposely been omitted from this drawing since it has not been possible to establish beyond doubt which regiments actually used these vehicles in Europe. (Art by Peter Sarson, © Osprey Publishing)

was stripped to hull level and decked over the turret ring. Raised, armoured headcovers were provided for the commander and driver and the full width dozer blade was mounted on heavy duty brackets at each side. It was raised and lowered by a winch, driven off the tank's engine and located in the fighting compartment, via a short jib at the front. Following a disastrous fire at the Royal Ordnance Factory at Kirkby one of these dozer tanks was modified to remove sensitive munitions. The blade was fixed, extra armour and sandbags added to the front and an extended jib fitted with a carrier suspended well ahead of the vehicle. In an effort to produce a hydraulically operated dozer blade, one of the Crusader Gun Tractors was adapted but production ultimately centred on the cable operated system, fitted to the Centaur tank.

The only countries, apart from Britain, to employ the Covenanter bridgelayer were Australia and New Zealand. The latter are recorded as having 13, and used them

The Crusader 5.5in SP gun. The driver's seat and gear lever may just be seen alongside the nearest air cleaner. The gun mounting is clearly quite substantial.

A Crusader III taking part in towing trials with a 17-pdr anti-tank gun and limber.

A Crusader gun tractor used to test the hydraulic dozer operating gear.

well into the post-war period which must have been a maintenance achievement, if nothing more. The Australians had eight, and used them operationally on two occasions as part of Special Equipment Squadrons on Bougainville and Balikapan. This is thought to be the closest any Covenanters came to seeing active service.

The strangest fate of all awaited a batch of Crusader gun tractors which were purchased by Argentina after the war. Some were rebuilt as SP guns, mounting pre-war French weapons of 75mm and 105mm calibre along with three Madsen machine guns. Information is scarce and very few pictures are known, but it would appear that the superstructure was both raised and extended with the gun mounted centrally at the front, above the driver's and commander's hatches. It seems probable that the vehicle was open at the top. Even so the weight factor was doubtless critical.

A Crusader dozer tank from the rear. The blade is raised and both armoured hatches are open.

The modified Crusader Dozer at ROF, Kirkby. It managed to clear the entire site without one single fatality.

CHAPTER 4

THE TANKS OF THE OLD GANG

Early in World War II many influential soldiers believed that it would carry on where World War I left off, with the apparently impregnable Maginot Line and the Germans' daunting Siegfried Line marking the edges of a new No Man's Land, between which the ground was likely to become as inhospitable and shell-torn as its progenitor in the Great War. The lessons of mechanised mobility thrashed out on Salisbury Plain and elsewhere were disregarded by this faction so heavy tanks such as A20, or Churchill's powerful trenching machine 'Nellie' were favoured instead. Quite how Sir Albert Stern was drawn into this is not entirely clear; some say that he imposed himself and his band of like-minded veterans on the authorities, while others hold that he was invited to assemble a group and design a super-tank specifically for these conditions, which he knew well. However the former, given the sort of man he was and the fact that his tanks were built independently of the mainstream of British tank production, is very suggestive. It may be that it was not as cut and dried as that and there was indeed some official encouragement based upon his earlier experience and that of his team.

Whatever it was, Stern created the Special Vehicle Development Committee consisting of Sir Eustace Tennyson D'Eyncourt, the former Director of Naval Construction, General Sir Ernest Swinton, Sir William Tritton and Mr Harry Ricardo among others. They were known collectively as The Old Gang, hence the 'TOG' name adopted for their tanks. Walter Wilson, whose specialist skills in tank transmission would not be required in this instance, joined to begin with but soon left. Wilson was still a busy man, and he had never seen eye to eye with Albert Stern.

At first, as one might expect, a design was drawn up which was essentially an enlarged World War I tank, with a rhomboid-shaped hull devoid of superstructure, unsprung rollers in the track frames and large, flat track plates. Weapon sponsons were to be fitted on each side and a 75mm howitzer was mounted on the right side at the front, with the driver seated alongside it on the left. This gun was in fact the French 75mm weapon as fitted in a similar position in their Char B. Power was supplied by an enormous Paxman-Ricardo V12 diesel normally rated at 450hp but increased to 600hp for this purpose. C.H. Merz of Merz and McLellan designed the electric final drive, two English Electric generators which powered two of the same company's electric motors, a combination that provided both acceleration and steering. It is said that electric drive was selected on account of the great weight of the tank (63.5 tons), but as Sir Albert Stern had been a forceful promoter of the system during World War I, his rivalry with Walter Wilson may have also played a part. Diesel-electric drive theoretically provides the best answer for a tank driving system. It offers smooth acceleration without the complication of changing gear and infinitely variable steering. But it can be heavy and bulky, resulting in a longer and heavier tank. And not only was TOG1 long, it was also relatively narrow to conform to the British railway loading gauge and this combination made it difficult to steer.

TOG I on a demonstration run on waste ground outside Fosters' Works in Lincoln. Notice the hull mounted howitzer and the unarmed turret on top. Members of The Old Gang, and a dog, can be seen gathered in the background.

ABOVE TOG I giving a trench crossing display, still watched by members of The Old Gang. The large opening in the side shows where the right side sponson was supposed to go, but what the reclining figure sitting inside is doing makes no sense. There is an inclinometer, for demonstration purposes, further back. Note the World War I style tracks.

When the tank was completed, by William Foster and Co. of Lincoln in October 1940, the design had been altered to some extent. No sponsons were fitted at the sides although the openings for them remained, but the turret from an A12 Matilda tank had been perched on top, probably because it was one of the few turrets available. It was also small enough to fit the narrow hull between the tracks and still be capable of rotating, although for demonstration purposes it was not fitted with a 2-pdr gun. Trials in Lincoln proved the tank to be excellent at trench crossing, with a top speed of 8.5mph, but the electric motors were burned out, due perhaps to the strain of steering. The tank is said to have carried a crew of eight, but without the side sponsons two of the crew seem to lack employment, unless they were required to service the engine and electrical components.

TOG I was therefore rebuilt as TOG IA with a hydraulic transmission by the Hydraulic Drive and Engineering Company, using their Fluidrive system. Hydraulic drive had also been tried in tanks in World War I but had been found wanting due to heat. This time the problem seemed to be response delay, caused by the time it took for oil to refill the fluid couplings. This made steering uncertain, so it was also abandoned. By this time the German invasion of France had rendered the concept of these heavy assault tanks redundant. But development went on in the hope that other engineering lessons might be learnt.

A second prototype, to be known as TOG II was being designed from June 1940, by which time German forces, spearheaded by tanks, had virtually overrun France and the now totally useless Maginot Line was already far in the rear. One is forced to ask why the TOG project was allowed to continue but, apart from the strong personality of Sir Albert Stern, no logical answer is forthcoming, beyond research knowledge that might be gained for future tank design.

The wooden mock-up of the front part of TOG II showing the triple gun mounting in the turret, the howitzer in the front of the hull and the 'female' sponson on the left hand side.

A wooden mock-up of the front half was built at Lincoln and it shows a tank with what appears to be one of the fashionable triple mountings in the turret, comprising a 3in howitzer, 2-pdr anti-tank gun and a Besa machine gun. Another 3in howitzer is fitted in the front of the hull on the right-hand side, with machine-gun sponsons on either side, each equipped with two Besas. It was a formidable armament for a tank at that time, although Major-General Vyvyan Pope, the Royal Armoured Corps adviser to the British Expeditionary Force, was opposed to it, as he was to any multiplicity of weapons in a single tank.

Once again the tank was to be built by William Foster & Co. of Lincoln, and this in itself is odd since, although the firm was still making agricultural machinery as a sideline, it was now focused primarily on the manufacture of pumps, some of enormous size, having taken over the London firm Gwynne & Company in 1927. But certain key employees, such as William Rigby, who had been a senior draughtsman during World War I, were still with the firm and involved with the TOG project.

One feature of TOG II that was at variance with the original version was the arrangement of the tracks. Although they were still of World War I pattern, they did not pass all the way around the hull. Instead, after passing around the idler at the front they seemingly vanished down a dark tunnel until they were running close to the top of the tank's road rollers. At the rear of course they rose up again to pass around the drive sprocket and then followed their normal course underneath the tank until they reached the front idler again. Whether this caused much rolling resistance is not known although the new tank only ever had a top speed of 8mph and lacked any form of sprung suspension. The main reason for this arrangement was so that a larger turret ring could be fitted to carry a bigger turret, so that side sponsons could still be mounted and, incidentally, leaving room for a spacious fighting compartment.

When the tank was first completed in March 1941 it appears to have been fitted with an enormous dummy turret, made of wood, containing another version of the triple mounting. This featured a Besa machine gun, what appears to be a wooden representation of a 3in 20cwt anti-aircraft gun, a 2-pdr anti-tank gun and another Besa machine gun. Since the 3in 20cwt had an armour-piercing performance about the same as the new 6-pdr, the inclusion of a 2-pdr is somewhat difficult to understand. But then this only was a wooden mock up. No hull gun was ever mounted, and nor were the machine-gun sponsons ever fitted; the openings where they would have been are still visible, but are now covered by doors.

TOG II again with a bigger turret and three wooden guns. Notice at this stage that the tank is running on World War I-style tracks and that the side sponson opening has been filled in.

Mechanically TOG II was identical to TOG I, with the Paxman-Ricardo V12 diesel powering two English Electric generators which in turn powered two electric motors that drove the tank. One does not read of any problems with the electric motors burning out, but due to its hull length of

33ft 3in and restricted width of 10ft 3in (just within the revised loading gauge) the tank was still difficult to steer, particularly over soft or muddy ground. A dummy cast iron turret brought the total weight up to 62 tons.

By May 1941, with another wooden turret but this time only fitted with a replica 3in 20cwt gun, and a Besa machine gun on either side, the tank was taken down to Aldershot for trials. After these it was returned to Lincoln, where new manganese steel tracks with a more open pattern were fitted, along with a new turret that appears to be of steel construction mounting a real 3in 20cwt gun and inevitably two Besa machine guns.

Now running on new pattern tracks TOG II is camouflaged and fitted with a proper turret and real 3in gun. The turret is reversed and one can see the engine exhaust pipes above the hull.

In September 1941 even greater changes were introduced that resulted in a designation change to TOG II*. These included changes to the final drive arrangements, the fitting of a system of torsion bar suspension underneath the hull of the tank to give a better ride, and reversal of the tracks, as was done with A20. In this form TOG II* still survives, at the Tank Museum, although now mounting a prototype of the 17-pdr gun turret as later fitted to the A30 Challenger tank. This turret was made by Stothert & Pitt of Bath, who probably made the earlier TOG II turrets and used a centrally pivoting base at floor level, instead of the usual turret ring filled with a crowded ball race. This Big Gun Turret, as they called it, rotated on a large ball on the floor of the fighting compartment; in order to avoid any problems with the turret becoming stuck if an enemy round hit the join between turret and hull, it was possible to jack the turret up to clear it. In this form the modified tank weighed around 80 tons.

TOG II (R) was designed as a new model of TOG II, 6ft shorter but still with the torsion bar suspension. In the event it was never built, but had it been the idea was to offer it as a heavily armoured tank, perhaps armed with the 6-pdr Mark 5 anti-tank gun, which had a slightly better armour-piercing performance than the 3in 20cwt, except perhaps at longer ranges. Winston Churchill, writing in April 1943 about heavy tanks in general, although the 'Stern Tank' as he called it was the only one then in existence, said that 'development of a heavy tank … cannot be laid aside. Occasions will almost certainly arise when it would be a solution of particular problems. We shall be much to blame if the necessity appears and we are found to have fallen behind the enemy. ' Nevertheless the TOG programme was ultimately abandoned, and although other heavy tanks were developed later, they were never used.

TOG II* outside the Tank Museum mounting the prototype 17-pdr turret which is not quite located in the right place. Since this photograph was taken the tank has been moved inside a museum building.

CHAPTER 5

VALENTINE INFANTRY TANK

BY BRUCE OLIVER NEWSOME PH.D

INTRODUCTION

More tanks and their derivatives were produced during World War II on the Valentine tank platform than on any other British tank platform. Valentines and Valentine derivatives accounted for about 25 per cent of all the tank platforms produced in Britain during the war, about 25 per cent of those produced in Canada, and almost 75 per cent of the tanks exported by Britain and Canada to the Soviet Union. Valentines saw service across North Africa and Italy, through France to Germany, from India to Burma, from New Zealand to Guadalcanal, and from Russia to Berlin.

Yet the design started out in 1938 as a stop-gap infantry tank, with inferior specifications to the Infantry Tank Mark II (Matilda II), on the promise of quicker, cheaper production, and more reliable automotive performance, which it certainly achieved.

DESIGN AND DEVELOPMENT

FROM A10 TO VALENTINE

In April 1937, Vulcan Foundry refused the Mechanization Board's invitation to develop a new medium tank until it had completed the Matilda II. On 10 February 1938 the War Office, desperate for more medium tanks, invited Vickers to develop a derivative of the Matilda II or the Vickers A10 (Cruiser II). Vickers naturally chose to develop the A10. Vickers judged the capacity of the A10 platform at 16 long tons (17.92 short tons; 16.26 metric tons), which would limit the armour standard to 60mm – the minimum specification – and limit the turret crew to two, when the

A Valentine I and Matilda II have been loaded on the same Warflat wagon, indicating the Valentine I's lower profile and simpler production, but inferior protection and cramped interior.

specification was for three. Vickers suggested a Vickers 40mm cannon in place of the Royal Ordnance 40mm 2-pdr gun, to allow an even smaller turret.

The second meeting occurred the day before Valentine's Day, 14 February 1938. 'Valentine' was also the middle name of Sir John Carden, who had led the design of the A9 and A10, although he had died before theValentine was designed. 'Valentine' was also an acronym of the supplier (Vickers Armstrong Limited (Engineers), Newcastle-upon-Tyne).

The project aimed at a stop-gap Infantry Tank Mark III. As inducements, Vickers promised that the automotive line would need no development, and promised production from March 1939. Vickers also estimated a cost of about two-thirds of the Matilda's (although the price of production in the first contract of 1939 would be about nine-tenths). Accepting these promises, the War Office agreed to a mock-up tank with a 50mm basis and a Vickers 2-pdr.

However, when the mock-up was shown on 24 March 1938 to user and mechanization authorities they rejected the thin armour and the inadequate vision for the commander (limited to a single periscope). For a while the project was dormant, although the Superintendent of Design was working on a mounting to a 75mm armour standard.

In April 1939, after more delays to the Matilda II, the War Office invited Vickers back. Vickers offered a four-man 50mm turret or a two-man 60mm turret. The General Staff settled on the latter.Vickers estimated full production from April 1940, at four tanks per month. The Director of Staff Duties (DSD) doubted whether such a low rate of production justified such a design. He noted that the A10's running gear was vulnerable to wire, and asked whether skirting plates could be added. Vickers claimed that the platform could not afford the extra weight of skirting plates unless ammunition were reduced, and estimated that 3mm-thick plates would weigh not more than 0.2 long tons. DSD agreed to a reduction of ammunition to 50 rounds in order to add skirting plates and Vickers guaranteed a speed of 15mph. The meeting discussed also an attachment to carry a plough, which would be raised and lowered hydraulically through a power take-off from the gearbox, but Vickers opposed this attachment. The meeting agreed that it could be omitted only from training vehicles.

The DSD kept wondering out loud why Vickers could not produce the Matilda II, which was fully developed and more capable, but Vickers claimed that it could

Valentine Mark	Infantry Tank Mark	Deliveries (excl. conversions)	Evolutionary basis	External differentiation			
				Main armament	**Coaxial machine-gun**	**Turret front**	**Turret sides**
I	III	308	A10 (Cruiser II)	40mm 2-pounder gun, without muzzle brake or counter weight	7.92mm Besa on right of main armament	internal mantlet, behind a wide rectangular curved opening	On right side: square revolver port. On left side: either no port (tanks T15946 to T16555 and T20419 to T20493); or a D-shaped port (mostly Valentine IIs)
II	III*	1,511	Valentine I plus AEC diesel engine				
III (New Zealand converted 18 to III CS)	-	536	Valentine II plus 3-man turret	40mm 2-pounder gun (III CS had 76mm howitzer), without muzzle brake or counter weight		Internal mantlet, behind an almost square flat mounting; narrow elliptical casting at base of main gun	Circular revolver ports on both sides
IV	III**	524	Valentine I plus GMC engine	40mm 2-pounder gun, without muzzle brake or counter weight		As Valentine I/II	As Valentine I/II
V	-	1,208 (including 212 DDs)	Valentine IV hull, Valentine III turret			As Valentine III	As Valentine V
VI	III***	30	Valentine IV adapted to Canadian capacity		7.92mm Besa; 7.62mm Browning from sixteenth vehicle on	As Valentine I/II, except after first 100 vehicles the rivets were eliminated, although still bolted around the top and bottom	As Valentine I/II, except D-shaped port added after first 100 vehicles,
VII	III***	1,390	Valentine VI adapted to Number 19 radio		7.62mm Browning		
VIIA	-		Valentine IV with changes to exterior and engine compartment				
VIII	-	0	Valentine III plus 57mm gun	57mm 6-pounder gun, with counter-weight on muzzle (Mark III was shorter than Mark V)	None	External mantlet	Circular revolver ports on both sides; backwards-sloped bracket for two 4-inch smoke projectors on right side
IX	-	1,323 (including 236 DDs)	Valentine V plus Valentine VIII's turret			External mantlet; Mounting Number 1 Mark 1	
X	-	135	Valentine IX with Besa machine-gun		7.92mm Besa in protruding box on right of main armament	External mantlet; Mounting Number 4 Mark 1	
XI	-	295 (including 175 DDs)	Valentine X with 75mm gun	75mm gun with muzzle brake (1 hole each side)		External mantlet; Mounting Number 1 Mark 5	
Heavy Valentine (Valiant)	-	1 pilot	Valentine IX's automotive line, with independent concentric coil/ wishbone suspension and thicker armour	75mm gun, without muzzle brake, until added after war	7.92mm Besa mounted internally to left of main armament	Internal mantlet within curved casting; on each side, a column of 5 large bolts affixed the front casting to turret sides	Semi-elliptical casting without apertures
Heavy Valiant	-	0	Valiant with thicker armour and same running gear as US T1/M6 heavy tank and British Heavy Cromwell	57mm gun, 75mm gun, or 95mm howitzer			
Bishop	-	1 pilot and 149 production vehicles	Valentine III hull with tall fixed superstructure for a 25-pounder gun	87.6 mm 25-pounder gun/howitzer; no muzzle brake; box-shaped cradle extending partway under barrel	None	External mantlet; protruding gun cradle; tall narrow vertical mounting; upper plate slopes backwards towards roof	Tall vertical sides, each welded to front plate; roof is bolted to internal angle plates
Archer	-	2 pilots and 665 production vehicles	Valentine V hull with new superstructure and mounting for 17-pounder gun	76mm 17-pounder Mark II gun with muzzle brake (2 holes each side)		No turret; superstructure extended at hull front	No turret; superstructure extended from hull sides

Valentine Mark	External differentiation		Internal differentiation		
	Turret rear	Hull	Crewmen in fighting compartment	Radio	Engine compartment
I	Armoured cover hanging down over the air exfiltration slit: earlier design ended with a straight edge (T15946 to T16013, T16221 to 16233, T16356 to T16378, T16381, T16390, T16393, T20419 to T20423, T20427, T20430 to T20432); most covers had a curved lip; Army workshops would add bracketed boxes on each corner (each for 2 Bren magazines)	All riveted and bolted; 100 Valentine Is (T15946 to T16045) had hinges and handles on only the nearside rear access door, and a fuel tank filler under a flap towards the offside; 75 Valentine Is (T16046 to T16120) had hinges and handles on both doors, and fuel filler on inside	2	Number 11 low power with 6-foot rod aerial	AEC spark-ignition engine, with fuel tanks either side, Meadows gearbox
II		As final Valentine Is; Desert Service vehicles had sandguards, auxiliary fuel tank on left trackguard, and container for 5 water cans below the access door		Number 11 or Number 19	AEC diesel engine with fuel tank on nearside, Meadows gearbox
III (New Zealand converted 18 to III CS)	Commander's rotating hatch set towards rear; bulge slopes backward and downward towards straight edge; one large box for Bren magazines bracketed centrally and horizontally.		3	Number 19	
IV	As Valentine I/II, except all had curved exfiltration cover		2		GMC 6.71S diesel, Spicer gearbox
V	As Valentine III		3		
VI	As Valentine IV, except first vehicle had straight exfiltration cover	As Valentine I/II, except cast nose after first 100 vehicles; otherwise riveted and bolted; splash angles in front of turret ring	2	Number 11	
VII				Number 19	
VIIA		As above, with: protective cages over headlamps; convoy lamp; ice-studs on tracks; auxiliary fuel tank			As above, except: extra engine oil cooler; batteries moved to rear
VIII	As Valentine III, except box is bracketed at a slope; Vickers welded all these tanks, but Metropolitan Cammell welded only the last Valentine Xis	as Valentine III			AEC diesel
IX		as Valentine V			540 vehicles had GMC 6.71S; 783 vehicles had GMC 6.71A
X		as Valentine IX, except: mostly welded, some rivets; protective cages over headlamps; splash angles in front of turret ring			GMC 6.71A diesel
XI		as Valentine X, except cast nose			
Heavy Valentine (Valiant)	Large cast bin, welded to rear	Cast and welded front with concave driver's plate; trackguards but no side skirts; 6 evenly spaced wheels, each with vertical springs	2		GMC 6.71M diesel, governed at higher speed and power than in Archer
Heavy Valiant		Side skirts; 3 evenly spaced bogies, each with 2 parallel pairs of wheels, and horizontal volute springs (HVSS)			Rolls-Royce Meteorite
Bishop	vertically split doors opening outwards; the container carrying five water cans was affixed to the lefthand door, but sometimes relocated to a trackguard	As Valentine III	3	Number 18 Mark III, gradually replaced in field by Number 19	AEC diesel, Meadows gearbox
Archer	No turret; gun mounted rearwards over engine compartment	Hull superstructure extended at front and sides, all welded	3		GMC 6.71M diesel

This Valentine I is at Lulworth in Dorset, after completion of gunnery trials. Its Bren machine gun is in the sprung, angle-poised 'Lakeman' mounting.

BELOW This Bren (without magazine) is being demonstrated on the 'Lakeman' mounting by 'A' Squadron, 2nd Lothian & Border Horse, 6th Armoured Division, in September 1942.

ABOVE RIGHT This Valentine I illustrates the wide internal mantlet common to the Valentine I, II, IV, VI and VII. This tank has the first design of track, which was lightest but least durable. The malleable cast iron shoes were materially softer than steel shoes, and the double pin link suffered more stress than a single pin link.

produce two of its design to one Matilda II. News of delays in the supply of armour for the Matilda II was the final justification for an agreement to order 100 tanks as soon as Vickers could assure fulfilment of the General Staff minimum specifications, which it did on 4 April.

The Director of Mechanization (Major-General Alexander Davidson) had been decisive in warning of the Matilda II's risks. On 4 April, he promised that the War Office would almost certainly order 200–250 Valentines, following Treasury approval, of which Vickers should produce 50, with deliveries from May or June 1940, while other contractors would assemble the rest. On 9 April, the General Staff settled on 300 Valentines. On 15 May, Vickers was put on notice to produce 50 tanks, while Metro-Cammell and Birmingham Railway Carriage & Wagon Company (BRCWC) were put on notice to make 125 each. In July 1939, an order was placed with Vickers alone for 275 vehicles to be delivered in May 1940. No pilot vehicles were ordered. By September 1939, the skirting plates had been dropped. Instead, the Ministry of Supply asked if a fender bar could be incorporated to mitigate the chance of wire becoming entangled in the tracks. Also in September the Fowler plough attachment was deleted.

NEW ENGINES AND GEARBOXES

The Valentine Mark I (Valentine I), as delivered from May 1940, had a spark-ignition engine (A189) by AEC. The Valentine II had the slightly less powerful but more economical diesel version (A190). Both had a 5-speed clash-type gearbox by Meadows. AEC was already an unreliable supplier, so, early in 1940, the Directorate of Mechanization (in July 1940 this became the Department of Tank Design or DTD) tried a diesel engine of the same capacity by General Motors Corporation (GMC). AEC carried out the trials under DTD's supervision. The Valentine IV was a Valentine II adapted for the GMC engine and a gearbox by Spicer (another American company). The Spicer gearbox had clash gears in first and fifth, and syncromesh gears in second, third and fourth gears.

ABOVE This Valentine II illustrates the distinctive engine compartment of all Valentines: air was taken in over the engine and expelled by fans through the sloping rear. The armour covering the air exfiltration slit at the rear of the turret has a curved lip; earlier covers had a straight lip.

All 308 Valentine Is received the A189 spark-ignition engine. All Valentine IIs, Valentine IIIs, and Bishops had the AEC A190 diesel engine. All Valentine IVs, Valentine Vs, Valentine VIs, Valentine VIIs, and 540 of the 1,323 Valentine IXs received the GMC 6.71S engine (the 'S' type of the Type 6004 engine). The remaining 783 Valentine IXs, all Valentine Xs, and all Valentine XIs received the more powerful 'A' type (thanks to larger fuel injectors and a higher governed speed). The Archers (self-propelled 17-pdr guns) received the more powerful 6.71M, which was uprated further for the Valiant tank.

CANADIAN VERSIONS

In early September 1940, a British detachment landed in Canada with a Valentine I and a Matilda II, which shortly travelled to the US, while the Valentine stayed at Camp Borden with part of the detachment.

The British Ministry of Supply's tank mission ordered the Angus Works of the Canadian Pacific Railway Company (a subsidiary in Montreal of American Locomotive) to assemble 300 Valentine hulls. The British mission ordered British-designed armaments and ammunition from suppliers on the other side of the St Lawrence River, but sourced the GMC engine, the Spicer gearbox and suspension arms from America. The British at home redesigned the Valentine II as the Valentine IV to accommodate the American-sourced sub-assemblies.

This is one of the first 50 Valentine Is out of Vickers, with the slightly heavier and more durable steel shoes (still with double pin links). It is being followed by a Matilda II on a cross-country course in Northern Command.

This Valentine I is towing a Cruiser IVa during recovery trials in late 1940.

Late in 1940, they despatched a pilot Valentine IV with drawings, which the Canadians redrew for metric units and locally sourced armour. L.E. 'Ted' Carr was despatched from the British Tank Mission in the US to help, resulting in a cast nose after the first 100 vehicles. The Canadian version was designated as Valentine VI, until the turret was redesigned slightly to accept a No. 19 wireless set, producing the Valentine VII. The Valentine VIIa was adapted slightly for Soviet use.

UPGUNNED VALENTINES AND SELF-PROPELLED GUNS

In September 1941, the General Staff declared the Valentine obsolete, and urgently required a replacement. In the meantime, they urged rearmament with the 6-pdr gun as a stop-gap. However, in December 1941, the Ministry of Supply reported that the tank's turret did not offer room for a larger gun, and was working out how to mount a 6-pdr on a turretless platform as a self-propelled gun (SP or SPG).

On 4 June 1942,Vickers (of Chertsey) sent a self-propelled 6-pdr gun on a Valentine I hull for automotive trials, but after just 76 miles it was sent back on 6 June without further interest. Around then, the Ministry authorized a Valentine with a 6-pdr in a turret. DTD's design accommodated the 6-pdr gun, but only two crewmen and no coaxial machine-gun. The prospect of this turret and the Valentine II/III hull was known as Valentine VIII, but the Valentine V hull was substituted in order to standardize the GMC engine, except that the side armour was reduced further. This combination was the Valentine IX, which was delivered from late 1942 to mid-1943.

The Valentine X, which was delivered from July 1943, benefited from a coaxial machine-gun. The Valentine XI, which was delivered from February 1944, had a 75mm gun.

The Valentines IX, X and XI were the first British tanks to be assembled with armoured ammunition bins, although each successive mark lost stowage in favour of guns.

In December 1941, the Director of Artillery suggested a 6-pdr gun in a partial turret on the rear of a Valentine; the engine compartment would be relocated forwards. Instead, Vickers (at Chertsey) took a 6-pdr gun off its towed carriage, and placed it atop a fabricated pedestal affixed to the top of the driver's compartment of a Valentine I. Pivoting in this pedestal, the gun has been traversed to face the photographer. To shield the crew, plates were affixed vertically, by means of angle plates, to the trackguard and along the forward edge of the engine compartment. The central of the three plates at the rear was hinged as a door. The shields were not completed on the offside for this photograph, although presumably the vehicle was complete for its only known demonstration, at Farnborough, from 4 to 6 June 1942.

The Valentine IX had a 6-pdr gun but no machine-gun or 2in smoke projector to its offside. Instead, a bracket was affixed on the side of the turret for two 4in projectors.

THE VALIANT (A38)

On 7 May 1942, the Tank Board had approved development of an assault tank (eventually the A33 or Heavy Cromwell), but its basis – the Cruiser VIII – was still developmental. On 26 June 1942, Vickers formally proposed an 'assault tank', to be developed from the Valentine, with thicker armour and a 6-pdr gun, at 23 long tons altogether (25.76 short tons; 23.37 metric tons), and without growing wider than the railway loading gauge. In the proposal, Vickers emphasized the low risk of an unambitious development with existing components, as it had emphasized in 1938 when marketing the Valentine tank. Vickers anticipated a pilot vehicle in 12 months.

The outline drawings and wooden model looked like the Valentine X, except for a door in the left turret side for the gunner, a single split hatch in the turret roof, a glacis sloping backwards and left and right from the longitudinal centre line, independently sprung larger roadwheels, and a wider track. In August 1942, the Ministry of Supply contracted with Vickers for three pilot tanks in mild steel, shortly amended to six: four Valiant Is were to be fitted with either the GMC or the AEC diesel engine; two Valiant IIs were to be fitted with prospective V8 engines by either Ford or Rolls-Royce.

On 25 September 1942, Vickers proposed that 'the initial batch of production vehicles' (Valiant I, the same as specified in June) should be powered by a GMC engine uprated to 210bhp, while a Valiant II would be developed with an engine developing 400 to 500bhp (presumably the Rolls-Royce Meteorite) and an adjusted transmission.

On 22 October 1942, the Ministry of Supply placed an order with Vickers for 500 Valiants, but soon cancelled it. In January 1943, the Ministry transferred the automotive part of the project to Rolls-Royce's engine facility at Belper, then under contract with the Ministry of Supply. W.A. Robotham was head of research at Rolls-Royce, and since November 1941 also Chief Engineer Tank Design at the Ministry of Supply, at which point Belper had become a contracted research and development facility. Nobody there had ever designed a tank until Belper started designing the Heavy Cromwell in September 1941, but Robotham's official ethos was strong after his leadership of the development of a tank engine (the Meteor) from the Merlin aero-engine.

VALENTINE I, 3RD TROOP, 'A' SQUADRON, 1ST ROYAL GLOUCESTERSHIRE HUSSARS, 20TH ARMOURED BRIGADE, 6TH ARMOURED DIVISION, IN ENGLAND, 1941

On 1 September 1940, Home Forces established 6th Armoured Division (AD) with 20th and 26th Armoured Brigades. By the start of November, 6AD had 123 Valentines – more than half of deliveries up to then. By February 1941, 6AD had 195 Valentines; by April it had 300; in September, during its final manoeuvres of the year, it had 340 tanks.

The assemblers had finished the tanks in khaki-green, over which the Army's workshops painted curvaceous patches in a darker shade. The unit has painted tactical signs in red, to denote the senior regiment in the brigade: the triangle denotes 'A' Squadron, within which is a number denoting the troop. On the offside nose of the tank is the transport weight; on the nearside nose and tail is painted the divisional sign; in the middle of the nose and tail, this unit was supposed to paint the number '51' in white – designating the senior armoured regiment – but this was not present on all vehicles. (Art by Henry Morshead, © Osprey Publishing)

VALENTINE III, 2ND TROOP, 'C' SQUADRON, 17TH/21ST LANCERS, IN TUNISIA, DECEMBER 1942

The Allied landings in Morocco and Algeria started on 8 November 1942. The most easterly landings were at Algiers. On 13 November, 6AD and 78th Infantry Division landed through Algiers, aiming for Tunis. 6AD had one Armoured Brigade (26th), with three armoured units: 16/5th Lancers, 17th/21st Lancers, and 2nd Lothians and Border Horse. Their left flank was screened by a battle group ('Blade Force'), whose main tank unit was 17th/21st Lancers, with a mix of Valentine IIIs and Crusader IIIs. Blade Force advanced 300 miles before being held up short of Tunis, when the battered units were returned to 6AD for the rest of the campaign.

In Britain, this tank was configured for 'Desert Service' with sand-coloured paint. For the greener conditions of Tunisia, patches of khaki have been painted. The unit has painted a number '2' on the left revolver port to denote the 2nd Troop, and a circle to denote 'C' Squadron, all in yellow to denote the middle regiment of the brigade in terms of seniority. (Art by Henry Morshead, © Osprey Publishing)

In March 1943, the Ministry of Supply wrote to Vickers relating that Ruston & Hornsby would be parent designer. Effectively Belper remained lead designer, while Ruston & Hornsby (which specialized in agricultural equipment) would be the co-developer and producer. Both should be blamed for the impractical driving and fighting arrangements, unnecessarily tall turret, and unnecessarily proud driver's compartment.

OPPOSITE The Valentine X had a coaxial machine-gun on the offside of the 6-pdr.

LEFT The Valentine XI's main armament was a 75mm gun, identifiable by its muzzle brake.

The Valiant was replete with shot traps, the driver's hatches fouled the gun, and the driver's controls fouled each other.

The Valiant's tail was impractically low and extended.

Belper planned delivery of three different pilots: Valiant I later in 1943, Valiant II around the end of 1943, and Heavy Valiant in 1944, with even thicker armour and the running gear common to the US T1/M6 heavy tank and the Heavy Cromwell. The Heavy Valiant was known, by various confused authorities, as Heavy Valiant, Valiant Mark III and Vanguard. Belper ignored the Tank Board's current requirement for a version with 17-pdr gun, and specified a 57mm 6-pdr gun, with allowance for a 75mm gun or a 95mm howitzer, each with coaxial machine-gun. For no good reason, Belper proposed an alternative armament of twin Oerlikon cannons with coaxial machine-gun, multiple machine-guns or machine-guns with a 20mm Oerlikon cannon.

Only one Valiant was produced, late in 1943 or early 1944 by Ruston & Hornsby. This survives with a 75mm gun, although possibly it had been assembled with a 57mm gun.

No report of the first trial survives, probably because it could not proceed safely. Vision through the periscopes was limited to 10 yards ahead. When changing down from fifth gear, the gear change lever came back so violently, with so little space between it and the right steering lever, that the driver might break his wrist in trying

In 1944, an Archer was tried with a 25-pdr gun, but the Sexton already offered better elevation and a roomier compartment.

to operate it. (The Valiant steering levers were either side of the seat, instead of between the driver's knees.) The footbrake pedal was positioned such that the driver could depress it only with his heel, where it could become trapped between the pedal and the footplate. The driver was forced to sit in a crouched position that was liable to injure him by contact with the rear edge of the escape hatch.

There were other problems. The ground clearance was impractically low, as low as 8.75in below the final drive at the rear. Furthermore, the tail projected beyond the tracks, so the tank grounded on almost any rise. The turret contained no stowage, no seats, and no turntable (just a wooden platform). Gunnery would have been practically impossible, since the turret traverse control was fitted underneath the armament.

In April 1945, Ruston & Hornsby returned Valiant for trials of the suspension only, probably because Vickers had persuaded the Ministry of Supply that the suspension had been neglected, but a drive of 13 miles revealed the dangers, and the trial was abandoned. The suspension was too exposed and fragile for an assault tank anyway.

The School of Tank Technology retained the Valiant for the purpose of demonstrating to students how not to design a tank, before transferring it to the Tank Museum.

PRODUCTION

In May 1940, Vickers delivered a Valentine I for trials, which proved satisfactory, at which point it was recorded as a delivery (12 June). The Ministry of Supply counted ten deliveries by the end of June, 39 by the end of July.

Metropolitan-Cammell – a Vickers subsidiary – and BRCWC, both specializing in rolling stock, delivered one vehicle each for inspection in July 1940. By the end of 1940, about 350 vehicles had been delivered, far more than expected. As of 2 August 1941, 1,156 Valentines had been accepted. Vickers production peaked in December 1942 at 81 Valentines for the month, eased off most rapidly at the end of 1943, and ran out in May 1944, when production switched to the Archer, which ran out in September 1945.

VALENTINE IX OF 50TH ROYAL TANK REGIMENT, IN TUNISIA, MARCH 1943

Valentine IX tanks arrived in North Africa in January 1943, but saw no operational use until the assault on the Mareth Line in Tunisia. On 16 March, infantry captured the approaches to the Wadi Zigzaou. At 2315 hours on 20 March, 9th Battalion, Durham Light Infantry (DLI), of 50th Division, advanced over the wadi to the strongpoint of Ksiba Ouest, while 8th DLI advanced to Ouerzi – one mile to the left (west). In between, 50th RTR, with Valentines – a few of which were Valentine IXs, was supposed to advance into the rear of both positions, after which 6th DLI was supposed to consolidate. The tanks moved forward in the early hours of 21 March. Under increasing artillery fire, the engineers blew gaps in the wadi, and constructed a causeway with fascines and earth, but only three tanks gained traction up the muddy bank before the causeway collapsed under the fourth tank. The other tanks withdrew at first light, hoping for another attempt on the following night. At 2330 hours, 5th East Yorkshires advanced to the right of Ksiba Ouest, while 9th DLI expanded its lodgement, and 6th DLI advanced to strongpoints behind Ouerzi, but 50th RTR again failed to get across. At 0145 hours 22 March, 15th Panzer Division drove back the Valentines, while the infantry took cover in the wadi with high casualties. Before dawn on 23 March, 50th Division completed its withdrawal. (Art by Henry Morshead, © Osprey Publishing)

	Vickers	Metropolitan-Cammell	Birmingham Railway Carriage & Wagon Company (BRCWC)	Canadian Pacific Railway Company	Ruston & Hornsby	TOTAL new assemblies
Valentine I	175	66	67	0	0	308
Valentine II	350	494	667	0	0	1,511
Valentine III	0	0	536	0	0	536
Valentine IV	375	149	0	0	0	524
Valentine V	450	546	0	0	0	996
Valentine V DD	0	212	0	0	0	212
Valentine VI	0	0	0	30	0	30
Valentine VII	0	0	0	1,390	0	1,390
Valentine VIII	0	0	0	0	0	0
Valentine IX	965	122	0	0	0	1,087
Valentine IX DD	0	236	0	0	0	236
Valentine X	100	35	0	0	0	135
Valentine XI	100	20	0	0	0	120
Valentine XI DD	0	175	0	0	0	175
Valiant	0	0	0	0	1	1
Bishop	0	0	150	0	0	150
Archer	667	0	0	0	0	667
Bridgelayer	0	80	160	0	0	239
TOTAL	3,182	2,135	1,580	1,420	1	8,317

VALENTINE XI OF 2ND ANTI-TANK REGIMENT ROYAL CANADIAN ARTILLERY, 2ND CANADIAN INFANTRY DIVISION, IN GERMANY, FEBRUARY 1945

2nd Canadian Infantry Division was mobilized at the start of the war, and deployed to Britain from August to December 1940. After its bloody baptism at Dieppe on 19 August 1942 (where the only Allied tanks were Churchills), it did not see combat again until after landing in Normandy in July 1944. Thereafter, it was one of the leading 'assault' divisions in almost every operation, so in October its anti-tank regiment was prioritized for Archers, which were accompanied by Valentine XI tanks for use by each of the four battery commanders. These vehicles were incorporated during the division's long period of deserved rest from November 1944 to January 1945. This Valentine XI was used on the first day of Operation Veritable (the offensive into the Rhineland) on 8 February 1945, when the division was tasked with assaults on Wyler and Den Heuvel. (Art by Henry Morshead, © Osprey Publishing)

This Valentine II in Egypt shows wear on the sides and gun due to the crew mounting and dismounting.

Orders and deliveries of Valentines and derivatives, by contractor and vehicle number

Assembler	Date of order	Orders	Deliveries	Period of delivery	WD numbers
Vickers	1 July 1939	275	175 Valentine I, 100 Valentine II	12 June 1940 to January 1942	T15946 to T16120 (Valentine I), T16121 to T16220 (Valentine II)
	31 May 1940	300	250 Valentine II, 50 Valentine V	29 February to 20 September 1941	T27121 to T27370 (Valentine II), T27371 to T27420 (Valentine V)
	13 December 1940	250 Valentine II	250 Valentine IV	By 22 September 1942	T47098 to T47347
	7 May 1941	755 Valentine III	125 Valentine IV, 400 Valentine V, 230 Valentine IX	1941 to 1942	T66466 to T66590 (Valentine IV), T66591 to T67220 (Valentine V and IX)
	7 October 1941	460 Valentine V	460 Valentine IX	By 4 January 1943	T122698 to T123157
	6 February 1942	475	275 Valentine IX, 100 Valentine X, 100 Valentine XI	By 23 September 1943	T123158 to T123632
	October (?) 1942	2 pilot Archers	2 pilot Archers	September to October 1943	S279594 to S279595
	November (?) 1943	800 Archers, reduced to 670, reduced to 665	665 Archers	May 1944 to September 1945	S279596 to S280260
	22 October 1942	500 Valiant/Vanguard, cancelled	0		
Metro-Cammell	29 June 1939	125 (67 Valentine I, 58 Valentine II)	44 Valentine I, 81 Valentine II	1 August 1940 to March 1941	T16221 to T16345
	2 November 1939	25 Valentine II	25 Valentine II	May to June 1941	T18071 to T18095
	28 December 1939	75 Valentine II	22 Valentine I, 53 Valentine II	14 October 1940 to March 1941	T20419 to T20440 (Valentine I); T20441 to T20493 (Valentine II)
	12 June 1940	300	214 Valentine II, 86 Valentine V	15 May to November 1941	T27421 to T27524, T27571 to T27674, T27679 to T27684 (Valentine II); T27525 to T27570, T27675 to T27678, T27685 to T27729 (Valentine V)
	6 March 1941	250 (101 Valentine II, 149 Valentine IV)	81 Valentine II, 20 Bridgelayer, 149 Valentine V	1941 to 1942	T32531 to T32595, T32685 to T32720 (Valentine II); T32471 to T32530, T32596 to T32684 (Valentine V)
	26 June 1941	645	40 Valentine II, 60 Bridgelayer, 460 Valentine V, 85 Valentine V DD	20 November 1941 to 11 March 1942	T67221 to T67260 (Valentine II), T67261 to T67320 (Bridgelayer), T67321 to T67865 (Valentine V)
	7 October 1941	455 (52 Valentine V, 75 Valentine V DD, 16 Valentine IX, 312 Valentine IX DD)	127 Valentine V DD, 92 Valentine IX, 236 Valentine IX DD	1942 to 1943	T82163 to T82617
	9 January 1942	460 Valentine V, reduced to 260 on 9 January 1943	30 Valentine IX, 35 Valentine X, 20 Valentine XI, 175 Valentine XI DD	1943 to 1944	T120690 to T120949
BRCWC	29 June 1939	70 Valentine I, 145 Valentine II	67 Valentine I, 133 Valentine II	3 August 1940 to 6 June 1941	T16356 to T16422 (Valentine I); T16423 to T16555 (Valentine II)
	2 November 1939	25	25 Valentine II	By May 1941	T17360 to T17384
	12 June 1940	300	299 Valentine II, 1 pilot Bishop	June to October 1941	T17385 to T17684 (Bishop was T17474)
	6 March 1941	250	210 Valentine II, 1 bullet-proof turret for pilot Bishop, 39 Bishop	1941 to 1942	T32721 to T32969 (Valentine II); random S-numbers including S32888 to S32969 (Bishop)
	26 June 1941	500 Valentine II	313 Valentine III, 77 Bridgelayer, 110 Bishop	By 26 May 1942	T59684 to T60183 (Valentine III and Bridgelayer); S59689 to S60029 (Bishop)
	7 October 1941	450, reduced to 305 on 9 January 1943	223 Valentine III, 82 Bridgelayer	By 11 February 1943	T121823 to T122127

In the end, 8,316 Valentine tanks and variants were produced (6,896 British and 1,420 Canadian), of which 7,260 were turreted tanks (5,840 British, 1,420 Canadian), of which 3,665 were exported to the Soviet Union (2,302 British, 1,388 Canadian), and two Canadian tanks were retained by Britain. Thus, effectively, 3,540

This Valentine II is configured for Desert Service with auxiliary fuel tank, sandguards over the tracks, and a container for five water cans on the rear; it has not yet been finished in sandcoloured paint. The tracks are of the third type, designed by the Department of Tank Design (DTD), with more links and single pins, for more reliability, but more weight. All later tanks, including all Canadian tanks, were delivered with this track. Most shoes were cast manganese steel, but some were stamped from slightly heavier 30-carbon steel, identifiable by slightly rounded ends.

Valentine turreted tanks were assembled on British account, 30 on Canadian account. Ruston & Hornsby assembled the only Valiant, for a total of 8,317 newly assembled vehicles developed from the Valentine platform.

USE

BRITISH USE

In 1940 and 1941, the War Office allocated most Valentines to armoured divisions, pending deliveries of cruiser tanks. Their use as infantry tanks remained doubtful: the Matilda II was better protected; the Infantry Tank Mark IV (later known as 'Churchill') was under development with even thicker armour. Both accommodated three men in their turrets, unlike the Valentine, and were more mobile across country, although the Valentine was easier to transport and its automotive line was more mature.

Repeatedly, from November 1940 to June 1941, the Director of Armoured Fighting Vehicles (DAFV), Major-General Vyvyan Pope, recorded Valentines as stop-gaps, and denied their suitability as infantry tanks, mainly because of inferior protection, particularly due to the lack of skirts protecting the running gear.

This Valentine XI is serving in north-west Europe as the command tank for a battalion of M10 Tank Destroyers.

VALENTINE VI AT THE CANADIAN ARMOUR SCHOOL AT BORDEN CAMP, CANADA, IN 1942

The first Valentine VI was paraded for the press on 27 May 1941. The second vehicle was delivered in July, and probably sent straight to the Royal Canadian Armoured Corps School at Camp Borden in Ontario to familiarize personnel with the type. (Art by Henry Morshead, © Osprey Publishing)

At that time almost all Valentines were being used as stop-gap cruisers in three of the five armoured divisions at home. As of 1 May 1941, 772 Valentines were in service (307 Valentine Is; 465 Valentine IIs). As of 1 June 1941, 902 were in service, of which only four were overseas (for trials or demonstrations).

In June 1941, following a request from Middle East Command (ME or MEC) for more cruisers, Pope allowed for Valentines to be sent overseas as stop-gap cruisers, although the first 50 Valentine IIs enshipped as infantry tanks to replace the Matildas of 8th Battalion Royal Tank Regiment (RTR) that had been sunk in transit the previous month. They were not used in action until the next offensive in Libya codenamed as Operation Crusader (18 November 1941).

1st Army Tank Brigade's other two battalions (42nd and 44th RTR) were equipped with Matilda IIs, until replacement by Valentines during 1942. 7th RTR was converting from Matildas to Valentines when captured at Tobruk on 21 June 1942. A Special Service tank squadron (about 15 Valentines) was used during the invasion of Madagascar in May 1942.

These Valentine VIs are giving a flaming salute at Camp Borden in Canada.

VALENTINE VI, SOVIET 139TH TANK BATTALION, 146TH TANK BRIGADE, IN RUSSIA, 1942

British Valentine IIs first reached the Soviet Union in October 1941. 139th Tank Battalion was the last of the six battalions to be issued with Valentine IIs that year. In 1942, it received Valentine VIs from Canada. Most of these tanks went into action as received. With time and experience, this unit painted tactical numbers on the sides. After the first snowfall, the tanks were whitewashed. (Art by Henry Morshead, © Osprey Publishing)

By 21 June 1942, 660 Valentines had shipped to Egypt, although perhaps half had been knocked out or captured. For the offensive from Alamein (23 October 1942), 8th Army held 223 Valentines, of which 169 were employed by 23rd Armoured Brigade, whose four battalions supported infantry divisions as doctrinally prescribed.

Another 20 Valentines were held by 8th Army as ready replacements, 31 were in repair, and three were training tanks. Another two Valentines had been evacuated on 21 October. As of 7 November, 23rd Armoured Brigade had lost 171 tanks: 19 tanks completely destroyed, 55 awaiting recovery, 29 in third-line workshops, and 68 already repaired and returned. This brigade was withdrawn from the frontline until 23 February 1943.

The 2-pdr, two-man turreted versions (Valentines II and IV) were still the most numerous versions through to the end of the North African campaign in May 1943. Late in 1942, Valentine IIIs and Vs (three-man turret) were issued to squadron and troop commanders. On 13 November 1942, 6th Armoured Division disembarked in the port of Algiers with Valentine IIIs and Crusader IIIs.

In December 1942, MEC's armoured warfare authority reported the Valentine as 'definitely obsolete' because of its thin armour and weak armament, even with the 6-pdr. Independently, MEC's technical authority reported:

> Valentine is an extremely dependable tank and mechanically superior to either Grant or Sherman petrol-engined tanks. As a fighting proposition it falls between two stools, being neither fast enough for a cruiser nor sufficiently well armoured for an assault tank. Of the two roles, the latter is the more suitable, as it is less likely to involve a conflict with enemy AFV, in which the tank has neither the striking power to make a stand nor the speed to get away.

In New Zealand, a Valentine II is leading two Valentine IIIs or Vs, another Valentine II, and another Valentine III or V, ahead of a column of M3/M3A1 (Stuart) hybrids.

Valentine IX tanks had arrived in January 1943, and first saw combat during the assault on the Mareth Line in Tunisia in March 1943, but 'also failed to find favour owing to their deficiency in fire power. From the point of view of reliability they were every bit as good as Sherman, and though less well protected in front, they had better side armour.'

By then, two tank brigades were ready in Tunisia with Churchill tanks, which carried the 6-pdr gun, a coaxial machine-gun, and a third crewman in the turret, and were better protected. These took the lead in subsequent assaults. By June 1943 the War Office had deleted Valentines from British tank units, although many remained in Soviet, Australian, New Zealand and Indian service, while British units in Europe retained Valentines as artillery observation vehicles (main armament removed), Bridgelayers, amphibious tanks, and tractors.

Valentine XI tanks (with 75mm guns) were used by anti-tank battalion and battery commanders in the campaigns in north-west Europe and Italy from late 1944 onwards.

CANADIAN VALENTINES

The first Valentine VI was paraded for the press at Angus Works on 27 May 1941, although counted as a delivery in June, the only one for that month; this was followed by five more in July, ten in August and 14 in September, for a total of 30 (CT138916 to CT138945). 16 were held by the Armoured Corps School at Camp Borden, the other 14 apparently distributed to units.

None was delivered in time for Canadian 1st Tank Brigade which enshipped for England in June 1941 without any tanks. There it was equipped with British tanks, until finally re-equipped with Churchills. In fact, 13 Canadian armoured units were in England by the end of 1941, most of which never trained with Valentines, apart from familiarization at Borden.

The 1,390 Valentine VIIs were allocated for export, starting in late November 1941: Britain retained two; 1,388 were enshipped to the Soviets, although only 1,208 arrived. In total, Canada produced 1,420 vehicles (73 in 1941, 943 in 1942 and 404 in 1943).

NEW ZEALAND USE

In October 1941, 20 Valentine IIs arrived in New Zealand (NZ), ahead of Valentine IIIs, Valentine Vs and Matilda IV Close Support (CS) tanks. All were required for the 1st Army Tank Brigade, but this never filled, and was disbanded in October 1942, leaving 2nd Battalion with Valentine tanks and Stuart Hybrids (US M3 light tanks with M3A1 turrets), for service with the 3rd NZ Division in the Pacific Rim. (The NZ Division in North Africa was supported by British tank units.)

In 1943, 25 Valentine CS tanks were required for regional operations (19 to be issued to one squadron; six to be held by the Ordnance Field Park), although, due to lack of time before deployment, the requirement was reduced to 18.

The first nine vehicles were converted from 1 to 19 August 1943, and issued to the Tank Squadron upon arrival in Wellington: two tanks were issued to the tank squadron HQ, one to each of the five troop leaders, and two to the Ordnance Field Park. The final nine were converted in September, and stayed in New Zealand. In early February 1944, the squadron landed in Guadalcanal with 25 Valentine IIIs, including nine CS. The squadron fought only one action, on 20 February 1944, when four CS tanks were engaged.

The first batch of Valentine VIs for the Soviet Union was entrained at Angus Works in Montreal on 18 November 1941, with dashed lines containing loading information that the Soviets rarely obscured.

SOVIET USE

The General Staff had already declared the Valentine obsolete when the British government expanded production as aid to the Soviet Union after the Axis invasion of 22 June 1941. On 24 August 1941, the Ministry of Supply asked (as a courtesy) for the War Office's agreement to order another 1,325 Valentines, for total production of 5,600 Valentines through July 1943.

British Valentine IXs and Xs arrived in 1943, and remained in Soviet use through to the end of the war, but always in second-rate units. In total, 3,690 Valentine platforms were sent, equivalent to 71 per cent of all British and Canadian platforms sent.

On 28 October 1941, the first 20 Valentines arrived at the tank training school in Kazan, while another 120 were unloading at Arkhangel'sk. As of 20 November, the Soviets had issued 97 Valentines to six tank battalions (131st had 21 Valentines, 132nd had 19, 136th had 9, 138th had 6, and 137th and 139th, both of 146th Tank

Supplies of Valentines and derivatives to the USSR, by period and type

	October 1941 to June 1943			July 1943 to June 1944			TOTAL		
	Shipped	Lost at sea	Arrived	Shipped	Lost at sea	Arrived	Shipped	Lost at sea	Arrived
Valentine II	161	25	136	0	0	0	161	25	136
Valentine III	135	0	135	211	0	211	346	0	346
Valentine IV	520	71	449	0	0	0	520	71	449
Valentine V	234	113	121	106	0	106	340	113	227
Valentine VI–VII	1,213	170	1,043	175	10	165	1,388	180	1,208
Valentine IX	201	0	201	635	18	617	836	18	818
Valentine X	0	0	0	74	8	66	74	8	66
Bridgelayer	0	0	0	25	0	25	25	0	25
TOTAL	2,464	379	2,085	1,226	36	1,190	3,690	415	3,275

Brigade, had 21 Valentines each). By the end of 1941, the Soviets had unloaded 259 Valentines and issued 216.

The Soviets preferred their own tanks, followed by the Matilda II, so relegated the Valentine to defensive operations during summer 1942 against second-rate enemies. By then, Canadian Valentines were arriving quicker. In the second half of 1942, Canada shipped 298 Valentine VIIs directly to Russia, followed by 460 in the first half of 1943, and 155 in the second half.

The Soviets attempted to install a 76.2mm gun, and manufactured stronger track pins and spurs to help traction in winter conditions, to which the Canadians responded with a track fitted with small 'ice spikes', and other minor changes, which were standardized on the Valentine VIIa.

AMPHIBIOUS VALENTINES

VALENTINE DD

Early in 1942, Nicolas Straussler converted a Valentine II to the amphibious configuration later known as Duplex Drive (DD); another was converted with an adapted flotation screen. Both were destroyed during trials. Metropolitan-Cammell subsequently converted another two Valentine IIs, of which the last became the final design. None of these conversions was counted in DD production.

The trackguards were replaced by a platform extending around the hull, fabricated from mild steel plates, welded together into sections that were bolted to the tank's hull. The platform was braced by angle iron struts atop the platform. Another two struts on the underside of the platform at the rear protected the propeller. On a flange on the outer edge of this platform was erected the screen, secured by steel beading bolted to the flange by countersunk bolts, the joint being made watertight by strips of sponge rubber.

The screen was constructed from rubberized flax canvas and supported by 33 pneumatic tubes that made up 'air pillars'; 16 long pillars extended from the air base to the top frame of the canvas, 17 short pillars to the lower frame. The support was completed by two tubular frames running around the inside of the screen, and four

These Valentine V DDs are training near Gosport in January 1944. The turret would be traversed to the rear when raising the screens.

mechanical struts (two each side of the vehicle). The total displacement was about 600cu ft, with the entire hull below the waterline.

The propeller was a three-bladed, right-handed prop, 24.5in in diameter, with a pitch of 16in, driven by a power take-off from the rear of the transmission, giving a vehicle speed afloat of up to 4.5mph. The driver could steer via hydraulic linkages, by swivelling the propeller within a universal joint contained within a spherical housing, to which was attached a stub axle pivoted on fulcrum pins at top and bottom of the housing. The joint between housing and stub axle was closed by a spring-tensioned oil seal.

By similar hydraulic linkages, the driver could tilt the propeller up to prevent damage when the vehicle was out of the water. A mechanical lock held the propeller in the raised position.

This Valentine V is driving off a landing craft, with the propeller raised until the tail clears the ramp.

During assembly, the hull was waterproofed with Bostik compounds up to the level of the platform. Joints between sections of the platform and between the platform and the hull were made watertight with sponge rubber strips and Bostik adhesive. However, Bostik deteriorated with age, running, and contact with fuels or hydraulic fluid, so older vehicles were reserved for training on land.

USE

In summer 1942, the General Staff ordered 450 Valentine DDs. In the end, Metropolitan-Cammell assembled 623 Valentine DDs (212 Valentine V DDs, 236 Valentine IX DDs and 175 Valentine XI DDs). The added equipment was the same in all cases.

Most were retained in England for training. By then the Sherman DD was clearly more seaworthy, roomier and better armed, but due to the late acquisition of Sherman DDs, some British units trained with Valentine DDs at Frinton-on-Sea as late as May 1944, even though only Sherman DDs would land in Normandy in June 1944. British units generally trained with Valentine DDs in inland waters before taking Sherman DDs to sea, although Valentine DDs were used during the largest Allied amphibious exercise ('Exercise Smash 1' at Studland Bay, Dorset, on 4 April 1944), when six Valentine DDs sank (all operated by 4th/7th Royal Dragoon Guards), causing six fatalities.

In late 1943, 105 Valentine IX DDs were sent to Italy, where 75 of them were considered operational, the other 30 being reserved for training. As late as mid-1945, Valentine DDs were the only DDs in India and Burma, but none was used in an opposed landing. British forces there were still converting to Sherman DDs when Japan surrendered.

SELF-PROPELLED GUNS

BISHOP

In June 1941, the DAFV (Pope) required 'assault artillery', meaning self-propelled direct-fire weapons, inspired by the 'startling successes gained by the German assault artillery'. The requirements for direct and indirect fire could be filled by one weapon

This newly delivered Bishop gives a true impression of the high profile of the superstructure. The gunner's ports are closed; the driver's visor is open.

– the 25-pdr gun/howitzer. In June 1941, the Ministry of Supply asked BRCWC to develop a self-propelled 25-pdr on a Valentine platform. In August, this was ready for firing trials at Shoeburyness, Essex.

On 9 September 1941, the Tank Board agreed to place a requirement for 100 vehicles 'as soon as the design had been approved'. The Minister of Supply stated that the vehicles could be produced by December 1941 if the order were given at once. On 4 November, an order for 100 vehicles was placed, but on 12 December, the Chief of the Imperial General Staff (Alan Brooke) chaired a meeting on all self-propelled artillery projects (25-pdr on Valentine; 6in howitzer on Churchill; 3in 20cwt in Churchill 'Special Type'). After reading the Ministry's view that the Valentine was too small and light, Brooke directed that the Valentine 25-pdr order should be reduced to 60, 'if this could be done economically and without upsetting production. The equipments should be tried out and used in the Middle East and kindred theatres and a report should be rendered on their suitability for desert action.'

In Tunisia in 1943, a troop of muddy Bishops has taken position on a slope, which will help to increase range.

Over winter 1941–1942, Allied forces started to use more 25-pdrs in direct fire support, but this increased the guns' exposure and prevented their ready concentration for indirect fire. Thus, the requirement for self-propelled 25-pdrs was more urgent by spring 1942. In July 1942, the order was extended to a cumulative total of 150.

This Bishop in 'Desert Service' configuration is undergoing trials in Egypt. This view shows the limited elevation of the 25-pdr.

Production started in March 1942, using the platform of the Valentine III. Deliveries seem to have been completed by May 1942. Bishops were first used in Egypt in October 1942. Already, Allied units there were using US M7 SP 105mm howitzers ('Priests'), which offered superior throw-weight, stowage and reliability. On 20 June 1943, 8th Army's technical authority reported that the Bishop 'was found to be quite unsuitable and was scrapped. The chief disadvantages were the limits of both range and traverse.' However, other units continued to use Bishops in Italy until they were scrapped in 1944, leaving no surviving vehicles anywhere.

ARCHER

On 25 June 1942, the General Staff agreed that the Ministry of Supply should explore self-propelled 6-pdr, 17-pdr or 3in 20cwt anti-tank guns, or 25-pdr field guns/howitzers, using the platforms of the Matilda II, Valentine, Cruiser VI (Crusader) or Cruiser VII tanks. On 14 August, the AFV Division of the Ministry of Supply submitted its proposals to the War Office and on 16 September the War Office required 400 self-propelled anti-tank guns, 1,000–1,500 self-propelled field guns and 2,000 infantry guns. On 6 October, the two ministries agreed to develop a self-propelled 17-pdr gun (eventually Archer) and a 25-pdr (eventually Bishop) on the Valentine platform, and a self-propelled 95mm gun/howitzer (eventually the useless 'Alecto') on the Light Tank Mark VIII platform.

The Archer was piloted in September 1943, before a second pilot, which was accepted for production, although this was delayed by production of tanks for Soviet receipt until May 1944 (26 Archers). Production peaked in September (63), and reached 349 for the year. Another 178 were produced in the first third of 1945. Upon the surrender of Japan in August, the order for 800 vehicles was reduced, allowing for the 665th vehicle to be completed in September.

ARCHER (SP 17-PDR), 102ND ANTI-TANK REGIMENT ROYAL ARTILLERY, 15TH (SCOTTISH) DIVISION, IN GERMANY, FEBRUARY 1945

From October 1944, Archers replaced M10 Tank Destroyers in anti-tank battalions of prioritized infantry divisions in Italy and north-west Europe, including 15th (Scottish) Division, which had been a leading 'assault' division since mid-June. It was one of the five 'assault' divisions for the offensive into the Rhineland on 8 February 1945, when it was part of British XXX Corps under 1st Canadian Army, 21st Army Group. On 19 February, during the division's assault on Goch, Churchill tanks supported the infantry during the assault, while the Archers were used to fire indirectly on German positions. After the assault units had captured their objectives, the Archers moved forward to take defensive positions in case of enemy armoured counter-attacks.

This particular vehicle is designated 'L1' as the first gun of 'L' troop, which was usually the self-propelled troop in each battery, while other troops might be using either towed 17-pdrs or towed 6-pdrs. Each battalion had four batteries, each of three troops. The vehicle designation was sometimes painted below the driver's visor, or on the side towards the gun mounting, but not on this particular vehicle. (Art by Henry Morshead, © Osprey Publishing)

The Bishop's fighting compartment does not look as spacious inside as outside. Ammunition occupied most of the side walls, in two rows. The recoil normally varied between 16 and 19in, although the recoil strip was graduated from 10 to 24in. Cartridge cases were expended through a chute into the lowest part of the compartment, behind the driver. The gunner sat on a fixed leather-covered seat to the left. Behind him, the loader could sit in a tip-up, leather-covered seat –this pivoted vertically and was normally clamped into a bracket on the left wall. The commander could sit on a similar seat to the right. The gun was fired with the rear doors open, for ventilation, and to allow for resupply from the trailer over the engine deck.

Archers were used by anti-tank battalions within prioritized infantry divisions in Italy and north-west Europe from October 1944. Archers replaced US M10 Tank Destroyers in the assault infantry divisions of northwest Europe towards the end of 1944, and replaced towed guns in the other frontline infantry divisions early in 1945.

BISHOP (SP 25-PDR GUN), 142ND (ROYAL DEVON YEOMANRY) FIELD REGIMENT (SP) ROYAL ARTILLERY, 1ST CANADIAN INFANTRY DIVISION, IN SICILY, JULY 1943

Bishops were shipped to Egypt over summer 1942, and first used in action in support of the offensive around El Alamein on 23 October 1942. These Bishops were converted to 'Desert Service', just the same as Valentine tanks (see page 117), except the container for water cans was on the left-hand door at the rear. By the time they reached Tunisia, some users had painted patches of green. 1st Canadian Division deployed to Britain towards the end of 1940. 142nd Field Regiment was one of two British Royal Artillery units assigned to the division. The division enshipped in June 1943 for the Mediterranean, to join XXX Corps (sailing from Egypt, Tunisia and Malta), under 8th Army. The division was one of the seven divisions that landed in Sicily on 10 July, taking the left of the British force, on the right flank of the Americans.

The division's Bishops deployed with an auxiliary fuel tank and water container, but no sandguards or new paint. The turret sides of this battery 'master gun' have been marked in chalk with a code for gun-laying. Field regiments were structured with three batteries, each of eight guns. Bishops remained in service on the Italian mainland throughout most of 1944, until US M7 Priests (SP 105 mm howitzers) and Canadian Sextons (SP 25-pdr guns) equipped all frontline units. (Art by Henry Morshead, © Osprey Publishing)

Users liked its cross-country performance and reliability, particularly in mud and uphill climbs. The Archer's rear-heaviness actually improved its cross-country mobility compared to the tank; however, the Archer was not as fast or reliable as the M10 on hard roads. The gun was mounted with limited traverse, facing backwards, which meant that the Archer backed into a firing position, although users liked being able to drive forward out of trouble. They liked the low silhouette and the well-arranged fighting compartment, although they disliked the thin armour, the incomplete overhead protection, and the exhaust smoke that gave them away when changing positions.

CAPABILITIES

DRIVING

Access

The driver sat centrally, with two doors either side, opening up to the sides. Each door was sprung by torsion bars to assist opening and closing. The door could be

This display illustrates the Archer's advantages and disadvantages compared to the M10 Tank Destroyer at left, and the 'Alecto'. The Archer has a lower silhouette than the M10, and mounted the most powerful gun. Although the M10 could be rearmed with the same gun (to produce the 'Achilles'), its fighting compartment was smaller. The M10 had a fully traversing turret, although the Archer's 45 degrees of traverse was plenty in most defensive positions. The Archer offered the best mobility off road. None of these vehicles was assembled with a complete roof, although separate kits were produced later to rectify the M10 and Archer.

locked in the closed position by a bolt, or retained in the open position by another bolt. The door was supposed to be locked, otherwise the motion of a door swinging to and fro would wear out the torsion bars. The doors could not be opened from the outside.

To access the emergency hatch below, the driver would need to vacate his seat to the offside, fold the back rest forward on top of the seat, grasp the whole seat and swing it up to the vertical position, and release the hatch's two locking levers. At this point, the door was supposed to fall away, although it could remain stuck if buckled by blast or heat. To move between the driver's compartment and the fighting compartment the driver would need to lay the seat's backrest flat.

Vision

The driver had two periscopes – one looking forward right, one looking forward left – and a rectangular aperture in the front vertical plate, closed by a visor. The right-hand periscope could be rotated freely, but was supposed to be aimed at the rear-view

This Archer is protecting the flank of a road near Nutterden, on 9 February 1945 – the second day of the offensive into the Rhineland. The crewmen have thrown the cover over the mounting, on top of which they have rested the Bren. They have gathered stowage towards the front to clear the arc of fire.

The Valentine III received a larger turret for three men, with a narrower aperture in front of the internal mantlet.

mirror on the right trackguard. As a precaution, the periscopes could be remounted back to front to present the armoured backside of the mounting to the enemy.

In all the Valentines, the visor could be swung out to the side, controlled from the inside by a lever. If open, the driver was protected by a 'look-out block'. The look-out block was considered an emergency option if the periscopes were damaged and the driver was unable to repair them. This consisted of a bullet-proof shield, with four vision slits, in front of a Triplex block. In case of damage, the whole look-out block could be lowered by releasing the finger catch underneath. The Triplex block could be removed by releasing a finger catch at bottom left of the shield. Two spare Triplex blocks were carried beside the driver.

The Archer had the same arrangements as the Valentines, except the visor opened upwards, and had no vision slit or look-out block. Some sources have reported incorrectly that the driver was obliged to leave his seat during firing, but the recoil was arrested at 14.5in by a hydraulic buffer and two steel springs, and the driver was needed to realign the vehicle if the target moved outside of the limits of the gun's traverse, to drive the vehicle out of trouble, or to operate the radio in an emergency. All the proposed Valiants lacked visors, so vision was reduced to two periscopes.

Controls

The driver's feet operated the clutch pedal (leftmost), the auxiliary brake pedal (in the middle) which was rarely needed, and the accelerator pedal (rightmost).

The two levers between his knees acted as steering and braking levers, operating on respective sides. These levers pivoted on a rod attached to a bracket secured to the floor plate, and were connected by rods, turnbuckles and chains to the steering clutch and brake operating gears.

The levers started in the 'hard on' or 'parked' position: pulled back (towards the driver) in order to engage the pawls in the central rack (ratchet). To release the brakes, the driver squeezed together the grips of each lever to withdraw the pawls, flipped over the catch on each lever to hold the grips in the squeezed position, placed his thumbs on top of the catches, and pushed the levers fully forward (engaging the clutches in the final drives). When ready to move, the driver depressed the clutch pedal, selected a gear, let out the clutch, and pressed on the accelerator. To steer towards one side, he pulled back the lever on that side. To stop, he pulled back both levers.

VALENTINE IV

Key

1. Four track links (spare)
2. Driver's hatch
3. Driver's seat
4. Driver's brow pad
5. Steering levers
6. Gear change lever
7. Driver's visor
8. Driver's periscopes
9. Driving mirror
10. Wood blocks for jack
11. Driver's hatch
12. 40mm 2-pdr gun
13. 7.92mm Besa coaxial machine gun
14. Gunner's rotating periscope
15. Gunner's sighting telescope
16. Two 2in smoke bombs
17. Commander's rotating periscope
18. Four distinguishing flags
19. Bren gun for AA use
20. Signal satchel
21. Commander's 'revolver port'
22. Aerial for No. 24 radio
23. No. 19/24 radio set
24. Aerial for No. 19 radio
25. Stowage bin
26. Air inlet louvres
27. Camouflage net inside tarpaulin
28. GMC 6-cylinder diesel engine
29. Fan
30. Water cans
31. Pyrene fire extinguisher
32. Jack
33. Tow rope
34. Crowbar
35. Shovel
36. Pick head
37. 51 rounds of 2-pdr ammunition around turntable
38. 10 boxes of 7.92mm around turntable
39. Gunner's seat
40. 16 2in smoke bombs

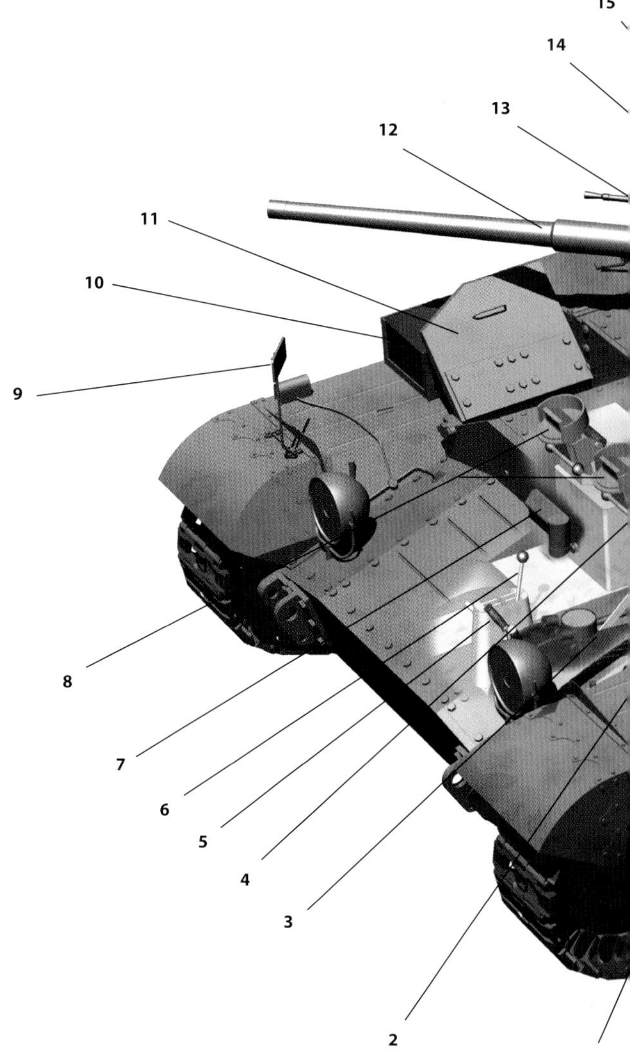

To its nearside is the large container for the coincidence rangefinder, to its offside the 2in mortar is stowed. The towing cable is attached on both sides in order to hang below the tow hook. On the front of the trackguard are a fire extinguisher and a jack. The camouflage net is folded atop a stowage bin. The gun is elevated fully, to the same limit as allowed by the Bishop's mounting.

The clutch pedal was depressed to release a gear, let out, depressed again to select a

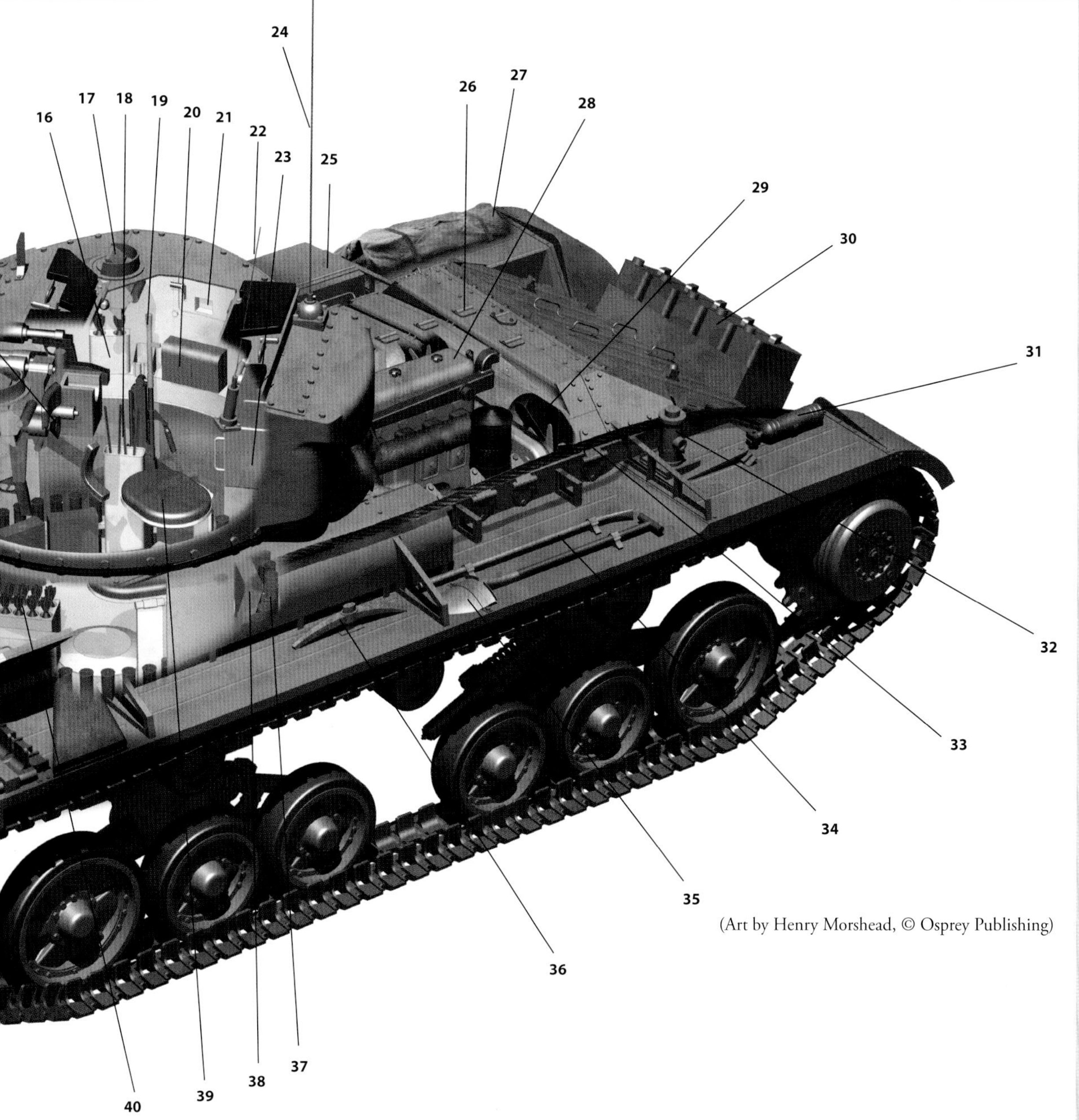

(Art by Henry Morshead, © Osprey Publishing)

gear, and let out again to engage the gear. The gear change lever was located in a gate on the right side of the driver. The lever was connected by universal couplings, selector rods and an adjustable actuating lever to the gearbox. The advance normally started in second gear, with the lever in the middle bottom of the gate. First gear (top right corner) was provided for uphill or heavy going. The reverse (bottom right corner) and fifth (top left corner) gears could not be engaged until the driver squeezed a catch on the lever.

This photograph shows the front and nearside of a fully stowed Archer from the first full-production batch. The driver's visor is open. Above him are two periscopes. Below the visor is a length of track.

Instruments

Forward of the driver, an instrument panel was mounted to the left, a smaller one to the right. The left panel was provided with an ammeter (reading 0 to 60 amps), oil pressure gauge, speedometer, starter button, an ignition switch for the 'flame primer' for cold weather starting, a flame primer hand pump knob, four switches for the exterior lights, a socket for an inspection lamp, and a five-way fuse box. On the Valentine IX, a light switch was added for the convoy lamp, two buttons were added for the tail smoke generators, and a red warning light indicated the master switch was on.

On the right panel was a water temperature gauge, an eight-day clock, and the engine shut-down control, which had three definite positions: if fully out, the fuel injectors and air valve were open; if partially depressed, the fuel injectors were closed but the air valve remained open, as a way to stop the engine normally; if fully depressed, the fuel injectors and air valve were closed, in order to stop the engine in an emergency.

In the Valentine IX, the right panel had only the temperature gauge, a lamp and a lamp switch (off, dim, or bright). The engine shut-down control was a lever to the

BOTTOM The crew of this Valentine I of 20th Armoured Brigade, 6th Armoured Division, in summer 1941, has gathered so much stowage on the engine deck as to obstruct the turret's traverse.

BOTTOM RIGHT Archer's roof kit was designed with the gap shortest over the gunner's plate, tallest over the driver's cover plate, and two hatches – here shown open. This kit reached 21st Army Group too late to be installed before the surrender of Germany.

left of the driver's seat, connected mechanically to the governor; the lever was manipulated forward and down to run the engine, or back and up to stop. At the rear of the turret, underneath the radio, was another emergency shut-down button.

The Valentine XI's hull looked the same as the Valentine IX's, with the container for five water cans affixed below the air outlet louvres.

Electrical power

On the left side hull plate, a master switch was located, which controlled all electrical power in the driving compartment, including the push-button circuit controlling the motor-starting solenoid, but excluding the main current to the starter motor. If the electrical battery was low, two tanks could be connected to share electrical power via a special cable, stowed on every tank, which could be plugged into the 24-volt socket on the left side of the driver's compartment. The generator was located on the right side of the engine, supplying electricity through a base junction underneath the turret floor.

FIGHTING

Vision

In Valentine I, II, IV, VI and VII, the commander was provided with a hatch, a rotating periscope in the hatch, and a large square 'revolver port' in the right side of the turret. Early Valentine Is had three sighting vanes in front of the periscope, whose gaps equated to one degree. All other Valentines had one larger sighting vane. Two spare prisms were stowed – one at the rear, one on the gunner's side.

The gunner looked out via a coaxial sighting telescope or a rotating periscope above, or a D-shaped port to the side (known misleadingly as a 'rear-view look-out'). This look-out was missing from most Valentine Is and some Valentine IIs (tanks numbered T15946 to T16555 and T20419 to T20493).

Since the rear-view look-out lacked splash proofing, bullets impacting around it were likely to find their way inside the turret. Under heavier impact, the parts could fail. In trials, the impact of a 40mm shot dislodged the securing pin of the operating lever on the inside. By the fourth round, the hinge bolts had sheared, and the door had fallen away.

By 1942, MEC was welding shut the ports and look-outs. At home, designers replaced them both with a circular revolver port, outside a circular aperture, with a

On exercise in England in 1941, these Valentine Is and IIs have the curved cover over the exfiltration slit at the rear of the turret, and the centrally located bulbous base for the 6-foot rod aerial used with the Number 11 wireless radio. The Number 19 set was used with a shorter thinner aerial on the offside of the turret roof for higher echelon traffic, and a yet shorter aerial on the nearside for traffic within the troop.

This is a late-production Archer at Vickers' Elswick Works before completion of its stowage. This vehicle has a tow bar on the rear, as well as the hook at the front.

This elevated view shows Archer's roof plates and an alternative stowage scheme. Just over the top of the gunner's roof plate can be seen the plate above the driver's position, on top of which the cover for the fighting compartment has been rolled up and secured with straps. On the left is the camouflage net, atop the folded cover for the engine compartment, within which are the blankets. These are strapped atop a bin containing most of the rations, electrical spares, cleaning kits, and other sundries. To the rear of this bin are two wooden blocks for use with the jack, which is obscured by some bundle forward of the silencer. Behind the air outlet louvres are rolled ground sheets. Behind this are the two smoke generators. The track adjusting tool is atop the right-hand bin, which contained most of the tools and spares. A reel of electrical cable has been affixed to the offside of the fighting compartment. On other vehicles it was affixed adjacent on the glacis or the trackguard. This vehicle does not have either a tow hook or a tow bar.

flap that closed down within the bracket. This port was designed into both sides of the turret. This configuration was introduced on the three-man turret, which entered production late in 1941 on Valentine IIIs and Valentine Vs, and continued on the Valentine IX, X and XI, but was forgotten by the designers of the Valiant. The Valentine IX's commander had a hatch, a rotating periscope in the hatch, a fixed periscope (without any handle) behind the hatch facing rearwards, and a circular revolver port in the right side.

The gunner of the Valentine XI had a small hatch in the leftmost part of the turret roof, a rotating periscope forward of the hatch, and a circular revolver port in the left side of the turret. Two spare prisms were stowed in the turret, as before, except that both were stowed together at the rear of the turret.

Vickers first proposed the Valiant with a single split hatch in the roof of the turret, centrally placed, with a periscope in the roof to the right. The pilot Valiant had a rotating periscope ahead of a split hatch for the commander on the right, and another behind his hatch. Vickers had proposed two periscopes for the gunner, and a large door in the left side of the turret, but the Valiant's had a single rotating periscope forward of his split hatch.

The Bishop's roof had a hatch above the gunner's head, and a visor in the sloping plate, but these were good for little more than ventilation. The commander had a rotating periscope, to the right of the ventilating fan towards the forward edge of the superstructure. The periscope could be locked at any bearing or attainable elevation with two clamping screws. In front of the periscope, a vane sight was mounted on the roof. The gunner's only vision was through a telescopic sight, protruding through a port to the left of the gun. If the sight was too dangerous to use, the port could be closed by a sliding shield on the inside of the superstructure. This shield was secured in the open or closed position by means of a T-handled screw.

In every Valentine, binoculars were stowed above the radio. In the Archer, they were stowed on top of the 2in bomb box in the right-hand side of the fighting compartment.

Controls

The gun was elevated via manually operated gears, and traversed via electrically or manually operated gears. For electrical control, the operator engaged the trigger inside the handle, then twisted (pivoted) the handle from vertical (clockwise for rightwards, counterclockwise for leftwards). The powered speed was controlled by the degree to which the control handle was twisted.

The control unit was bracketed to the turret floor in front of the gunner; the electric motor and gearbox were secured to the turret wall in front of the gunner.

Rangefinders

The Archer was designed with stowage for a coincidence rangefinder (Number 2 Mark VII). This could be mounted on a small socket on the upturned plate above the gunner, or on a stand that was normally stowed in the nearside stowage bin. Its container was attached to the left front of the superstructure, which filled with water and ruined the rangefinder. In the short ranges of Normandy and Italy it was reported to be more of an encumbrance, to the extent that users usually left the rangefinders behind in storage.

The Valentine XI was the first British tank to be designed with stowage for a rangefinder (Number 12, Mark VIII), but since this was deployed only as a command tank the rangefinders were appropriated for other tanks.

OTHER VARIANTS

The Valentine, due to its availability and reliability, was chosen as a platform for many conversions and experiments, although the larger US M4 Sherman medium tank and Churchill infantry tank superseded it in almost every case. More variants were converted in the field or tried at home than could be explained in this whole book, but only three conversions were standardized at home: flamethrowers, bridgelayers and mine-clearing flails.

The CSRD flamethrower was better protected than the PWD/AEC version, but less effectively pressurized.

FLAMETHROWER

The Petroleum Warfare Department (PWD) was established on 9 July 1940 to develop flamethrowers to defeat any invaders. In early 1941, a longer-range flamethrower was required for the Churchill tank, and a shorter-range flamethrower for the Valentine. The PWD ordered AEC to install its Heavy Pump Unit in a Valentine I.

The Ministry of Supply's Chief Superintendent Research Department (CSRD) had an Experimental Station at Langhurst, Sussex, which developed its own 'smaller flamethrower', which the Experimental Station at Chertsey, run by Vickers, installed in a Valentine I early in May 1941. In both cases, the projector was mounted on the offside trackguard, and the fuel was carried in a two-wheeled armoured trailer.

The PWD system developed pressure from compressed hydrogen, whereas the CSRD system developed pressure from slowly burning cordite, which proved

This is the PWD/AEC flamethrower, identifiable by the armoured cover over the projector, the external piping, and the incompletely armoured fuel tank.

spasmodic, so the PWD was preferred, even though it was more difficult to package and protect (due to the large hydrogen bottles). Photographs suggest that the CSRD flame reached targets 60 yards away; the PWD flame reached somewhat further. 12 Valentine IIs and IVs were allocated for conversion to the PWD system, although depot records survive for only two converted Valentine Is (T15998 and T16409); none was deployed, and none survives.

In March 1942, Langhurst was transferred to the PWD. Their projects for the 'longer-range flamethrower' were combined as the superior 'Crocodile' system, which was piloted on a Valentine before transfer to the more spacious Churchill.

BRIDGELAYER

In 1940, the Experimental Bridging Establishment developed the No. 1 scissors bridge, which folded out to 34ft long and 9.6ft wide, and was rated for 30-foot (9.1 metre) gaps and loads of 30 imperial tons. The new bridge was tested on a de-turreted Cruiser II, but by September 1941 this platform had been abandoned in favour of the Cruiser V (Covenanter). The bridge was fully developed for the Covenanter, and entered production, before orders were received around January 1942 to redesign the mechanism for the Valentine II.

Mechanism

The mechanism was operated by power taken off the fan drive, through a small oil-bath clutch and a 2-to-1 reduction gear, to a reversing gearbox directly behind the driver, beneath the screw feed gearbox. Deploying and recovering the bridge took 2.5 minutes each.

Use

This was tried on a Valentine I (T16278), with a bridge manufactured in 1941. All subsequent Valentine Bridgelayers used the Valentine II/III platform, since the diesel engine developed more torque to operate the mechanism. After the pilot conversion, 239 Bridgelayers were produced from January 1943 to August 1944; another 30 spare bridges were ordered in that period.

In January 1943, some Valentine Bridgelayers arrived in Egypt, but without bridges, which had been loaded on to another ship and sent somewhere else. A complete Bridgelayer landed there in March. 25 Bridgelayers were exported to the Soviet Union late in 1943.

Some Valentine Bridgelayers were used in north-west Europe from 1943 to 1945, when the supply of Churchill Bridgelayers could not meet demand, but the Valentine's launching gear was inferior, it lacked the speed to keep up with fighting tanks, its epicyclic steering gave inferior agility to the Churchill's controlled differential, and spares were in short supply.

Each armoured brigade in Italy and India/Burma had six Valentine Bridgelayers. Meanwhile, British forces in India developed a turretless Valentine bridging vehicle nicknamed 'Burmark', with ramps for other vehicles to climb over the hull.

ANTI-MINE FLAIL

In the field, Valentines were used to push or tow various rollers and ploughs against landmines. From late 1942, MEC was sending glowing reports of its flail ('Scorpion') on Matilda IIs and US M3 mediums. The Scorpion was preferred over the home-developed Matilda 'Baron', whose boom was too wide for landing craft.

Bridgelayer '30' is shown without its bridge, revealing the launching mechanism. All these vehicles are serving with 11th Armoured Division in England.

The War Office wanted AEC to develop and assemble two ME-pattern Scorpions within two months, towards a requirement for around 500 Scorpions, of which the first 25 kits were to be despatched urgently by air to the western front in Tunisia, for attachment to M3 or M4 medium tanks.

Instead the Ministry of Supply authorized a home-pattern Scorpion, for attachment to a turretless Valentine II, the combination known as UK Scorpion Mark III. On 3 March 1943, the AFV Liaison Meeting (led by the Ministry of Supply, with representatives from the War Office) decided that a contract should be given to AEC.

In April 1943, the Valentine Scorpion started trials at the Obstacle Assault Centre. The pilot was driven over two Tellermines twice without detonating them; on the third run, the flail detonated one of the landmines, which sympathetically detonated the second landmine under the belly of the tank, killing all three crewmen. The next pilot, and subsequent conversions for issue, were given plates of mild steel (0.5in thick), with an air space of 2in, below the belly.

The flail

The flail utilized 32 chains attached to a drum-like rotor carried in front of the tank by the two side arms. The rotor assembly consisted of a solid drawn steel tube (6.5in in diameter at its outsides), stiffened by four quarter angles (2in by 2in) that were welded to the 32 rotor blades (each 0.5in thick), which in turn were welded to the tube. Bolted to the rotor blades were the rotor blade extension pieces, to which the chains were secured by means of a coupling which clamped the last link of the chain and pivoted on a hardened steel brush in the rotor blade extension.

Each chain was about 4ft 9in long, with about 35 links made from steel bars 9/16in in diameter. It was supposed to be replaced before it was reduced to shorter than 4ft or 29 links. Two Ford V8 engines in the main compartment drove the flail via transmissions running inside respective side arms. The engines were governed to a speed of 3,100rpm, at which they developed 80bhp each. The operator was supposed to keep the engines operating at 2,900 to 3,000rpm, so that the flail rotor would revolve at 165 to 170rpm, but they were prone to overheating, despite various attempted solutions. The driver was supposed to advance at up to 1.5mph when flailing mines, 0.75mph against wire.

This Scorpion, converted from a Valentine II (T18072), is being used by 79th Armoured Division, early in 1944.

The turret was replaced by a taller superstructure housing the commander and flail operator. The superstructure was fabricated from flat plates in a complex six-sided plan, with overall dimensions of 8ft wide, 5ft long and 3ft 9in tall, and a weight of 1.3 imperial tons. The superstructure was secured to the hull by belting in place of the turret ring.

Access was gained via hinged flaps in the roof. The commander stood on the left, the flail operator on the right, upon a raised platform, above the bevel gearbox. The central part of this platform was hinged to allow access to the driver's compartment.

Use

Twenty-five vehicles were ordered from T.C. Jones & Company of Shepherds Bush, Middlesex. The first entered service in summer 1943. 79th Armoured Division wanted the Scorpions only for training of 30th Armoured Brigade, pending Sherman Crabs. As of 19 February 1944, 118 Scorpion kits had been delivered to Chilwell Depot, which had completed 37 Valentine Scorpions. 21st Army Group had issued 35 vehicles towards a requirement of 90 Scorpions; it took only Sherman Crabs to the continent in June 1944.

	Specification, 14 April 1939	Valentine I	Valentine II	Valentine III	Valentine IV	Valentine V	Valentine VI and VII	Valentine IX	Valentine X	Valentine XI
Veight, aden (inc. rew)*	16.00 long tons (17.92 short; 16.26 metric)	17.05 long tons (19.10 short; 17.32 metric)						17.20 long tons (19.26 short; 17.48 metric)		
ength**	17ft 9in (5.41m)	17ft 9.5in (5.42m) to tracks; 18ft 9.7in (5.73m) to sandguards						19ft 5in (5.92m) to 6-pdr Mark III muzzle at front and sandguard at rear; 20ft 9in (6.32m) to 6-pdr Mark V muzzle		20ft 10.625in (6.37m) to muzzle at front and sandguard at rear
Vidth †	8ft 5in (2.57m)	8ft 5in (2.57m) to tracks; 8ft 7.5in (2.63m) to track guards; 9ft 1in (2.77m) to sandguards								
eight ††	7ft 2in (2.18m)	6ft 7.6in (2.02m) to top of turret; 6ft 10.5in (2.10m) to periscope cover; 7ft 5.5in (2.27m) to top of sighting vane		7ft 3.5 (2.22m) to periscope cover	As Valentine I	7ft 3.5 (2.22m) to periscope cover	As Valentine I	6ft 11.5in (2.12m) to periscope cover; 7ft 1in (2.16m) to sighting vane		
ngine type	AEC A189	AEC A189 9.64 liter, 6-cylinder, spark ignition	AEC A190 (diesel version of A189)		GMC 6-71S (Model 6004 "S" type) 6.96 liter, 6-cylinder, diesel			GMC 6-71S (Model 6004 "S" type) or 6-71A (Model 6004 "A" type)	GMC 6-71A (Model 6004 "A" type)	
orque (lb-ı.)	-	4,960 at 1,000 rpm; 4,920 at 1,200 rpm	4,980 at 1,250 rpm		5,460 at 900 rpm			5,460 at 900 rpm ("S" Type); 6,300 at 1,000 rpm ("A" type)	6,300 at 1,000 rpm	
ngine ower brake horse ower)	150 at 2,000 rpm	135 at 1,900 rpm (governed speed)	131 at 1,800 rpm		130 at 1,900 rpm			130 at 1,900 rpm ("S" Type); 165 at 1,900 rpm ("A" type)	165 at 1,900 rpm	
ower/ veight ratio bhp per ong ton)	9.4	7.9	7.7		7.6			7.56 ("S" Type); 9.6 ("A" type)	9.6	
Aain earbox, ype	-	Meadows Number 22 (clash), 5 forward, 1 reverse			Spicer (syncromesh and clash), 5 forward, 1 reverse					
teering	-	Clutch and brake, operated mechanically by steering levers; multi-disc clutch and epicyclic double reduction gears in final drive, minimum turning circle 13ft (3.96m)								
rakes	-	Internal expanding shoes (4), by Girling, with nickel-chrome steel drums, with bonded asbestos linings by Ferodo								
uspension	Coil spring and hydraulic shock absorber (by Newton) acting on 3 wheels at a time ("slow motion" system)									
racks	Six road wheels each side; track width14in (0.36m)									
round ressure (lb/ q. in)	-	10.5	11.15					11.3 (11.5 for DD)		

DD Valentines weighed 17.50 long tons (19.60 short; 17.78 metric)

* with DD screens, Valentines measured 20ft 3in (6.17m)

DD, Valentines measured 9ft 5in (2.87 m) to DD skirts

† with DD screens raised, Valentines measured 9ft 7in (2.92m) at front, 9ft 3in (2.82m) at rear, 7ft 10in (2.39m) at sides

	Valentine Bridgelayer	**Valentine Scorpion (UK Scorpion Mark III)**	**Valentine Carrier 25-pounder (later: "Bishop")**	**Archer as delivered in 1944**	**Valiant "Assault tank" as proposed by Vickers in 1942**	**Valiant as piloted by Rolls-Royce and Ruston & Hornsby in 1943**	**Heavy Valiant designed by Ro Royce and Rus Hornsby in Ma 1944**
Weight, laden (inc. crew)*	19.25 long tons (21.56 short; 19.56 metric)	unknown	17.50 long tons (19.60 short; 17.78 metric)	16.50 long tons (18.48 short; 16.76 metric)	23.00 long tons (25.76 short; 23.37 metric)	26.90 long tons (30.13 short; 27.33 metric)	42.27 long tons (short; 42.95 metr
Length	23ft 7in (7.19m)	27ft 0in (8.23m)	As Valentine III	18ft 8in (5.69m) to trackguards; 21ft 11.25in (6.69m) with gun	17ft 7in (5.36m) without gun; 18ft 4in (5.59m) with gun	16ft 10in (5.13m) without gun; 17ft 4.5in (5.30m) with gun	20ft 10in (6.35m) 57mm gun forwa 19ft 4in (5.89m) gun aft
Width	9ft 8.25in (2.95m)	11ft 10in (3.61m)	As Valentine III	8ft 5.5in (2.58m) to tracks; 9ft 0.5in (2.76m) to trackguards	9ft 3in (2.81m)	9ft 5.5in (2.88m) to trackguards	10ft 7.75in (3.24 detachable final cover plates; 10ft 1.75in (3.09m) to skirts
Height	11ft 3in (3.43m)	8ft 3in (2.54m)	10ft (3m)	7ft 3in (2.21m) to top of mounting, 7ft 4.5in (2.25m) to top of sloped roof	7ft 0in (2.13m) to periscope cover	7ft 5.5in (2.27m) to turret roof plate; 8ft 1in (2.46m) to aerial base	8ft 2.4in (2.50m) periscope cover
Engine type	AEC A190 9.64 litre diesel			GMC 6-71M 6.96 litre diesel	GMC 6-71M (Valiant 1) or Rolls-Royce Meteorite V8 (Valiant II)	GMC 6-71M 6.96 litre diesel	Rolls-Royce Mete V8
Torque (lb-in.)	4,980 at 1,250 rpm			6,624 at 1400 rpm	11,160 (Meteorite) or 6,624 at 1400 rpm (GMC)	6,624 at 1400 rpm	6,458 at 1,500 rp
Engine power (brake horse power)	131 at 1,800 rpm			192 at 1,900 rpm	400 (Meteorite) or 210 at 2200 rpm(GMC)	210 at 2,200 rpm	330 at 2,200 rpm
Power/weight ratio (bhp per long ton)	6.7	unknown	7.5	11.6	17.4 (valiant I) or 19.6 (Valiant II)	7.8	
Main gearbox, type	Meadows Number 22 (clash), 5 forward, 1 reverse			Spicer (syncromesh and clash), 5 forward, 1 reverse			Merritt-Brown Z5, forward, 1 reverse
Steering	Clutch and brake, operated mechanically by steering levers; multi-disc clutch and epicyclic double reduction gears in final drive						Controlled differer
Turning circle	13ft (3.96m) minimum				unknown		
Brakes	Internal expanding shoes (4), by Girling, with nickel-chrome steel drums, with bonded asbestos linings by Ferodo				Internal expanding (Vickers had specified external contracting in the first proposal of June 1942)		
Suspension	Coil spring and hydraulic shock absorber (by Newton) acting on 3 wheels at a time ("slow motion" system)				Independent concentric coils acting on each wheel		HVSS acting on 2 at a time
Roadwheels	Six each side						
Track width	14in (0.36m)				20in (0.51m)		25.5in (0.65m)
Ground pressure (lb/ sq. in)	12.6	unknown	11.5	10.3	10.5	unknown	13.6

	Specification, 14 April 1939	Valentine I	Valentine II	Valentine III	Valentine IV	Valentine V	Valentine VI and VII	Valentine IX	Valentine X	Valentine XI
nax	15mph (24.1km/h)									
	-	3ft (0.91m)								
step	-	3ft (0.91m)								
ce under	16.5in (0.42m)	16.5in (0.42m) centre, 8in (0.20m) under suspension bracket								
tal gap	7ft 6in (2.29m)	7ft 9in (2.36m)								
t or slope s)	-	32								
ks / (imperial)*	As tested: 26+26	31+31 (2.5 gals unusable)	31 + 5 (2.5 gals unusable)		40 (2.5 gals unusable)		46	40		
onal range on, road	-	1.16 miles (1.87km)	3.14 miles (5.05km)		2.5 miles (4.02km)					
onal range on, across	-	0.82 miles (1.32km)	1.9 miles (3.06km)		1.5 miles (2.41km)					
onal range	70 miles (112.7km)	102 miles (164.1km)	199 miles (320.3km)		158 miles (254.3km)					
onal range country	(terrain not specified)	72 miles (115.9km)	121 miles (194.7km)		95 miles (152.9km)					
ary tank gave 32.5 gallons, of which 30 were useable										

	Valentine Bridgelayer	Valentine Scorpion (UK Scorpion Mark III)	Valentine Carrier 25-pounder (later: "Bishop")	Archer as delivered in 1944	Valiant "Assault tank" as proposed by Vickers in 1942	Valiant as piloted by Rolls-Royce and Ruston & Hornsby in 1943	Heavy Valiant as designed by Rolls-Royce and Ruston & Hornsby in March 1944
maximum	10mph (16.1km/h)	15mph (24.1km/h)		21mph (33.8km/h)	16mph (25.7km/h) for Valiant I; 20mph (32.2km/h) for Valiant II	unknown	13mph (20.9km/h)
g	3ft (0.91m)						
step	3ft (0.91m)			2ft 9in (0.84m)	3ft (0.91m)	Unknown	2ft 6in (0.76m)
ce under	16.5in (0.42m) centre, 8in (0.20m) under suspension bracket				Unknown	17.65in (0.45m) at centre front to 8.75in (0.22m) at rear suspension bracket	Unknown
ital gap	7ft 9in (2.36m)	Unknown	7ft 9in (2.36m)		8ft 0in (2.44m)	Unknown	7ft 6in (2.29m)
it or slope es)	32	Unknown	32		30	Unknown	33
iks capacity ial gallons)	36 + 30	31 + 5 (2.5 gallons unusable)		50	Unknown		63
onal range lon, road	Unknown			2.9 miles (4.67km)	Unknown		
onal range lon, across	Unknown	1.41 miles (1.83km)		1.5 miles (2.41km)	Unknown		
ional range	150 miles (241.4km)	Unknown		140 miles (225.3km)	100 miles (160.9km) (terrain not specified)		60 miles (96.6km) (terrain not specified)
ional range country	Unknown	47 miles (76km)		75 miles (120.7km)			

	Specification, 14 April 1939	Valentine I	Valentine II	Valentine III	Valentine IV	Valentine V	Valentine VI and VII	Valentine IX	Valentine X	Valen XI
Main armament	Royal Ordnance 40mm 2-pdr Mark IX or Mark X (76mm howitzer in Mark III CS)							Royal Ordnance 57mm 6-pdr gun Mark III or Mark V		75mm Mark V
Rounds for main armament	50	53	60	62x 40mm or 35x 76mm	62			53	44	46
Coaxial MG	7.92mm calibre Besa MG Number 1 Mark 1 or Mark 2 with 3,150 rounds (14 boxes)							None	7.92mm Besa MG Number 1 Mark 2 with 1,575 rounds (7 boxes; 11 boxes on later vehicles)	7.92mm MG Nur Mark 2 2,700 r (12 box
Anti-aircraft armament	0.303in (7.7mm) calibre Bren LMG Mark I or II, with 6x 100-round drums									
Personal weapons	0.45in (11.43mm) Thompson SMG stowed with 8x 20-round magazines (or 9mm Sten with 8x 30 round magazines from Valentine X onwards); revolvers on some crewmen									
Smoke, obfuscatory	either one internal or two external smokes dischargers	2-inch smoke projector with 18 bombs; 9 hand grenades (some mix of smoke or fragmentation)						two 4-inch smoke dischargers, Number 2, Ma and two smoke generators, Number 8 Mark I Mark III, with 6 rounds; 6 (Mark X) or 9 (Mark hand grenades (some mix of smoke or fragmentation)		
Turret mounting	-	2-pdr Number 5 Mark I or II		2-pdr Number 7 Mark I	2-pdr Number 5 Mark I or II	2-pdr Number 7 Mark I	2-pdr Number 5 Mark I or II	6-pdr/75mm Number 1 Mark 1	6-pdr/75mm Number 4 Mark 1	6-pdr/7 Numbe Mark 1 Numbe
Gunner's sight	-	Number 30 Mark I, Number 30 Mark IA, Number 33 Mark I, or Number 33IS telescopic						Number 39, Mark I or Mark II, telescopic		Numbe Mark I c Mark II telescop
Main armament traverse	360 degrees, electric and manual geared control system by Lucas									
Main armament elevation/ depression	elevation 20 degrees, depression 15 degrees (5 degrees at rear); controlled freely by shoulder piece							elevation 17 degrees, depression 8 degrees, c degrees at rear; by geared handwheel (MG co be moved freely via the pistol grip after relea locking catch)		
Crew	3			4	3	4	3			

	Valentine Bridgelayer	Valentine Scorpion (UK Scorpion Mark III)	Valentine Carrier 25-pounder (later: "Bishop")	Archer as delivered in 1944	Valiant "Assault tank" as proposed by Vickers in 1942	Valiant as piloted by Rolls-Royce and Ruston & Hornsby in 1943	Heavy Valiant designed by R Royce and Rus & Hornsby in M 1944
Main armament	None		87.6mm 25-pdr gun/howitzer Mark II	76mm 17-pdr gun Mark II	57mm 6-pdr gun	75mm gun Mark V	57mm 6-pdr gur 75mm gun, or 9 howitzer
Rounds for main armament	None		32 inside	39	55	Unknown	50
Coaxial MG	None	None	None	None	7.92mm Besa MG with 1,800 rounds		
Anti-aircraft armament	0.303in (7.7mm) calibre Bren LMG Mark I or II, with 6x 100-round drums		Unknown	0.303in (7.7mm) calibre Bren LMG with 24x 30-round magazines	Unknown		
Personal weapons	Thompson or Sten SMG stowed with 10 magazines		Thompson SMG with 16 magazine	2 Sten SMGs with no magazines except those on crew	Unknown		
Smoke, obfuscatory	9 hand grenades (some mix of smoke or fragmentation)		Unknown	One 2-inch mortar Mark VIII, and four smoke generators, Number 8, with 18 rounds (nominally illumination rounds, potentially smoke); no grenades		2-inch mortar with 18 bombs	
Turret mounting	None		25-pdr Valentine, Mark 1	17-pdr SP Number 1 Mark 1	Unknown		
Gunner's sight	None		Telescopic, dial, and clinometer	Number 51 Mark I, telescopic; Number 10 dial sight; clinometer sight Mark IV	Unknown		
Main armament traverse	None		4 degrees right and left	45 degrees (22.5 each side of longitudinal centre line), by handwheel, with electrical power assistance	360 degrees, electric and manual geared control system by Lucas		
Main armament elevation/depression	None		Elevation 15 degrees, depression 5 degrees	Elevation 15 degrees, depression 7.5 degrees; by handwheel	Unknown		Elevation 20 degre depression 12 deg
Crew	2	3	4		3		

	Specification, 14 April 1939	Valentine I	Valentine II	Valentine III	Valentine IV	Valentine V	Valentine VI and VII	Valentine IX	Valentine X	Valentine XI
ose	60mm basis (60mm rolled or 65mm cast)	60mm; 20mm to floor								
acis		30mm								
plate		60mm								
des		60mm vertical; 30mm sloping sides of engine compartment		50mm vertical; 30mm sloping sides of engine compartment				43mm vertical; 30mm sloping sides of engine compartment		
ar		17mm towards roof; 60mm vertical; 17mm sloping towards floor								
or		20mm under driver's compartment; 7mm rearwards								
of		20mm above driver; 30mm sloping sides of engine compartment; 17mm louvres and covers; 10mm roof elsewhere								
or tructure nd mantlet		65mm						65mm turret front and bottom mantlet; 41mm upper mantlet; 14mm MG cover plate		
sides		60mm								
rear		65mm						65mm vertical, 32mm sloped upper		
roof		20mm forwards, 10mm centre, 15mm rearwards								20mm, except 10mm rearwards

	Valentine Bridgelayer	Valentine Scorpion (UK Scorpion Mark III)	Valentine Carrier 25-pounder (later: "Bishop")	Archer as delivered in 1944	Valiant "Assault tank" as proposed by Vickers in 1942	Valiant as piloted by Rolls-Royce and Ruston & Hornsby in 1943	Heavy Valiant as designed by Rolls-Royce and Ruston & Hornsby in March 1944
ose	60mm; 20mm to floor			20mm; 10mm sloping to floor	114mm (4.5in) basis		216mm (8.5in)
acis	30mm			20mm	114mm (4.5in) basis		114mm (4.5in)
plate	60mm			20mm	114mm (4.5in) basis		229mm (9in)
des	60mm vertical; 30mm sloping sides of engine compartment		50mm vertical; 30mm sloping sides of engine compartment	20mm	102mm (4in) basis		140mm (5.5in) forward, 127mm (5in) around engine compartment (including 1in skirt)
ear	17mm towards roof; 60mm vertical; 17mm sloping towards floor			14mm sloping towards top; 20mm vertical; 15mm towards floor	76mm (3in) basis		102mm (4in) vertical, 83 mm (3.25in) to floor, 51 mm (2in) to roof
oor	20mm under driver's compartment; 7mm rearwards	12.7mm mild steel plus 20mm armour (driver's compartment) or 7mm (rearwards)	20mm under driver's compartment; 7mm rearwards	10mm	20mm below driver's compartment; 10mm to 20mm below engine compartment		40mm below turret, 25mm elsewhere,
oof	20mm above driver; 30mm sloping sides of engine compartment; 17mm louvres and covers; 10mm roof elsewhere			10mm	20mm		30mm forward, 25mm above engine compartment
or superstructure nd mantlet	(turret ring only) 65mm	14mm	20mm	(see hull front)	114mm (4.5in) basis		254mm (10in)
sides		14mm	20mm	20mm	102mm (4in) basis		152mm (6in), except 102mm (4in) on box at rear
rear		14mm	14mm	(rear-facing over engine compartment) 20mm	76mm (3in) basis		152mm (6in) vertical, plus 102mm (4in) on box
roof	(covering turret ring) 9.5mm	8mm	10mm	No roof except two 10mm plates: above gunner; and above driver	20mm		30mm, except 14mm above box

CHAPTER 5

CHURCHILL INFANTRY TANK

THE ORIGINS OF THE CHURCHILL

Harland & Wolff of Belfast were offered the chance to build a new tank for the British Army with the designation A20 late in 1939. It went through a number of modifications in the early stages, but was similar in some respects to the A12 Matilda design. Yet A20 was a new style of British tank, being neither a cruiser nor an infantry tank. Instead it was described as a Char de Fortresse, meaning that it was designed for a rather World War I-style direct attack upon an defended enemy position, with crumped and muddy ground to cross over first for which the lowest possible ground pressure was required. Consideration was even given to fitting the tank with subsidiary track beneath the hull to assist it if it sank too far in soft ground. As a result it was also referred to as a shelled-area tank. The idea behind it was typical of the outlook in Britain early in the war. Still imbued with the legacy of World War I, the authorities foresaw the war as being a new version of the Western Front, with the new trenches being the French Maginot Line and the German Siegfried Line. And it was to assault the Siegfried Line that heavy tanks such as A20 were projected.

The engine and transmission for the tank, which one might have thought was fundamental to the design, remained in abeyance since nothing was then quite ready. The plan had been to use the new Meadows DAV flat-12 which was then being produced for the new Covenanter tank, but as this only developed 300hp there were doubts about its suitability. At the same time Vauxhall Motors of Luton had been asked to design an engine which was to deliver 350hp, and having been given the dimensions of the engine compartment in A20 concluded that only another flat-12 would do. Vauxhall claims to have built the first engine from scratch in 89 days, but in fact it was created from two six-cylinder lorry engines, bolted together and altered to side-valve configuration. Still, it was a remarkable achievement. The first prototype, A20E1, was fitted with the new Vauxhall engine, rated at 350hp, and a regenerative transmission devised by Dr Henry Merritt while A20E2 was fitted with the Meadows power unit and the Wilson transmission, by way of comparison.

The original idea was to complete the tank to a turretless design, although the concept of fitting a gun in the hull was regarded as a problem since the barrel of a longer gun (such as the newly developed 6-pdr Mark I, the barrel of which was to be 50 calibres long) was likely to become embedded in the ground, and Vyvyan Pope suggested that the barrel be shortened although this could have ruined the ballistic properties of the weapon. Having a barrel that stuck out ahead of the hull of the tank was not regarded as a wise idea early in the war, although this attitude changed later. Even so the turreted design, which appeared in a drawing that accompanied an official report dated 15 May 1940, included a weapon mounted in the hull of the tank. This hull gun was to be another 2-pdr anti-tank gun in a gimbal mount between the driver and his mate, although as far as one can see it was never fitted.

The hull gun did not extend beyond the front of the hull but it was well forward. Being confined between the front track horns, it could only traverse 7.5 degrees either side of its centreline, which rather limited its effectiveness. Indeed, it is hard to imagine the point of fitting two guns of the same type in the tank, giving it no close support capability at all. Yet the authorities wanted a weapon capable of destroying concrete and suggested the 3in howitzer, but were told that no high explosive rounds were yet available for that gun. They then suggested the old 3.7in close support weapon until they were told that it lacked the muzzle velocity to destroy concrete structures. Side machine-gun mounts are shown in each side of the tank, more or less in line with the driver's position, each with an arc of fire of about 90 degrees. The guns are specified as .303 weapons which at that time suggests the water-cooled Vickers; however the mounting looks too small for such guns so the 7.92mm Besa, which was available by then, seems more suitable. The tank was to weigh around 32

A rare drawing of A20E1 as it was hoped to finish it, complete with hull gun, with a limited arc of fire, at the front, and side-mounted machine guns.

Photographed from the rear in Harland & Wolff's Belfast yard, A20E1 displays its enormous tail skid, but notice the Churchill-like appearance and the A12 Matilda turret on top. Notice also the silencer at the back of the hull, which is not shown on the drawing.

The turretless hull of A20E1 running on new tracks and with a large ballast box in lieu of a turret.

tons with sufficiently thick armour to resist penetration from a 40mm anti-tank gun such as the British 2-pdr. One prototype was built in Belfast, now fitted with the A12 Matilda turret, although plans were announced to develop a turret capable of mounting the new 6-pdr gun. But in the meantime events in France showed that Britain would need to embark on a new style of warfare, one in which the Char de Fortresse had no place. During a meeting of the Tank Board in June 1940 it was announced that although the A20 prototypes would be completed the 100 production tanks would be cancelled.

In due course a second, turretless hull had been produced which was now said to weigh around 40 tons. But the cupola on the turret of A20E1 meant that it was too tall to travel by rail; when this tank was shipped over to England for delivery to Vauxhall Motors, the turret had already been removed. Since the A20 project had come to an end and the order for 100 production machines had been cancelled, the order was reduced to four prototypes of which only two appear to have been built. Although it was essentially a new type of tank, it did owe something to earlier designs; the suspension, for instance, had already been foreshadowed in the type fitted to the medium tank A7E3.

Vauxhall Motors appear already to have designed the suspension for A20 and subsequently designed an engine for it rated at 350hp. All they seem to have done to the prototype when it arrived was to fit the tracks the other way round. From Luton the hull was transported to the MEE at Farnborough but it was only there for about 12 weeks and is recorded as doing very limited mileage. Since the purpose of MEE was to test samples of new tanks it is not entirely clear what A20E1 went there for, being already redundant. From there it went to the Experimental Bridging Establishment at Christchurch, perhaps connected with the development of the Bailey Bridge for heavier tanks such as the Churchill. After that it was sent to the Wheeled Vehicle Experimental Establishment, again at Farnborough, where it seems to have been used as a heavy test load on the new 70-ton Transporter Trailer developed by Cranes of Dereham.

A Churchill hull, seen here on the back of a lorry, giving some idea of its strong construction. The right-side pannier, around which the tracks were fitted, can clearly be seen, plus the opening for the side door.

Here we see an early Churchill hull with the suspension fitted. This hull even carries the first style of air intake on the side.

A20 TO CHURCHILL

The German invasion of France and Belgium rather put paid to the ideology that gave rise to heavy assault tanks such as A20 and TOG. It now became clear that this new war was not going to be anything like World War I with the churned-up no-man's land and the extensive defences of the German lines. It would be a more mobile style of warfare and needed tanks more suited to the conditions.

Following the A20 cancellation, the Honorary Advisor on Tank Production to the Ministry of Supply, Major John Dodd MP, told Harland & Wolff that production of 100 A20 tanks would now be held in abeyance since plans were being discussed 'for modification of the A20 to something different, although similar in construction'. Discussions were also going on at Tank Board level on the design of a new infantry tank, but no contractors had yet been considered. Despite Vauxhall Motors' lack of experience building armoured vehicles, in July 1940 it was named as the designer of the new tank and the parent company to supervise its construction.

The pilot model of A20, with a dummy turret in place of the Matilda turret originally specified, arrived at Vauxhall Motors in August 1940. It was tested in the neighbourhood and for some reason had its tracks reversed but was using up prodigious quantities of fuel and lubricating oil. It was at that time fitted with a Meadows flat-12 engine rated at 300hp, linked to a Wilson transmission, since the new Bedford engine was not ready yet and would in any case be linked to the new transmission devised by Dr Henry Merritt. Following these trials the tank was passed on to the MEE in Surrey and ultimately to the Experimental Bridging Establishment in Hampshire; the way was now clear for the construction of the new infantry tank, the first one of which was ready for testing in March 1941, in accordance with the Prime Minister's wishes, and after whom it would be named.

The Churchill appears to have been initially given the term 'assault tank', and then later 'infantry tank'; a term which was only ever used once again for the A43 Black Prince, although that was essentially a 1943 design which never got beyond the prototype stage, so effectively Churchill was the last infantry tank to see service. Since it is difficult in practice to find any difference between an assault tank and an infantry tank, it seems that the new term was adopted in deference to the Americans.

THE CHURCHILL DESCRIBED

The Churchill was produced in such large numbers and in so many marks with different turrets that it is virtually impossible to describe them all within the compass of a single chapter, and it would involve a lot of duplication. However, the construction of the Churchill's hull, suspension and transmission was virtually the same in all variants.

The hull was immensely strong and originally at least, was of bolted and riveted assembly. The basic hull was built on what is known in tank design as pannier construction. This involved a central box, stepped at the front with armoured boxes on each side which doubled as the track frames. There were side access doors in each pannier and seats in the central hull for two crew members, the driver and the hull gunner, with the other three men in the turret. The top plate of the hull included overhead hatches for these two men and a little further back a slightly wider part that encompassed the turret ring. Behind the turret the hull roof consisted of four large hatches that provided access to the engine, and at the back a shorter panel that included two hatches above the transmission and a central section for the stowage of pioneer tools.

If the heart of a tank is its engine then the unit supplied for the Churchill was remarkable. It was a flat-12, often described as a twin-six, since it is effectively formed from two blocks of six cylinders bolted together. It was a petrol engine with two spark plugs in each cylinder head to ensure dual ignition and steady running. Vauxhall-Bedford had never required nor built such a large engine at this time, so it was essentially made from the blocks of two six-cylinder (27.3hp) Bedford lorry engines bolted together. It was a side valve unit although by this time the firm was employing overhead valve layout. The engine employed four Solex carburettors to control fuel supply and was rated at 350bhp at 2,200rpm, which was considered powerful enough to drive a 35-ton tank. However during its development the Churchill's weight approached 40 tons and was soon to go a lot higher. Yet the power output from the engine could not be increased and no larger engine would fit.

Fitters working on the engine and transmission of a Churchill tank. The transmission is further away, behind the flywheel with part of the final drive at each end.

Outboard of the engine on each side were four radiators and six interconnected fuel tanks. Above the engine decks were the two exhaust pipes, each of which came up through the engine compartment roof at two points. Pipes then carried the exhaust into a pair of silencers arranged crosswise with their tail pipes pointing upwards.

Behind the engine was a large flywheel which incorporated a Sirocco fan that provided air circulation but also whipped up much of the dust which became a curse of the Churchill. The flywheel was also connected to a Borg & Beck dry plate clutch which controlled drive to the gearbox. On the first tanks (either 100 or 115) the tank was equipped with a Merritt-Brown 301c transmission incorporating a five speed gearbox linked to steering epicyclics and from them to the steering brakes on each side. However since the five-speed box kept jumping out of gear in top it was replaced in subsequent vehicles by the Merritt-Brown H4 transmission which employed a four-speed box. This transmission took its names from Henry Merritt, Director of Tank Design and a transmission specialist, and David Brown Tractors Ltd, his erstwhile employers. This transmission also gave the option of a neutral turn which meant that the tank, with one track rotating in each direction, could spin around in its own length without engaging a gear.

The suspension of the Churchill appears to have been unique but was actually foreshadowed on the prototype Medium Tank A7E2, built shortly before the war. It consisted of pairs of flanged, all-steel rollers on short trailing arms acting against a nest of springs. It looked archaic, was frightfully noisy, but suited to a heavy, slow moving infantry tank with a good cross-country performance. There were 11 such bogies on each side, all of which required regular greasing. Nine of these were in contact with the ground via the tracks while the other two, at front and back, only came into play when the tank was crossing rough ground. The return run of the

LEFT A single Churchill suspension unit showing the nest of coil springs and the steel-rimmed bogie wheels.

BELOW Suspension units in place on an early Churchill hull and the toothed idler wheel.

Fitting the tracks to a Churchill hull. This tank is being fitted with later-pattern tracks even though it is not the final model.

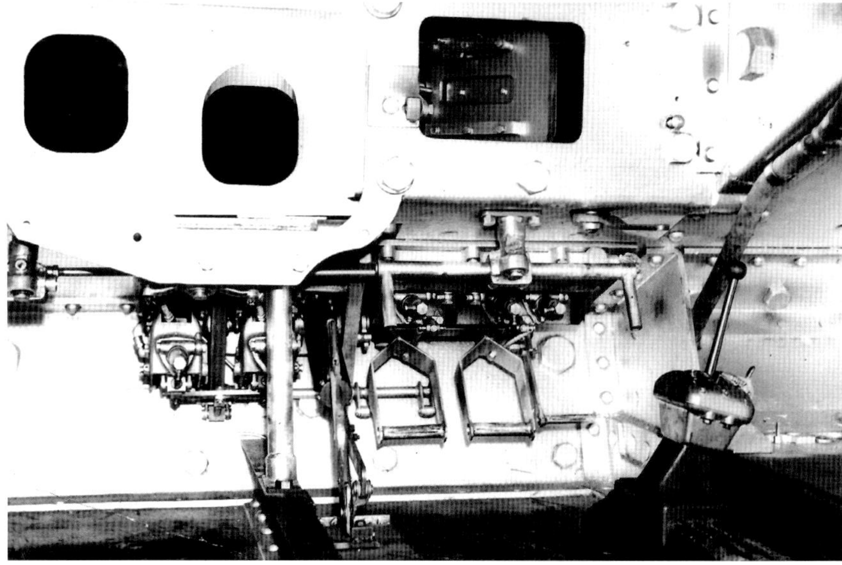

The driver's controls in a new Mark I Churchill. The hull gun has yet to be fitted, likewise the seats, but the driver's lookout door can be seen, partially opened.

BELOW An early Churchill cast turret, with the Prime Minister in the cupola. There is a hinged pistol port near the back and just ahead of it the canvas tube that holds signalling flags. Many of these turrets were produced by foundries in the United States. But notice that this one has the 'Caution Unarmoured' triangle attached.

track, along the top of the frame, was supported by five phosphor bronze skid bumps although these were subsequently replaced on later models by full-length steel skids.

The tracks supplied with the first tanks had been designed with the muddy conditions in France in mind, no doubt based on recollections of World War I. They had large, aggressive spuds that made contact with the ground and flat areas between to provide the greatest possible floatation. Proving unsuitable, they was soon replaced by a new design in pressed steel with a less aggressive tread, but since each link was shorter it was also necessary to replace the toothed idler and drive sprockets at the same time. The idler also served as a moveable track adjuster to control the tension of the track. It would slide horizontally in the track frame, controlled by a threaded rod and a substantial nut.

On all the early Churchill tanks (Marks I to VI) the side doors were square, as was the driver's look-out door. Each side door featured a pistol port while the driver's

An early Churchill hull on test, it is fitted with the early pattern air intakes and is fitted with a temporary ballast box instead of a turret.

look-out included a protected vision slit for use when closed. In order to reduce the width of the tank for rail travel the only thing that had to be done was to remove the air intakes sticking out from each side. These appeared in two forms; the early ones drew air in from underneath but also drew up water, mud and dead leaves which did not do the engine any good at all. Later these were replaced by a more substantial type which drew air in from above. When unbolted for rail travel these items were normally stowed on the rear deck of the tank.

A22 AND A22A: CHURCHILL MARK I AND MARK II

It is not easy to give precise numbers since some orders were increased, others cancelled and many covered tanks of more than one mark. However it seems that production of the Churchill Mark I was limited to about 300 machines. This was due to a shortfall in production of the 3in howitzer, the close-support weapon mounted in the front of the hull. The original plan had been to fit this weapon to all Churchill tanks although this was opposed by a Royal Armoured Corps advisor General Vyvyan Pope who felt that having two different calibres of ammunition in the same tank was a recipe for disaster.

In any case the location of the howitzer was not ideal. Situated low down in the front of the hull, it meant that the tank could not fight from a proper hull-down position without masking the fire of this gun. The gun was also restricted in its traverse by the enclosed front hull of the tank, while its mounting limited it to only 9 degrees of elevation – insufficient for a howitzer at the best of times. Following trials there were complaints about the amount of dust blowing in through the aperture at the front, and the extent to which depression of the gun left the gunner vulnerable to incoming fire. The run-out valve, located beneath the barrel, was also inaccessible due to the mounting and even the firing mechanism was impossible to use while the gunner was leaning forwards to look through the sighting telescope.

Figures suggest that 303 Churchill Mark I tanks were built before they reached the limit of 3in howitzer availability. The weapon itself was rifled but in a parallel barrel 75in long. It fired smoke or high explosive rounds only, and no armour-piercing projectile of any sort was available. Firing shot weighing nearly 14lb it had a muzzle velocity of 700ft/sec and a maximum range of 2,500 yards.

As a result a new Mark was created to complete the order for these 2-pdr-armed Churchills without the howitzer. This was the Mark II which featured a second 7.92mm Besa machine gun in the hull front instead of the howitzer. Evidence suggests that some 1,100 of this version were built.

Both the Mark I and the Mark II were fitted with the same type of turret. It was formed as a single casting, except for a section of rolled plate inserted into the roof, and was about 100mm thick at the front and around 90mm thick at the sides and rear. Three slots were cast in the front. The central one held the main 2-pdr (40mm) gun; the right slot was for the co-axial 7.62mm air-cooled Besa machine gun; while to the left was the slot for the No. 30 sight. On top on the left side was a circular commander's cupola and on the right side a two-piece rectangular hatch for the loader/wireless operator. On the sloping front roof of the turret, over to the right, was the aperture of the 2in smoke bomb thrower, while on the back was a mild steel stowage bin with a smaller one on the right side. On the left side, within reach of the

RIGHT An early Churchill, climbing onto a transporter trailer behind a Diamond T tractor. Twenty-four-wheel trailers such as this one, a Mark II originated by Dyson, were rated at 40 tons, so an early Churchill weighing around 38 tons was close to the limit.

BELOW Winston Churchill watching Churchill tanks roll by. The leading tank is a Churchill I, with a Churchill II following, but the censor has masked all regimental identification on both tanks.

This reworked Churchill I clearly belongs to a Canadian regiment – the Three Rivers Regiment or 12th Canadian Tank Regiment in the Canadian Army Tank Brigade. The two tanks are taking part in an exercise in Britain.

A Churchill II of 9th Royal Tank Regiment, moving across country. The square symbol on the stowage bin on the side of the turret, and on the hull front, denotes B Squadron.

ABOVE A Churchill II, with no obvious regimental affiliations, with an anti-aircraft machine-gun on the turret secured by a Lakeman mount. The asymmetrical outline of the first Churchill turret is quite obvious from this angle.

ABOVE LEFT A clear side view of a Churchill crossing a double-track railway line, probably at a regular crossing place. The flagman looks rather ineffective, standing where he is.

tank commander, was a vertical tube holding flags and poles. There is evidence to suggest that at least 1,000 of these turrets were manufactured in the United States, the Pressed Steel Company being one of the foremost contractors. This appears to have been before the Lend-Lease Act came into force, so they would have been paid for in the normal way.

Later, in North Africa, some Mark I tanks were modified by exchanging their guns: the 2-pdr being installed in the hull while the 3in howitzer replaced it in the turret. This created a close support tank with a more flexibly mounted armament. In Italy a few tanks were fitted with cupolas taken from captured German Panzer III tanks. Although it raised the profile of the vehicle to a dangerous level it gave the commander a clear all-round view. A few tanks were also adapted to mount 3in howitzers in the hull and in the turret.

A rework scheme was instigated in November 1941 to improve 1,000 of the first Churchills but not the very first 300, which presumably were considered beyond redemption. This should have excluded virtually all of the Mark I version but we know from photographs that some Mark I Churchills show signs of having been reworked so the process must have been carried out on a few. From a visual point of view only two features serve to identify a reworked tank; these are extended mild steel trackguards covering the entire top run of the tracks and new-style air intakes at the

Another early Churchill, without its guns, going over some uneven ground.

An unusual arrangement, with a 3in close support howitzer in the turret and a 2-pdr anti-tank gun in the hull position. T30981 began life as a Churchill I, so this oddity could be classed as a Churchill I CS except that the genuine I CS, which was only used in Italy, retained the hull-mounted howitzer and carried a second one in the turret. This therefore appears to be a unique modification, probably developed at Lulworth.

Shearer, a Churchill I of 43rd Royal Tank Regiment, photographed in the New Forest while standing guard with another tank over a taped-off area.

sides. Less obvious was the fitting of full-length track return skids, the strengthening of some suspension units and other details which meant that the work had to be done by existing contractors.

A22B: CHURCHILL MARK III

The 6-pdr (57mm) gun was the weapon the Churchill tank had been designed for in the first place but a series of events had conspired to delay its introduction. It was February 1941 before fitting it to the Churchill was considered, and even then mounting it in a tank seemed to be beset by difficulties. The same appears to have been true of the new turret. Since at the time the idea of a cast turret was being discounted because of the extra weight, a turret made from flat panels of rolled armour plate was favoured, with welded construction a consideration. This was not popular; many believed that such a large, welded structure would not work, that the welds would break up under fire and the whole thing fall to bits. Only Babcock & Wilcox of Renfrew appeared to have any faith in welding and claimed that they had the capacity to build welded turrets; virtually everybody else advocated bolted construction. The only problem was that no firm capable of assembling bolted turrets had the capacity to make them, as they all had full order books. So welding it had to be.

To begin with a special version of the 6-pdr was fitted – the Mark 3, which was adapted for fitting in tanks. Later a Mark 5 version appeared, some 16in longer with a counterweight at the muzzle end of the barrel. The commander and his cupola were situated on the left side of the turret, as they would be in all future versions of the Churchill tank, with the co-axial Besa machine gun and the sighting telescope fitted to the left side of the gun. This meant that the gunner was also located to the left and in front of the commander, and that he was also responsible for loading and firing the co-axial machine gun. The loader was located on the right side of the gun and he also served as the wireless operator; the only other weapon he was responsible for was the 2in smoke bomb thrower at the front, right hand side of the turret.

BELOW A relatively early Churchill III, albeit with a later style of air intake, having used a pile of fascines to gain height in order to cross a wall.

BOTTOM A reworked Mark III, one of six Churchill tanks that formed Kingforce at El Alamein. Notice the canvas 'dodger' suspended across the front, which was supposed to prevent sand and dust from blowing into the driver's face.

RIGHT A reworked Churchill III of 145 Royal Armoured Corps (once 8th Battalion the Duke of Wellington's Regiment), in the unusual local camouflage scheme adopted in Tunisia.

BELOW Another picture of a Churchill Mark III in Tunisia, this time having just fired its gun. Notice the unusual camouflage scheme – achieved, it is said, by smearing local mud on an overall green paint finish.

A Churchill III named Esk of 3rd Battalion The Scots Guards in 6th Guards Tank Brigade. This photo dates from 1943, before the Brigade was reorganised.

Babcock & Wilcox began by assembling a turret-shaped box for firing trials, it had no openings for hatches or a gun mounting, but was the right shape and size. Since the 2-pdr was the only anti-tank gun available, 18 rounds were fired at the test turret, and one 25-pdr round for luck. It was found that the welds stood up to the impact well and that damage was only in localised areas. This was enough to confound the doubters.

Firing trials against Mark III welded turrets began in October 1941, but they were overshadowed by a report stating that there was likely to be a shortage of armour plate suitable for welding in the future, so production of the new turret would be limited. The trials also revealed that although the outer surface of the armour stood up well to the impact, on the inner face it was a different matter. Although a projectile might hit the outer surface and not penetrate, it could cause fragments to break away from the inner surface with enough force to do considerable damage within the tank. To make matters worse the Bullet-Proof Plate Technical Committee announced that they were unable to guarantee the supply of armour that would not break up in this way; the only thing they could suggest was to fabricate each turret in two layers with an inner one of mild steel that would not flake. This was rejected on the grounds of weight, but in any case the likely shortage of weldable armour remained. As a result a new type of 6-pdr turret would have to be designed.

A Churchill III, fitted with the shorter Mark 3 gun, during firing trials at Lulworth in Dorset.

Precise figures for the number of Mark III Churchills built is not easy to compute although it appears to have been fewer than 700. One source gives 692 while a later one offers 675. Some were ultimately converted to Armoured Vehicles Royal Engineers (the famous AVRE), mounting a 290mm demolition charge projector.

In the summer of 1942 it was announced that six Churchill tanks were to be sent out to the Middle East for 'operational experience' to serve as a Special Tank Squadron. They arrived in Egypt by sea on 1 October 1942 and were originally sent to the Mechanisation Experimental Establishment in Cairo. After a couple of weeks they were sent forward to take part in the battle of El Alamein. Now known as Kingforce, and commanded by Major Norris King, they were sent to operate on the northern part of the front. Advancing along the Moon track with orders to deal with some dug-in Axis tanks near Kidney Ridge, one tank had to withdraw due to mechanical trouble, and another was hit and burned out. But the others, although hit repeatedly, gave good accounts of themselves and absorbed a lot of punishment. The five survivors saw action again about a week later at Tel el Aqqaqir but after that the pace of the advance increased and it was too much for slow tanks like the Churchill. They were withdrawn to Alexandria and Kingforce disbanded.

ABOVE A posed view of a fully reworked Churchill Mark III, not yet fitted with additional applique armour. This would be the definitive version of the Mark III as a 57mm gun tank.

LEFT A photo from Normandy showing a battle-damaged Mark III being towed away by a recovery tractor. The hull features added panels of applique armour and although the gun is the longer Mark 5 it is still only a 6-pdr.

T38178R COMPANY is a Churchill Mark I, left behind at Dieppe. It is shown with some deep wading gear rigged, it has the new-style air intakes on the old-style hull with no trackguards, and was obviously recovered and restored by the Germans.

They were, however, not the first Churchill tanks in the Middle East. Earlier in the year two Mark II tanks were sent out from Britain, upgraded with all-over mudguards, which were now styled as 'sand guards'. They were shipped as deck cargo and went the long way round Africa. Suffering during the voyage from liberal doses of sea spray, they required a lot of remedial work when they arrived in Egypt but on trials performed better than anyone expected. Perhaps the Churchill was not such a bad tank after all.

THE DIEPPE RAID

Operation Jubilee, the raid on Dieppe, scheduled for 19 August 1942, was the combat debut of the Churchill tank. At first seen as a totally British affair, it was to include the Churchill tanks of 48th RTR, but at the end of April 1942 it was decided to give the opportunity to the Canadians. One of their Churchill regiments, the Calgary Regiment or 14th Canadian Army Tank Regiment, was chosen instead. Originally planned as Operation Rutter it was scheduled for June 1942, postponed until July and then cancelled altogether. But such was the disappointment of the Canadians, along with other pressures, that it was revived in August under the new name.

About 20 vessels, Landing Craft Mark II, were involved, ten of which would hit the beach. The remainder were to stay out to sea carrying 28 tanks from A Squadron and part of C Squadron as a floating reserve. Dieppe has always been seen as a tank landing that went horribly wrong, but perhaps it should not be forgotten that other elements were involved and that they were successful. However, the 29 tanks that landed or tried to land struggled to cross the beach, which was composed of chert (like shingle only bigger), which trapped some tanks and broke the tracks of others, so many were disabled without coming under fire. Fifteen tanks climbed the sea wall and reached the promenade, and although most of them were hit by anti-tank guns only two had their armour penetrated. Ten even managed to get back to the beach to cover the withdrawal, but the German fire was so intense that this proved virtually impossible.

The beach at Dieppe showing two abandoned Churchill tanks and a burning Tank Landing Craft Mark II, a type that was chosen in preference to the newer Mark III. German soldiers are picking their way among the wreckage.

Of the tanks involved 18 were Mark III, five Mark II and seven Mark I, all of which had to be left behind. Although with hindsight it may seem strange that the latest British tank, still effectively on the Secret List, should be abandoned in this way, one should remember that the force was supposed to have landed and withdrawn before the Germans reacted. But the Germans were prepared for any such landings, there were more troops in the vicinity than British Intelligence had calculated, and they were well armed. The Germans were scathing about their captured Churchill tanks, regarding them as old-fashioned, slow and noisy, and armed with archaic weapons. Only their armour protection seems to have impressed them, according to a report which later came into British hands. Dieppe is said to have provided some useful lessons for those planning the Normandy landings in 1944, but it is difficult to see what these were. However, the Germans were destined to meet the Churchill tank again and find it not so easy to defeat as they first thought.

ABOVE LEFT A view along the beach at Dieppe, taken from on board a Landing Craft, showing abandoned Churchill tanks and a Dingo scout car, with the promenade and the dominant casino building in the background.

TOP Blondie, a Churchill Mark III left behind at Dieppe, here being tested by a German crew.

A22C: CHURCHILL MARK IV

The decision had already been reached: Churchill production would end when 3,500 tanks had been built, but the problems with the welded turret of the Churchill Mark III, in particular the non-availability of weldable steel plate meant that only 675 tanks of this Mark could be built. The final 1,422 tanks would require a new type of

The cast turret of the Churchill Mark IV had a more rounded look but it still fitted the 54.25in turret ring. The 6-pdr mounting was developed by Stothert & Pitt of Bath. The tank at the far end is fitted with a 75mm gun and is experimentally covered in an anti-magnetic coating, the British equivalent of Zimmerit.

Churchill Mark IV tanks, with camouflaged turrets, serving with A Squadron, 51st Royal Tank Regiment, lining up to attack the Gothic Line in Italy.

turret, and the only alternative seemed to be a casting. Cast armour was not unknown in Britain, having been used on the A11 and A12 turrets; on the smaller turrets fitted to Churchill Marks I and II (although most of these appear to have been made in the USA, as were many A12 turrets); while larger, more complex castings were used in the construction of the A12 Matilda tank hull. But the use of larger castings had been developed in the United States and it is said that by the time a cast turret for the 6-pdr Churchill was being considered, British casting techniques had caught up with the best American practice.

This is odd because the Americans had learned this technique for producing larger castings from the British tank engineer L.E. 'Ted' Carr, who had been sent down from Canada to impart this knowledge to American foundries. The Americans may have improved the practice, but the basis of their knowledge had been acquired from a British engineer, and that is what British producers were now learning. The new turret was a complex, asymmetrical shape with different thickness of armour on

Another Churchill Mark IV in Italy. Notice that with the 6-pdr and all subsequent mountings the co-axial machine gun was fitted to the left of the main weapon.

Churchill Mark IV tanks with Royal Tank Regiment crews hurrying to mount up. The tanks are in a marshalling area from where they will move out, perhaps into battle.

different surfaces and three substantial openings: two in the roof for hatches and one on the front for the gun mounting, and a number of smaller openings for such things as ventilators and a smoke bomb discharger. It still fitted the 54.25in turret ring diameter and weighed about half a ton more than the welded version. Since weight was one of the reasons given for not adopting a cast turret in the first place, perhaps a little more should be said about this. Evidently the new practice, learned in part from the Americans, meant that the different thicknesses of armour could be more accurately controlled, but it was still necessary to grind away excessive armour from some places. The unitary construction of the turret meant that it was remarkably strong, however, and not very different in terms of armour thickness than the welded version. Indeed diagrams show that on top, it was thicker than the welded type, and about the same thickness everywhere else.

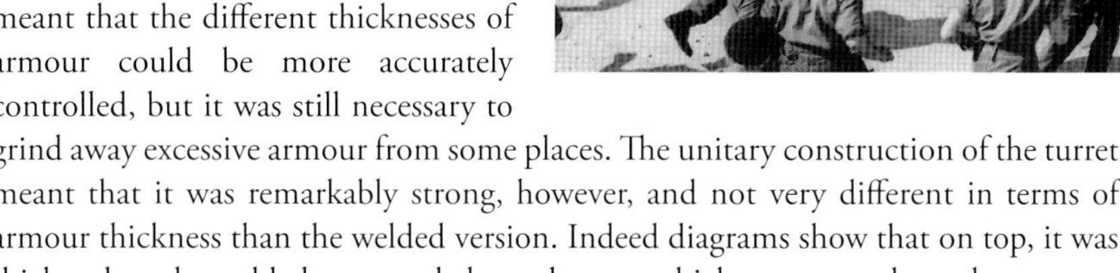

Two versions of the 6-pdr gun were fitted, as they were on the Mark III version. These were the 43-calibre Mark 3 and the 50-calibre Mark 5. And although both guns fired the same ammunition the longer gun had a slightly higher muzzle velocity: 2,965ft/sec against 2,800ft/sec in the Mark 3 with a correspondingly better armour-piercing performance of 87mm at 500 yards. In June 1944 an Armour Piercing Discarding Sabot round was introduced for the Mark 5 gun which gave it a better armour-piercing performance than the newer 75mm gun.

The forecast end of Churchill tank production relied to a large extent on having something to replace it with. In fact there seems to be no one tank selected to replace the Churchill; instead, a selection of Assault Tank projects were begun over a period of about two years, most of which came to nothing. Indeed the A33 of 1943 was one of the few that even reached the prototype stage.

The latter part of 1943 seems to have been crunch time for the Churchill tank. With no suitable replacement by then produced, the total number built was steadily increased and in November 1943 a new version, the Mark VII, first appeared. Although in many respects a new tank it had the same mechanical components as the earlier Churchills and naturally looked similar. In addition the advent of the 75mm gun, both as part of a rework package and as the principal armament of the new tank, meant that the Churchill was going to see out World War II.

Also at the end of 1943 Vauxhall Motors was required to develop a successor to the Churchill, which they did in the form of the A43, known as 'Black Prince'. It was, in effect, an enlarged version of the Churchill, armed with a 17-pdr gun but powered by the same engine. A43 was abandoned when the war ended after six prototypes had been built. Although Vauxhall Motors dabbled in the Cromwell Cruiser tank in 1942, they only ever built two prototypes and otherwise remained faithful to the Churchill for the rest of the war.

Since it was numerically the most significant version of the Churchill ever built the Mark IV is generally seen as the archetypal Churchill tank. It saw service from

Tunisia onwards and, particularly in Tunisia and Italy, demonstrated an amazing ability to climb steep hills, for which it became famous. It was also in Tunisia that Churchill tanks first encountered the formidable German Tiger tank, the PzKfw VI. On 21 April 1943 Churchills belonging to two troops of B Squadron, 48th Royal Tank Regiment came up against a Tiger and other, lesser German tanks at an average range of 200 yards, on the Jebel Jaffa feature. The Tiger knocked out two Churchills, but fortuitous rounds from other Churchills damaged the German tank so its crew abandoned it while the crews from nearby tanks also made their escape. The tanks they abandoned were captured by the British regiment.

THE REWORK PROGRAMME

Although sometimes called the Great Rework Scheme, and referred to officially as a Major Rework Scheme, as it was first conceived, in a list supplied by Vauxhall Motors, it seems to have been largely cosmetic. No mention was made of improvements to the power unit, transmission or suspension, the features that seem to have caused most trouble with the Churchill tanks. In fact a gradual process of improvement had been going on almost since the Churchill was introduced, but this major scheme, which embraced all but the first 300 tanks, was a much more organised affair. Two firms, Vauxhall Motors and Broom & Wade of High Wycombe, were to be removed from the list of tank manufacturers and given over entirely to reworking existing tanks. The new programme appeared as a list of 71 items, including modifications to the engine, gearbox and suspension. Outwardly the manifestation of this programme could be seen in the provision of new side air intakes, drawing air from above instead of underneath, full-length track guards in three sections, and additional panels of applique armour, each about 20mm thick, welded on at the sides.

Out of sight, new full-length skid rails were fitted to support the top run of the tracks to replace the old intermittent raised bumps (known as 'camel backs' in North Africa); new carburettors, improved petrol pumps and an improved starter motor were fitted; and, probably most fundamental of all, the hull was waterproofed, every seam on the lower hull being caulked with a mastic substance called Bostik. This was so fundamental it suggests that every tank that went through the process was effectively rebuilt as a new tank.

A Churchill Mark IV gun tank of 79th Armoured Division uses a Churchill ARK to tackle a replica sea wall during training.

This was a time of uncertainty in tank production. Vauxhall Motors asked whether production of new tanks should be slowed down in order to incorporate these modifications, to which the Ministry of Munitions said 'No'. General Richardson of the General Staff in London was told that new tanks with all the latest improvements would begin coming off the production line in March 1942 but reworked tanks, to the latest specifications, would not be available for a year. Yet the first reworked tanks, which could be identified by the letter R added as a suffix to the War Department number, were being issued to 21st Army Tank Brigade by July 1942, and it was agreed that user trials should be conducted with 25 Churchills from the brigade undergoing long distance road and cross-country runs, under the codename

A Churchill Mark V with the 95mm close support weapon on the left with a 75mm gun Mark VII on the right. Notice that additional track plates are being used to improve protection. Whether they did any good or not remains unproven, but crews believed that every little helped.

'TRENT' to ensure that the rework did in fact work. The trials were conducted over a six-week period, interrupted by other exercises, and they seemed to show that the rework was not as comprehensive as everyone had hoped. However, a senior instructor from the Driving and Maintenance Wing from Bovington was very critical of 'TRENT' and the way it was conducted; as well as saying that the tanks were driven too fast and the cross-country courses were not tough enough, he was very critical of the standards of Parade Maintenance within the regiments themselves.

A trial under the codename 'Pussyfoot' involved a Churchill tank fitted with solid rubber tyres on all its rollers. Earlier trials conducted by Vauxhall Motors seemed to show that rubber tyres made a significant difference to the noise level, the ride of the tank and crew comfort. However the Pussyfoot report claimed that a reduction in noise from the suspension only emphasised the noise of the engine and exhaust, and that in any case as the tank went faster the tyres became hotter and then started breaking up, so the project was abandoned.

THE 75MM GUN

The idea that the next stage in Churchill tank development should be to up-gun it to 75mm would seem to be a logical progression, but in 1942 no such British weapon existed. In any case the Churchill had been designed to accept the 6-pdr, so unless a 75mm gun could be developed to fit the 6-pdr cradle, the task would be impossible.

A project was announced in December 1942 whereby the 6-pdr was to be converted to 75mm calibre and chambered to accept the American ammunition from the Sherman. This was a project initiated by Vickers-Armstrongs for a medium-velocity gun of 36.5-calibre barrel length, not to be confused with the 75mm high-velocity gun that they were also developing, which had a 50-calibre barrel that would not fit any existing British tank because the turret ring diameter was too small. One advantage of the modified 6-pdr was that it would be able to fire high-explosive rounds in addition to armour-piercing, which no British gun had ever been able to do before, at least with a shell with a respectable explosive content. Even so the British 75mm had an inferior armour-piercing performance to the older 6-pdr – 61mm at 1,000 yards – whereas the earlier gun could penetrate 80mm at the same distance. Measured in calibres the new gun had a shorter barrel than the 6-pdr Mark 5 (36.5 calibres against 50 calibres) and the American 75mm M3 (40 calibres).

Now, in theory, it would be possible to convert any armoured fighting vehicle (AFV) currently mounting a 6-pdr gun to a 75mm weapon by simply changing over the barrel, replacing the sight and adapting the ammunition stowage to suit. Priorities were established in February 1943, with the Churchill listed first, the Cromwell second and then the Centaur and Valentine in that order; after that the gun would be available for certain armoured cars and other vehicles.

ABOVE A Churchill Mark III re-armed with a 75mm gun, serving in North West Europe. In this guise they were designated Mark III*.

ABOVE RIGHT The first 75mm-gun Churchill, the NA75, created by inserting the complete Sherman 75mm gun and mounting into a modified Churchill Mark IV turret. Developed in North Africa it saw service in Italy, where this photograph was taken.

However with the advent of a 75mm barrel that would replace the 57mm 6-pdr it proved possible to up-gun Churchill Marks III and IV. The Mark III with a 75mm gun was designated Mark III*; however in the case of the Mark IV two distinct types are officially recorded. Some are referred to as the Churchill Mark IV (conversion to 75mm) while others were completed as the Churchill Mark VI and it is extremely difficult to tell them apart.

The figure of 242 is given as the number of Churchill Mark III tanks converted to accept the 75mm gun, whereupon it became known as the Mark III*. Exactly the same figure is given for the up-gunned Mark IV, although this was known as the Mark IV (75mm). A post-VE-Day report dated July 1945 announced that 'a Field Conversion Scheme' had been introduced that enabled guns in the Mark III and Mark IV tanks to be changed from 6-pdr to 75mm (including new sights and revised ammunition stowage) by unit workshops in the field, but whether this was ever done or not is unclear.

The up-gunned Churchill Mark IV should not be confused with the Churchill Mark VI which was undergoing acceptance trials at Lulworth in September 1943. Whether the Mark VI was a rebuilt Mark IV or a new type of tank that just happened to look like a Mark IV we do not know, but it was armed with the 75mm gun with geared elevation. According to the official stowage diagram it also carried an infantry telephone in a box on the back, a crowbar on the offside trackguard, and one 4-gallon water tank instead of a pair of 2-gallon ones. These were all features found on the next model, the Mark VII, but not on the Mark IV.

Since there seemed to be little hope of any of these guns reaching Italy in the immediate future, the British Army there would have to manage with the 6-pdr gun in the Churchill and the 75mm Shermans, unless they could find some way of creating 75mm Churchills from their own resources. Captain P.H. Morrell was a REME officer serving at what was then called Bone, Algeria, in 1943. One of Morrell's jobs involved breaking up wrecked tanks, and he noticed that among the Shermans that were brought in many were equipped with 75mm guns that had hardly been fired and appeared to be as good as new. Morrell also noted, and confirmed by measuring, that the cast turret of the Churchill Mark IV would accept the Sherman gun with a bit of modification, and he set about persuading those in authority that it was possible. In due course he was authorised to carry out the experiment on a new tank and it was successful, although not easy. The Churchill turret had to be modified to accept the new gun mounting, including enlarging the opening in the front. Ammunition stowage had to be modified, and even the hull machine-gun mounting had to be altered to accept a Browning to bring it into line with the new co-axial weapon. Finally a production line was established at Bone and 210 up-gunned Churchills were built. The entire M34 mount from the Sherman was lowered into place in the modified Churchill turret and then bolted down. Classified as the Churchill NA75 (NA for North Africa) they began to arrive in Italy in April 1944 and appear to have given a good account of themselves.

A Churchill Mark IV (75mm) photographed in North West Europe. Extra track links have been added, all over the front, in an effort to enhance armour protection.

A new close support weapon, ultimately entering service as the 95mm Mark I tank howitzer, was first considered in January 1942, the old 3in weapon now being declared obsolete. The new gun was designed by mating a short section of the barrel of the 3.7in anti-aircraft gun with the breech and firing mechanism from the 25-pdr field gun and chambered to fire ammunition from the 3.7in mountain howitzer. The original plan was to produce two versions – one on a towed, wheeled carriage and a tank-mounted version that would be carried in a 6-pdr turret.

A towed gun, the Mark 2 version, was built in quite large numbers, but long-term trials started to show up faults. Under tow across country the gun carriage proved to be unstable, the track of the wheels being too narrow. Firing trials, which were not completed until November 1944, revealed that the recoil system was faulty, due to insufficiently strong springs. As if that was not bad enough, limited elevation of the piece restricted its range. As a result the gun was declared obsolete in April 1945 without ever being issued for service. In the towed version of the gun (and the Mark 3 version later mounted in the Alecto self-propelled gun) ammunition came in two units – a projectile and a separate loaded charge, albeit in a brass cartridge case. For the tank-mounted weapon a one-piece round was developed, while a High Explosive Squash Head and a smoke round was also available. Despite its limitations the same weapon was also fitted to the Churchill Mark VIII.

For a while the future of the tank-mounted howitzer, the Mark 1, was also in doubt, when it was revealed that the new weapon could not be made to fit the welded turret of the Churchill Mark III. Indeed there never was a close support version of the Churchill III with any type of weapon that we know of. However it was possible to mount the 95mm howitzer into the cast 6-pdr turret resulting in a new version of the Churchill, the Mark V, and although limited elevation (37 degrees) of the gun in the cast turret restricted the range to 6,800 yards this was considered

The Churchill Mark VI is a difficult tank to identify, although this is said to show them. The censor has been at work on this photo. The tanks, with infantry tank-riders, were photographed approaching Venlo in November 1944.

quite satisfactory for a tank. What is odd is that the new weapon fitted quite happily into the welded and bolted turret of the Cromwell/Centaur tank so why it could not be fitted into the welded turret of a Churchill is unclear.

Of course the 75mm gun was standard fit in the Churchill Mark VII, although this in many respects was an entirely new tank. The Mark VIII was the same tank but mounting the 95mm close support howitzer although it is difficult to find evidence of it ever actually being used.

ABOVE A Churchill Mark V with 95mm howitzer, photographed from a low angle. The markings suggest a tank of 7th Royal Tank Regiment in 31st Tank Brigade. The purpose of the fitting on top of the turret is not known.

RIGHT A Churchill Mark VII on the road in France. The circular door in front of the driver is as good a recognition feature as any, but note that the centre section of the track guard has been removed. This has been done to prevent it from buckling under fire and jamming the turret. Its 152mm thick frontal armour made this the most heavily armoured British tank to see service during the war.

A22D: THE CHURCHILL THREE-INCH GUN CARRIER

Although it was not a tank the Carrier, Churchill, Three-Inch, 20cwt, is included for completeness. It was in fact the old 3in anti-aircraft gun mounted in a rectangular box-like structure on the hull of a Churchill tank. The gun was carried low down on the left side, alongside the driver, pointing forwards and the Gun Carrier was intended as a mobile anti-tank gun for dealing with German tanks in the event of an invasion. Yet only 50 were ever built, starting in May 1942, by which time the threat of a German invasion was virtually over. By the time the last one was completed in November 1942 nobody was quite sure what to do with them.

Apart from the prototype built by Vauxhall Motors the 49 production machines were built by Beyer Peacock & Company of the Gorton Works, Manchester, delivered at the rate of about one per week. The 3in anti-aircraft gun is said to have been capable of penetrating 84mm of armour plate at 1,000 yards, which was in fact little better than the 6-pdr gun but good enough to deal with a Panzer III or an early Panzer IV. The only concrete evidence we have for their proposed later use comes from the War Diary of the 14th Canadian Army Tank Regiment (better known as the Calgary Regiment). It records a request for volunteers to form a Tank Brigade Heavy

Support Company but, with the Dieppe raid in the offing, it is questionable whether they were ever introduced to the new vehicles, never mind trained on them.

Issued on the scale of one company per brigade suggests one troop (three tanks) for each regiment, or roughly one per squadron, although it is suggested elsewhere that the 3in mounting was only temporary pending replacement by self-propelled guns mounting the 17-pdr. In fact it seems unlikely that anything of this sort ever happened and some were rebuilt as armoured recovery vehicles. One, with its gun removed, served as a carrier for 50 lengths of Snake mine-clearing tubes under the name Wurlitzer while a few more were used as hard targets, including those dug up recently at Folkestone.

ABOVE LEFT A Churchill Three-Inch Gun Carrier showing how the gun was mounted, low down at the front, and the box-like superstructure.

TOP A Churchill Three-Inch Gun Carrier aboard a landing craft in Poole Harbour, with Brownsea Island in the background. The naval officer climbing over the side of the LCT to board the LCM alongside is Lord Louis Mountbatten, Chief of Combined Operations until October 1943, when he went to the Far East.

A22F: CHURCHILL MARK VII AND MARK VIII

The A22F, sometimes called the Heavy Churchill, was regarded by many as a new tank, but it still looked like a Churchill and by awarding sequential Mark numbers, those responsible seemed to be implying the same. Yet soon after the war it was awarded a new General Staff number, A42, which seemed to suggest that it was a new tank after all.

The hull was now of all-welded construction, which had been done experimentally some years earlier. However welding saved weight so despite being more heavily armoured (152mm across the front of the hull and the front face of the turret, and

A view inside the Vauxhall factory showing A22F hulls under construction. Engines are being fitted from the stock on the right. Notice the rails along the floor upon which the new hulls move forward until the tracks are fitted.

Newly built Churchill Mark VII tanks on a cross-country driving exercise in Britain, all looking remarkably clean and free from additional stowage.

an inch thicker on each side and on the sides of the turret), at 40 tons it was only about one ton heavier than the Mark IV. It was also fitted with a new gearbox (type H41) on account of the greater weight and the new gear ratios reduced the overall top speed from 15.5mph down to 13.5mph. The new Churchill also had improved suspension with stronger springs although these were not interchangeable with earlier Marks, whereas such developments as there were with the engine and other parts of the transmission could be applied to all types of Churchill.

Externally the main visual difference was that the side hull doors and the driver's visor were now circular, instead of square or rectangular. This had been suggested earlier by the contractors Babcock & Wilcox, since it alleviated the problem of weak zones in the armour at the corners, but it was not acted upon while the future of the Churchill remained uncertain, and was only introduced on this late model.

An even more drastic change concerned the turret, although the solution was not new. As already mentioned, one of the problems with casting was controlling the thickness on all surfaces. In the case of a turret this was especially true of the roof, which required a lot of man-hours grinding it down to the right thickness. For this new turret the four upright walls were cast as a single piece, so that some grinding was still necessary, but a 20mm roof of steel plate, in two sections, was fitted inside a lip running around the interior of the cast turret and welded in place so that it did not present a vulnerable edge from any angle. Something similar, although on a smaller scale, was done with Matilda tank turrets from about 1938. A lip of thicker armour was also provided all around the bottom edge of the turret to partly shield the turret ring, and this is very distinctive. On top of the turret the commander was now provided with a rotating All Round Vision cupola with periscopes all around the circumference.

Although they were identical in terms of hull and turret structure the Mark VII mounted the 75mm Mark V gun while the Mark VIII was equipped with the 95mm

A posed view of one of the new Churchill Mark VIII close support tanks showing clearly the stubby 95mm howitzer and, incidentally, the round mounting for the hull Besa machine gun.

A very unusual picture of a Mark VIII Churchill in India. Since most Churchill tanks have positions for a crew of five, one of these men is an imposter.

Mark I howitzer. Both types seem to have been equipped for easy conversion to the Crocodile flamethrower.

A number of documents published at the end of the war refer to three more Marks of Churchill, Marks XI, X and XI, which mounted respectively the 6-pdr gun, the 75mm dual purpose weapon and the 95mm howitzer. Each type was further subdivided into those fitted with the new-style A22F turret and those that carried the original turret fitted with an All Round Vision cupola and identified by the letters LT (for Light Turret) after the Mark number. So, for example a Churchill Mark IX would be fitted with an A22F turret mounting a 6-pdr, while a Mark XILT would have the original turret, suitably modified, mounting a 95mm howitzer.

All Marks of modified tank were supposed to have the front hull plate of an A22F, with round driver's visor and machine-gun mounting, stronger suspension and H41 gearbox, but no photograph of one has ever been seen. A document published in 1945 (DRAC News Letter) says that while some Mark X and XLT tanks had been built (32 according to a contract card) it was unlikely that any Mark IX or Mark XI tanks would be so converted. The absence of corroborative photographs hardly constitutes evidence that this was never carried out, but the fitting of the heavier A22F turret would require some strengthening of the hull roof to support it and fitting the new, thicker front plate would also be difficult. Yet four 75mm gun tanks described as Mark XLT were supplied to the Irish Army, but since they appear to have the original style of front hull plate they have more in common with a Mark VI, with the addition of an All Round Vision cupola.

A43 BLACK PRINCE

Towards the end of 1943, with all Churchill development more or less in the bag, the Department of Tank Design approached Vauxhall Motors with the suggestion that they develop a new heavy infantry tank to mount the 17-pdr gun. The Director of Tank Design was showing interest in a tank with a sloping front plate that would be better suited to defeating the armour-piercing rounds of the German 88mm gun; another tank, A41 Centurion, was already under development with this feature, but lacking a hull-mounted machine gun which it was felt might destroy the integrity of the sloping front plate.

Vauxhall Motors, on the other hand, decided to design their new tank 'as much like a Churchill as possible, so that we could profit by all the lessons we had learnt'.

Black Prince alongside a measuring pole. This is Pilot No. 3 with a canvas cover over the mantlet. Note in particular the stronger suspension, although it is still recognisably of the Churchill family, and the way the air intakes have been moved to the top of the hull.

Designing an infantry tank with a high-velocity anti-tank gun would seem to be a contradiction in terms but the British had always done it, arguing that such a tank was better equipped to fight off counter-attacking tanks when the infantry had captured a defended position. Even so, a proportion of the ammunition carried in the tank was to be High Explosive, which was more use when attacking a defended position. Thus Black Prince, as the new tank was to be named, looked like a scaled-up Churchill – even down to the layout of the hull, the style of the suspension, and, most controversially of all, the fact that it was built around the same Bedford 350hp flat-12 engine that had been used in all Churchill tanks since the very first.

The Bedford engine was now trustworthy and reliable, but since it was already working hard in a 40-ton tank (the Churchill Mark VII) was it really good enough to power a 50-tonner? There were those who did not think so and argued in favour of the 600hp Rolls-Royce Meteor instead. The main argument against the Meteor was that it was a bit too tall to fit into the engine bay of A43. One suggestion was that by tilting the Rolls-Royce engine a mere 4 degrees it would fit, while it was also suggested that the roof of the engine compartment could be raised a little bit to accommodate it. But it was never done and the six prototypes were all fitted with the Bedford engine, albeit linked to a new Bedford five-speed gearbox and the inevitable Merritt-Brown triple differential steering system. The choice of engine limited the top speed to 11mph. Although an order was discussed for 300 production machines, none were ever built, but they might have been fitted with Meteor engines which, it was calculated, could raise the top speed to 22mph (with a proportionate increase in reverse speed, which at that time the authorities were most concerned about).

The hull of Black Prince was similar to the Churchill, although noticeably bigger. Total width was now 11ft 3in, well outside the railway loading gauge, but necessary for the larger turret ring that was required to accommodate the 17-pdr gun. Yet the armoured panel across the front, ahead of the driver and machine-gunner, was 152mm-thick (near enough 6in) the same as a Churchill Mark VII and still good enough to resist most guns. The crew remained at five, the same as in the Churchill – three in the turret and two in the front of the hull. Experienced Churchill crewmen remarked on how much roomier it was. The front of the hull was still stepped, despite the wishes of the Director of Tank Design. There was a Besa machine gun in a ball mounting to the left of the driver. To improve the driver's view, although not by very much, the front end of the track frames, and the idler wheel, were lowered very slightly. Behind the turret aperture, the engine decks were clear and uncluttered, and the exhaust system was now internal, apart from the engine air intakes which were located on the top instead of at the sides. The suspension components, although essentially similar to the Churchill tank, were much heavier and with one extra pair of rollers on each side, each pair of rollers acting against a stout bracket. The tracks were much wider, at 24in, which helped to spread the weight.

The turret on Black Prince was perhaps not the most imaginative part of the design, the only novel feature being the new style of mounting at the front. This was made by Stothert & Pitt of Bath, and had a heavy duty cast mantlet with prominent trunnions set in a cast frame; a similar arrangement had been designed for the A34 Comet, and was also seen on the Mark I Centurion. However, it was invariably protected by a canvas cover to keep dust out, and is therefore rarely seen. The rest of the turret was a large but simple welded box, slab-sided and square at the back, with a mild steel bin attached. Since they both mounted the same 17-pdr anti-tank gun, the Department of Tank Design wanted to know why the turret fitted to Centurion was a different shape to Black Prince's. They were told that the turret originally proposed for Centurion was also slab-sided, but it had been altered to provide an illusion of even better protection, but there must be more to it than that. Centurion's turret was cast whereas that on Black Prince was constructed from large flat plates of armoured steel, welded together. There is no good reason why a Centurion-style turret could not have been fitted to Black Prince, as both tanks had the same diameter turret ring and the designers at Vauxhall had already seen drawings of the proposed Centurion turret.

The new infantry tank mounted a Mark 6 version of the 17-pdr gun, specially designed for tanks but with a shorter breech block. A co-axial 7.92mm air-cooled Besa machine gun was fitted to the left of the main gun. But in contrast to all other versions of the Churchill tank the commander's hatch and All Round Vision cupola were fitted to the right side of the turret, placing the tank commander directly behind the gunner, as he was in most tanks.

Black Prince without its mantlet cover, stopped alongside the wreck of a Mark I Churchill on a target range.

CHAPTER 7

CHURCHILL CROCODILE

INTRODUCTION

As a weapon, the flamethrower exercises far more power over the imagination than it can actually deliver in reality. It exploits our most primeval fears and, when mounted in a tank, becomes a formidable psychological threat. This is no new thing; when the Landships Committee discarded their huge Pedrail machine in 1915 it was handed over to the Trench Warfare Department at Porton Down, and they planned to complete it as an armoured flamethrower. In the event nothing came of this and there is little evidence for interest in flame as a weapon until World War II was imminent.

Even then flame was regarded essentially as a defensive weapon and in a very short time some 40,000 Flame Fougasse installations were hidden away in the British countryside, along with Defile Flame Traps and Hedge Hoppers where appropriate. In addition, the Home Guard had mobile flamethrower units in the form of trailers carrying drums of petrol and hand-operated pumps, although these were truly last-ditch weapons. Winston Churchill questioned the flamethrower's defensive capability: in a minute to General Ismay in August 1940, he pointed out that in the event of invasion enemy infantry would not move through disputed territory without having scouts and flank guards posted, so surprise with flame traps might not be achieved. Indeed, if the use of flamethrowers in war proved anything, it was that they were primarily suited to the offensive role.

ORIGINS

Surprisingly perhaps, in light of later events, huge quantities of petrol existed in Britain in 1940. Stocks had been built up during the immediate pre-war period while exports to the Continent had ceased. Should the Germans invade, these reserves would have to be destroyed and many felt that this was best done in direct action against the enemy. Thus, all over the country, various experiments were taking place, and in a move to concentrate this effort the government decided to create a Petroleum Warfare Department (PWD), which came into being on 9 July 1940.

1: AEC HEAVY PUMP UNIT, 1941

During an official demonstration at Leeds Castle in Kent, this pump-operated system discharged flame fuel through its main projector at a range of 100 yards (91.4m) at the rate of 750 gallons (3,409 litres) per minute. Fuel was carried in a large tank at the back, but no capacity is given. The small, auxiliary projector had a range of 75 yards (68.5m). The main projector, which is sometimes shown with a curved shield, could be elevated to the vertical position to discourage low-flying aircraft but, at a similar demonstration for the Royal Navy, an American stunt pilot showed that it was perfectly safe to fly an aircraft through flame. The chassis was the regular AEC Model 0854 six-wheel drive diesel. One source claims that 25 of these were built, but that cannot be confirmed. The vehicle is shown in a khaki brown finish typical of the period, but it never entered military service so no markings were applied. (Art by Tony Bryan, © Osprey Publishing)

2: AEC BASILISK, SOUTHALL, 1942

AEC are reputed to have built their first armoured car as a private venture in 1941. It subsequently entered service as the Mark I, on a rear-engined version of the Matador chassis, type 0855. The Basilisk appears to have used the same chassis but with a modified hull and turret. This, in turn, led to the development of the AEC 0856 chassis, with a 170bhp (127kW) engine that became the basis of the AEC Mark II armoured car. Thus the Basilisk may be seen as a link between the two. It was photographed in company with other mobile flamethrowers during demonstrations at Moody Down, but is shown here in grey primer paint as it would have looked on first being rolled out from AEC's Southall factory. A claim by AEC that development of the Basilisk was halted by the end of the war would seem to be a fiction. The project was probably killed off when a plan to include flamethrowers in armoured car regiments was dropped. (Art by Tony Bryan, © Osprey Publishing)

Two schemes should interest us because they each had a bearing on subsequent events. One was based upon the work of Reginald P. Fraser of London University's Imperial College, who was also a director of the Lagonda car company of Staines. Fraser was developing an annular flamethrower that projected petrol with an outer layer of thickened fuel. This, it was hoped, would eliminate the supposed risk of fire working backwards to the fuel tank. But in fact, since oxygen would not be present here, this could not happen. However, Fraser had an experimental vehicle put together by Lagonda on a Commer lorry chassis that was fitted with a flame-thrower turret.

ABOVE Reginald P. Fraser's original, mobile flamethrower on a Commer lorry chassis. Never a military vehicle in the official sense, it was the prototype for virtually all such equipment in British service.

RIGHT The big AEC Heavy Pump Unit thrills its military audience with a high-angle shot. One demonstration, at Leeds Castle in Kent, caused considerable damage to the garden.

This is the Mark IA Heavy Cockatrice, an odd, asymmetrical vehicle that used the same AEC 6x6 chassis as the Heavy Pump Unit. The flame-projector turret is behind the cab and the two machine guns are worked from an open section at the back.

At around the same time the gifted bus designer and ex-Tank Corps officer G. J. Rackham of the Associated Equipment Company (AEC) was developing a design of his own using a powerful Mather & Platt pump, powered by a Napier Lion engine, to produce something quite awe-inspiring: the jet of blazing liquid was expelled at 750 gallons (3,409 litres) per minute. Fitted into an armoured AEC 6x6 chassis and known as the Heavy Pump Unit, it also featured a smaller projector on a two-wheeled carriage that was carried on the back of the vehicle. This could be manhandled by its crew as far away as the hose would stretch. A suggestion, in one source, that 25 of these big vehicles were built seems doubtful.

Fraser's work at Lagonda was highly significant, as we shall see. Developed from his original Commer prototype, Fraser now designed what came to be known as the Cockatrice, based on an armoured Bedford QL vehicle with flame-projector, 60 of which were ordered for the protection of Royal Naval Air Stations. Six more, on the bigger AEC 6x6 chassis, went to the Royal Air Force for similar work. These were described as the Heavy Cockatrice (Mark IA), but apart from the fact that they could carry more flame fuel there was no difference in performance between them and the Mark II (Bedford) or

Light Cockatrice. The Admiralty also ordered a version of the Light Cockatrice that could be dismounted from a lorry and carried aboard a landing craft. The result was the Landing Craft Assault (Flame-Thrower) or LCA (FT). The Cockatrice flamethrower, a sample of which was shipped to the United States, used carbon monoxide as a propellant, employed a rotating weapon mount with elevation to 90 degrees and had a range of about 100 yards (91m). Unfortunately, by the time this equipment was in production the need for it had virtually disappeared. The War Office had never shown any interest at all, so mass production was out of the question.

Finished in the so-called 'Mickey Mouse Ear' camouflage, this is a Mark II Light Cockatrice of the Royal Navy on the four-wheel drive Bedford QL chassis. Although unproven, it has been suggested that for some of these vehicles other 3-ton (3.05-tonne) 4x4 chassis may have been used.

The final attempt to produce a wheeled flamethrower in Britain is attributed to Rackham who, in response to a requirement that armoured car regiments should have their own flame capability, designed the Basilisk, based on the AEC Mark I Armoured Car chassis. It was a strange-looking vehicle: rear engined and with a large armoured body surmounted by a tiny, one-man turret that housed the flame-projector and a Besa machine gun. The commander occupied the turret, so he was the flame-gunner; there was also a driver, of course, and a third man known as the observer, but it is not clear where he was located or what he could observe. The flame fuel capacity was 300 gallons (1,363 litres) and the flame jet was propelled by compressed air. Official documents claim a range of 120–130 yards (109–118m), but one commentator reckoned that the effective range was closer to 75 yards (69m). The prototype vehicle was fitted with a 105hp (78kW) AEC diesel, but the report claims that production machines would have been fitted with a 170bhp engine that would have lifted the speed from 30 to 50mph (48 to 80km/h) but, in the event, it was decided not to include flamethrowers in armoured car regiments and the project was dropped. The Basilisk was apparently never issued with a War Department number, nor tested by the Mechanisation Experimental Establishment (MEE) at Aldershot.

THE FIRST TANK FLAMETHROWERS

The concept of having a tank fitted with a flamethrower goes back to 1938, when the General Staff issued a requirement for a tank with a turret-mounted flamethrower based on the current design of infantry tank, the A12 Matilda. The specification was suitably vague since no such weapon existed at the time, but the flame-gun was required to be co-axial with a Vickers .303 machine gun, capable of firing on the move or with the tank stationary, and have a range of between 200 and 300 yards (188 and 274m). The flame fuel would be carried in tanks mounted externally on the vehicle or in a two-wheeled trailer towed behind. One sentence implies that some sort of pump device driven by one or both of the tank's engines would propel the flame jet, but later it was suggested that slow-burning

Rackham's Basilisk armoured car on the AEC Matador chassis. The flame-projector is in the turret and it may be that the third crew member, designated as observer, would be located alongside where a periscope head may be seen. If so, his view would be very limited.

INFANTRY TANK MARK III, VALENTINE. MINISTRY OF SUPPLY FLAMETHROWER DESIGN, LANGHURST, MARCH 1942

The tanks used for these experiments did not display numbers, but appear to have been of the Mark I type. Shown here at Langhurst, the MoS version is towing the second type of trailer design. Very few details appear to have survived of the internal arrangements of the trailer, or of the way it coupled up to the tank, although the flame projector was photographed in some detail. Traverse and elevation employed a gear train, apparently operated by remote control from the driver's position. Other photographs of this tank show it with a different pattern trailer and the main armament removed from the turret. (Art by Tony Bryan, © Osprey Publishing)

cordite be used to raise the pressure. The problems created by a turret-mounted weapon can be understood if one considers the design of a rotary junction. The designer has to create something that will permit fuel to flow into a turret capable of 360-degree rotation. The junction has to be well engineered to eliminate any risk of leaks, which would be extremely dangerous in the confined space of an armoured vehicle. The pre-war design work on the Matilda took place at Woolwich under the Superintendent of the Research Department, in what soon became the Ministry of Supply (MoS). However, it is interesting to note that the document mentioned above also suggests that the authorities purchase an Italian flamethrower in order to gain experience.

The onset of the Blitz in the summer of 1940 saw a number of institutions moving out of London. Among them, the MoS department concerned with flamethrower development found itself transferred to a site at Langhurst in Sussex. At around the same time the PWD, under Brigadier Donald Banks, was established on a disused landing ground at Moody Down near Winchester. Up to this time they had operated in whichever part of the country required their services, but things were now changing. The requirement for a tank-mounted flamethrower had been revived and the two organizations became rivals as each set to work on its own design.

Since the prototypes were not completed for some time and were not tested competitively until March 1942, the actual descriptions can be saved for later, but before other experiments are discussed it may be worth looking at the rival propellant systems. Experts at the MoS, where the original Matilda project had first been considered, still favoured a method whereby pressure for the flame fuel was achieved by slow-burning cordite. Unfortunately no detailed explanation has been found as to

CHURCHILL MARK II OKE FLAMETHROWER BEETLE OF 8 TROOP, B SQUADRON, 14TH CANADIAN ARMY TANK REGIMENT, DIEPPE, 19 AUGUST 1942

Beetle displays a comprehensive set of markings as it sits, disabled, on the beach at Dieppe with a track broken. T68875 is the tank's own War Department number and the red/white/red display a form of national identification. The gold maple leaf and ram insignia is that of 1st Canadian Army Tank Brigade. The 14th Canadian Army Tank Regiment (CATR), the Calgary Regiment, as junior regiment in the brigade, is identified by the number 175 on a divided blue over khaki rectangle: the blue square signifies B Squadron while the number 8 is that of the particular Troop to which Beetle belongs. The armoured container on the rear of the tank, which housed the flame fuel reservoir and pressure cylinders, proved a very convenient place to paint this array of markings, which would also be repeated at the front. (Art by Tony Bryan, © Osprey Publishing)

how this system worked. The PWD, on the other hand, favoured some sort of gas pressure system such as Rackham had used in the Basilisk although, ultimately, nitrogen was preferred as the propellant.

Meanwhile, as this long-term research progressed, other people were at work upon less sophisticated projects. Among them was Lieutenant-Colonel Martin, commanding 47th (London) Division, who in conjunction with a Mr S. W. Adey produced a device for covering anti-tank ditches with fire, which became popularly known as the Adey-Martin Drainpipe. Developed in response to a requirement for mobile, offensive weapons rather than the static defensive kind, the equipment was mounted on a vehicle of the Universal Carrier family and demonstrated by a crew from the Welsh Guards at the Guards' Depot on Sandown Park racecourse.

There was, at this time, no official requirement for such a weapon and indeed the very future of the PWD was in some doubt, but the vehicle was taken to Moody Down and demonstrated to an audience of senior officers that included General A. D. L. McNaughton, commander of Canadian Forces in Britain, whose enthusiasm for the project effectively saved it. At the time of this demonstration, May 1941, the British Army's interest in flamethrowers was limited to the man-pack type.

THE RONSON

On 5 August 1941, an order was placed for 17 prototype flamethrowers installed in the Universal Carrier vehicle. The project was handed to Fraser, who based it on his original Commer design. Since the systems were intended for the Canadian Army, it was agreed that Canadian-built Carriers would be used.

RIGHT The original caption claims that this is a Wasp, in action in France. In fact it is a Canadian Carrier equipped with Fraser's Ronson device, demonstrating its powers in Britain. Notice the pipe linking the two tanks at the rear.

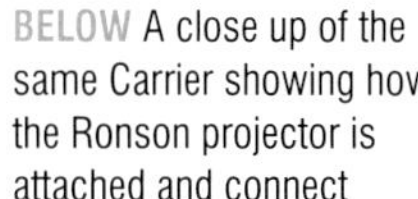

BELOW A close up of the same Carrier showing how the Ronson projector is attached and connect

A Précis for Junior Leaders, issued by the Royal Canadian Engineers, gave basic details of the equipment. Two fuel containers at the back of the Carrier contained 60 gallons (272 litres) of fuel and the propellant took the form of a carbon dioxide (CO_2) pressure cylinder stowed in the front compartment of the vehicle. In fact, every effort was made to keep the interior of the Carrier free for its regular crew so that the pipe, carrying fuel from the left hand of the linked tanks, passed along the outside of the vehicle to a pivoting projector on the edge of the front gunner's position, where the operator sat. This projector had a range of about 50 yards (45.7m) and there was sufficient fuel and propellant for about 40 short bursts.

A Ronson Dragonfly with the flotation screen folded down. Seaworthiness must have been questionable, even in a flat calm. A marine propeller was driven off the differential at the back.

The Précis accepted that 50 yards was not much range, but pointed out that the vehicle would be moving at the time and would therefore be difficult to hit. The effect of this mobility was enhanced by the Canadians, who removed the governors from their Carriers' engines and, styling themselves the 'Ronson Cavalry', put on some impressive demonstrations at Moody Down. Orders for 1,300 sets of Ronson equipment were placed in Canada, based on information supplied by the Lagonda company, but in the end no Ronson ever saw active service. Despite fluctuations in interest from the authorities, it seems that Fraser blithely worked on with the project and before long had a new system, with far greater range, on the drawing board, which would be known as the Wasp.

Meanwhile one of the more bizarre British developments was the Dragonfly, which was a Duplex Drive (DD) amphibious variant of the Ronson Carrier. Nicholas

Fraser's Twin Ronson Churchill Mark II in the markings of 102 Officer Cadet Training Unit, which later became the Westminster Dragoons. It may have had a short range and carried a limited amount of flame fuel, but with both projectors working this vehicle must have been an impressive sight.

Straussler had already produced drawings for a DD adaptation of the Universal Carrier, but there was no requirement. On the other hand, adding a flamethrower to the package might be regarded as a step too far. Some prototypes were built and tested, first on a pond in the New Forest and subsequently in the Solent, but one wonders how well they might have performed in the sea conditions prevailing on D-Day and it is probably a mercy that the project was not taken up.

DIVERSIONS

Early in 1942, it seems that priorities changed once again and Fraser was informed that as far as the British Army was concerned a tank-mounted flamethrower was preferable to a Universal Carrier, since it was a lot less vulnerable. He got down to work at once and produced a design that featured two complete Ronson units fitted to a Churchill tank. Work went ahead quickly using a Churchill Mark II tank and, since the modification did not involve any major alterations to the tank itself, the prototype was completed by 24 March 1942.

The projectors were mounted, one either side, on the inner track frames at the front of the tank so that they were visible to the driver and his mate. As with the Ronson, a pair of containers, each holding 30 gallons (136 litres) of flame fuel were located at the rear of the tank, feeding the flame-projectors via pipes running along each side of the hull. Since it would be

An unusual photograph apparently showing two Churchill II Okes newly converted. It provides an excellent view of the armoured cover for the fuel tanks, but the non-standard trackguards were not fitted in service. The second Churchill has its air intakes resting on the engine deck.

difficult for one man to control the movement of two projectors they were fixed in place so it was up to the driver, directed by the tank commander, to take aim by turning the tank, while the hull machine-gunner was responsible for firing them electrically. Following a demonstration on 26 March, the Chief of the Imperial General Staff asked Fraser if a single projector with greater range might not be better.

Nothing had been done at this stage to improve the range: it was still 50 yards (45.7m) and presumably two projectors would use up fuel twice as fast so the combat effectiveness of the arrangement would be very limited. At about this time a Royal Tank Regiment (RTR) officer and veteran of World War I, Major J. M. Oke, appeared on the scene. According to the records Oke suggested that instead of fitting Ronson fuel containers to the rear of the tank it would make more sense to employ the reserve fuel tank, which was a standard fitting on early Churchill tanks anyway. If this resulted in an increased fuel capacity it would make sense, but it did not. The reserve fuel tank was capable of holding 32.5 gallons (147 litres), not much more than half the capacity of a pair of Ronson tanks. A photograph of one of the converted Churchills clearly shows that the tank actually fitted was a good deal larger than the original type, albeit carried in the same way. Whatever the reason Oke must have had more to do with the design than is immediately obvious, since the Ronson-equipped Churchill tanks were known in some quarters as the Oke type thereafter. Some sources suggest that the fuel tank could be jettisoned once it was empty, but this cannot be correct. Photographs taken at around this time show quite clearly that the fuel container and its attendant pressure cylinders were enclosed in an armoured cover, which certainly would not have been dumped when the fuel ran out.

The first Churchill Oke with a single projector was demonstrated on 24 May 1942 and resulted in an order for two more. Impending events were starting to sweep things along and matters were not improved by a certain amount of secrecy and subterfuge. The so-called Dieppe Raid, Operation Jubilee, was to include a battalion of Churchill tanks manned by 48th RTR, who commenced amphibious training on the Isle of Wight. It was decided that as soon as they were ready the three flamethrowers would accompany this regiment. In the meantime, however, it had been agreed that the majority of troops for Dieppe should come from the Canadian Army in Britain and an order announced that 'the three Churchill tanks now being fitted with flame-throwing apparatus should be transferred, for operational reasons, from the 48th RTR to the 14th Canadian Army Tank Battalion', the dull alternative title to what was, in fact, the Calgary Regiment.

Tintagel was with B Squadron, 48th Royal Tank Regiment when photographed as an Oke flamethrower. Here the fuel tank is unprotected, but one can follow the pipe as it runs forward to the projector. T32049 was renamed Boar when it went ashore at Dieppe with 14th Canadian Army Tank Regiment.

There is neither space nor need to tell the entire Dieppe story here. Instead it is only necessary to focus on No. 8 Troop in B Squadron, which consisted of the Churchill tanks Bull, Boar and Beetle, all of which were equipped with the Oke flamethrowing device. All three tanks, along with a Caterpillar D7 Bulldozer, went ashore in Landing Craft Tank (2) No. 159 on 19 August, but what should have been a significant occasion, the first time British armoured flamethrowers would see action, was blighted by fate. Bull was just too eager, launched early and was swamped, Boar managed to knock off its armoured fuel tank and was unable to use its flamethrower, while Beetle got ashore safely and then broke a track.

The MoS Valentine showing the first type of trailer, blazing away with its flame-projector. The main turret is traversed rearwards, but at this time did not mount a gun.

The story of the Oke ends there; no more were produced and indeed its Carrier contemporary, the Ronson, was also in the process of being replaced. However, it is necessary to bring the tank flamethrower story up to date, and for this we must go back to March 1942 and to Hangmore in Surrey. Donald Banks portrays the event as a cross between a duel of honour and a horse race in which the palm was awarded to the PWD's pressure-operated system.

Both contenders employed Valentine tanks, early models with the 2-pdr gun, but in each case the projector was mounted independently of the main turret. The flame fuel was also carried in a two-wheel trailer towed behind the tanks, but in other respects the vehicles were quite different. The MoS version towed what was known as the Flame-Thrower Trailer No. 3 Mark I at the trial, although photographs reveal at least two types of trailer. The No. 3 Mark I had a capacity of 150 gallons (681 litres)

This is the PWD Valentine putting up a fearsome show, but the trailer is a clumsy affair and the fuel hose curls over the engine deck.

A photo that is not easy to explain; one of three views, none of which are captioned. The vehicle may be a transitional design between Wasps I and II or possibly Reginald Fraser's ill-fated Hornet.

of 'coal tar and petroleum oils', but whether this was a mixture or alternatives is unclear. The operating pressure of 260psi was achieved by the use of cordite, and the system was described at the time as follows: 'a charge of cordite displaced 15 gallons [68 litres] from the fuel tank into a small tank, from which it was discharged through the gun.' Just how this worked is not explained. What we do know is that the flame-projector had a discharge rate of 6 gallons (27 litres) per second, but after each discharge pressure had to be built up again. A simple sum will show that there was sufficient fuel in the trailer for a total of 25 seconds flaming, but this could not be continuous.

The PWD's effort, produced in conjunction with Rackham and Stock of AEC, featured a large, cylindrical tank containing 685 gallons (3,114 litres) of fuel oil carried in an open trailer. Besides the normal towing link, an enormous hosepipe connected the trailer to a large projector mounted on the offside front mudguard of the Valentine. Pressure was supplied at 300psi using compressed hydrogen, which gave a discharge rate of 12 gallons (54.5 litres) per second and a duration of fire lasting 56 seconds, which could be delivered continuously if need be.

Oddly enough, despite the greater pressure behind the PWD system there was not a lot to choose between the rivals when it came to effective range. The MoS system could manage 80 yards (73m) against 85 yards (78m) for the PWD projector. By the curious laws of physics it appears that an accurate balance of pressure with flame fuel and the size of nozzle on the projector were the keys to greater range, not simply increased pressure itself. It is also curious to note a comment, apparently made at the time, to the effect that the trailer towed by the MoS Valentine 'interfered seriously with the movements of the armoured tank'. Why this should not apply equally, if not even more so, to the PWD arrangement is not at all clear.

The MoS contender, with its professional-looking trailer and turret-like projector on the offside, bore all the hallmarks of a finished product. The PWD entry, by contrast, with a crude trailer containing the fuel tank and what looks like a rough-and-ready projector that only appears to fire straight ahead, gave a distinct impression that it was only half finished. Even so, three days later, on 30 March 1942, Sir Andrew Duncan of the MoS announced that the demonstration proved beyond doubt that the PWD system was better and that in future the two departments would merge under Banks. The enlarged PWD would continue development of tank flamethrowers and Reginald Fraser would work on the Carrier variants while offering advice to the PWD. Yet this very confirmation of importance now accorded to tank flamethrowers inevitably involved contact with other bodies, notably, for obvious reasons, the Department of Tank Design (DTD). On 23 June the DTD announced that their preference for future development would be for a flamethrower based upon the Churchill tank, hauling a trailer with either a castor action single wheel or two wheels, something Reginald Fraser had already suggested.

In fact there was so much going on that it was nearly the end of July before authority was given for the next stage to go ahead. The PWD was permitted to order 12 tank flamethrowers for development purposes, only to have the entire project squashed a month later when the War Office Policy Committee announced that it was now only prepared to encourage the development of man-pack flamethrowers and those mounted on Carriers. The reason given was that, in the view of the War Office, no tank could be sufficiently protected to prevent its destruction while a faster vehicle, such as a Carrier, might be able to employ its mobility to avoid getting hit.

To what extent the War Office had been influenced by events at Dieppe earlier that month is impossible to say. After-action reports contained very little of relevance because few of those who returned appear to have seen the flamethrowers or known much about them. Even so, it seems reasonable to assume that they would have noticed if flame had been employed, so the conclusion must have been that they had failed to get into action. Since success depended upon getting very close to the target, then it could only be that the Churchill tanks, despite their thick armour, had been knocked out before they were within range to flame. This at least would be consistent with the War Office decision, and the theories were confirmed after the war when the survivors returned from the Prisoner of War camps.

Since work on the Carriers was still going ahead, despite previous War Office scepticism, roles were now somewhat reversed. Publicly everyone concentrated on Fraser's very promising Wasp design while a smaller team of enthusiasts quietly went ahead to develop a flamethrowing version of the Churchill that would have greater range – just in case.

THE WASP

The link between Fraser's original design, the Ronson, and the ultimately successful Wasp appears to have been a device known as the Hornet. Fraser first mentions it in a proposal dated 19 March 1942, where it is described as a long-range Ronson. However, another source explains that Hornet involved permanent conversion of the Carrier to the flamethrowing role. Four days later the project was given 'High Priority' and it was subsequently confirmed that 75 Ronson devices would be cannibalized into Hornets.

Fraser must have been working flat out at this time. His Cockatrice vehicles were now being delivered, too late to be of much use; Ronson production was getting under way and he must have been involved to some extent in the various tank flamethrower projects. Even so, the first Hornet was ready in May and at the end of that month Fraser was asked to come up with a revised design that would result in the Wasp. Some time

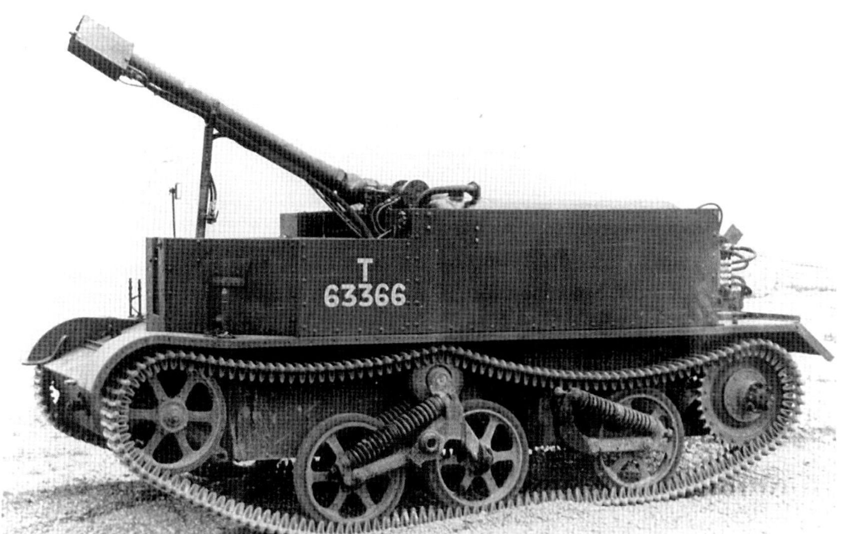

A Wasp Mark I with the projector on full elevation and one of the fuel tanks just visible inside. The pressure cylinders are located outside at the back but note that on this very basic version a deep slot has been created in the front gunner's position so that the projector could be depressed to some extent.

1: WASP IIC CARRIER, WESTMINSTER REGIMENT, 5TH CANADIAN ARMOURED DIVISION, ITALY, 16 DECEMBER 1944

The large flame fuel tank across the rear of this Canadian version of the Wasp also proved an ideal place to paint vehicle markings, but there is some doubt about those shown. When 5th Canadian Armoured Division arrived in Italy, the Westminster Regiment was its Motor Battalion and the markings shown are correct for that role. However, at one stage, in keeping with local practice, British and Commonwealth armoured divisions in Italy added a second infantry brigade to their strength because infantry proved to be more effective than armour in the prevailing conditions. Thus, at the time of this action, the Westminster Regiment was part of the newly created 12th Canadian Infantry Brigade. Unfortunately, it has not proved possible to establish beyond doubt the numbering system employed for a second infantry brigade in an armoured division, because it was peculiar to Italy. If it followed the practice in infantry divisions then 60 on a green square might be appropriate, since the Westies were the senior regiment in their brigade. On the other hand, such markings may never have been applied, since the entire Canadian Corps in Italy transferred to northwest Europe shortly after this action and 12th Brigade ceased to exist. (Art by Tony Bryan, © Osprey Publishing)

2: WASP II CARRIER, 1ST BATTALION HIGHLAND LIGHT INFANTRY, 53RD WELSH DIVISION, NORMANDY, JULY 1944

It is an indication of the complexity of British Army organization that by 1944 a dedicated Scottish regiment should find itself a significant element in a Welsh infantry division. The white 57 on a red square tells us that 1st Highland Light Infantry (HLI) at this time was junior regiment in the first brigade (71st Brigade) of the division, whose famous Red W insignia adorns the Carrier's other track guard. It is believed that 1st HLI was the first ever to use Wasp flamethrowers in action, when they were supporting 2nd Battalion the Monmouthshire Regiment, from the same division, in fighting west of Caen. (Art by Tony Bryan, © Osprey Publishing)

in June the Hornet prototype was burned out during trials and on the 10th of that month Fraser submitted his Wasp design, which is described as a modified version of the original Commer projector that would be a temporary fit.

Clearly, however, the Hornet was not quite dead because on 19 June the chief engineer of First Canadian Army contacted Reginald Fraser and, as a result, staff from the Canadian Petroleum Warfare Experimental Unit (PWEU) were sent to Lagonda at Staines to develop an improved Hornet, which was later demonstrated to General McNaughton. Since no more is heard of the Hornet after this, it must have been eclipsed by the Wasp design. The DTD ordered a Wasp prototype on 12 June followed by an order for 30 on 22 July.

Now that Carrier flamethrowers were once again in the ascendant, another consideration arose. One of the problems of employing a prolific and ingenious

A view of a Wasp II showing how the two fuel tanks and gas cylinders fill up the interior. It also shows how relatively inconspicuous the new projector was. This is clearly a demonstration vehicle since it lacks all conventional stowage and any markings apart from the WD number.

inventor is that invariably his quest for perfection leads him ever onwards until he does not know when to stop. Thus, even before the prototype Wasp had been subjected to any trials, Fraser came up with an improved design. Donald Banks had to take a more practical view. Bearing in mind that a cross-Channel invasion was not out of the question for 1943, he preferred to go with what he had in the form of Fraser's original Wasp design, rather than wait for something new in the hope that it might be better. With hindsight it is clear that this was not the correct decision, since the 1,000 Wasp Mark I units manufactured were only ever used for training, but this was not clear at the time. It is also worth reminding ourselves that since the Wasp, like the Ronson, came as a kit to be fitted to Universal Carriers as required, this did not require large numbers of vehicles to be tied up.

Following yet another change of emphasis from the War Office, it was now decided that it would be better if the flame fuel containers, and indeed all of the equipment associated with them, should be contained within the armour of the Carrier. Thus what was known officially as the Flame-Thrower, Transportable, No. 2 Mark I or Wasp Mark I had two cylindrical tanks located on either side of the engine. That on the right contained 60 gallons (272 litres) while that on the left was shorter and held 40 gallons (181 litres), but it shared that side of the vehicle with the pressure bottle and other related items. The flame-gun itself was a relatively large piece of equipment that rose out of the rear hull, rested on the bulkhead that separated the front compartment and poked out over the flame-gunner's head. By packing the rear of the Carrier with equipment there was room for only two crew members – the driver and flame-gunner – and access to the engine was virtually impossible. Worse still, the flame-gun was such a large and conspicuous object that it would be obvious to the enemy, even before it flamed, that here was some sort of weapon a good deal more lethal than a Bren gun, and hence marked the Wasp I as a priority target.

The flame-projector could be traversed, elevated and depressed to a limited extent and, using a thickened fuel, in ideal conditions could squirt out fuel to ranges up to 150 yards (137m). Pressure was supplied by CO_2 and later compressed-air cylinders that, as in the original Ronson, used a heat exchanger to vaporize the propellant.

However, although using this system it was theoretically possible to eject the flame fuel in one long squirt, the process developed and patented by Fraser did not permit the Wasp to flame in this way. In the original scheme as developed by AEC, ignition at the nozzle of the flame-projector was constant, but Fraser preferred an arrangement whereby the ignition system only ignited once flame fuel was ejected. So, in all Wasp-type projectors, the correct process was to fire short bursts of flame and not one long, continuous burn.

Orders for 1,000 Wasp Mark Is were placed and, as soon as they realized that it was a great improvement on the Ronson, the Canadian Army also took an interest although, as we shall see, they had other designs of their own in the pipeline. Deliveries were completed by late 1943.

Due to the delays imposed by Donald Banks, it was August 1943 before prototypes of the new Wasp Mark II were ready for testing. The projector itself was a good deal smaller than that used on the Mark I, although it had a slightly increased bore. It was also possible to install it in the weapons slot at the front of the Carrier, rendering it a good deal less conspicuous. Yet it had improved elevation, depression and traverse when compared with the Mark I. Another factor that Fraser had to take into account was weight. This steadily reduced, as far as the equipment was concerned, with each successive model. Partly this improvement was connected with handling. The complete flamethrower kit for the conversion of a Universal Carrier came packaged in crates that unit fitters had to handle and install. Thus, the lighter they were, the better. On the other hand, increased fuel capacity meant extra overall weight on the vehicle so any compensatory reduction in material weight was welcome.

Although it was an entirely different discipline within the scientific community, the development of a suitable fuel for flamethrowers was of equal importance and also came under the umbrella of the PWD. Thin, highly inflammable fluids such as petrol produce an impressive result in the form of great billowing clouds of flame and smoke. It impresses the observer, but in reality does relatively little harm. Something thicker that ejects from the projector like a rod of fire not only travels farther but is also far easier to aim and, in the form of an inflammable gel, sticks to what it hits and goes on burning for a while. British and American scientists, working in what might be termed cooperative competition, came up with two solutions that were suitable for use in both flamethrowers and bombs. The British contribution was Fuel Research Aluminium Stearate (FRAS) while in the United States Napthenic and Palm Oil Acid was produced as Napalm. For reasons of security and surprise it was agreed that this thickened flame fuel would not be released for use until D-Day, when it would be employed in another surprise package, the Churchill Crocodile.

This is definitely a prototype Churchill II Crocodile and trailer taking part in an official demonstration at Langhurst. Flame fuel trailers used for these early trials lacked the various details seen on those issued for active service.

ENTER THE CROCODILE

The official decision of August 1942 notwithstanding, the PWD continued work on tank flamethrowers and, in keeping with the DTD preference, concentrated on the Infantry Tank Mark IV: the A22 or Churchill. Donald Banks admits that progress was slow, for priority had to be given to the Wasp while that was the official favourite. There is some evidence to suggest that work on the Churchill was carried out at the old MoS establishment at Langhurst rather than the PWD's site at Moody Down, perhaps to keep the unofficial project out of sight.

Since this was a somewhat clandestine affair, surviving records are limited, but what evidence there is suggests that the prototype was developed around a Mark II Churchill, the version with a cast turret and 2-pdr gun. It appears to have been completed by December 1942 and cannot have been too secret, as it is mentioned in the Royal Armoured Corps' (RAC) six-monthly report for the second half of 1942, which states that although it was not then a General Staff requirement the PWD was hoping to change their minds by means of a demonstration in the near future. The same report also states that in a recent trial flame had been projected for a distance of 200 yards (182m).

One condition of the project was that it should not inhibit, in any way, the normal fighting capabilities of the tank. As recorded earlier, the DTD had stated in June 1942 that it favoured the idea of a tank with some sort of trailer to carry the flame fuel. A single-wheel, castoring type had already been tested and found wanting, so a two-wheeler based loosely on the old MoS design was developed. It was a substantial item in its own right, armoured to 0.47in (12mm) standard and weighing in the region of 6.4 tons (6.5 tonnes). The shape will be obvious from the plates. Inside were two large fuel containers which, between them, held 400 gallons (1,818 litres) of flame fuel and five compressed-air cylinders to deliver propellant. There was also a good deal of plumbing and a series of control valves along with a hand-operated pump, in a compartment at the front, that could be used for filling the fuel tanks.

In an ideal world no tank should ever tow a trailer. It is always a nuisance and inhibits the tank's ability to move at will across country, but there are times when it

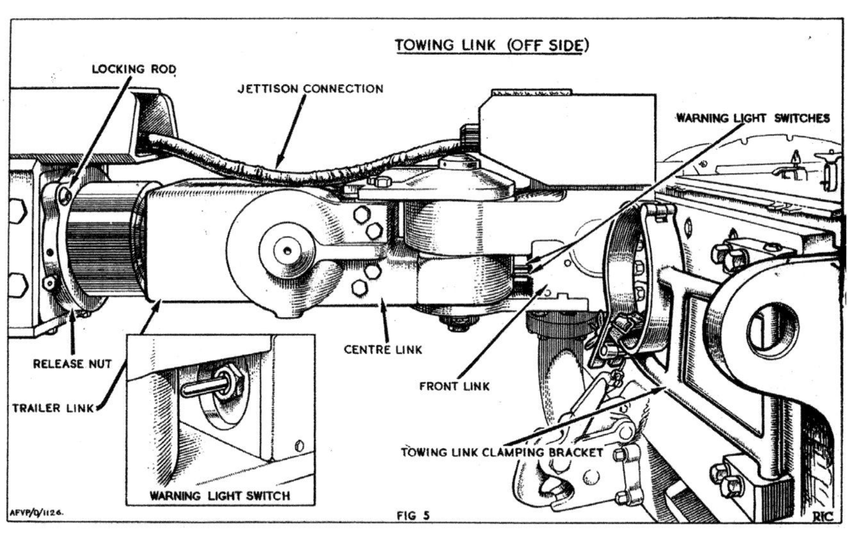

The Link: the connection between a Churchill and its trailer which truly defines the Crocodile. Inset we see the little micro-switch that defines the limit of turning.

CHURCHILL MARK VII Crocodile Flamethrower and Trailer

Essentially this tank is an Infantry Tank Mark IV, type A22F, the final production version of the Churchill. It retains virtually all the standard features of that tank including the 75mm gun and co-axial Besa machine gun in the turret. The only difference is that the hull machine gun, at the front, alongside the driver's position, is replaced by a flame projector. Since the interior of the tank remains standard we have elected to show mostly those hidden features that are peculiar to the flame-thrower role. One of the most impressive features of the design was the complicated Link which not only served as a drawbar between tank and trailer but also as a secure conduit for flame fuel and compressed air.

The object is to expel blazing fuel from the nozzle of the projector which is set in a ball mounting (43) that includes the original machine-gun cradle and is free to move around to a limited extent, controlled by the gunner. His right hand grasps the trigger mechanism (37) at the back of the mounting while he aims the weapon using the long arm (41), reaching outwards to the left. Bearing in mind that red represents sections of the tank cut away to reveal detail then yellow shows the plumbing associated with fuel supply, blue the piping for compressed air and pale green the electrical circuitry required to ignite the fuel. On the trailer, with the upper armour removed, we can see two large fuel containers (22) and the compressed air cylinders (20) sandwiched between them. A complex network of pipes carries the pressurized air into a system of valves and filters that provide propulsion for the fuel mixture which, by means of a large-diameter pipe, now passes through a series of universal joints known as The Link (29/30), which connects the Crocodile trailer to the tank. At this point the fuel is directed downwards, at the rear of the tank and, mostly in a protective duct, beneath the hull until it re-enters, through a hole in the floor protected by a deflector (36). Here the fuel pipe splits in two so that unexpended fuel can be circulated back through the system, although at this stage it is not under serious pressure. Meanwhile another, smaller pipe, also passing through The Link delivers compressed air to a reservoir (38) situated close to the flame gunner's seat. There is no electrical connection with the trailer but there is an independent circuit around the tank that carries power from the tank's own system, aided by its auxiliary generator as required and via a series of control boxes available to certain crew members, to a final junction at the front, including two coils which generate the ignition spark. Here it all comes together, along with a supply of petrol pumped from the Churchill's own fuel tank, which initiates ignition. In reality the rear end of the projector would be covered by a shield in order to protect the flame gunner but this is not shown in the interests of clarity. The Link is an impressive combination of considerable strength, remarkable flexibility but very fine engineering that enables fuel to pass from the trailer to the tank no matter how many twists and turns the pair undergo, nor what strain the junction may be under on very difficult ground. Yet, at the same time, should it prove necessary to ditch the trailer in a hurry this was easily done with the loss of only a few drops of fuel. Once separated from the trailer, and as time permitted, the segment of towing Link still attached to the rear of the Churchill could be folded aside and secured by a special bracket (15). (Art by Tony Bryan, © Osprey Publishing)

Specifications

Crew: five
Combat weight: 45 tons 15 cwt. (46,484kg)
Overall length: 40ft 6.1/2 in. (12.3m)
Width: 10ft 8in (3.2m)
Height: 8ft 2in (2.4m)
Engine: Bedford Twin-Six 350bhp
Transmission: Merritt-Brown H41
Fuel capacity: (Churchill tank): 150 gallons (682 litres)
Maximum speed: 13.5mph (21km/h)
Maximum range: 90 miles (144k)
Fuel consumption: 0.6mpg (0.2k/l)
Fording depth (unprepared): 3ft 4in. (1m)
Armament: 75mm Mark V & 7.92mm Besa MG
Ammunition: 84 rounds
Muzzle velocity: 2,030fps (618m)
Effective range: 2,000 yards (1,828m)
Gun elevation/depression: 20 deg/12.5 deg
Flame fuel capacity: 400 gallons (1,818 litres)
Duration of fire: 4.7 gallons (21 litres) per second
Effective range: 110 yards (100.5m)

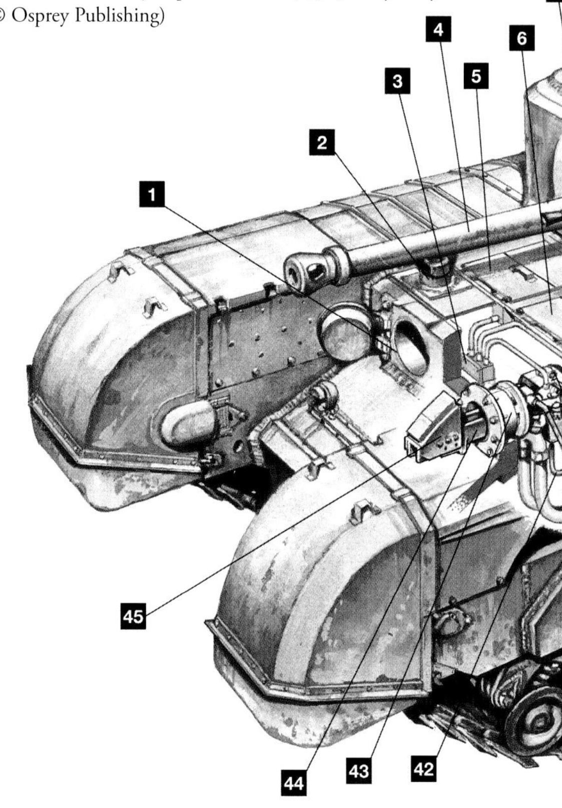

Key

1 Driver's aperture
2 Driver's periscope
3 Driver's control box
4 75mm main armament
5 Driver's hatch
6 Flame gunner's hatch
7 Co-axial machine gun
8 Twin (50.8mm) smoke-bomb thrower
9 Loader's periscope
10 Turret ventilator
11 Gunner's periscope
12 Loader's hatch
13 Commander's hatch
14 Ethyl bromide fire extinguisher
15 Towing Link support bracket
16 Jettison block
17 Trailer jettison release gear
18 Main control valve
19 Control panel
20 Compressed air cylinders
21 Manhandling tube.
22 Flame fuel tanks
23 Rear access door opening
24 Manhandling tube socket
25 Drain valve
26 Fuel valve
27 Trailer support leg
28 Spill box
29 Rear Link
30 Front Link
31 Rear junction box
32 Fuel pipe conduit
33 Commander's control box
34 Side hull door
35 Flame gunner's control box
36 Deflector (where fuel pipe enters hull)
37 Flame gun trigger
38 Low pressure gas reservoir
39 Flame gun controller
40 Flame fuel pipes
41 Flame gun direction control handle
42 Gas pipe
43 Flame gun ball mounting
44 Flame gun cradle
45 Counterweight

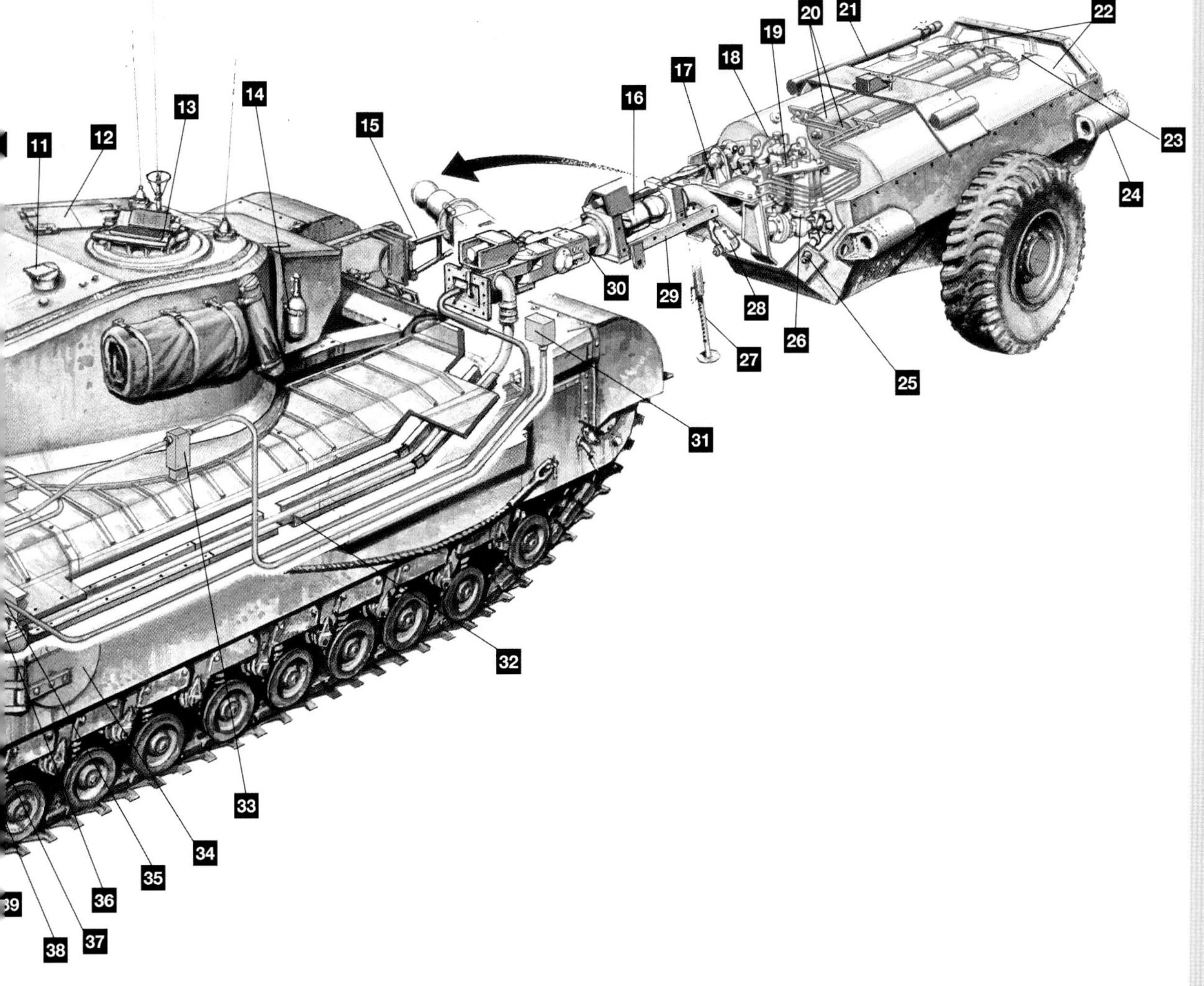

A Churchill VII Crocodile demonstrates the range and lethal effect of a solid jet of thickened flame fuel, which continues to burn where drops fall to the ground. Squirting fuel and setting fire to it afterwards was referred to as a 'wet shot'.

is unavoidable, the case of the Crocodile being one. It was now up to the designers to devise something that would follow the tank more or less anywhere and yet provide an uninterrupted flow of flame fuel and pressurized propellant. The connection between trailer and tank, always referred to as The Link, was a substantial affair as might be imagined. Formed almost as an extension of the front end of the trailer, it was connected by three large, swivelling joints to a final section that bolted onto the rear plate of the tank. It was, at least in theory, possible for the tank to twist and turn in virtually every direction without upsetting the trailer or doing anything to stop the flow of fuel and gas, but there were limits. If the trailer got into a situation where it was turned either side as far as it could go, and in danger of damaging itself against the rear of the tank, a micro-switch was activated that caused a red or green light to appear in front of the driver, who knew that he could turn no farther, either left or right depending on the light. Also, it probably goes without saying, the tank was quite unable to execute a neutral turn while the trailer was attached. No brakes were fitted to the trailer, nor shock-absorbing springs. For the former it relied on the mass of the tank to hold it in check and it was assumed that the large Runflat pneumatic tyres would be sufficient to cushion the ride at the speeds envisaged.

From the back of the tank a pipe ran down, beneath the bottom of the hull and up through an opening in the floor (normally used to dispose of used shell cases). From here the tube rose up, passed over the hull gunner's right shoulder and entered the base of the projector located in front of the gunner. Although it was hoped to modify tanks to the flamethrower role with as little structural work as possible, it was essential that the front plate, containing the driver's visor and hull machine-gun mounting, be changed. The reason was that in this early design it was intended to make the flame-projector co-axial with the hull machine gun. Maybe this was overstretching the requirement not to interfere with the tank's normal fighting arrangements, but it did mean that the hull gunner, using the same sighting telescope for both, could fire the flame-gun or the Besa machine gun as necessary.

This revealing photograph is another mystery. It is assumed to show the prototype Crocodile, which employed a Mark II Churchill, but the boss on the near side just above the headlamp suggests that it was once an Oke and clearly not one of those sent to Dieppe.

To operate the flamethrower the gunner first had to activate a series of switches, one of which produced a fine spray of petrol from the vehicle's fuel tank. Another set up a circuit for the spark to ignite the petrol spray, which in turn set the main fuel jet alight once that was turned on. With the flame jet ignited the gunner placed with his eye to the sighting telescope, and moving the projector in its mounting he could squirt long bursts in a flaming rod directly at the target or lob small blobs of flame higher to drop behind an obstacle or into a trench. Another method was to first soak the target in unignited fuel and then set it alight with a quick burst of flame. From the victims' point of view it was, by any standards, a terrifying experience to be on the receiving end of a jet of blazing oil. But aiming and firing flame was a slow process and easy to see, so anyone who kept his nerve, at least in the open, stood a chance of avoiding it. Cooped up inside a pillbox under flame attack might be another matter.

Once the trailer had expended its contents, or if it became damaged or caught on an obstacle, it could be disengaged by means of a quick release, activated by a Bowden cable. In theory it was then possible for the tank to continue in action as a conventional gun tank, while the trailer was recovered from the battlefield by a lorry or tractor. To this end the trailer came complete with an additional tow bar that could be fitted at the front and linked to the standard tow hook of a suitable vehicle. Poles were provided that could be used to manhandle the trailer, should the need arise, and a set of tubular legs was also carried, which would support the trailer on an even keel when it was not attached to a tank.

The PWD retained a crew of RTR personnel at Langhurst to man the tank and among those who witnessed one of their demonstrations was Major-General P. C. S. Hobart, commander of the specialist 79th Armoured Division, who would later control the Crocodiles in action, at least vicariously. He is reported as being enthusiastic. However, the key figure at this time appears to have been Major-General Alec Richardson. As Richardson was an RAC advisor to the General Staff, his opinion carried a lot of weight, but he had been overseas at the crucial time when tank flamethrower development was in the doldrums and he was not due to return before December 1942. When he did, and discovered the state of play, he was quite horrified. Banks laid on a special demonstration of the Crocodile for him at Langhurst on 14 January 1943, which clearly made the right impression. On 23 March Hangmore was again the venue for a demonstration for the War Office and, as a result, the project to develop a flamethrowing tank was reinstated in April. Time, however, was running out.

Two days after the Hangmore demonstration the prototype Crocodile was taken to Dunwich, where the commanding officer of 54th Division wanted to try out an armoured sledge. This appears to have been an open-topped box, with a hinged ramp at the front like a landing craft and capable of carrying 12 infantrymen. The trials revealed that the sledge could be hitched onto the back of the Crocodile trailer and towed along quite happily, even over rough country and trenches. It may not have been

Crocodiles of B Squadron, 141st RAC, which took part in the American attack on Brest. Extra stowage soon got added to the trailers, as well as the tanks. For a while some of these Churchills were fitted with Culin hedgerow cutters.

terribly comfortable for the men inside, and one wonders how happy they might have been travelling so close to 400 gallons (1,818 litres) of highly inflammable liquid on a live battlefield, but in the event there is no evidence that it was ever used. However, one other lesson came unbidden from this experience. The east coast of England is renowned for its weather, not entirely to its credit. One demonstration took place in a gale of wind estimated at between 60 and 80mph (96 and 128km/h) and it was found that when it blew as a cross-wind the range of the flamethrower was very much reduced and the jet of flame itself whipped away without ever touching the ground.

The prototype Crocodile was taken over for examination by MoS specialists, since it was appreciated that if any were to be ready for operations the following summer there would be no time to develop an alternative design. Permission to go ahead was given in August 1943 with an order for 250 units, and this before any more prototypes could be produced or troop trials undertaken. Indeed, before production work could begin drawings would be required, most of which would have to be taken directly from the prototype. It was now agreed that the production Crocodile would be based upon the current production Churchill, the 57mm gun Mark IV.

Later in the year plans changed as a new version of the Churchill tank, the A22F Mark VII, was entering production and it was now decided that this, too, should be adaptable to the Crocodile role. At about the same time it was decided to drop production of a new flame-projector in the Crocodile in favour of the tried and tested Wasp unit. This change involved some reduction in maximum range, to about 120 yards (110m) in ideal conditions, but it was felt that the Wasp already worked so well that there was nothing to be gained by developing yet another weapon. However, this meant that it would now no longer be possible to fit the flame-projector in the hull mounting with a co-axial Besa, so the machine gun was dropped. Since the flame-gun fitted the same mounting it was perfectly possible to replace one with the other as required.

CHURCHILL VII CROCODILE, B SQUADRON, 1ST FIFE & FORFAR YEOMANRY, RIVER RHINE, MARCH 1945

The US Ninth Army, operating immediately alongside British and Canadian forces in the advance into Germany, made considerable use of Crocodiles, and in particular those of B Squadron, 1st Fife & Forfar Yeomanry, in March 1945 part of 31st Armoured Brigade, 79th Armoured Division. The advantage of this proximity was that supplies of flame fuel and pressure cylinders were easier to maintain. We view the tank as it flames. Notice that divisional insignia and unit codes are repeated on the trailer. As the second most senior armoured regiment in the 31st Armoured Brigade (as formed in February 1945), 1st Fife & Forfar wear 992 in white on a green square. (Art by Tony Bryan, © Osprey Publishing)

OPERATIONAL USE

Six prototype Crocodiles were said to be nearing completion in October 1943, but there was still some uncertainty about the arrangements for operating them. It seems that for a while the War Office favoured the idea of supplying the flame equipment to units equipped with the right type of tanks, to be fitted as required, and a complicated drill evolved, at least on paper, to effect this. What it amounted to was that a given regiment would be notified that Crocodile equipment was on the way so that it could start preparing some of its tanks by removing the front armour plate (no mean task in itself) along with the Besa mounting and floor hatch. One trailer would arrive for each tank, towed by a D7 Caterpillar tractor, and this would be parked in front of the tank. Stowed on top of the trailer was everything required to complete a Crocodile, including the new front armour plate. There was some doubt as to whether this procedure really could be done in the field and if it was deemed beyond the capabilities of the regimental Light Aid Detachment (LAD) then it would have to become a Base Workshops task.

Had this practice been adopted then Crocodiles might have operated when required by any Churchill tank regiment in the same way that it was planned to incorporate Wasp Carriers into infantry battalions. This appears to ignore the fact that the Crocodile was a highly specialized weapon, to be used sparingly and requiring a very high level of crew training. In any case, things changed when it was discovered that a conversion kit to cover both Mark IV and Mark VII versions of the Churchill was not feasible, and in the end it was agreed that Crocodile conversions should be limited to the new Mark VII. In practice, of course, this meant that the same conversion could be applied to the Mark VIII, which was essentially the Mark VII armed with a 95mm howitzer, although Crocodile versions of the Mark VIII are very rare. It is also quite likely that no Mark IV Churchill Crocodiles ever existed. Indeed it seems highly unlikely that field conversions were ever carried out. Late-production Churchills came complete with all the basic fittings necessary to convert into Crocodiles with a minimum of extra work, even down to holes, drilled and tapped into the machine-gun mounting, to which the armoured counterweight of the flame-projector could be bolted.

In fact, as the War Office soon realized, it made a lot more sense to dedicate specific regiments to operate the Crocodiles rather than simply spread them around to all and sundry. This policy came as a considerable surprise to the first regiment so dedicated: 7th Battalion The Buffs (otherwise known as the Royal East Kent Regiment), for the duration of the war to be known as 141st Regiment, RAC, was doing gunnery training in their Churchill tanks at Warcop when the commanding officer and the intelligence officer were summoned to London. They returned with news that the regiment would be converting to operate flamethrowers and that speed was of the essence. Some of them would be required to go ashore on D-Day, which was just ten weeks away.

According to an anonymous chronicler of 141st RAC, Crocodile training was confined both in terms of time and space available. Although 79th Armoured Division was not involved with flamethrowers at this time, it is probable that 43rd Royal Tank Regiment, which was the division's experimental regiment, may have done some of the initial work. But according to The Buffs much of this training proved to be wrong, at least at the outset. An officer who wrote some initial historical notes says that they trained to attack buildings and strongpoints, but in Normandy the regiment spent most of its time dealing with woods, trenches and similar obstacles.

The regiment was in fact suffering from precisely those difficulties that had been anticipated with the other 'Funnies' administered by 79th Armoured Division. For example, 141st RAC assumed that it knew best about the operational employment of flamethrowers and found that it was constantly in conflict with divisional commanders who were also trained to believe that they knew best about everything. In particular, it was difficult to make infantry understand that they needed to stay up close with the Crocodiles and actually advance through the flame to take advantage of the initial shock. Furthermore, one should not forget that, as part of the original design, the Crocodile was also a fighting tank, and that may well have been a tactical mistake.

By this time, naturally, 141st RAC had accumulated a great deal of experience, not only in dozens of minor actions but in at least two major ones. In the first, B Squadron, at the request of General Omar Bradley, supported the US Ninth Army in an attack on the fortified port of Brest. Then in September 1944 Operation Astonia, the attack on Le Havre, involved most of the regiment in a massive and highly formalized assault embracing all the resources of 79th Armoured Division.

On 14 June 1944 (D-Day + 8) three Crocodiles of 15 Troop, 141st RAC, advanced on the occupied village of La Senaudiere in Normandy on the incorrect understanding that British infantry were about to attack. Instead, the three Churchills found themselves sharing the village with German tanks. One, a Panther, put two rounds through a Crocodile trailer that, contrary to expectations, did not burn, but one Crocodile was later lost and went up in flames very quickly. Fear of fire was the

normal condition for most tank men, but in the Crocodile it had an extra dimension. It was hardly surprising that the regiment felt ill used and it was also suffering from too much dispersion.

As a regular Churchill regiment the 141st was trained to fight as an entity or at least in squadron strength, but now that everyone wanted a few Crocodiles, even when the rest of the regiment arrived in France later in June, it would often find itself spread across a three-division front, fighting as individual troops. Certain details aside, the organization was based on an armoured regiment in a tank brigade: that is three squadrons, each responsible for five troops each of three Crocodiles, one of which in each troop would be equipped with an extra No. 19 radio set to act as a Control Tank.

To begin with 141st RAC was something of an orphan among the armoured units in France, although more or less under the control of 31st Army Tank Brigade. This relationship was formalized in August 1944, and then in September the 141st became part of the all-embracing 79th Armoured Division. This organization made a great deal of sense, since Crocodiles could be classed as 'Funnies' the same as Flail tanks or Armoured Vehicle Royal Engineers (AVREs). They also needed the same kind of administrative control to reduce the incidence of poor employment. Divisional commanders who believed they had the authority to retain the Crocodiles once a specific operation was over soon learned that a 79th Armoured Division advisor had what amounted to absolute power over the loaned equipment and was not to be tangled with. Not that this helped with the regiment's desire to fight as a body, indeed it made it worse. From October 1944 the squadron organization was modified so that it now comprised three troops, each of four Crocodiles and a fourth troop of three. The reason was that now it would be possible, at least in the majority of cases, to field half-troops of just two Crocodiles when required. However, the pressure this created on Crocodile crews was eased to some extent in October, when a second Crocodile regiment joined the brigade in the form of 1st Fife & Forfar Yeomanry.

ABOVE LEFT Topping up the trailer with flame fuel was also hard work. The bulk of the fuel was poured straight from 45-gallon (204-litre) drums when possible, but in action every drop was precious so it was essential to fill it right up to the top, another back-breaking duty.

ABOVE Two troopers, with their cap badges conveniently blotted out by the censor (but probably 141st RAC), demonstrate that fitting pressure cylinders, all five of them, into a Crocodile trailer is no easy task.

CHURCHILL VII CROCODILE, 15 TROOP, C SQUADRON, 141ST REGIMENT ROYAL ARMOURED CORPS, NORMANDY, 6 JUNE 1944

Preparing a tank for deep wading, as from landing craft to shore, was a long, tiresome and messy business. Every hatch and orifice had to be sealed, every crack filled with a sticky, mastic compound and extensions added to air intake and exhaust pipes. Special books were printed to ensure that everything was done properly and the object, with all types of vehicle, was to ensure that it could keep going while immersed in up to 6ft (1.8m) of water. Three Crocodiles of 141st RAC were included in the D-Day plan to come ashore at Le Hamel on Gold Beach, where they unconsciously re-enacted events at Dieppe. One tank drowned when it took to the water, the second got itself bogged down in a shell crater while the third, having made it across the beach, broke a track. Virtually all markings are below water level in this case, but the tank still presents a colourful sight with the silver, waterproof fabric around the turret ring, mantlet and weapons. Tyres on the trailer were so large that it was almost buoyant. (Art by Tony Bryan, © Osprey Publishing)

LESSONS LEARNED

'Lessons learned' is a popular military phrase – often quoted, sometimes heeded. From the point of view of the Crocodiles, there was a lot to learn. In action, for example, crews soon realized how important it was to shield the trailer as much as possible with the tank. Armoured to withstand nothing more potent than small-arms fire the trailer was a very vulnerable item. Both driver and commander were constantly aware that it must not be exposed to enemy fire and there was need for considerably more manoeuvring than the crew of an ordinary tank needed to worry about.

There was also the business of preparing for action. It is not known how often the special pump was used, but it soon became normal practice to fill the containers in each trailer direct from 45-gallon (204-litre) drums. A framework of scaffolding pipes was constructed so that the drums could be rolled direct from the transporting lorry to a position above the trailer and the liquid poured straight in, topping up being done from smaller drums. But that was only the half of the procedure; next came the job of pressuring up. Gradually, carefully, the five pressure cylinders were turned on (nitrogen was now preferred to compressed air). Do it too quickly and one was liable to damage many of the valves and piping. That done, however, it was imperative to get into action as soon as possible. During training one officer from 141st RAC had referred to the Crocodile trailer as a mobile air leak, and if the action was delayed for any time pressure would steadily drop until the flame fuel emerged as a pathetic trickle. If that happened the tank would have to withdraw from action while the crew went through the back-breaking process of replacing the cylinders. It called for fine judgement and,

CHURCHILL VII CROCODILE, A SQUADRON, 7TH ROYAL TANK REGIMENT, HOLLAND, JANUARY 1945

The use of whitewash to camouflage tanks against a snowy background was common but of dubious value on such large and noisy machines. In any case it has started to wash off this Crocodile. A section of the trackguard alongside the turret has deliberately been removed. Churchill crews discovered that if it was damaged and bent upwards this section of trackguard could prevent the turret from traversing. Whitewash has also been applied to the Crocodile trailer, but this has been compromised by a sheet of canvas laid to protect whatever is stowed there. All markings on the tank would have been obliterated by the whitewash, but as senior regiment in the brigade the 7th RTR would show 991 on a green square and red squadron symbols. No name is shown on this tank but it is worth recording that in its new guise as 7th RTR the regiment seems to have retained its old 10th RTR names, which all began with J. (Art by Tony Bryan, © Osprey Publishing)

as best they could, crews liked to wait until they were within about 30 minutes of action before turning on the pressure. At least in the Carriers, where the pressure cylinders were handy, one could more or less turn them on or off at will.

For long-distance moves, such as the journey to Brest undertaken by B Squadron, 141st RAC, the tanks went by transporter while the trailers were towed by lorries. Each squadron was provided with 15 AEC Matador Medium Artillery Tractors for this role, but written accounts indicate that when they were available the big Mack NM6 tractors were used because the unsprung, unbraked trailers could be quite a handful on the road. There is also some evidence to suggest that M3 half-tracks, of which each squadron had three, could be used, possibly to recover abandoned trailers from the battlefield.

Richard Harley's drawing of a Crocodile trailer being towed by a Mack NM6. This was a six-wheel drive truck in the 6-ton class issued to the British Army as a Medium Artillery Tractor, a role that it shared with the AEC Matador 4x4, which it sometimes also supplanted.

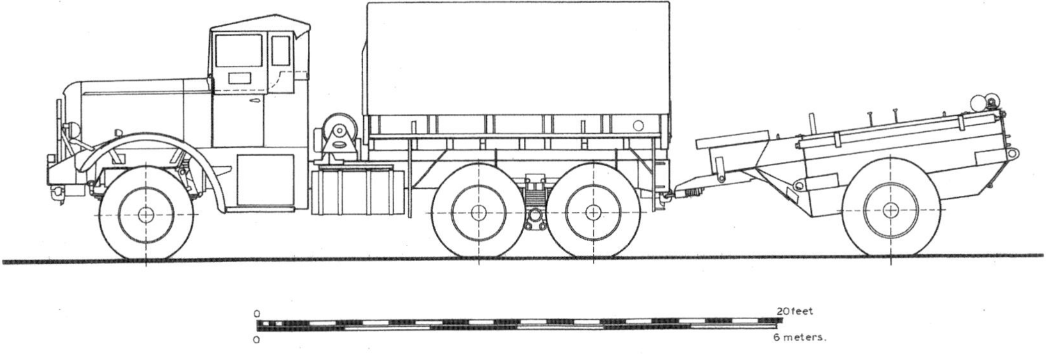

A Wasp IIC on a railway wagon. This example has panels of the so-called plastic armour applied, both inside and out around the crew compartment at the front.

CANADIAN WASPS

The Canadians accepted British developments with Carriers such as the Wasp II up to a point, but they were not sold on the need to put the fuel tanks under armour. They wanted to maintain the general utility of the Universal Carrier and decided to install a 75-gallon (340-litre) container crosswise, outside the armour at the back. The result was designated the Wasp IIC. In most other respects the two types were identical, but the Canadians saw two advantages to their design. In the first place it meant that the Wasp IIC could be used, to a certain extent, as a regular Carrier without having to dismantle all the flame equipment. They also pointed out that, even in the flamethrower role, the vehicle's ability to carry a third crew member in the rear, on the left side of the engine, meant that he could use a light machine gun or a 2in mortar, in addition to acting as an observer able to spot things that the driver or flame operator might miss.

Canada also developed a new Carrier flamethrower, which they called the Barracuda. Reginald Fraser examined the drawings for the PWD and reported to Banks in March 1943. He was not very impressed. The flame-gun, which he said was reputedly the Barracuda's best feature, was simply a modified Cockatrice and he doubted if it could meet the claims made on its behalf for range. A few days later a comparative trial was arranged between a prototype Barracuda and what Fraser referred to as a Wasp III – which we assume was in fact the Mark II. He told Banks that any suggestion that the two designs should be amalgamated was not a good idea: 'I can only suggest that the Barracuda is a badly brought-up child of too near a relationship for legal marriage!'

The first recorded employment of the Wasp II in action occurred in late July or early August 1944 near Hill 112 in Normandy. It seems reasonable to assume that, for flame operations at least, a section of three Carriers would be fitted with Wasp equipment. Even so, on this scale flame was very much a weapon of opportunity and it would make sense that every battalion, once convinced of the value of flame, would maintain at least one section ready for action at all times.

With the buildings of Belsen Camp blazing in the background, the crew of a Wasp IIC belonging to 4th Battalion, Somerset Light Infantry, 43rd Wessex Division, take a break. Notice how they have adorned their Carrier with spare links of tank track to enhance protection.

This option would certainly become easier after August 1944 when the Canadian Wasp IIC became available. Definitive evidence is wanting, but it seems likely that Wasp equipment was issued as supplies arrived in theatre, so that British battalions could be found operating the Canadian Wasp IIC and vice versa. While the Crocodile, by its very nature, was best suited to formal, pre-planned attacks, the Wasps appear to have been employed on a more immediate basis. For example, a nest of enemy machine guns, tucked into a hedgerow, would be an ideal target. While one or two guns might suffer the full treatment of flame, the rest would rapidly evacuate the area as soon as the flame started to belch forth.

A posed photograph by an official photographer shows a Crocodile of 7th Royal Tank Regiment and its extended crew outside Belsen, which they had helped to burn to the ground.

M4A4 SHERMAN V ADDER PROTOTYPE

As a Sherman flamethrower, the Adder seems to have been a much more practical proposition than the Crocodile. It may not have had the capacity of a Crocodile trailer, but it was much more self-contained and interfered very little with the fighting capabilities of the tank. Eighty gallons (363 litres) of flame fuel was carried in a hull extension made from 14mm (0.55-in.) armour plate, which also contained the pressure cylinder and valves. The fuel pipe, where it ran along the edge of the hull, was also protected by an armoured duct while the flame-projector itself replaced the hull machine-gunner's periscope. Modifications to the tank itself were minimal. An additional grille was fitted on top of the hull at the very back and one of the internal stowage bins had to be moved so that four rounds of 75mm ammunition were lost. This was to make room for a flexible pipe that curved around inside the hull to connect up with the projector. The projector, incidentally, was fitted with a No. 35 sighting telescope in place of the periscope. The tank, which has appliqué armour panels on the side, is finished in standard US olive drab and the only visible marking is the British War Department (WD) number T147340. (Art by Tony Bryan, © Osprey Publishing)

THE CROCODILES EXPAND

Like other elements of 79th Armoured Division the Crocodiles soon attracted the attention of the division's inventive engineers. Trials were conducted with Crocodiles towing stores sledges, or even gutted Universal Carriers as stores trailers behind the fuel trailer, which must have been a driver's nightmare. Another idea was to use flame to cook-off and explode German Schu mines. A Crocodile was tested for this purpose, but it did not work.

The revived 7th RTR (it had been 10th RTR until April 1943) was the third Churchill regiment to convert to Crocodiles. This took place in February 1945, shortly after the regiment had withdrawn from its part in the investment of Dunkirk. In their training they were assisted by 1st Fife & Forfar Yeomanry. So, for the final four months of the war in Europe, 31st Armoured Tank Brigade included three Crocodile regiments. Not that it ever operated as a complete brigade, or its constituent regiments even as complete regiments come to that. To pick an extreme example, one gets the impression that 1st Fife & Forfar Yeomanry invariably had one squadron supporting elements of the US Army who, by now, seem to have become totally sold on flamethrowers.

The Americans had shown a lot of interest in flame early in 1944, when a Committee on Special Equipment reported to General Eisenhower that Britain would be able to supply equipment to convert 100 Sherman tanks to the Crocodile role, starting in March 1944. It appears to have been an optimistic promise, for although a prototype was soon ready, on an M4A4 (Sherman V) tank, the supply of

LVT IV SEA SERPENT, AMPHIBIAN SUPPORT REGIMENT, ROYAL MARINES, STUDLAND BAY, DORSET, 1945

Since this unique regiment never got the chance to see action with its vehicles, the Sea Serpent is shown as it looked during trials in Britain, at a secure location near Poole Harbour on the south coast. The capacious hold of the Buffalo has been altered to fit a pair of Wasp flamethrowers with fuel tanks and pressure bottles at the front and a simple structure to hold a .30-in. Browning machine gun at the rear. The Wasp projectors were in small turrets, each open at the back, which could be rotated through a limited arc and fired independently. The machine gun appears to have been included for anti-aircraft defence. In service Sea Serpent would carry a crew of five. The regiment's badge, which may have been worn as a shoulder flash, showed a fouled anchor in yellow on a red triangle, itself outlined in yellow along each side and superimposed on a dark-blue shield. It is not clear when this was adopted since the regiment began as the Royal Marine Armoured Support Group, which landed on D-Day. It went out to India in 1945 and saw some action in an infantry role on Java, but returned to Britain in 1946 to become part of the School of Combined Operations at Fremington in north Devon. (Art by Tony Bryan, © Osprey Publishing)

trailers alone was bound to interfere with British requirements. The Sherman Crocodile was arguably a somewhat clumsier conversion than the Churchill due to its design and, in order to keep things simple, the Churchill-type trailer was used and the same coupling but from there everything was external. The flame fuel pipe ran along the right side of the hull in an armoured cover and was connected to a projector located on the sloping hull front plate, close to the hull machine-gunner's position.

Subsequently, American interest declined. The idea of tanks pulling trailers did not appeal and, until the assault on Brest, the activities of British Crocodiles did not inspire

An M4A4 Sherman V fitted with what appears to be a wooden mock-up of the Sherman Crocodile equipment. This was an odd decision in a sense, since the US Army, for whom it was intended, would not use the M4A4 in action if they had any choice in the matter.

The Sherman Crocodile DD sets sail on a very calm day upon the Solent, with the Isle of Wight just visible across the water. The trailer, in this instance, is floating with the aid of an inflatable rubber dinghy lashed to the top.

them. On the other hand, attempts to employ an American-designed tank flamethrower in Normandy were dismissed as pathetic, so interest in the British design was rekindled and four M4 Crocodiles delivered to 739th Tank Battalion in November 1944. They formed a special platoon, but despite requests no more were ordered and their use was limited. Even so, there is evidence that British attempts to improve the design continued after the war and included an amphibious, DD version.

In Italy, where the writ of 79th Armoured Division did not run, it was arranged to kill off the 25th Army Tank Brigade and recreate it as 25th Armoured Engineer Brigade, composed of RAC and Royal Engineer (RE) elements. Although this formation was not officially created until March 1945, most of its constituent regiments had been undergoing conversion a good deal earlier and the one that interests us, 51st Royal Tank Regiment, learned that it would be operating Churchill Crocodiles and Sherman Crab flail tanks. It finally settled on A and C Squadrons for the former which, in keeping with typical Crocodile practice, were subdivided in half-squadrons named Green and Black in A Squadron, Red and Blue in C Squadron.

Calgary is believed to be a Crocodile of C Squadron, 51st Royal Tank Regiment and it was photographed on the River Senio in April 1945. Always regarded as the poor cousin in relation to northwest Europe, Italy would probably never have acquired Churchill Mark VII tanks had they not obtained Crocodiles.

At first few opportunities arose to test the flame weapon in action, and the Crocodiles seem to have remained on stand-by most of the time. The same seems to have been true of the Wasp Carriers with the infantry. The Canadians say that before 16 December 1944 it had not been possible to bring the Wasps up in time to take part in any actions. However, on that date the Westminster Regiment of 5th Canadian Armoured Division employed four Wasps against German positions on the far bank of the Munio Canal, as a result of which the crossing at this point was virtually unopposed.

This action, however, pales into insignificance when compared with the use of flame in support of the crossing of the Senio river on 9 April 1945. Following a massive barrage of bombs and artillery, 28 Churchill Crocodiles and 127 Wasps took up positions on top of the friendly flood bank, spaced roughly 70 yards (64m) apart along a 5-mile (8km) front. They poured out such a deluge of flame that 2nd New Zealand Division, supported by C Squadron 51st RTR, suffered no fatalities at all during the

A version of the Sherman Salamander in which the 75mm gun is replaced by what is described as a 'Long Wasp' flame-projector.

crossing. For the remaining weeks of the campaign in Italy flame was in favour all round but in particular with New Zealand, Indian and Polish forces.

OUT EAST

The potential value of flamethrowing tanks for use in the Far East was quickly appreciated in Britain, but based upon recent experience, particularly in Burma, it was agreed that a trailer would not be a good idea on grounds of manoeuvrability and that a Carrier would be a liability because it lacked overhead cover.

Late in 1943 the PWD, in conjunction with the DTD, proposed a light tank flamethrower, perhaps along similar lines to contemporary American developments. Whether this implied that the light tanks would be American Stuarts or earlier and smaller British types is uncertain, but the former would seem to be more likely. The authorities also stated a preference for cordite rather than gas as the source of pressure since, they reasoned, heavy gas cylinders would be very difficult to transport and handle in jungle conditions. Not that any of this mattered very much. The project was dropped early in 1944 when it was concluded that a more heavily armoured tank would be more suitable so, under the code-name 'Salamander', another project was initiated involving Sherman and Churchill tanks.

The Salamander scheme is not worth studying in great detail since, despite evolving into nine different designs of considerable complexity, it was ultimately dropped. Even so, a rough outline helps to indicate how people were thinking at the time. No trailer was to be used and the flame fuel had to be carried within the tank, under armour. At first it was hoped to install the flame-projector in a fully rotating turret, still retaining the main armament, but this proved impossible and most of the later designs involved a flamethrower replacing, but usually disguised as, the main gun. Naturally this meant that the installation would be permanent. Cordite CO_2 propulsion was rejected since it could not generate sufficient pressure and the majority of versions would have used CO2. The endless succession of designs rather implies indecision, but in any case the scheme was defeated because of difficulties in

A Sherman V (M4A4) Adder with ballast weights to represent stowage is hoisted clear of the ground by a crane, probably to establish the centre of gravity. For details of the additions refer to page 208. Surviving publications also refer to an M4A2 (Sherman III) version of Adder.

producing a safe rotary base junction. The entire scheme was closed down by the end of 1944. Incidentally, the Churchill was only included as an alternative on the first design. All the rest were based on Shermans.

Whether the 'Adder' project began as a result of the demise of Salamander or independently in its own right is not clear, but it was different to the extent that the Adder was a bolt-on arrangement intended to be fitted to a tank as required, at a base workshop if need be. It had much more in common with the old Churchill Oke than anything else and the armoured cover, shielding an 80-gallon (363-litre) fuel container and pressure cylinder at the rear, is almost identical. The rear housing, armoured to 0.55in (14mm), also contained the various valves and controls, although

Hill-climbing trials at Chaklala, India, on 2 April 1946. The Churchill was always a good climber, but it was not regarded as suitable for the Far East on account of the trailer. Even so, some 250 units were earmarked for use in Burma if the Japanese had not surrendered when they did.

The Sea Serpent prepares for a demonstration at Studland Bay in Dorset, while a gaggle of observers prepare to follow it into Poole Bay and witness events from a DUKW.

the master switch could be activated by the flame-gunner. He sat alongside the driver at the front. The hull machine gun was removed but the flame-projector, which had a 180-degree arc of fire, was mounted in place of the periscope in the hatch above the gunner's head and it was fed by a pipe, in an armoured cover, that ran from the tank at the back, along the edge of the hull and through the hull just to the right of this hatch. The weapon had an effective range of 80 yards (73m).

As before, with the Far East in mind the original plan was to develop Adder for the Sherman and the Mamba (later renamed Cobra) for the Churchill. Parts were to be interchangeable as far as possible, but Adder took priority because Shermans were already operational in the Far East whereas Churchills were not. Although 500 kits were ordered the Adder was still not ready when the war ended, but development continued, including an improved version again designed for both the Sherman and Churchill, for issue to India.

One cannot leave this region without mentioning two Australian contributions, the Frog and Murray. Perhaps less well known was Sea Serpent, a British modification to the American Landing Vehicle Tracked (LVT) Mark IV, known as the Buffalo in British service. In 1945 the Royal Marines formed the 34th Amphibian Support Regiment, largely from members of the old Royal Marine Armoured Support Group, supplemented by specialist Army personnel. Transferred to India early in 1945 it was to be equipped with the American LVT (A)4, mounting a 75mm howitzer in the turret, a rocket-firing version and the Sea Serpent itself – the basic LVT IV that mounted a pair of Wasp projectors and an additional Browning machine gun. The war ended before the regiment had a chance to employ its amphibious equipment, but it returned to Britain after the war and remained as a Combined Operations demonstration unit until 1947.

Just to illustrate the amazing versatility of the Wasp, it might be worth recording here that the Royal Electrical & Mechanical Engineers (REME) adapted it to fit the little M29C Weasel amphibian (a device that was more or less copied by the French for use in Indo-China). Most bizarre of all, No. 1 Demolition Squadron, commanded by Vladimir Peniakoff, managed to fit one to a Jeep.

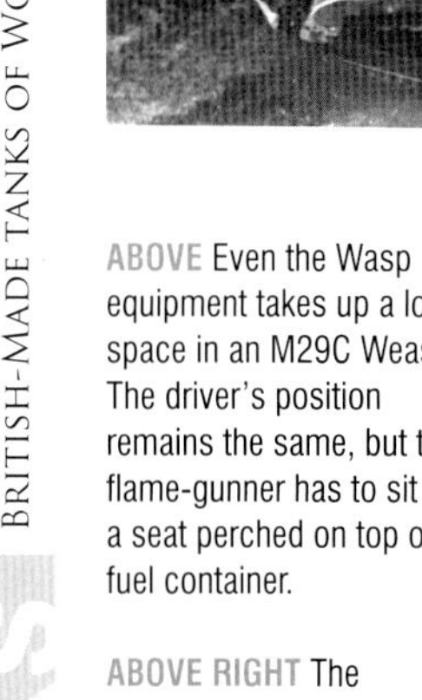

ABOVE Even the Wasp equipment takes up a lot of space in an M29C Weasel. The driver's position remains the same, but the flame-gunner has to sit on a seat perched on top of the fuel container.

ABOVE RIGHT The Crocodile trailer, towed by a Comet, becomes airborne during towing trials over a prepared course.

OPPOSITE The only surviving diagram showing the flame-throwing version of FV201, essentially a Centurion turret on what would become the Conqueror chassis. The flamethrower variant was to have a small turret ahead of the main one, operated by a crew member located to the left of the driver.

THE FLAME GOES OUT

Considering the enthusiasm expressed about the value of flame by so many influential individuals at the end of the war, its rapid disappearance from the scene is difficult to explain. Maybe, under the threat of nuclear war, the flash from a bit of blazing petrol was hardly noticed.

Not that flame was extinguished at once. In August 1946 *The Tank* (the RTR journal) republished an article that first appeared in a Royal Air Force magazine concerning a demonstration laid on for a party of RAF officers by 7th RTR in Germany. It involved a mock flamethrower attack that certainly made a striking impression, although it is often the case that members of one service find the activities of another either baffling or awe-inspiring. Yet by the time this article appeared, 7th RTR was in India operating light tanks and armoured cars, while the rump of 79th Armoured Division, now known as the Specialised Armour Establishment (SAE), continued to experiment and improve the equipment.

As far as flamethrowers were concerned, SAE, when it issued its final report in 1951, was trying out various improvements to the Crocodile. These included a remote-control method of pressuring up, a pressure gauge for the flame-gunner and an offset sighting telescope that would not be obscured by flame and smoke. The Sea Serpent flamethrowing amphibian was still being tested (now under the designation FV502) and attempts were being made to create a DD swimming version of the Sherman Crocodile. Once SAE was disbanded its role was to be taken over by 7th RTR again, now based at Bovington, which became responsible for all of those examples of specialized armour operated by the RAC. Yet it becomes clear, reading between the lines, that the plan was to make flame available to all armoured regiments rather than employing dedicated regiments as was done during the war.

In the intervening years 7th RTR had been busy. Late in 1950 C Squadron, equipped with Crocodiles, had been shipped out to Pusan as part of the British contribution to the United Nations force in Korea. It took quite a while to get everything together and in fact the squadron never operated as a flamethrower unit. Trailers were detached and for the time that they were there the Churchills only ever operated as gun tanks.

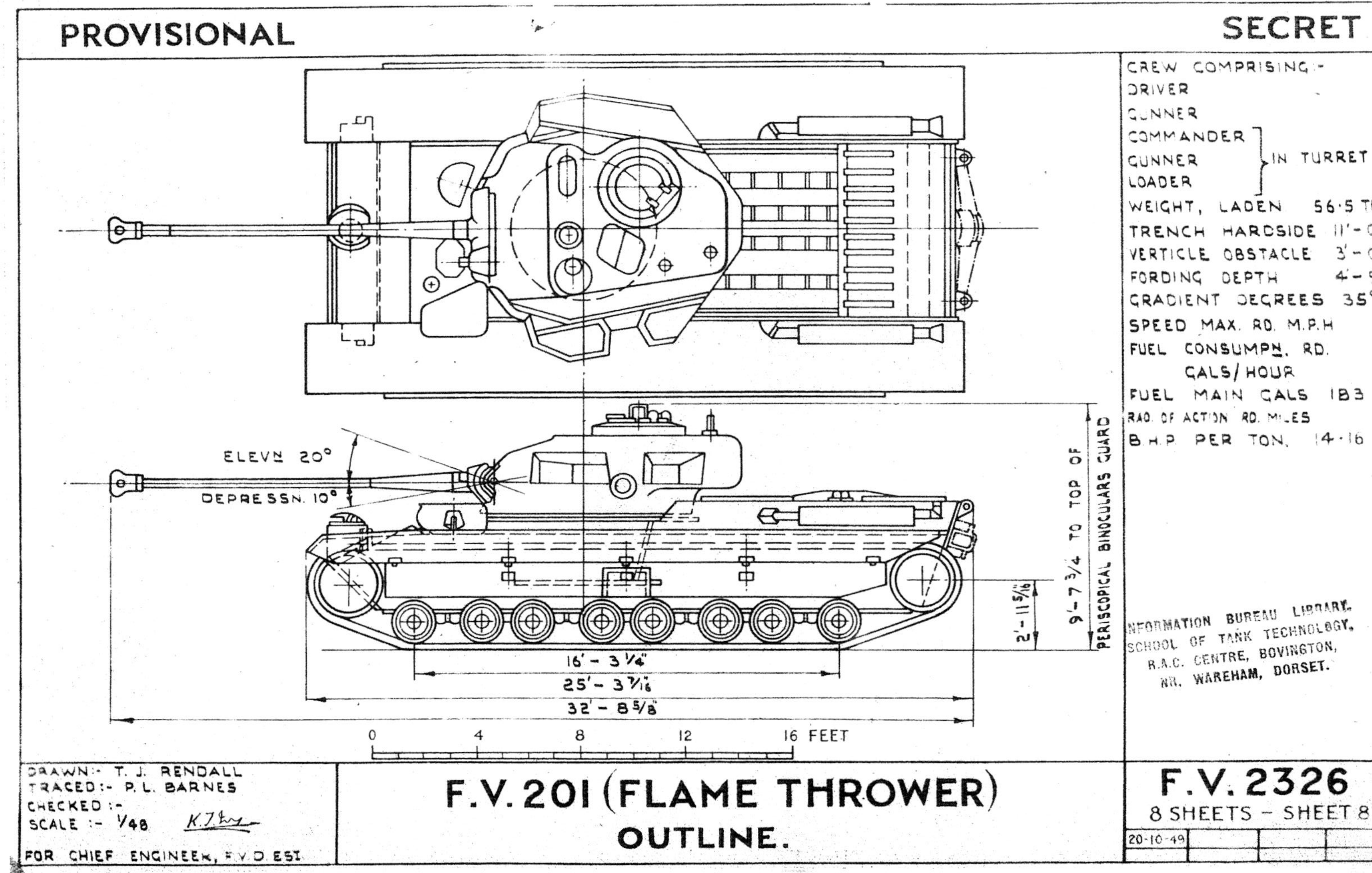
PROVISIONAL
SECRET
CREW COMPRISING:-
DRIVER
GUNNER
COMMANDER
GUNNER
LOADER
IN TURRET
WEIGHT, LADEN 56·5 TON
TRENCH HARDSIDE 11'-0"
VERTICLE OBSTACLE 3'-0"
FORDING DEPTH 4'-9"
GRADIENT DEGREES 35°
SPEED MAX. RD. M.P.H
FUEL CONSUMPN. RD.
GALS/HOUR
FUEL MAIN GALS 183
RAD. OF ACTION RD. MILES
B.H.P. PER TON. 14·16
ELEVN 20°
DEPRESSN. 10°
9'-7 3/4 TO TOP OF
PERISCOPICAL BINOCULARS GUARD
2'-11 5/16
16'-3 1/4"
25'-3 7/16"
32'-8 5/8"
0
4
8
12
16 FEET
INFORMATION BUREAU LIBRARY,
SCHOOL OF TANK TECHNOLOGY,
R.A.C. CENTRE, BOVINGTON,
NR. WAREHAM, DORSET.
DRAWN:- T. J. RENDALL
TRACED:- P. L. BARNES
CHECKED:-
SCALE:- 1/48
FOR CHIEF ENGINEER, F.V.D. EST.
F.V.201 (FLAME THROWER)
OUTLINE.
F.V. 2326
8 SHEETS - SHEET 8
20-10-49

The dubious Comet Crocodile. It may have been nothing more than a tank and trailer combination created to try out the effect of speed on towed trailers. There is no evidence of a flame-projector at the hull machine-gun position.

The Director Royal Armoured Corps (DRAC) used to publish what were known as Liaison Letters, which kept everyone up to date on developments. One issue that came out shortly after the war contained a brief note on flamethrowers. It announced that the Churchill Crocodile would be the main weapon for the immediate future, with a few Sherman Adders in India, while work on the Sherman Crocodile would be suspended and the design of the Churchill Cobra abandoned. But most interesting of all, it went on to say that since Cromwell, Comet and Centurion regiments would not have integral flame equipment it would be necessary to issue Churchill Crocodiles.

There is, in theory, no obvious reason why Crocodile equipment could not be applied to these tanks since, suspension systems aside, the basic hull form was much the same. Granted the Cromwell was already cramped inside and should in any case be phased out of service very soon, but there was not a great deal wrong with Comet in the late 1940s, and of course Centurion was the coming thing. In fact there is evidence, in the shape of one photograph, that a Comet Crocodile existed. No date is given and, beyond the fact that it is towing a trailer, there is no evidence to prove whether it was in fact complete and able to flame. It may have been no more than an experimental test rig – such a thing is known because a report survives concerning a trial in which a Crocodile trailer, attached to a Comet, was towed at speed (well, 8mph/12.8km/h) over a series of obstacles to see what happened. The trailer appears to have spent most of its time airborne and bounced with such violence that it finally broke away from the tank and went off on its own. Maybe this was the reason why the fast cruiser tanks were not considered suitable as Crocodiles. But what of the Centurion?

Originally the idea was rejected because it cut down the amount of ammunition that the tank could carry. In any case, there was a rival. Based on a firm 21st Army

The Ram Badger was a Canadian modification. Wasp projectors were installed in place of the hull machine gun in late-production Rams, indicated here by the arrow. However, this example also has a projector, protected by a shield, mounted on top of the hull.

Group requirement, a heavier tank designated A45 was on the drawing board, probably better known as the Universal Tank, in response to Field Marshal Montgomery's oft-expressed wishes. The idea was to fit the tank with a built-in power take-off so that all manner of attachments and adaptations could be employed. In the case of a flamethrower this would be a pump, operating a Crocodile-type projector mounted on the co-driver's hatch. This projector would traverse to give an arc of fire of 120 degrees. DRAC insisted that a trailer with a capacity of about 400 gallons (1,818 litres) was essential.

By 1946 the A45 designation had been changed to FV201, but as the peacetime economy kicked in many of the features were trimmed and a number had been rejected before the first mild steel pilots appeared. The project was officially dropped in 1948, although a drawing described as FV201 (Flame Thrower) dated October 1949 survives. This, in turn, rejuvenated the Centurion project and a Mark 3 tank was put aside for conversion, albeit with an old Churchill Crocodile trailer. The projector was mounted on top of the hull at the front and the problem next to be solved was who in the crew should operate it? Trials were conducted throughout 1953 and 1954. To begin with they offered the job to the commander, but his vision while closed down proved inadequate. Next they tried the driver, but he was always cutting himself on the control switch and found it difficult to drive and work the flame-gun at the same time. Finally they turned to the loader who had a good view and nothing else to do. The trouble was that with the tank moving he was thrown about all over the place, which did not help his aim. The obvious answer might have been to install another crew position alongside the driver, as they did with the Centurion AVRE, but this was not accepted. Maybe it would have reduced

The post-war variation of the Badger developed by the Canadians gives an impressive demonstration. It is tempting to suggest that this is a lot of tank to modify to the flamethrower role with no other offensive capability.

ammunition stowage to an unacceptable level, but the chances are that it was an economic decision: the budget would not run to such a drastic conversion.

In post-war Canada, flame was still regarded as a viable weapon and an improved version of the Wasp IIC, known as the Iroquois, was taken into service. It was described as being cheaper, simpler and lighter than the Wasp with a capacity of 80 gallons (363 litres) and a range of 190–200 yards (173–182m) in good conditions. The best feature, as described by a Canadian report, was the way in which the flame fanned out when it was fired. Even so, the need for greater protection, which had already manifested itself during the war in the shape of the Ram Badger, was now fulfilled by a late-production M4A2 Sherman III hull. This operated without a turret and with a Wasp IIC projector installed in the front machine-gun position. Also known as the Badger, it was a self-contained unit with a creditable performance, but when it was demonstrated in Canada in June 1949 the report was annotated by one officer 'I would not ask troops to go into battle sitting on top of 150 gallons [681 litres] of fuel,' and in the event only three prototypes were built.

The final chapter in the British flamethrower saga concerns a period, starting in the 1950s, when a vast range of potential weapons came up for consideration, all identified in part by a colour: Orange William, Green Archer and Blue Steel are among the better known. At least three were flamethrowers – there was Red Cyclops, about which nothing more is known, and Red Hermes, which is described as a trailer-type unit capable of attachment to various British AFVs. The fuel of this unit, in the form of thickened petrol, and pressurizing gas consisting of carbon dioxide dissolved in acetone, shared a common tank but were separated by a flexible membrane. Operating pressure was 500psi and the effective range about 200 yards

(182m). There was also Blue Perseus, which again involved a trailer, this time for a medium tank, and contained both fuel and propellant held apart by a membrane but in such a way that 400 gallons (1,818 litres) of fuel occupied the centre, surrounded by compressed air. The performance figures were calculated as being similar to those of Red Hermes. And at the very last there was a return to a cordite-operated system, as discarded in 1942. This one does not appear to have qualified for an exotic code-name and it turned out to be of such complexity that it was never developed, but the plan was to produce a system that would fit inside an AFV and deliver flame up to a range of 100 yards (91.4m).

As each of these projects died, the popularity of flame as a weapon seems to have decreased. Only the US Army kept the faith and still had flamethrowing versions of the M113 Armoured Personnel Carrier (APC) operational in Vietnam at least up to 1969. Maybe, in peacetime, we find the idea of burning men alive a bit too unpleasant to contemplate, although if wartime evidence is any guide flame was more deterrent than killer, except in the case of the most fanatical resisters. Possibly it was simply more trouble and more risk than it was worth. Whatever the case, it had its day and is now gone.

The last of the line, the prototype Centurion Crocodile. The front-end layout was rather clumsy, but the trailer was the conventional type.

CHAPTER 6

CROMWELL CRUISER TANK

BY DAVID FLETCHER AND RICHARD HARLEY

GENESIS

Before he left France in the summer of 1940, Brigadier Vyvyan Pope sent an urgent letter to a colleague at the War Office in London. One key paragraph read, 'We must have thicker armour on our fighting tanks and every tank must carry a cannon. The 2-pdr is good enough now, but only just. We must mount something better and put it behind 40 to 80mm of armour.' Pope, who was Lord Gort's advisor on armoured fighting vehicles at General Headquarters of the British Expeditionary Force, had the letter delivered by hand. Things had gone so badly in France that Pope was not even certain he would get home.

If it sounded like a counsel of despair it probably was, but Pope had learned some unpleasant facts in France. Unfortunately he was too late; the next generation of cruiser tanks was already on the stocks. Granted, both the Covenanter and Crusader were up-armoured as an emergency measure, but nothing could be done about the gun; not at that stage anyway. With the country stripped of tanks following events in France and under imminent threat of invasion, it made more sense to continue production of existing types than risk the inevitable delays of producing new ones. In any case, there was the demand from the Middle East to consider. It has been estimated that losses in France arrested tank development in Britain by two years, and what applied to tanks was equally true of anti-tank guns.

An improved anti-tank gun, a 57mm weapon known as the 6-pdr, was ready for production in 1939. But, again due to events in France, nothing could be done until November 1941 and even then priority went to towed anti-tank guns rather than guns for tanks. And to jump ahead briefly, it is sad to record that Vyvyan Pope never lived to see the new gun in a tank. He was killed in an air crash in October 1941 and the first 6-pdr Crusaders did not reach the Middle East until the summer of 1942.

Muffled against the cold, the crew of this early production Cavalier await the arrival of the king and queen at a site on Cannock Chase. Her Majesty will unveil the name CROMWELL, which was the original title for this tank.

A curiosity of Pope's letter is the emphasis he appears to give to the importance of thicker armour over a better gun. Covenanter and Crusader were already in the design stage when war began and the 2-pdr was the only gun available. This is excusable. What is not is that these tanks were designed without the ability to up-gun built in. Such was typical of the lack of technical acumen and the laissez-faire attitude that infested the War Office in those early days.

Even so, Pope's words hit home and very soon after the fall of France in July 1940, the War Office issued basic specifications for a new cruiser tank with up to 75mm of frontal armour and a 60in-diameter turret ring. No actual gun was mentioned although the 6-pdr was an obvious choice. Lurking in the wings, however, was a hideous alternative, a triple mounting comprising a 2-pdr anti-tank gun, a 3in howitzer and 7.92mm Besa machine gun – a tank gunner's and loader's nightmare. And that was not all.

Hovering in the background, like ghosts at the banquet, stood Colonel Sir Albert Stern and his Special Vehicle Development Committee, or 'The Old Gang' as they were known. These survivors of the original tank design programme of 1915, most well past retirement age, had already perpetrated two crimes against the British Army in the bulky shapes of the super-heavy breakthrough tanks TOG 1 and 2. These had failed at enormous cost, but their designers would not go away and, although it conflicted with their own ideas of future tank design, offered specifications for a cruiser tank that were forcibly promoted by Stern.

In the end common sense prevailed and the project quickly slimmed down to three contenders. These were:

- Vauxhall Motors for a Cruiser Tank based on an infantry tank design they were already working on – the Churchill.
- Nuffield Mechanization & Aero for what was, in effect, an improved Crusader.
- Birmingham Railway Carriage & Wagon Company (BRCW) for a design like Nuffield's offering, but lighter and with their own preference of suspension and tracks.

Cavalier Type B tanks modified to the OP role at No 8 AFV Depot in Leicester. They are being kitted out for service with 65th (Highland) Medium Regiment, Royal Artillery.

It takes time for such designs to evolve, but even so one senses a peacetime lack of urgency in the fact that they were not considered until a Tank Board meeting on 17 January 1941. By this time the Department of Tank Design had somehow become involved with the Nuffield project and it is probably no surprise that it was their proposal, with the General Staff specification number A24, that was accepted. An initial order for six tanks was placed on 29 January and the firm was told that the new tank must be in production by the spring of 1942.

This may go a long way to explain why the Nuffield project was accepted. Despite the debacle in France the previous year, British cruiser tanks were making their presence felt in North Africa. Even as the Tank Board was meeting, cruisers of 7th Armoured Division were tearing across the trackless wastes of Cyrenaica to head off, and ultimately destroy, a huge Italian Army retreating around the coast. Inspired by both this and a new sense of urgency, the Minister of Supply and his Tank Board selected the tank that, as far as possible, was based on existing components. In their view this eliminated the need to work through the tedious and time-consuming stages of prototype testing; one simply produced a handful of pilot models in order to check details and then swung straight into production.

Geoffrey Burton, as Director of Tanks and Transport, agreed that this was a short cut, but only to disaster; he was overruled. He could have made his case a lot stronger had he realized that the Crusader itself was seriously flawed.

CAVALIER DESCRIBED

Cruiser Tank Mark VII, A24 Cromwell, as it was first known, looks at first glance like a child's sketch of a tank. A simple, rectangular hull surmounted by a boxy turret with the requisite gun sticking out the front and a series of big wheels along the side. Gone was any attempt to give the tank that sleek, racy look of Crusader. Virtually every surface was either vertical or horizontal and although it was only 6in taller than Crusader the visual effect was of something a lot bigger. It was also longer and wider than Crusader, which was essential to accommodate the larger-diameter turret ring required to receive the bigger gun and allow for recoil. This was the big problem.

In keeping with Royal Armoured Corps doctrine, gun mountings in British tanks had free elevation. That is to say when the gun lock was released the gun pivoted on its co-axial mounting, slightly breech-heavy, so that it could be moved up and down with ease by the gunner. This design was dictated by the requirement that British tanks should be able to fire on the move and it meant that the gunner, gripping the gun mounting and with his knees slightly bent, acted as a human stabilizer, balancing the gun against the movement of the tank as it raced across country. With his forehead pressed against the brow pad of the sighting telescope and one hand on the power control of the turret traverse gear, he could track his target, fire and hit it on the move. At the same time his fast-moving tank should prove a difficult target for the enemy to hit. And there is nothing wrong with that, as doctrines go, always provided that the gunner has been given sufficient time, and practice ammunition, to hone his skills, and the tank itself can be relied upon.

Fully stowed Cavalier ARV Mark I. Ahead of it the big Caterpillar D8 tractor represents an earlier period of tank recovery. Visible stowage includes Hollebone towing bars at the rear, front jib arms to the left and the tow cable with snatch blocks.

Since Cavalier, as it became, and Centaur and Cromwell were physically similar, this first model will be covered in detail and only the differences noted when the others are described. Much will be obvious from the illustrations, but what cannot be seen so clearly is the way the tank was divided up inside. From front to back the hull contained four unequal compartments, separated by incomplete bulkheads that acted as internal stiffeners. The front compartment was the smallest, and stepped to conform to the seated attitude of the driver on the right and hull machine gunner on the left. A short, longitudinal bulkhead divided these two. Amidships was the fighting compartment into which the turret fitted and the bulkhead behind that acted as a firewall between the crew and the engine compartment. A final bulkhead separated the engine compartment from the transmission and final drives.

ARMOUR

British practice on armour originally favoured homogeneous plate, the type best suited to resist attack by capped armour-piercing shot as used by the Germans. The Germans preferred face-hardened plate, which was better at keeping out plain AP shot. British armour quality was not all it might have been in 1941 and plate over 35mm thick tended to flake from the back under impact; thus the hull front and visor plates on the new cruisers were made up from two thinner plates. The sides were also double layered, as they had been on Crusader, with the Christie suspension units sandwiched between the inner and outer plates.

GUN AND TURRET

The turret was little more than a six-sided box constructed in a similar manner to the turret on Covenanter or Crusader, with an inner shell of welded plate to which was bolted an external skin of thicker armour. The Department of Tank Design was still struggling with the concept of welding armour plate and for the present favoured riveting. However, the turret was built this way to avoid the need for a frame and rivets that, if hit from outside, could fly around inside just like bullets. The bolts, by contrast, were enormous things with huge, bevelled caps that stuck out like carbuncles on the outside. The main armament was the new Ordnance QF rifled 57mm, 6-pdr Mark 3, the first version designed for use in tanks. It was mounted co-axially with a 7.92mm Besa air-cooled machine gun and a sighting telescope (No. 39 Mk IS) on the left. A second Besa was placed in the hull, to the left of the driver and in the roof of the turret was a breech-loading 2in bomb thrower used primarily to launch smoke rounds.

The gun mounting was unusual to the extent that it employed an internal mantlet behind a relatively large, square opening in the front of the turret. It was never popular with tank crews, who believed that the shadow created by the aperture provided the enemy with an aiming point, although this was probably a piece of tank crew mythology.

ENGINE, TRANSMISSION AND SUSPENSION

Mechanically Cavalier was identical to Crusader, although an improved version of the Nuffield Liberty (the Mark IV) engine delivered greater horsepower at higher revolutions. A multi-plate clutch carried the drive to a five-speed and reverse gearbox and then through Wilson two-speed epicyclic steering gear to the final drive reduction and finally to the drive sprockets. Gearshift and steering brake controls were pneumatically operated. Suspension was simply a stronger version of the Crusader's Christie system that Lord Nuffield had introduced into Britain. To allow for the additional weight Nuffield's engineers reduced the length of the swing arms, which meant that Cavalier gave its crew a much bumpier ride than its predecessor. The tracks were manganese steel, dry-pin skeleton type 14in wide and 4in pitch – 124 links per side.

CAVALIER PRODUCTION

Tank production in Britain worked on what was described as a Parentage system. The Parent was the company with overall responsibility for a particular tank. In the case of Cavalier this was Nuffield Mechanization & Aero. The Parent had two types of

Winston Churchill is shown a Cromwell IV of No 2 Squadron, 2nd Welsh Guards, in March 1944. Notice how this regiment kept all markings as low down as possible, making them less eye-catching to the enemy. The aptly named Blenheim was the squadron commander's tank. The fitting on top of the turret is a PLM mounting, lacking its machine guns.

sub-contractor. Some provided components, and as far as Cavalier is concerned the only one worth noting was Morris Motors Ltd which provided the Liberty engines. The other firm, Ruston & Hornsby Ltd of Lincoln, manufactured complete tanks.

Production of Cavalier does not seem to have been pressed with serious effort. Indeed it was December 1941 before the prototype was ready for gunnery trials at Lulworth. Back in August it had been claimed that the Naval Land Equipment (Nellie) programme had affected Cavalier production, but the problem seems to have been the turret, which clearly was not ready until December. Within weeks, early in the New Year, it was agreed to cut production back to 500 tanks – for reasons that will become clear. In March 1942 the first pilot model was at Farnborough for trials and the Cavalier programme was now running four months late. By this time, too, the problems with Crusader were manifest, with endless complaints emanating from the Western Desert theatre. Cavalier's faults were identical: water cooling, fan drive and engine bearings. Sent back to Nuffield's for remedial work the prototype then suffered a major engine failure. Not yet satisfactory was the verdict of the Mechanization Experimental Establishment.

Cavalier's fate was sealed at a meeting of the AFV Liaison Committee on 13 February 1943. Things had moved on quite a bit by then and it was agreed that, unlike its rivals, the A24 Cruiser would not be adapted to take the new 75mm gun or the 95mm howitzer. Final production would be 160 tanks with 6-pdr guns and the balance of 340 to be completed as Observation Post (OP) tanks. This decision meant that the tank had been written off as a combat type but was still deemed suitable for an important auxiliary role.

OBSERVATION POST TANK

The OP Tank was a mobile signal station that operated in the front line passing information back to gun batteries in the rear. It looked like any other tank, but it was in fact a sheep in wolf's clothing. In a fast-moving battle situation it was invaluable, able to summon artillery support at a moment's notice in response to a difficult situation. It was operated by the Royal Artillery and carried a FOO, or Forward

Although the vehicle here is in fact an OP tank, this photograph provides a good view of a Cromwell Mark IV with Type F hull in post-1948 condition. Prominent on the turret is the All-Round Vision cupola, late-style vane sight and eight turret stowage boxes.

Seen at the Rolls-Royce Clan Foundry at Belper, Derbyshire, in August 1943 this is the experimental Cromwell Pilot D, which displays the frontal appliqué armour, wider tracks and, of course, the welded turret.

Observation Officer. The 'office' was the turret from which the 6-pdr gun was removed to make more space, although the Besa was retained and a dummy gun fitted to disguise its special role.

The turret contained two No. 19 and one No. 18 wireless sets with seats for the commander and operator. The front machine-gun position was removed and here was located an auxiliary charging engine, three sets of extra batteries and three cable reels. The exhaust and silencer for the charging set – either the Tiny Tim or Chore Horse model – were located on the hull roof. Brackets for the cable reels were mounted on the rear mudguards. Outwardly the only other modification was an extra aerial on the turret.

ARMOURED RECOVERY VEHICLE

Following a decision by the War Office Recovery Committee that a protected towing vehicle was required to move disabled tanks from the battlefield, an Experimental Recovery Section tested a range of turretless tanks for this role. The general principle was to provide an armoured recovery vehicle for each class of tank, so a prototype Cavalier ARV duly appeared. The towing powers of these tanks were limited so a system of blocks and tackle was carried to enhance power. The tank also carried a portable jib and hoist to handle heavy components. In the event the Cavalier ARV was abandoned as rapidly as the tank it would have supported.

ENTER ROLLS-ROYCE

The next stage in the Cromwell saga represents the only truly inspirational moment in the wartime British tank story, and it was due to what might be called the old boys' network of the British motor industry. Henry Spurrier, third in line in the Leyland Motors dynasty, was critical of official British policy on tank design, particularly in respect of engines. Leyland Motors was already deeply involved in tank production and Spurrier related his fears to W.A. Robotham of Rolls-Royce; the result was remarkable. Robotham was head of the Rolls-Royce experimental department, which the war had effectively sidelined. Taking a fresh look at the problem Robotham and his team came to the conclusion that their magnificent aircraft engine, the V12 Merlin, could be modified to suit tanks. The result was the 600hp Rolls-Royce Meteor.

From this elevated angle there is a good view of the Vauxhall-designed turret and the A33-style driver's hatch on one of the two single-skin welded Cromwell hulls from BRCW. The tank was photographed at Chertsey sometime in 1943.

The Ministry of Supply (MoS) was so proud of this development that it published a book about it at the end of the war. A chart comparing the two engines showed that the main modifications involved removing the supercharger, changing the gear case and adding a belt drive for cooling fans and accessories. It sounds ideal, but there was a problem. Although the MoS controlled tank production, aero engine manufacturers like Rolls-Royce came under the Ministry of Aircraft Production (MAP). The Meteor shared 80 per cent of the Merlin's components and MAP's insatiable demand for Merlins meant that Meteor production continually fell behind schedule, which affected Cromwell production until an MoS manufacturer, Henry Meadows Ltd, began producing Meteors in 1944.

For trial purposes Meteor engines were installed in two Crusader tanks in May 1941. Running against the clock one tank was believed to have reached 80km/h (50mph), but it also became clear that Robotham's team still faced a major problem. A means had to be found to ensure adequate cooling for the powerful engine. Cavalier's radiators, sandwiched between the engine and fuel tanks, would have needed 80hp (13 per cent) of the Meteor's output to cool them. Rolls-Royce developed a new layout of transverse radiators with a highly efficient fan drive that only absorbed 32hp (5 per cent) while ramming air through the engine compartment at the incredible rate of 509.7m^3 (18,000ft^3) a minute. Added to that was the problem of transmission. The system adopted for Cavalier, derived from Crusader, was simple but wasteful of power and in any case far more sophisticated types now existed. The most promising was designed by Henry Merritt of the David Brown tractor company. It was a triple differential steering system with a five-speed-and-reverse gearbox that provided the tank with a range of turns depending on the gear selected, and a neutral turn (where the tank spins on its axis with one track turning in each direction) instead of the cruder skid turns.

CRUISER MARK VIII A27M CROMWELL

It would have made a lot of sense to apply the new engine and transmission to Cavalier, but Lord Nuffield would not hear of it. Major alterations would have been required to the original design but this was not impossible and production could have been speeded up. Yet Lord Nuffield insisted and he was indulged. His company spent the next two years producing 500 totally useless Cavaliers.

CENTAUR MARK I, 1st FIFE & FORFAR YEOMANRY, 28th ARMOURED BRIGADE, 9th ARMOURED DIVISION, GREAT BRITAIN, APRIL 1943

This Centaur I, built by English Electric of Stafford, exhibits the Type A hull, with stowage boxes extending right to the front of the upper hull on both sides. The air-intake cover behind the turret is more typical of Cromwell tanks, although it was seen on this maker's Centaurs as well. The red/white/red flash on the side, more common in the desert and Italy, was an identification mark later replaced by the white star in Europe.

The distinctive Panda's head device of 9th Armoured Division was never seen outside the United Kingdom, but 1st Fife & Forfar later converted to Crocodile flame-throwers and served as part of 79th Armoured Division. The red square with 53 in white indicates the junior regiment in the armoured brigade. (Art by Peter Sarson, © Osprey Publishing)

CENTAUR III AA TANK MARK I, GREAT BRITAIN, 1944

According to contemporary reports Centaurs were due to replace Crusader tanks in the anti-aircraft role in time for the invasion of Europe, but this never happened. Markings shown here are therefore limited to the War Department number, a graduated scale on the mantlet and the symbol, a black cannon on the Royal Armoured Corps colours of the Gunnery School, Lulworth Camp, Dorset.

In addition to the gunner/commander the turret contained two loaders who sat in very cramped positions, vulnerable to injury from the rapidly moving guns and the difficulty of handling large ammunition drums in confined spaces. Thus the No. 19 wireless set was located close to the driver and the aerial base may be seen on the glacis plate. Directly behind it is the exhaust pipe for the auxiliary generator, which was also situated close to the driver's position. Rate of fire per gun was 450 rounds per minute. (Art by Peter Sarson, © Osprey Publishing)

Inevitably, however, Cromwell was almost indistinguishable from its predecessor at first glance. Built by BRCW the first example was actually running by January 1942, and following extensive trials it was declared to be 'exceptionally good' by those responsible. Not, it has to be said, that this necessarily meant very much in view of what else was available. Nevertheless, things looked so promising that by May 1942 it was agreed that production of Cromwell must be expanded and, as a result, more firms were drawn into the group.

This expansion brought with it certain problems due, according to one commentator, to 'obstinate practices'. Few are actually specified but the impression is given of firms, set like concrete into reactionary Victorian habits, that could not be persuaded to change with the times nor, indeed, on account of the war. One example will suffice: that of a steelworks in the north-east of England producing armour panels for the front plates of Cromwell. These proved to be so poor that 100 of the new tanks were immediately fitted with the red warning triangle to inform would-be users that they were not adequately armoured.

Diversity of suppliers appears to have lain at the root of the problems. Faced with a vast increase in demand for armour plate, the relevant authority, the Iron and Steel Control, brought together an odd assortment of small producers that they referred to as The Cromwell Pool. None of these firms had the capacity to run the whole gamut of armour plate production, but they could all play a part. Thus plate from one steelworks would go to another for heat treatment, a third for rolling and so on. The initial result was a chronic muddle, compounded by

OPPOSITE One of the participants in the Fighting Vehicle Proving Establishment Three Thousand Mile Trial. A welded Cromwell VIIw, it lacks appliqué armour, hence the additional ballast to make up the weight. This view also reveals the tow hook and rear smoke emitters.

desperate variations in quality, which took a long time to sort out.

Cromwell had an anticipated top speed of 40mph that, for a 27-ton tank, implied some serious punishment to the suspension. The designers therefore decided to double up the springs on all road-wheel stations and incorporate shock absorbers on all but the central suspension units on each side. A return to longer suspension arms compared with Cavalier meant that the Cromwell gave its crew a much more comfortable ride. As Cromwell improved and received heavier suspension, springs were strengthened and on some Marks wider 15.5in tracks were fitted to better spread the weight.

CRUISER MARK VIII A27L CENTAUR

Centaur might well be described as a throwback. Having brought W.A. Robotham on board and encouraged the development of the Meteor, Henry Spurrier and Leyland Motors now expressed doubts about the possibility of providing adequate cooling for the Rolls-Royce engine. In July 1941 they abandoned the project. In the light of subsequent events this was not just a foolish decision: it was idiotic of the authorities to agree to it.

Leyland Motors was not lost to tank production; the General Staff agreed to a compromise whereby Leylands would produce a tank similar to Cromwell that took the old Nuffield Liberty engine, now in an improved model, the Mark V. A curious result of this was the requirement that Cromwell tanks, starting with the second pilot model, should be capable of accepting the Liberty engine, as Centaur was of taking the Meteor. Thus where there was one, now there were three, all known as Cromwell at first. Ultimately they entered service as:

- Cruiser Tank Mark VII A24 Cavalier (originally Cromwell I)
- Cruiser Tank Mark VIII A27L Centaur (originally Cromwell II)
- Cruiser Tank Mark VIII A27M Cromwell (originally Cromwell III).

(L and M signify Liberty and Meteor engines respectively.)

Abandoned on Gold Beach on D-Day, this Centaur of 1st Armoured Support Regiment, Royal Marines, has been selected to display the Deep Wading trunking and the Porpoise reserve ammunition sledge that it towed ashore behind it.

Centaur was not simply a Cromwell tank with a Liberty engine, there were numerous detail differences. For example Centaur employed the worm-operated track tensioning system adopted for Crusader and Cavalier where Cromwell used a ratchet wheel and lever. Likewise Centaur did not require the additional air intake and armoured cover on the rear deck, and since it was lighter at the rear than Cromwell it lacked the extra springs on the last two wheel stations and only had three shock absorbers on each side to Cromwell's four.

As will be seen, Centaur was never accepted as a front-line tank and even before the trials that finally condemned it an official announcement was made to the effect that the first 300 Centaurs would only ever be regarded as training tanks while the next 166 would all have to be reworked. With hindsight the entire Centaur project was a complete waste of time and material, and this at a critical period in British history.

THE HYBRIDS

Given the shared features it is tempting to imagine that converting a Centaur to a Cromwell was simply a matter of switching engines, but naturally it was not as straightforward as that. It was done, but only as a means of examining the possibilities and resulted in a few early Centaurs being fitted with Meteor engines and taking designations Cromwell Mark III or Cromwell Mark X. They were put through a series of trials in 1942.

In early 1943 English Electric broke ranks with the Centaur Group of manufacturers and joined the Cromwell Group. They continued building tanks with Centaur hulls and suspensions, but fitted them with Meteor engines, clutches and fan drives, delivering these newly built vehicles as Cromwell Marks III or IV depending on armament. This took some of the pressure off BRCW, freeing them to continue development of Cromwell and Challenger.

CROMWELL FAMILY MAIN ARMAMENT PERFORMANCE 1941–54

Weapons	Armament for	Ammunition	Muzzle velocities ft/sec (m/sec)	Penetration in mm (in) at 30 degrees to vertical 500 yards: (457m)	1,000 yards: (915m)	1,500 yards: (1,371m)	2,000 yards: (1,828m)
2-pdr Mks IX or X	Triple Mounting with 3in howitzer and Besa MG, proposed for A24 but not adopted	APCBC	2,600 (792)	53 (2.08)	49 (1.92)	44 (1.73)	40 (1.57)
6-pdr Mk.V	Cavalier I, Centaur I, Cromwell I, II and III	APCBC	2,700 (822)	87 (3.42)	80 (3.14)	73 (2.87)	67 (2.63)
		APDS	3,900 (1,188)	131 (5.15)	117 (4.60)	108 (4.25)	90 (3.54)
95mm Mk.I	Centaur IV, Cromwell VI and VIII	HEAT	1,075 (327)	110 (4.33)	110 (4.33)	110 (4.33)	110 (4.33)
75mm Mk.V or VA	Centaur III, Cromwell IV, V, Vw, VIIw, VII, A33E1 & A33E2	APC M61	2,030 (618)	68 (2.67)	61 (2.40)	54 (2.12)	47 (1.85)
76mm M1A1	US 76mm proposed for A34, but not adopted	APC M62	2,600 (792)	93 (3.66)	88 (3.46)	82 (3.22)	75 (2.95)
		APCR M93	3,400 (1,036)	157 (6.18)	135 (5.31)	116 (4.56)	98 (3.85)
17-pdr Mks. II and VII	A30 Challenger and SP2 Avenger	APCBC	2,900 (884)	140 (5.51)	130 (5.12)	120 (4.72)	111 (4.37)
		APDS	3,950 (1,203)	208 (8.19)	192 (7.56)	176 (6.93)	161 (6.34)
77mm Mk.I	A34 Comet	APCBC	2,600 (792)	110 (4.33)	105 (4.13)	91 (3.58)	89 (3.50)
		APDS	3,675 (1,120)	178 (7.01)	150 (5.91)	131 (5.16)	122 (4.80)
20-pdr Mk.1	FV4101 Charioteer	APCBC	3,346 (1,019)	196 (7.72)	183 (7.20)	169 (6.65)	156 (6.14)
		APDS Mk.3	4,692 (1,430)	295 (11.61)	277 (10.91)	260 (10.24)	243 (9.57)

THE GUNS

If the gun is what the tank is all about, then the Cromwell and its cousins were caught at an awkward stage of gunnery development. When the new tanks were being developed the cruiser was regarded as a tank fighter, but experience in the desert changed all that. Rommel's use of tanks mixed with anti-tank guns brought forth a cry for a dual-purpose weapon: one that could fire High-Explosive (HE) in addition to Armour-Piercing (AP) shells.

The original 6-pdr for tanks, the Mark III, was a 43-calibre weapon, which firing Armour Piercing Capped Ballistic Cap (APCBC) could penetrate 56mm of armour

CROMWELL FAMILY PRODUCTION TOTALS 1942–45

Manufacturers	Cavalier	Centaur	Cromwell (riveted)	Cromwell (welded)	Challenger	Comet	A33 'Excelsior'	Avenger	Totals
BRCW Co Ltd			256	123	200			80	659
English-Electric		156	647	1		276	2		1,082
Harland & Wolff		125							125
John Fowler & Co		529	274			150			953
Leyland Motors		643	735			610			1,988
LMS Railway Co Ltd		45							45
Metro-Cammell			300			150			450
Morris Motors		138							138
Nuffield M&A	203	150							353
Ruston-Bucyrus		35							35
Ruston & Hornsby	300								300
Vauxhall Motors				2					2
Grand Totals	503	1,821	2,212	126	200	1,186	2	80	6,130

CAVALIERS **Nuffield Mechanization & Aero, and Ruston & Hornsby**

Marks	Types	Main Armament	Notes
I	A, B	6-pdr Mk.III or V	Riveted hull, bolted turret, 14in (355mm) tracks.
II	A	6-pdr Mk.III or V	Trials vehicle with 15.5in (394mm) tracks. No series production.

CROMWELLS **BRCW, Metropolitan-Cammell, English Electric, and Vauxhall Motors**

Marks	Types	Main Armament	Notes
I	A, C	6-pdr Mk III or V	Riveted hull, bolted turret, 14in (355mm) tracks
V	C	75mm Mk.V	ditto
VI	C, D, E, F	95mm Mk.I	ditto
"Pilot D"	similar to riveted Type A	6-pdr Mk.III	Pilot welded double-skin hull, welded turret, applique armour, large canister springs, and 15.5in (394mm) tracks
"Cromwell II"	similar to rivetd Type B	6-pdr Mk.III	Pilot welded single-skin hull, composite cast/welded turret, large canister springs and 15.5in (394mm) tracks
VwD	Dw	75mm Mk.V	Production welded hull, bolted turret, applique armour, large canister springs and 14in (355mm) tracks
VwE	Ew	75mm Mk.V	Similar to Cromwell VwD but low-speed final drives
VIIwE	Ew	75mm Mk.V	Similar to Cromwell VwE but heavy-duty front axles and 15.5in (394mm) tracks

CENTAUR GROUP TANKS **Centaurs only: Harland & Wolff; LMS; Mechanization & Aero; Morris Motors; and Ruston-Bucyrus**
Centaurs and Cromwells: English-Electric; Fowler; and Leyland Motors

Tanks	Marks	Types	Main Armament	Notes
Centaur	I	A, B, C	6-pdr Mk. III or V	Riveted hull, bolted turret, and 14in (355mm) tracks
Centaur	II	not known	6-pdr Mk.III or V	Designation reserved for Centaur with 15.5in (394mm) tracks. No series production
Centaur	III	C, D	75mm Mk.V	Riveted hull, bolted turret, and 14in (355mm) tracks
Centaur	IV	C, D	95mm Mk.I	ditto
Cromwell	X	A	6-pdr Mk. III or V	Existing Centaur I converted for trials with Meteor engine
Cromwell	III	A, C	6-pdr Mk. III or V	New production Centaur I built with Meteor engine
Cromwell	IV	C, D, E	75mm Mk.V	New production Centaur III built with Meteor engine. Cromwell track adjuster on vehicles built to FS (Final Specification) standards
Cromwell	VI	D, E	95mm Mk.I	New production Centaur IV built to FS standards with Meteor engine and Cromwell track adjuster
Cromwell	IV	F	75mm Mk.V	New production Centaur III built to FS standards with Meteor engine and Cromwell suspension and track adjuster

REWORKED CROMWELLS		**Reworked by Royal Ordnance Factories, post-1945. (original manufacturers BRCW, English Electric, Fowler, Leyland and Metro-Cammell)**	
Marks	**Hull Types**	**Main Armament**	**Reworked from:**
7	C, D, E, F	75mm Mk. 5	Cromwells 4, 5 and 6 NO applique armour
7w	Dw	75mm Mk. 5	Cromwell 5w Applique armour retained
8	D, E, F	95mm Mk.1	Cromwell 6 NO applique armour

Riveted Cromwells Marks 4, 5, and 6 were reworked with large canister springs and 15.5in (394mm) tracks, low ratio final drives and late pattern trackguards. Some Type Cs were converted to Type Ds. Modified (push-out) driver's hatch fitted to all riveted Types C, D and E. Centaur track adjuster was replaced by Cromwell type.

FV4101 CHARIOTEER		**Robinson & Kershaw Ltd.**	
Marks	**Hull Types**	**Main Armament**	**Converted from:**
6	D, E, F	20-pdr Mk.1	Cromwell 6
7	D, E, F	20-pdr Mk.1	Cromwell 7
7w	Dw, Ew	20-pdr Mk.1	Cromwell 7w
8	D, E, F	20-pdr Mk.1	Cromwell 8

Cromwell Mark 6s were reworked to Mark 8 standard during conversion. All Type Cs were converted to Type Ds. All riveted Types D and E were modified with Cromwell 7w driver's escape hatches.

at a range of 2,000 yards. It was superseded, in 1943, by the longer Mark V that had a similar performance, but neither could fire an effective HE round. This problem was solved temporarily by Vickers who reamed out the 57mm gun to 75mm and chambered it to take the American ammunition used in Sherman tanks, both HE and AP. Unfortunately what was gained with HE was lost in terms of armour piercing. The best this gun could do, firing a 14lb APCBC shot, was 50mm of armour at 2,000 yards.

The free elevation arrangement already described was fine given a properly trained gunner, but it made the task of firing HE more difficult and in any case demanded a well-balanced gun. This could not be achieved with the hybrid 75mm, so a crude system of geared elevation was employed, which some believed gave the worst of both worlds. Yet this was not the gun the army wanted. In March 1942 Vickers-Armstrongs had offered a new, high-velocity 75mm gun with a 50-calibre barrel and there was a general belief that this would fit the new cruiser. It took until May 1943 to learn that it would not. Thus, with time pressing, it was the modified 6-pdr or nothing if the Cromwell was to carry a dual-purpose gun.

Meanwhile, there had been developments elsewhere. Experience in the desert showed that the old concept of close-support, with a breech-loading mortar firing only smoke rounds, was antiquated. In 1942, in keeping with the typically British skill at improvisation, a new gun was created by combining the breech of the Royal Artillery's beloved 25-pdr with the barrel liner of the 3.7in anti-aircraft gun. The result, known as the 95mm howitzer, proved to be a remarkable weapon. Firing a respectable HE shell it had a maximum range of 6,000 yards; firing High Explosive Anti-Tank (HEAT) rounds it could theoretically penetrate 110mm armour at any range it could reach.

Both guns had been standardized for Cromwell and Centaur by February 1943. The most interesting result of these changes was that no Centaur or Cromwell went to war mounting the 6-pdr gun. This was a pity since, with the introduction of Armour Piercing Discarding Sabot (APDS) ammunition in June 1944, the Mark V gun proved to be an excellent anti-tank weapon at close range. It could penetrate 108mm of armour (which over-matched even the Tiger's front plate) at 1,500 yards and at any range up to 2,000 yards was second only to the legendary 17-pdr.

MARKS AND TYPES

The sub-division of any given model of tank by Marks is, and has always been, common practice worldwide. Each succeeding Mark normally indicates some change in gun power, armour or other physical development. In Britain, at least up to the advent of Chieftain, these Marks usually showed up as visual differences that could be recognized by those in the know.

Cromwell, Centaur and even Cavalier to some extent were unusual in having a separate system of Types that indicated other modifications that cut across the succession of Marks and were not always instantly recognizable. Full details of all Mark and Type variations will be found in the accompanying tables, but notice that they are not random: combinations of Mark and Type relate to particular manufacturers.

Variations are highlighted in captions, but three might be mentioned here as general illustrations. Type B was one result of firing trials carried out against a sample Centaur tank at Shoeburyness. These revealed a number of vulnerable points, one of which was the hatch above the front hull machine-gunner's position. It was difficult enough to open and squeeze through at the best of times, but it was also easily fouled by the turret, making it impossible to open at all, especially in an emergency. The revised design involved replacing the hatch with a door that opened sideways, moving part of the roof with it. Nobody could describe this as a vast improvement, but it worked well enough and tanks thus modified were classified as having Type B hulls. Of course, in order to clear space for the hatch to open, one external stowage locker was deleted.

Naturally the problem repeated itself on the driver's side, but it was not possible to mirror the hull gunner's hatch because certain engine controls were in the way. Once modifications had been introduced it resulted in the Type F hull, which reached the troops in the summer of 1944. Meanwhile some of the older Types were retro-fitted with a new driver's hatch with flaps split diagonally; the rear flap simply dropped into place. In an emergency the driver pushed open the front flap and knocked the rear one aside as he baled out.

Not all Type modifications were improvements. The early riveted tanks were weighted to the limit of their suspensions and the addition of new operational equipment made them overweight. The Tank Board reluctantly approved a 50 per cent reduction of engine-compartment armour to compensate and this change was introduced on hull Type C.

A Centaur with Type A hull being used to test the new 95mm howitzer (without its counterweight). Notice the one perforated-tyre road wheel and the air intake, behind the turret, more typical of a Cromwell.

CROMWELL FAMILY WD NUMBERS AND MANUFACTURERS

WD No. Ranges	Tanks, Marks & Types	Manufacturers
T84618–84620	Cavalier IA (pilots)	Nuffield Mechanization & Aero
T120415–120689	Cromwell IC, VIC, VID, VIE, VIF	Metropolitan-Cammell Carriage and Wagon Co. Ltd
T188657–188681		
T121150–121406	Cromwell IA, IC, VC.	Birmingham Railway Carriage and Wagon Co. Ltd. (BRCW)
T121701–121822	Cromwell VwD, VwE, VIIwE	
T121863		
T129620–130119	Cavalier IA, IB	Nuffield M&A, Ruston & Hornsby
T130120–130164	Centaur IA	LMS Railway Co
T171962–171966	Centaur IA (pilots)	Leyland Motors, and English Electric
	Cromwell X (pilots)	
T183800–186510	Centaur IA, IB, IC	Gun tanks by English Electric, Fowler, Leyland, Harland & Wolff.
	Centaur IIIC, IIID	CS and AA tanks by Fowler
	Centaur IVC, IVD.	Dozer conversions by MG Cars
	Centaur III AA.I	
	Centaur Dozer	
T187501–188082	Cromwell IVD, IVE, and VIE	Gun tanks by Leyland and Fowler.
		88x CS tanks by Fowler
T188151–188656	Cromwell IVF	English Electric, Leyland, and Fowler
T188687–188926		
T189400–190064	Cromwell IIIA, IIIC, IVC, IVD and VID	Gun tanks by English Electric and Fowler. 3 x CS tanks by Fowler
T217801–217880	Centaur IIIC	Morris Motors, Nuffield M&A, and Ruston-Bucyrus
T218001–218562	Centaur III AA.I	Dozer and Taurus conversions by MG Cars
	Centaur Dozer	
	Centaur Taurus	
T255310	Cromwell VwE	English Electric
T271901–272100	Challenger I	BRCW Co. Ltd
T334901–335308	Comet IA, IB	Leyland, Fowler, English Electric and Metropolitan-Cammell
T335331–336108		
S348560–348639	SP, 17-pdr, Avenger	BRCW Co. Ltd

Chosen to illustrate the Great Swan, this shows a Polish Cromwell racing past a Jeep and an abandoned PaK 43 88mm anti-tank gun. The tanks move on one route, coating one another in great clouds of dust while support vehicles use a parallel lane.

CENTAUR MARK IV, No. 2 BATTERY, 1st REGIMENT, ROYAL MARINE ARMOURED SUPPORT GROUP, NORMANDY, JUNE 1944

The most striking feature of these tanks has always been the distinctive turret markings, graduated in degrees of the compass, which were a relic of the original plan to shoot from landing craft operating off-shore. The gunner's periscope was replaced by an artillery sight projecting through an armoured box located ahead of the commander's position. Each regiment comprised two batteries, each of four troops. Each troop included four 95mm Centaurs and a Sherman command tank. Individual troops were identified by letter and tank names were selected to match, usually those of Royal Navy warships, HMS *Hunter* being an H Class destroyer.

Hull machine guns were removed – they would have been useless on board ship. Extra stowage indicates the extent to which this unit had to function entirely on its own resources once ashore. (Art by Peter Sarson, © Osprey Publishing)

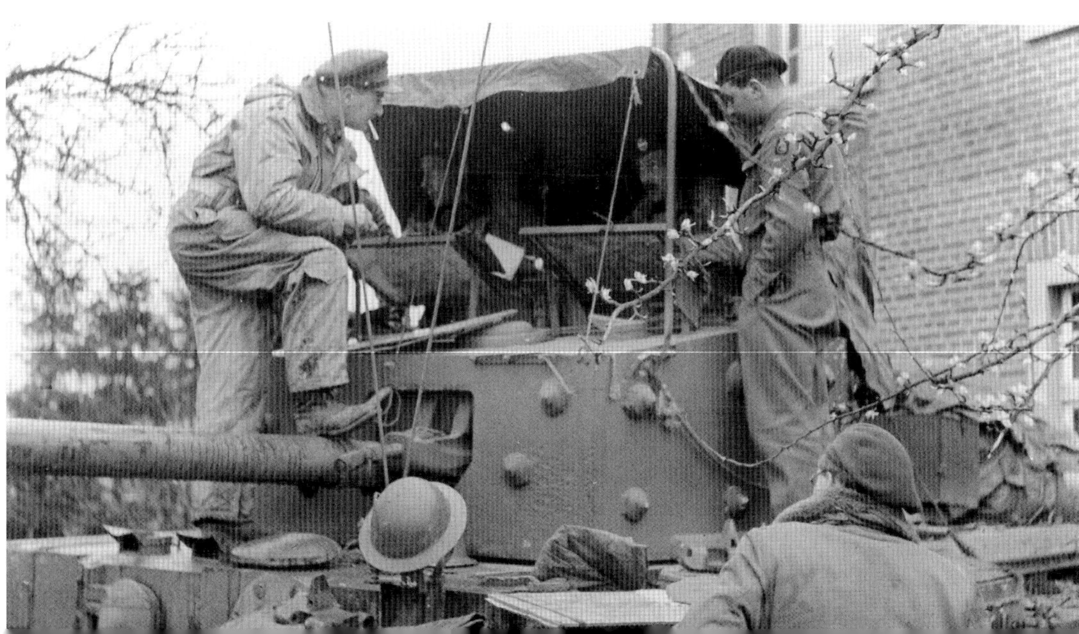

WELDED CROMWELLS

The Cromwell would change in many ways, but the most significant development was welded construction, which was first considered in December 1941 – even before the riveted pilot models had been completed. Welding offered several advantages including faster production, improved protection and a watertight hull for wading. The first welded Cromwell was Pilot D built by BRCW. Its hull followed the Type A layout and it also had a welded turret, wide tracks and a new, large canister spring suspension permitting a weight increase to 28 tons.

Seen at Harland & Wolff in Belfast a new Centaur I Type A, still awaiting its armament. This tank has perforated tyres on all road wheels and the Cromwell-type air intake that was also typical of Centaurs built by English-Electric and the LMS Railway.

BRCW had great difficulty welding Pilot D's double, homogenous front plates, but when Machineable Quality armour became available they built two further welded hulls with thicker, single front plates. These new hulls followed the Type B layout, but also had an improved driver's escape hatch copied from the A33 Assault Tank, as well as wide tracks and large canister springs. These hulls then went to Vauxhall Motors of Luton who, in 1942, had been instructed to build Cromwells instead of Churchills. Vauxhall completed them with a new composite turret featuring cast sides and a welded roof, but the resulting Cromwell II never went into production. Churchills proved successful in Tunisia so production was to continue and Vauxhalls would build no more Cromwells.

Yet the Tank Board still required welded Cromwells and told BRCW to build as many as possible without disrupting Challenger production. This was achieved when BRCW designed adjustable hull assembly jigs that meant that both types could be built interchangeably.

Even so there was indecision about the final form of these Cromwells. In August 1943 Pilot D was fitted with appliqué armour, increasing its frontal protection to 101mm and setting the pattern for a Stage I design with a welded turret. A Stage II design called Commodore was also proposed with 101mm of single-thickness armour. Neither was built. Instead BRCW modified their Vauxhall hull with a Type D engine deck and Pilot D's appliqué armour while retaining the bolted turret and built 123 Cromwell Vw and VIIw to that design.

GOING WEST

Throughout the period when these new cruiser tanks were being developed, British tanks were coming in for a barrage of criticism. As early as July 1942, the Director, Armoured Fighting Vehicles (Major-General Richardson AWC) was pointing out to the Tank Board the similarities between Centaur and the disgraced Crusader, and the fact that so far the Merritt-Brown transmission had been an unmitigated disaster on Churchill. He also reminded the Chief Engineer Tank Design (Robotham) 'neither the Government, War Office nor the Ministry of Supply could weather another storm such as the one we have just passed through...'

Late in February 1943, the Tank Board decided that Vickers-Armstrongs should turn their tank-building capacity over to Cromwell with the proviso that if in six months' time the tank should prove unreliable, production should be cut and America asked to supply more tanks. As late as September 1943 another senior officer

OPPOSITE Open for business, a Cromwell IV Type E Command Tank of Headquarters 22nd Armoured Brigade, 7th Armoured Division, photographed in 1945. Both turret weapons are dummies, and bent to prove it. There is a mass of intriguing detail in this picture.

Looking immaculate, even down to a polished muzzle brake, this is a Cromwell OP of 6th Armoured Division, seen outside the Battery Workshops after the war. Notice that it retains its Normandy Cowl.

Raising the jib on a Cromwell ARV I. The tank reverses until the wire, linking track and jib, raises the latter in the correct place, when the man on top will secure the stay. A chain hoist is secured to the jib, there is a vice on the hull front and the Besa machine gun is still in place.

wrote 'the most disturbing feature of the Cromwell tank is the fact that its inherent design will not permit the fitting of a better gun than the medium velocity 75mm'. There is no doubt that the Americans agreed. In March 1943 their General Somervell was urging Britain to stop making tanks altogether and accept American types in the interests of uniformity and reliability, although he did admit that Cromwell was better than Sherman in some respects. This request was not acceptable as far as Britain was concerned, although there was a general tendency to cut back tank production in Britain and take more from the USA as the war progressed.

As the attached tables show, many late-production Centaurs were completed as Cromwells, but none of this seems to have had any effect on Lord Nuffield. The Tank Board had compelled him to build Centaurs instead of more Cavaliers, possibly hoping for Cromwells in the long term, but he was still not reconciled with the Rolls-Royce engine. Instead he offered something called the Democrat, which sounds suspiciously like the Liberty by another name. Two were installed in Centaurs for trials early in 1944, but they showed no improvement over Meteor.

In the spring of 1943 six Centaurs and one Cromwell were shipped over to the USA. Only the Cromwell was complete, the Centaurs going without engines. This shipment was in connection with the Tank Engine Mission to the United States, headed by Sir William Rootes. Ford Motors had developed a new V8 and were anxious to interest the British. Four of the Centaurs were to be tested with the new V8, with two more laid aside for a proposed V12. The Americans were not impressed with the British tanks at all. The Cromwell let the side down so badly that General Richardson wrote a scathing report in which he described the British as 'the world's worst salesmen!' The Americans fitted one of the Centaurs

with their latest gun stabilizer but it was not adopted, and neither was the Ford engine. Compared with the Meteor it was underpowered and in Centaur or Cromwell the Ford would not be interchangeable with the Liberty or Meteor. In spite of this, Leyland continued to argue in favour of the Ford engine until the Tank Board ruled it out in July 1943.

The best sources of operational information on Cromwell are 21st Army Group Technical Reports. The Cromwell had few chances to show its spurs until the Great Swan, the amazing dash across France to Belgium. The tank was praised for its reliability, the only major problem being road-wheel tyres that began to crumble under the strain. A shortage of spare road wheels led to some units cannibalizing their Crusader AA tanks, so Cromwells began to appear with a mixture of solid and perforated tyres.

TRIALS AND TRIBULATIONS

The first production Centaurs and Cromwells began to replace Covenanters in 9th Armoured Division in April 1943, although some regiments had to wait until September for their first Cromwells. Both types were still under development, so the first tanks issued were built to prototype standards. Crews soon discovered that the Centaur was no more reliable than the Covenanter. Its clutch was weak and the Liberty engine sprayed oil over the radiators, causing overheating. Cromwell's Meteor was less troublesome, but both types suffered from gearbox and steering defects.

Worse still, the delivery ratio of Centaurs to Cromwells was five to one and this alarmed the divisional commander, Major-General D'Arcy. On 27 June he complained that while he understood that Centaur was only a stop-gap until sufficient Meteors were produced for the Cromwell to replace it, that policy did not appear to be accepted on the production side. He considered that Cromwell would develop into a first-class tank but that Centaur would be a second-rate one, and

The pilot model of the Centaur III Anti-Aircraft Tank Mark II, showing the enlarged turret. The gunner's sight is not in place, but one can see the auxiliary engine exhaust on the trackguard and the aerial base on the turret top.

CROMWELL MARK VW, 5th ROYAL TANK REGIMENT, 22nd ARMOURED BRIGADE, 7th ARMOURED DIVISION, NORMANDY, 1944

Typical of veteran Desert Rats, this tank is seriously cluttered with additional stores and also displays one version of the foliage-style turret camouflage adopted during the hedgerow fighting in Normandy. This tank also sports the so-called 'Normandy Cowl', a device to prevent exhaust fumes from cycling back through the turret when the tank was idling.

The battered state of this Cromwell's trackguards would be entirely typical of a tank that had come a long way with its crew. Made of light-gauge metal to save weight, they were easily damaged by enemy fire or driving incidents. At this stage in the war (from August 1944) 5th RTR was the junior armoured regiment in the brigade (No. 53) below 5th Dragoon Guards and 1st RTR. (Art by Peter Sarson, © Osprey Publishing)

reported that his 129 Centaurs had received 95 defect reports, including 23 clutch failures, while only three of his 26 Cromwells had given trouble of any kind. Centaur required far more maintenance and, because it was underpowered, its Liberty engine had to work flat-out all the time. Summing up he asserted that 'any attempt to saddle the fighting troops with an indifferent fighting machine for the sake of some consideration other than military, when a first-class machine can be produced, would be criminal', and he asked for the policy to be unequivocally clarified. The War Office duly obliged him with the hardest test it could devise, short of committing both tanks to battle.

OPERATION DRACULA

As titles go Operation Dracula seems to have been calculated to invite the ribald wit. In fact it probably derived from the title of the initiating officer, Major-General Richardson, the Director, Royal Armoured Corps or DRAC (previously the DAFV). Richardson had been posted to Washington by the time Dracula began in August 1943, but the man who mattered was the trials officer, Major Clifford. Dracula involved a comparative test in the form of a 3,700km (2,300-mile) tour in which Cromwell, Centaur, Sherman III (M4A2) and Sherman V (M4A4) tanks could be tested for reliability as they roamed around the country visiting armoured formations. Thus it could also be seen as a familiarization tour for the new types while, as a by-product, it was also used to try out the effectiveness of new items of tank-crew uniform.

Operation Dracula could have been the kiss of death for Cromwell and Centaur. Both tanks performed badly when compared with their American counterparts, and the Centaur was so bad that Clifford announced that he would not wish to take it into combat. Cromwell showed up well for its top speed, when it was running well,

CROMWELL MARK VI, A SQUADRON, 10th MOUNTED RIFLES, 1st POLISH ARMOURED DIVISION, NORMANDY, 1944

The 10th Mounted Rifles was divisional reconnaissance regiment to 1st Polish Armoured, hence the white squadron sign. Each squadron would include two 95mm close-support tanks. Organized along the lines of a typical British armoured division of the time, 1st Polish had three regiments of Sherman tanks in the armoured brigade and Cromwells (with A30 Challengers) only in the reconnaissance regiment.

The Poles used their armour with considerable verve. In debatable areas they tended to advance with all guns blazing, giving adjacent British units the impression that some terrible battle was taking place nearby. (Art by Peter Sarson, © Osprey Publishing)

but for pure reliability and staying power the M4A2 diesel Sherman took the palm.

Yet, although time was running out, both British tanks won a stay of execution while their designers strove to cure the mechanical problems. In November 1943 ten each of the latest Centaurs and Cromwells were subjected to a punishing 3,000-mile reliability trial in the abrasive mud of Long Valley, Aldershot. The Cromwells emerged with flying colours but the Centaurs failed again.

That was enough for the Tank Board, who declared that in the short term the battleworthy Cromwell should continue to be produced up to the limit of Meteor engine production. Centaur production would be scaled back from 2,700 to just 2,000 tanks and in May 1944 it was revealed in the press that 'Britain's latest monster

Excellent shot of a Centaur Mark I Type B at speed. It is demonstrating the effect of its rear smoke emitters at Porton Down on Salisbury Plain in May 1944.

Centaur Taurus 17-pdr Gun Tractor, one of nine converted by MG Cars of Abingdon. The full-length sand guards were designed for Cromwell, but were very rarely seen on gun tanks.

tank' had been removed from the Secret List. As this was a tank that had not yet seen action, the House of Commons began to ask awkward questions, not just about Centaur but the entire situation concerning British tank design.

BATTLE CROMWELL

In February 1944 Leyland Motors announced the specification for what they described as the Battle Cromwell, although the official designation was FS, for Final Specification. In essence it was a short catalogue of features (such as the type of Meteor engine and variant of transmission to be used and the practice of welding seams, even on riveted tanks, to enhance structural strength and waterproofing) that would be acceptable for use on active service. In effect this relegated all Cromwells prior to the Mark IV to the scrap heap. However, it set a standard and provided a tank that well-trained crews could rely upon.

Other features adopted at this time were the All-Round Vision cupola for the commander, along with the vane sight and rear smoke emitters. On certain marks an improved type of idler was seen and the perforated tyres were replaced by solids. Stronger trackguards and lockers were fitted, Cromwell-pattern track adjusters were standard and all tanks were prepared for deep wading. Evidence from reports suggests that a number of these improvements were not honoured one hundred per cent. Many Cromwells that served in North-West Europe were not up to Final Specification in all respects.

Leyland and Fowlers had now joined the Cromwell Group, but it was still a race against time. Four hundred FS Cromwells were required by D-Day but only 152 had been accepted by April 1944. Some regiments only reached full establishment on the eve of embarkation.

ROYAL MARINES

In an effort to provide Royal Marine Commandos with their own fire support on D-Day, the Marines acquired 80 Centaur 95mm close-support tanks and developed a system of gunnery based upon naval gunfire techniques. The plan was to remove the engines from these tanks and mount them on Tank Landing Craft, raised high enough to fire over the bulwarks. These craft would then operate off the beaches, bringing down fire on Marine objectives as required, and finally run ashore and continue firing from the shoreline. Since this would demand considerable expenditure of ammunition, the vacant engine compartments would be used to store additional rounds.

Then everything changed. Following an exercise on the Dorset coast, General Montgomery suggested it would make more sense for the tanks to land and drive ashore, so engines were refitted and Royal Armoured Corps drivers transferred to the Marines. Formed as the Royal Marine Armoured Support Group, it comprised two armoured regiments, sub-divided in batteries and one Independent Armoured Battery. Denied everything in the way of technical and material support, this gallant band still managed to do extremely well. Some of their distinctively marked Centaurs could still be found, more than two weeks after the initial landings, fighting up to 10 miles inland.

A Centaur III Type C being used to test Prong, the British version of Sergeant Culin's hedgerow cutter. Tested in September 1944, it was not produced until November for Cromwell, which was too late to be of any use.

When the unit was disbanded their surviving Centaurs were distributed to various units, including one special Canadian battery supporting 6th Airborne Division, before being handed over to the French.

CROMWELL IN ACTION

Reports on the effectiveness of Cromwell on the battlefield are compounded of official wishful thinking, personal loyalty or simple misunderstanding. One commentator, writing in the *Royal Armoured Corps Journal*, reported on the fate of those Cromwells destroyed in the debacle at Villers Bocage on 14 June 1944. The writer describes Cromwell as 'the new British Cruiser tank' but said that its armour was not in the same class as Panthers and Tigers. The fate of some 4th County of

This scruffy-looking Cromwell IV Type E is of no significance in itself except that it was used, at the end of World War II, to test a British version of the German Zimmeritt anti-magnetic paste. Apparently the stuff came off in chunks every time it was hit.

CROMWELL TANK

Key

1 Parking brake
2 Idling speed control screw
3 Right hand steering lever
4 Hand throttle lever
5 Choke control lever
6 Left hand steering lever
7 Driver's seat
8 Driver's periscope
9 Hydraulic fluid supply tank
10 Suspension lubrication tank
11 Besa MG 7.92mm
12 QF 75mm high explosive shells
13 Sighting telescope
14 Breech 75mm gun
15 Spare prism box for tank periscope
16 Radio equipment No19
17 Ammunition box for Besa in feed tray
18 4 gal water tanks x3
19 Box for spares and tools
20 Spotlamp
21 Air inlet cover door
22 Suspension units
23 Hull gunner's door
24 Starter motor
25 Gunner's seat
26 Ammunition bins (cut-away)
27 Base junction
28 Commander's seat
29 Telescope (spare)
30 Cylinder CO2
31 Besa ammunition boxes
32 75mm spent cartridge bag
33 Gear lever
34 Clutch pedal
35 Brake pedal
36 Accelerator

(Art by Peter Sarson, © Osprey Publishing)

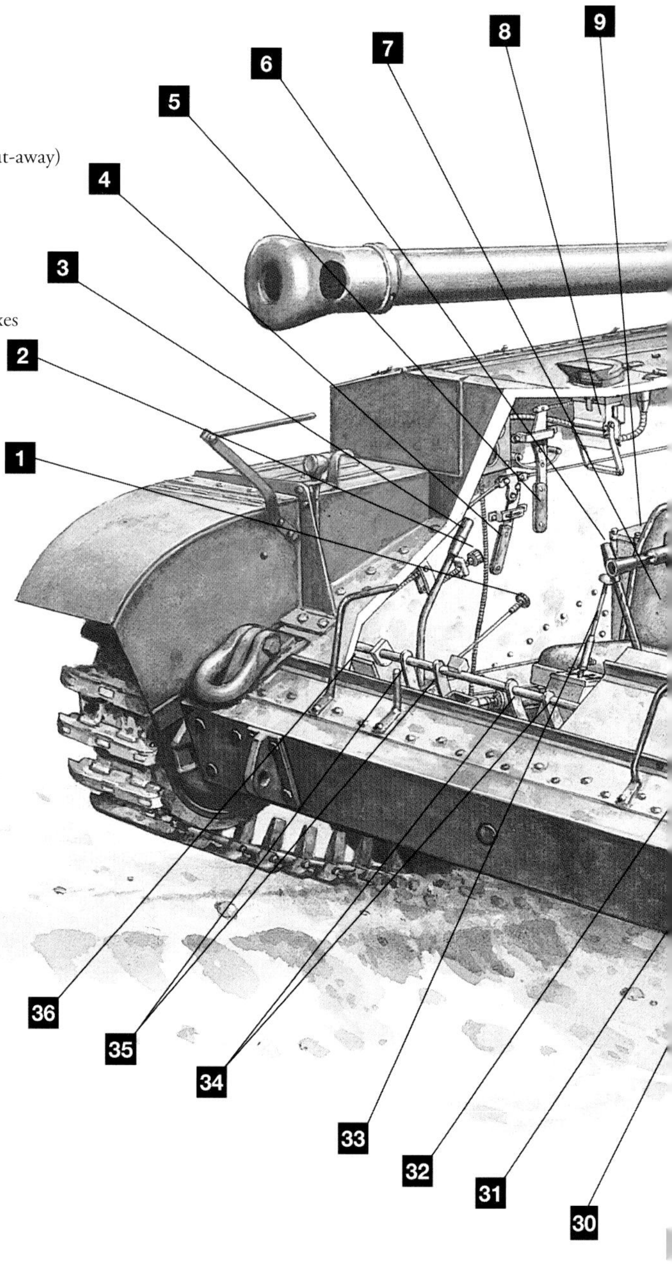

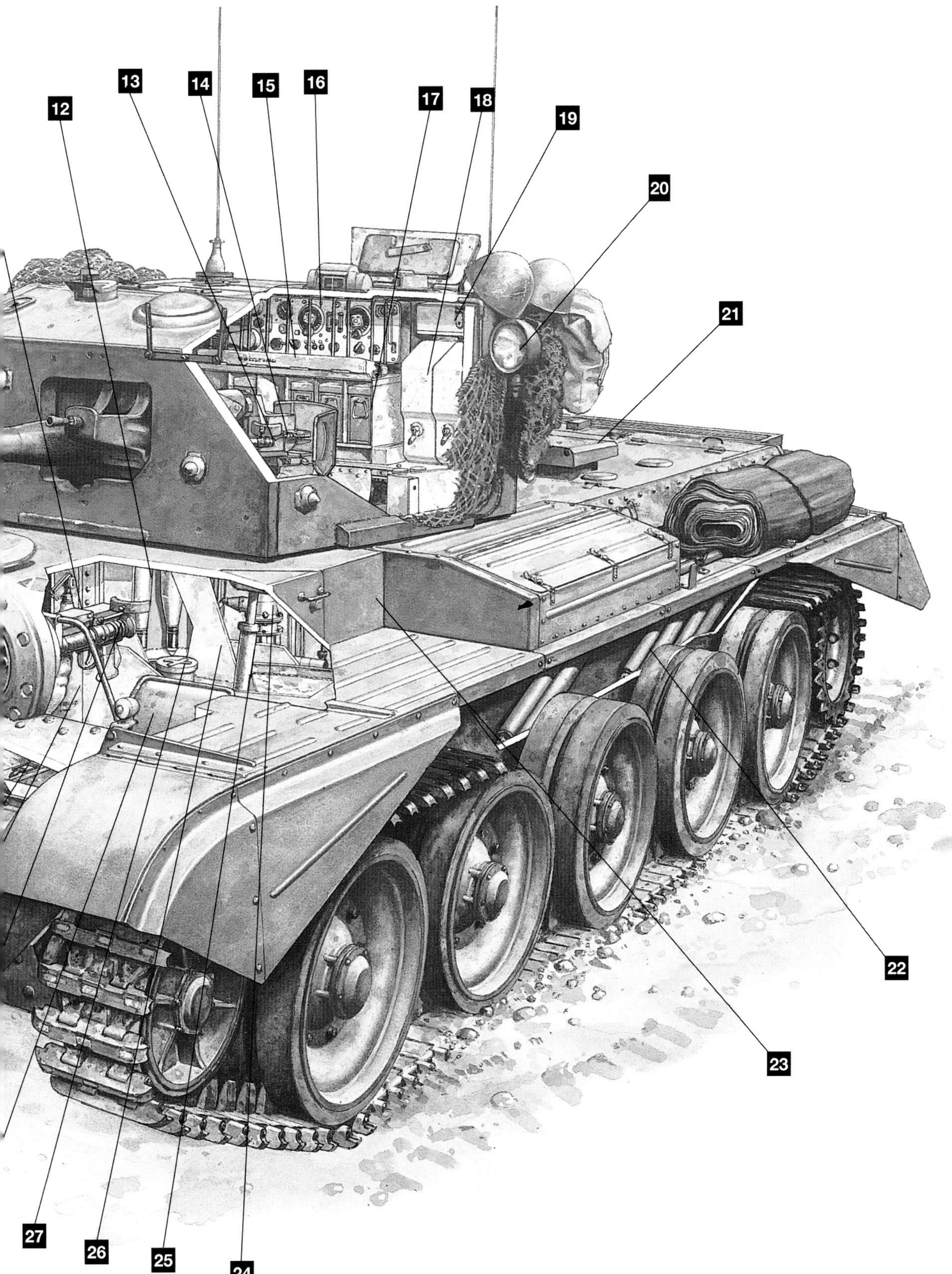
12
13
14
15
16
17
18
19
20
21
22
23
24
25
26
27

21st Army Group and Allied units operating Cromwell family AFVs, 1944–45

Formation	Regiments	Tanks	Remarks
Royal Marines Armoured Support Group (RMASG)	1st & 2nd Armoured Support Regiments, RM 5th (Independent) Armoured Support Battery, RM	Centaur IV	Normandy, D-Day to D+14
Free French Forces	13eme Regiment des Dragons	Centaur IV	Ex-RMASG, no combat service
51st Highland Division (attached)	6th LAA Battery, 27th Light Anti-Aircraft Regiment, RA	Centaur IV	Ex-RMASG, until 30/7/44
6th Airborne Division (attached)	(a) 'X' Armoured Battery, 53rd Light Regiment, RA (b) 1st Canadian Centaur Battery, RCA	Centaur IV	Ex-RMASG, transferred to Canadians on 6/8/44
6th Airborne Division	6th Airborne Armoured Reconnaissance Regiment	Cromwell	Divisional Recce Regt
7th Armoured Division	8th King's Royal Irish Hussars	Cromwell Challenger	Armoured Recce Regt
7th Armoured Division (22nd Armd Bde)	1st Royal Tank Regiment 5th Royal Tank Regiment 4th County of London Yeomanry 5th Royal Inniskillen Dragoon Guards	Cromwell Challenger Comet	4CLY replaced by 5RIDG 8/44. Challenger in 5RTR, 8/44. Comet in 1RTR, Berlin, 9/45.
11th Armoured Division	2nd Northants Yeomanry 15/19th Hussars	Cromwell Challenger	Armd Recce Regts. 2NY replaced by 15/19H 8/44
11th Armoured Division (29th and 159th Brigade Groups)	15/19th Hussars 23rd Hussars 2nd Fife & Forfar Yeomanry 3rd Royal Tank Regiment	Comet Cromwell Challenger	3/45 to 5/45. Challenger in 15/19H only.
Guards Armoured Division	2nd Battalion, Welsh Guards	Cromwell Challenger	Armoured Recce Regt
1st (Polish) Armoured Division	10th (Polish) Mounted Rifles Regiment	Cromwell Challenger	Armoured Recce Regt
1st (Czechoslovakian) Independent Armoured Brigade Group	1st, 2nd, and 3rd (Czechoslovakian) Armoured Regiments	Cromwell Challenger	1st Canadian Army, Dunkirk, 9/44 to 5/45
79th Armoured Division. (1st Assault Bde, RE)	87 Assault Dozer Squadron, Royal Engineers	Centaur Dozer	Germany, 4/45 to 5/45

London Yeomanry's tanks, he says, was 'a mishap that put the case against British tank design far better than a dozen speeches in Parliament could do'. Cromwell may have been Britain's latest tank, but it was hardly new, and on welded types the frontal armour was exactly the same thickness as Tiger. It was the gun that was the problem. In fact, given precisely the same circumstances, no tanks could have survived what happened outside Villers Bocage, not even if 4th CLY themselves had been equipped with Tigers.

The autumn of 1944 saw a return to positional warfare, with engines overheating as mud and fallen leaves clogged air intakes. This malfunction was made worse where crews piled on extra stowage that masked air intakes, until they were ordered to stop.

Mines were also a menace and Cromwells seem to have been particularly vulnerable; the explosion could twist a hull out of alignment, causing the tank to be written off. Mine blast would also buckle trackguards, jamming hatches and preventing escape. The Czech Brigade solved this by fitting tack-welded panels instead of trackguards; these would simply break off, leaving the hatch clear. The practice of welding spare track links to tanks as additional protection was popular, but frowned upon as ineffective by experts. Yet there is evidence of one Cromwell IV surviving five direct hits from a 75mm PaK 40 at 300 yards while a nearby tank, without such protection, was knocked out.

CROMWELL FAMILY HULL TYPES EVOLUTION: CAVALIERS, CENTAURS, AND RIVETED CROMWELLS

Type	Description	Applicable to:
A	Two escape hatches in driving compartment roof, belly escape hatch, four trackguard stowage lockers. Hull floor plate 6mm thick with additional spaced, 8mm layer below crew compartments. No.20 gimbal mounting for hull Besa with No.35 periscopic gunsight and separate vision periscope for hull gunner. Long-range fuel tank optional. Engine deck air intake standard on Cromwells but optional on Centaurs, depending on manufacturer.	Cavalier I Centaur I Cromwell I, III and X
B	Side escape hatch for hull gunner. Belly escape hatch deleted. three trackguard stowage lockers. No.20 gimbal or No.21 ball mounting for hull Besa. Hull gunner's vision periscope deleted. Long-range fuel tank optional.	Cavalier I Centaur I
C	Similar to Type B but engine compartment armour reduced and long-range fuel tank deleted to save weight. New pattern of engine deck air intake for all Cromwells and some Centaurs. No.20 gimbal or No.21 ball mounting for hull Besa. Hull gunner's vision periscope reinstated on later vehicles. Revised trackguards introduced on later Cromwell IVCs.	Centaur I, III and IV Cromwell I, III, IV, V and VI
D	Similar to Type C but engine deck redesigned to improve access to radiators. No.21 ball mounting for hull Besa, hull gunner's vision periscope and revised trackguards all standard.	Centaur III and IV Cromwell IV and VI
E	Similar to Type D but laminated floor plate replaced by a single-skin 14mm floor plate.	Cromwell IV and VI
F	Similar to Type E, but with driver's side escape hatch. Two trackguard stowage lockers. Two turret side stowage lockers. Towing ropes stowed on glacis plate. Late vehicles had WD Pattern sprung drawbar for guns and trailers. All Type F had Cromwell suspension as standard.	Cromwell IV and VI

WELDED CROMWELLS

Type	Description	Applicable to:
Dw	Welded hull similar to riveted Type D. A33-pattern driver's roof hatch incorporating one of his periscopes. Single-skin 10mm floor plate. Applique armour on hull and turret front. Large canister suspension with 14in (355mm) tracks.	Cromwell VwD
Ew	(a) Welded hull identical to Type Dw, but fitted with low-speed final drives and 14" (355mm) tracks.	Cromwell VwE
	(b) Welded hull identical to Type Dw but fitted with low-speed final drives, heavy-duty front axles and 15.5in (394mm) tracks.	Cromwell VIIwE

CHALLENGERS

WD No. ranges	Description
T271901–271940	Production A30 welded hull and turret design, with 60mm turret nose casting. Cromwell exhaust system
T271941–272000	As above, with turret nose casting increased to 102mm. Later tanks equipped for deep wading, fitted with Normandy cowls
T272001–272100	As above, with applique armour added to turret front, and hull front and sides. Very late vehicles had Comet Type B exhausts

COMETS

Mark and Type	Description
Comet 1 Type A	Original A34 welded hull design with Cromwell exhaust system. Normandy cowl was divided to clear the gun barrel
Comet 1 Type B	Revised A34 hull with fishtailed exhaust pipes and Normandy cowl deleted. Frontal armour joints reinforced with steel angles
	N.B. Early Type Bs were built with exhaust ports blanked off and Normandy cowls fitted until fishtailed exhausts became available.

WARTIME VARIANTS AND SPECIALIST VEHICLES

COMMAND AND CONTROL TANKS

The Royal Armoured Corps half-yearly report for the first half of 1944 lists Command, Control, Rear Link and OP (Observation Post) variants of Cromwell. It is a complicated subject to cover in a few words but, according to a table issued in 1943 these different Cromwell variants were fitted out as follows:

- Cromwell Command Tank. One each No. 19 Low Power (LP) and High Power (HP) wireless sets with the main armament removed. These were issued at divisional and brigade HQ level.
- Cromwell Control Tank. Two LP sets, armament and ammunition retained. Issued at regimental HQ level.
- Cromwell Rear Link Tank. One HP set with armament and ammunition retained. Issued to HQ of armoured reconnaissance regiments.

CROMWELL ARMOURED RECOVERY VEHICLE MARK I, C SQUADRON, 2nd NORTHANTS YEOMANRY, 11th ARMOURED DIVISION

Again the squadron symbol being in white indicates that 2nd Northamptonshire Yeomanry was acting as divisional reconnaissance regiment for 11th Armoured. This would be the only regiment in the division to be equipped with Cromwells and each squadron had one ARV.

When not in use the jib and hoist were stowed upon the vehicle along with many other items required for recovery operations. Since these vehicles were not equipped with power winches they used snatch blocks and holdfasts to recover the casualty and then tow it to a location from which it could be carried away by a tank transporter. The ARV was manned by REME, the Royal Electrical and Mechanical Engineers. (Art by Peter Sarson, © Osprey Publishing)

- Cromwell Observation Post (OP) Tank. Two No. 19 and two No. 38 portable sets, armament and ammunition retained. Issued to artillery regiments in armoured division and armoured brigade HQs.
- Later came Contact Tanks, converted in the field. These were equipped with one No. 19 Command set, one No. 19 Air Support Signals Unit (ASSU) set and a VHF set. Used by RAF liaison officers to control fighter-bombers, they also had a dummy gun and were fitted with telescopic aerials taken from captured German equipment.

ARMOURED RECOVERY VEHICLE

Outwardly it can be difficult to distinguish a Cromwell ARV from the Cavalier version, especially when fully stowed with recovery equipment, although the obvious

Cromwell T187820 was a Mark IV Type E issued to the Specialized Armour Development Establishment (SADE) and is here being used to test a version of the Canadian Indestructible Roller Device (CIRD), which has pulled the centre of gravity well forward.

CROMWELL MARK IV, KING'S OWN HUSSARS, 7th ARMOURED DIVISION, OPERATION BLACKCOCK, JANUARY 1945

Operation Blackcock involved some bitter fighting in harsh winter conditions around the Dutch/German border. Tanks were given a rough coating of whitewash to reduce contrast with the snowy landscape and this obliterated virtually all markings. The 7th Armoured Division was the only one to be equipped primarily with Cromwell tanks.

Although 8th Hussars were nominally the divisional reconnaissance regiment they had, by the winter of 1945, effectively become a fourth armoured regiment in 22nd Armoured Brigade, which reflected experience in the field. This Cromwell has the Type F hull, which can also be recognized by the small stowage boxes now carried on the turret sides. (Art by Peter Sarson, © Osprey Publishing)

differences in terms of engine, transmission and rear-end arrangements are there. Records show that 58 Cromwell ARVs had been delivered by the end of 1944 but these were not new construction. They were converted from existing gun tanks, usually Mark IV Cromwells with Type C hulls.

AA TANKS

Tanks fitted with anti-aircraft guns to provide air defence for armoured formations were not a new idea, but experience in France in 1940 stimulated development and, following experience with Light Tanks, this became a Cruiser Tank role that devolved upon the Crusader. Centaur was regarded as the natural successor and in October 1943 a prototype was inspected. It was similar to the Crusader AA Tank Mark III, but with Polsten cannon replacing the 20mm Oerlikons of the former. Since the turret was cramped, and liable to quite violent movement in action, the wireless set with its operator was installed in the hull. In Crusader the AA turret was powered by the tank's engine, but the Centaur employed an auxiliary generator located in the nose of the tank with its own exhaust pipe situated on the nearside trackguard.

No reason has ever been found to explain why Centaur AA tanks should not have replaced the unreliable Crusaders with the armoured divisions in Europe. However, by October 1944 the order for Centaur AA tanks Mark I had been cut back from 450 to 100 and its replacement, the Mark II, probably only existed as a single example. The Mark II mounted an enlarged turret that included an extra man, a gunner, sitting alongside the tank commander who now tracked the target for him. There are hints that Centaur AA tanks were employed as part of Operation Diver, the concentrated AA barrage mounted as an antidote to the V1 flying bombs. But if true, where they were deployed and who operated them is not known. There is one report of a Centaur

Business-end view of a Centaur Dozer or Trailbreaker showing various fittings. This is in fact the prototype, identified by the hinged hatch, replacing the normal blanking-off plate, which was unique to this vehicle. It was provided to give the commander a view forwards when he was not using the armoured box directly above.

AA Mark III, which also existed in prototype form and featured a new design of turret. All of these improvements went by the board when the AA tank programme was cut back.

CENTAUR DOZER

The demise of the anti-aircraft tank programme was followed quickly by a revival of interest in armoured bulldozer tanks. The Crusader had been tested in this role but found wanting, while the Centaur, with its greater weight, proved far more effective. Built on the hulls of cancelled AA tanks, the Centaur Dozers mounted a full-width blade that was raised and lowered by a powered winch in the fighting compartment via cables running over a small jib at the front. The driver sat in his usual place while the vehicle commander occupied the position on his left, covered by an armoured conning tower.

Taken from the special tower at the Lulworth Gunnery School, this top view of A30 Challenger shows how the central part of the hull had to be enlarged to take the bigger turret. Notice also how far forward the commander's cupola is located.

TOP LEFT Detail view of an A30 Challenger in service showing both turret hatches open and the curved strip of armour that protected the turret ring at the front. No unit details are available beyond the fact that the turret insignia suggests 4 Troop in C Squadron; a system typical of 15/19th Hussars.

TOP One of a series of classic pictures showing a Challenger of 4 Troop, C Squadron, 15/19th Hussars in Holland in October 1944. Considerable effort has been made to camouflage both gun and turret, which seems only to emphasize its apparent bulk.

The War Office requirement for 250 machines was met by MG Cars of Abingdon, who undertook the conversion. The Dozers were issued to 87 Assault Squadron Royal Engineers in 79th Armoured Division and they were used primarily for clearing rubble in bombed and shelled built-up areas. Even so, deliveries were slow and they did not go operational until April 1945. Centaur Dozers later saw service in the Korean War and even the 1956 Suez crisis, in Operation Musketeer.

Centaur Kangaroos, described as turretless personnel carriers, are mentioned at the end of the war. Some details also survive of a Royal Electrical and Mechanical Engineers (REME) programme to produce gutted, turretless personnel carriers to be towed, full of troops, behind battle tanks. A redundant Cromwell was converted in France, with engine doors from a Sherman tank fitted at the back, but a plan to modify Centaurs in the UK was dropped.

Drawings survive for other Cromwell projects, including one with an exposed, multiple machine-gun mounting and even a self-propelled gun with a 25-pdr in an enclosed structure. These were never built, but other experimental modifications will be found among the photographs.

A30 CHALLENGER

The origins of Challenger are open to various interpretations. The official line is that BRCW were asked to design a new tank 'with the minimum amount of design and development that would carry the 17-pdr gun'. On the other hand W.A. Robotham, then chief engineer at the Department of Tank Design, later claimed that it was his idea and that the design work was carried out by his Rolls-Royce team at Belper in Derbyshire. There may be an element of truth in both claims, but on balance one tends to favour the official line since there is more hard evidence to back it up.

It is that phrase about the minimum amount of design and development that should set the alarm bells ringing, yet it appears to have been British policy for tank design since 1940. Perfectly reasonable too, if one is improving upon the best, but not when it involves taking a short cut that results in something less than adequate. The matter was not improved by handing parts of the design to different firms in the hope that they could be made to harmonize afterwards. Thus work on the turret was entrusted to Stothert & Pitt of Bath, a firm that normally specialized in the manufacture of large cranes, while BRCW developed the chassis to receive it. This

TOP T187820 again, with CIRD brackets at the front, now modified to carry and fire four 76.2mm (3in) Typhoon rockets with 27kg (60lb) warheads. This was another SADE trial, staged in 1946.

TOP RIGHT A view inside the Birmingham Railway Carriage & Wagon Company works at Smethwick, Birmingham, showing A30 Avenger hulls on the production line with turrets waiting in the adjoining bay.

would be the big short cut since it was a modification to the A27M hull, which had to be enlarged to carry a bigger and much heavier turret.

The essential requirement was to increase the diameter of the turret ring from 60in on the Cromwell to 70in, and this was done by creating a new central superstructure, elevated above the level of the engine deck and extended outwards over the tracks. The design team also deemed it necessary to extend the tank to accommodate the new superstructure and reduce the ground pressure (on account of the greater weight) by putting more track on the ground. Since the hull had to be stretched, an extra wheel station was added on each side to support it. Lengthening a tank without widening it in proportion invariably leads to steering difficulties, but widening this tank ran the unacceptable risk of exceeding the British railway loading gauge, which had inhibited the design of British tanks since 1916.

Stothert & Pitt's turret was enormous, not just to accommodate the big gun but to leave enough headroom for the elevation and depression demanded by the War Office. Since the extra weight of this part-cast and part-welded turret could have been prohibitive the entire turret assembly rested upon a large steel ball, held in a special cradle on the hull floor to avoid the complication of a conventional ball race turret ring.

The ball device (described as a 'doubtful blessing' by one commentator) assisted with a secondary function unique (unless one includes the heavy tank TOG 2) to Challenger. This was the ability, from inside the fighting compartment, to jack up the

A Challenger, displaying the additional frontal armour used on the last hundred tanks to leave Birmingham. Alongside is the far lower profile of the prototype Avenger Tank Destroyer, which mounts the same gun in an open-top turret.

turret by up to 1in. The idea was that the risk of it jamming through accidental damage or enemy action could be obviated by raising the turret sufficiently to clear the problem and then lowering it again.

Tank Board representatives saw the prototype A30 at Farnborough in August 1942. It was an ungainly looking thing with the tall, solid turret dominating a long, low hull. Gunnery trials at Lulworth revealed that the new Metropolitan Vickers Metadyne electric turret traverse gear worked very well, but it was suggested that a second loader would be a sensible idea due to the weight of the projectile. In the event it seems that on active service the extra loader was dispensed with, and certainly other 17-pdr armed vehicles managed with just the one. The turret carried a co-axial machine gun that, oddly for a British tank at that time, was the .30-calibre (7.62mm) Browning, but there was no machine gun in the hull. Space in the new tank was at a premium, particularly for ammunition stowage, but it also saved weight.

By February 1943 A30 had been accepted for production and an order for 200 placed with BRCW, with the proviso that they took precedence over Cromwell production. Challenger's role was a specialized one: to provide long-range anti-tank support for the Cromwells in its regiment and not to replace them, as Montgomery seems to have believed at one time.

INTO ACTION

Challenger, like its more popular rival the Sherman Firefly, was described at the time as a hole puncher (the holes being in other people's tanks). On paper at least it could defeat 111mm of armour at ranges up to 2,000 yards firing APCBC ammunition, but when firing APDS that figure went up to 161mm. In practice it seems the gun was not as accurate as it might have been and the sights no better than average. Some suggest that the round could wobble in flight and ricochet from an oblique strike when it should have smashed straight through. It is also worth recalling what the Experimental Wing of the Gunnery School at Lulworth said of Challenger that 'under European conditions the performance at long ranges of the 17-pdr gun could not be relied on as a compensating factor for inadequate armour protection'. Even so the gun was regarded with a healthy respect by German tank crews.

In the interests of uniformity Challengers were only issued to Cromwell-equipped regiments in North-West Europe, starting with 15/19th Hussars in August 1944.

OPPOSITE Another SADE trial, a development of the wartime Canal Defence Light scheme, saw this Mark VIIw mounting a pair of mercury-vapour spotlights at the front. For experimental purposes power was supplied by two generators mounted on the rear deck.

A production Avenger adopts a hull-down position, providing a good view of the range of movement of the suspension stations. This example is fitted with the special roof added to provide protection from mortar rounds and air bursts.

Limited operational use revealed a weakness in the front idler assembly that resulted in the whole lot being withdrawn for a while. Half way through production other changes were introduced, notably increased armour protection to front-facing surfaces. In 1943 plans had been drawn up for a 36-ton Challenger Stage II with heavier armour to General Staff specification A40, but the project was abandoned.

A30 AVENGER SP2

In British service tank destroyers were the province of the Royal Artillery who operated the American M10, re-armed with a 17-pdr gun, and the Valentine Archer equipped with the same weapon, this last as an interim measure. Although a contemporary of the Archer in terms of design, A30 17-pdr SP (the name Avenger was not adopted until after the war) took longer to evolve. Essentially it was a low-profile version of the A30 Challenger's hull with a 17-pdr in an equally low turret that was open at the top. Following experience in North-West Europe, where the Germans employed air-burst shells to harm tank destroyer crews, the turret of Avenger, also known as SP2, was fitted with a spaced head cover. It was an impressive-looking machine, but arrived too late to see operational service and only served briefly with two anti-tank regiments when hostilities were over. The Royal Artillery Wing at Bovington Camp ceased teaching Avenger after 1949.

Comet and Diamond T tank transporter. The tank's turret has been reversed for travel and the gun locked to its cradle on the rear deck. Notice how the Normandy Cowl is split to accept the muzzle of the longer gun.

A34 COMET

Although it was too large to fit Cromwell, development of Vickers' 50-calibre, high-velocity 75mm gun continued. However, to confuse the issue, by the time it entered service the calibre had changed to 76.2mm, the breech modified to accept 17-pdr ammunition while the official description altered to 77mm, to distinguish it from the longer weapon fitted to Challenger. The new gun proved to be more accurate than the 17-pdr when firing HE rounds. Despite this the Tank Board at one point suggested that the new American 76mm gun should be considered. Fortunately, since this weapon failed to live up to expectations, the final choice of the new British gun helped to make Comet an excellent tank.

Photographed on parade with 3rd Royal Tank Regiment in Hong Kong, this Mark I Comet has its War Department registration on the side and a local registration marking on the front. This picture was taken in an era when Britain maintained garrisons in many parts of the world.

Leyland Motors was appointed manufacturing Parent, having evidently overcome their suspicion of the Meteor engine. Indeed in most respects, apart from the turret, Comet was little more than an improved Cromwell – proving that, if the job was done properly, a mediocre British tank could be improved. The result was impressive. The turret was a welded structure with an unusual cast front of quite complex shape containing an external mantlet recessed within the turret ring. There was an extension at the rear to contain the radio and counter-balance the heavier gun. An All-Round Vision cupola was fitted as standard, as were return rollers to support the top run of the wider 18in tracks. Subsequent trials suggested that these served no useful purpose at all, but they do help to identify the tank.

Issued first to 29th Armoured Brigade in 11th Armoured Division, Comet soon proved popular, even to crews with long experience of the Sherman. It was fast, manoeuvrable and above all it could fight. It was like having an entire regiment of Fireflies, easily a match for the Panther and perfectly capable of dealing with the Tiger at most ranges.

There is no hard evidence for the existence of Command and Control Comets before the end of the war, although regimental COs certainly used Comets and surviving post-war documents include illustrations to show the turret interior fittings of an official Command and Control Comet.

COMET CROCODILE

One surviving photograph reveals the existence of a Comet flame-thrower similar to the Churchill Crocodile, with a pressurized fuel trailer but no evidence of a flame projector mounted in place of the hull machine gun: almost certainly a post-war conversion. No documents have been discovered, but it would be in keeping with Montgomery's views on the Capital tank and his belief that all such tanks should be adaptable to tasks like flame-throwing, mine clearance or amphibious operations. This apart, no other special modifications of the Comet are known.

POST-WAR DEVELOPMENTS

The place of Cromwell and Comet in the post-war world might be summed up, as far as the British Army was concerned, in a Fighting Vehicle Design Establishment (FVDE) report c.1950 in which the two tanks were marked down as vulnerable at all ranges to every Russian anti-tank weapon from the old 76mm gun of the T-34 upwards. Nevertheless Comets served with many Territorial Army regiments up to 1954; many of these tanks were stockpiled in the Middle East.

A34 COMET, REGIMENTAL HEADQUARTERS, 2nd FIFE & FORFAR YEOMANRY, 11th ARMOURED DIVISION, GERMANY, 1945

The four patron saints of the United Kingdom were represented at RHQ. Saint Andrew is shown here, appropriately for a Scottish regiment. Although official Command and Control versions of Comet were introduced after the war there is no record of them earlier. However, an extra aerial mounting appears to have been fitted on the glacis plate of Saint Andrew, suggesting a field modification. The white 53 indicates that at this time 2nd Fife & Forfar was the junior regiment in 29th Armoured Brigade, a fact also reflected in the blue diamond symbol representing regimental headquarters.

From this low angle the wider (457mm/18in) tracks give the Comet a much more solid appearance than its predecessor the Cromwell. It was better armoured than A27M if not quite as fast, but the 77mm gun could penetrate 122mm (4.8in) of armour at 1,828m (2,000yd) firing APDS and was also renowned for its accuracy. Unfortunately, Comet arrived on the scene too late to take full advantage of this. (Art by Peter Sarson, © Osprey Publishing)

Fearnaught was a Comet of Headquarters Squadron, 6th Royal Tank Regiment, which was converted to the command role with a dummy 95mm gun, a weapon never actually fitted to Comet. The tank was photographed on a rail flat in Italy, just after the war.

POST-WAR CROMWELL REWORKING PROGRAMMES

Surviving, original Marks and Types			Not Reworked to later Marks	Reworked Cromwells				Cromwell Totals	Converted to Charioteers				Charioteer Totals
Manufacturer	Mark	Type		Mark 4D	Mark 7	Mark 7w	Mark 8		Mark 6	Mark 7	Mark 7w	Mark 8	
BRCW Co. Ltd	I	A	1	0	0	0	0	1	0	0	0	0	0
	I	C	1	0	0	0	0	1	0	0	0	0	0
	V, NFS	C	13	0	29	0	0	42	0	2	0	0	2
	Vw, FS	Dw	5	0	0	7	0	12	0	0	5	0	5
	Vw, FS	Ew	3	0	0	0	0	3	0	0	0	0	0
	VIIw, FS	Ew	36	0	0	0	0	36	0	0	36	0	36
English Electric	IV, NFS	C	26	2	19	0	0	47	0	0	0	0	0
	IV, FS	C	1	77	65	0	0	143	0	40	0	0	40
Fowler	VI, FS	D	1	0	0	0	2	3	0	0	0	2	2
	VI, FS	E	36	1	0	0	17	54	1	0	0	17	18
Leyland etc	IV, FS	E	50	0	87	0	0	137	0	60	0	0	60
	IV, FS	F	189	0	225	0	0	414	0	154	0	0	154
Metropolitan-Cammell	VI, NFS	C	0	0	0	0	5	5	0	0	0	0	0
	VI, NFS	D	5	0	0	0	2	7	0	0	0	0	0
	VI, FS	D	13	0	0	0	11	24	3	0	0	11	14
	VI, FS	E	13	0	0	0	14	27	2	0	0	14	16
	VI, FS	F	98	0	5	0	50	153	38	5	0	52	95
Grand Totals			491	80	430	7	101	1,109	44	261	41	96	442

A Cromwell V Type C, reworked to Cromwell 7 Type D for post-war service in the Middle East. The SA serial was normally issued to tanks that did not qualify for FS (Final Specification). The crew are chatting to the locals, but the tank is not mounting its machine guns.

However there were still Cromwells to spare and many of these were subject to a major rework scheme intended to bring surviving earlier Marks up to date. A total of 618 were rebuilt by the Royal Ordnance factories and 442 later converted to Charioteer. Note that from 1948, when a new War Department registration system was introduced, the British Army ceased to use Roman numerals for Mark designations and switched to Arabic. Thus, for example, a wartime Cromwell Vw might be reworked to appear as a Mark 7w.

Probably the last Cromwells to fire their guns in anger with British forces were those of the reconnaissance troop of 8th King's Royal Irish Hussars and 45th Field Regiment Royal Artillery (gun-armed OP tanks) in a desperate action against overwhelming odds in January 1951, during the Korean War. Comets lasted a good

TOP The bizarre-looking COMRES-75 vehicle on a Comet IB chassis. Ammunition is stowed in tubes, either side of the gun, and passed through an auto-loader at the back. The crew all remain inside the hull. The tank was part of an Anglo-German project of the 1970s that did not last very long.

TOP RIGHT Poor but rare picture of Charioteer in British service. Bulled up almost to Red Square standards it is serving with 23rd Armoured Brigade during a parade through Liverpool. It is probably 46th (Liverpool Welsh) Royal Tank Regiment.

deal longer, but were never called upon to engage in any serious action. A few long-term survivors were used for experimental purposes, the most significant being the installation of an externally mounted 83.8mm auto-loading gun, developed by the Fighting Vehicle Research and Development Establishment in 1968 under the name COMRES-75.

FV4101 CHARIOTEER

Early in 1951 the Director, Royal Armoured Corps, Major-General Nigel Duncan, announced that in the event of hostilities, presumably against Russia, it would be necessary to employ Cromwell tanks in at least one formation. DRAC was fully aware that the tank's 75mm gun was impotent against contemporary Russian tanks and had requested that the FVDE see if they could find a way of mounting the 83.4mm 20-pdr gun on the A27M. It was a tall order.

We have already seen the problems involved in fitting the 17-pdr, and the 20-pdr, which first appeared in 1947, was even bigger. It had been developed for the Centurion Mark 3 but Centurion production was in arrears so there were guns to spare. The most remarkable thing about the new design was the way in which FVDE managed to widen the hull above the fighting compartment to accommodate a larger turret ring without having to extend it. This meant that the basic Cromwell hull remained intact so that performance and reliability were not affected, but the overall result was dreadful.

The new turret was enormous, and to keep the weight down frontal armour was a mere 38mm and the sides just 25mm. This was not a tank in which the crew would be given a second chance. As for the crew, they originally numbered three: driver, loader/radio operator and commander/gunner. This is why, according to some, the turret does not feature a commander's cupola – in action neither he nor his loader had any time to look out. The loader had enough to do handling the large rounds, although there were only 25 of them, of which three were held on clips in the turret itself. When he was neither loading nor operating the radio, the loader could fire the co-axial machine gun mounted to the left of the main armament. There was no machine gun in the hull; the space to the left of the driver was earmarked for the crews' personal kit, although sometimes a fourth man travelled here. The 20-pdr's muzzle blast could obscure the target below 1,500 yards, so the commander would dismount and direct fire from the flank while this fourth man took his place as gunner.

CROMWELL FAMILY: OVERSEAS DELIVERIES & SALES, 1943–95

	Cavalier	Centaur	Cromwell	Challenger	Comet	Charioteer	Avenger	Totals	Notes
Australia			1					1	Evaluation vehicle, 1943
Austria						82		82	1956–65
Burma					22			22	1954–95
Cuba					14			14	Procured 1957
Czechoslovakia			188	22				210	Ex-1st CIABG, 1945–54
Denmark							2	2	Evaluation vehicles, 1950
Eire					8			8	1959–73
Finland					41	38		79	1958–79
France	43	71						114	1944–54, incl. Cavalier OP
Greece		52						52	1946–57
Hong Kong					69			69	RTR units 1949–59
Israel			2					2	Stolen from 4/7 Dragoon Guards, 1948
Jordan						49		49	1954–72, 23 Six-Day War survivors sold to Lebanon
Lebanon						20		20	1954–76 plus 23 ex-Jordan
Portugal		48						48	1945–55
Somalia					5			5	Procured 1962
South Africa					26			26	1954-1968 (MRV 1978–85)
USSR			6					6	Evaluation vehicles, 1944–45
West Germany					13			13	Procured 1961
Grand Totals	43	171	197	22	198	189	2	822	

Charioteer was also described as an anti-tank gun and it had a lot in common with the previous generation of tank destroyers, except that the turret was fully enclosed. However, the addition of a co-axial machine gun should qualify it as a tank and that was certainly how it was perceived when it first entered service with Territorial Army regiments of the Royal Armoured Corps. Even so, its service with the British Army was short and many were exported, as shown in the table at the top of the page.

Photographed in the Taw estuary in North Devon, with Appledore across the water, this Charioteer, with Type A barrel, is on Deep Wading trials at the Combined Operations Experimental Establishment (COXE). The turret crew are taking no chances – both men wear life jackets.

A30 CHALLENGER, 1st CZECHOSLOVAKIAN INDEPENDENT BRIGADE GROUP, DUNKIRK, 1944

Equipped entirely with Cromwells and Challengers, apart from some Stuart reconnaissance tanks, the Czech regiments spent most of their time investing the German garrison in the port of Dunkirk, which had been bypassed by the main Allied advance. When hostilities ended the Czechs and their tanks returned home.

Seen in profile the Challenger looks ungainly, although in fact it had a slightly lower profile than a Sherman. One problem common to all 17-pdr armed tanks was the length of the gun, which seemed to attract enemy attention. Among many attempts to disguise it the method shown, of painting half of the underside in a paler colour, was the most popular. (Art by Peter Sarson, © Osprey Publishing)

Tripoli is a Cromwell VIII Type F that started life as a Cromwell VI. It is shown here in company with Comets of 40th Royal Tank Regiment (23rd Armoured Brigade) on parade in Liverpool. Later still this tank became a Charioteer.

There are two instances of Charioteer being up-gunned to take the 105mm weapon that had replaced the 20-pdr in Centurion. Trials at Shoeburyness and Kirkcudbright in 1960 showed that despite the extra recoil force, believed to be too strong for such a light hull, the gun worked well with no detrimental effect. A British Army team sent out to the Lebanon in 1972 to examine a 105mm Charioteer apparently converted out there – using electric, instead of hydraulic, turret traverse – found the tank in such a poor state of repair that no sensible results could be achieved.

COMET 1 ARMOURED MAINTENANCE VEHICLE

Almost certainly the last manifestation of Comet in a service role was the Armoured Maintenance Vehicle employed by the Army of the Republic of South Africa. Note the word 'maintenance' as distinct from 'recovery'. The Comet AMV prototype was

FV4101 CHARIOTEER, 3rd TANK REGIMENT, JORDANIAN ROYAL ARMOURED CORPS, 1960

Following service with the British Territorial Army, 189 of the 442 Cromwell tanks converted to Charioteers were sold abroad. Austria took 82, Finland finished up with 38, Jordan 49 and Lebanon 20. The Jordanian tanks were among the most potent AFVs in the Middle East when they joined the Arab Legion in 1954, but they were worse than obsolete by the time of the 1967 Six-Day War and those that survived the Israeli counter-attack were passed to Lebanon where, following their civil war, some were taken over by the Palestine Liberation Organization.

The artwork shows a Jordanian tank fitted with the B-type 20-pdr gun, identified by the concentric fume extractor half way down the barrel. (Art by Peter Sarson, © Osprey Publishing)

developed by the Orange Free State Command Workshops at Bloemfontein in 1978. Once this vehicle had been evaluated it became one of three Comet AMVs to enter service with the South African Army in 1980. It was a dramatic conversion with a Continental V12 air-cooled engine linked to an Allison three-speed automatic gearbox replacing the original drive train. The turretless tank had a crew of four, a powerful Hydrovane hydraulic crane at the rear and a cradle capable of carrying a spare Continental diesel engine for the Olifant tank, South Africa's extensively modified Centurion. In addition to a range of tools, lubricants and water, the AMV carried welding and cutting equipment and its role was clearly to undertake maintenance on disabled Olifants in the field; it probably lacked the stamina to recover one in the usual way. The Comets were retired in 1985 when new, wheeled Armoured Maintenance Vehicles entered service.

Cromwell VIII Tripoli in its new guise as Charioteer 01ZW29. From this angle the turret looks perfectly reasonable while the 20-pdr gun appears positively massive. External stowage has not been fitted; normally there would be a towing cable at the front and camouflage netting on the sides of the turret, but the barrel clamp, used to secure the gun when the turret is reversed, is visible at the back of the hull. This tank ultimately went to Jordan.

CONCLUSION

In a clearing alongside a road in Thetford Forest, a Cromwell tank can be found, perched on a brick plinth. It is a memorial to the 7th Armoured Division, the Desert Rats, who trained in this area in the months leading up to D-Day in 1944. Sitting up there in the weather the tank looks small, with its narrow tracks and box-like turret; it does not dominate the scene, as some of its larger American or German contemporaries might. And yet it did the job.

CROMWELL AFV FAMILY SPECIFICATIONS 1942–54

	Cavalier Mk.I	Centaur Mk.IVD	Cromwell Mk.IVC	Cromwell Mk.VIIwE	Challenger Mk.I	Comet Mk.I	Avenger	Charioteer Mark 7F
Crew	5	5	5	5	5	5	4	4
Weight, laden (tons)	25.25	27.15	27.5	28	32.5	32.7	31	28.5
Engine	Liberty IV	Liberty V	Meteor	Meteor	Meteor	Meteor	Meteor	Meteor
Horsepower at rpm	410 at 1,700	395 at 1695	600 at 2550	600 at 2550	600 at 2550	600 at 2550	600 at 2550	600 at 2550
Power/weight, bhp/ton	16.23	14.2	22.1	21.42	18.5	18	22	21.05
Max road speed (mph)	22.5	27.3	38.75	32	32	32	32.3	32
Average cross-country speed (mph)		12.5	16.6	16	20	14	20	16
Fuel consumption (road/ cross-country mpg)		1.44/0.63	1.43/0.76	1.4/0.7		1.0/0.65		1.4/0.7
Range (roads/cross-country, miles)	100/n/k	167/73	165/88	165/88	150/70	125/70	105/n/k	150/70
Max gradient (degrees)		24	24	24	31	35	31	24
Vertical step)	3ft 0in	3ft 0in	3ft 0in	3ft 0in	3ft 2in	3ft 0in	3ft 0in	3ft 0in
Trench crossing	7ft 6in	7ft 9in	7ft 9in	7ft 9in	10ft 3in	8ft	8ft 6in	7ft 9in
Fording depth (flaps open/shut)	4ft 0in	3ft 5in/4ft 6in	3ft 5in/4ft 6in	3ft 7in/4ft 8in	3ft 5in/4ft 6in	3ft 8in/4ft 9in	3ft 0in/4ft 0in	3ft 7in/4ft 8in
DIMENSIONS								
Length gun forward	21ft 1in	21ft 4in	20ft 9in	21ft 4in	26ft 3in	24ft 6in	28ft 7in	29ft 0in
Length, hull	20ft 9½in	20ft 9in	20ft 9in	20ft 9in	23ft 6in	21ft 3/8in	24ft 3in	20ft 9in
Width overall	9ft 6½in	9ft 6½in	10ft ¾in	10ft ¾in	10ft ¾in	10ft 1½in	10ft 0in	10ft ¾in
Height overall	7ft 10in	7ft 10in	7ft 10in	7ft 10in	9ft 5in	8ft 9in	7ft 3in	8ft 6in
Ground clearance	16in	16in	16in	18in	16in	19in	18in	18in
Ground contact length	12ft 7in	12ft 3in	12ft 3in	12ft 3in	14ft 9¼in	12ft 3in	14ft 9¼in	12ft 3in
Track width	14in	14in	14in	15½in	15½in	18in	15½in	15½in
FIREPOWER								
Main armament	6-pdr	95mm	75mm	75mm	17-pdr	77mm	17-pdr	20-pdr
Ammunition (main)	74	46	75	75	51	61	55	25
Secondary armament	2x Besa	1x Besa (RMASG)	2x Besa	2x Besa	1x Browning	2x Besa	nil	1x Browning
Ammunition (secondary)	4,950	4,950	4,950	4,950	20 boxes	5,170	Nil	14 boxes
Elevation/depression	+20/-12.5	+20/-12.5	+20/-12.5	+20/-12.5	+20/-10	+20/-12		+10/-5
Power traverse	Hydraulic	Hydraulic	Hydraulic	Hydraulic	Metadyne	Electric	Metadyne	Hydraulic
PROTECTION								
HULL (mm)	(riveted)	(riveted)	(riveted)	(welded)	(welded)	(welded)	(welded)	(riveted)
Visor plate	64	64	64	101	90	76	64	64
Glacis plate	20	25	25	30	30	32	30	25
Nose plate	57	57	57	82	82	63	57	57
Toe plate	25	25	25	25	25	25	25	25
Upper side	32	32	32	44	51	32	44	32
Lower side (inner)	14	14	14	14	14	14	14	14
Lower side (outer)	32	25	25	32	14	29	32	25
Rear upper	38	25	25	38	38	32	38	25
Rear lower	32	32	32	32	32	32	32	32
Roof	14	14	14	20	14	25	20	14
Floor	6 + 8	6 + 8	6 + 8	10	10	14	10	14
TURRET (mm)	(bolted)	(bolted)	(bolted)	(bolted)	(welded)	(welded)	(welded)	(welded)
Nose casting/mantlet	n/a	n/a	n/a	n/a	102	101	64	n/a
Front	64	64	64	90	88	101	64	30
Sides	51	51	51	51	40	63	40	25 & 20
Rear	44	44	44	44	40	57	40	30
Roof	20	20	20	20	20	25	10	16
Inner plates	12.7	12.7	12.7	12.7	n/a	n/a	n/a	n/a

Once a Cromwell IV Type E, reworked to a Mark 7 and now an abandoned wreck in Korea in company with a Churchill Mark VII of 7th Royal Tank Regiment.

There is an old country saying that applies to almost any implement – that it is not the tool but 'the man behind un' that counts. This must be true of the Cromwell; it underwent a long period of preparation to the point that it was virtually out of date when it first went into action. Yet it led three British and one Polish armoured divisions, and a Czech brigade to victory in Europe. Good or bad this must be due in no small part to 'the men behind un'.

CHAPTER 8

OTHER TYPES

A17 TETRARCH, A25 HARRY HOPKINS, A33 EXCELSIOR, AND A39 TORTOISE

A17 TETRARCH

The idea that a light tank should carry a weapon larger than a heavy machine gun seems to have occurred to Vickers-Armstrongs shortly before World War II. Vickers had first fitted a 40mm (2-pdr) turret to the chassis of a Light Tank Mark VI in 1935, and a year later fitted a turret armed with their own 40mm gun to a commercial light tank which enjoyed some success. But a new tank with a larger turret for two men, mounting a 40mm gun and a co-axial machine gun, was not considered until a bit later, around 1937.

The tank began life as a private venture under the code PR, which has sometimes been interpreted as 'Purdah'. It was armed with Vickers' own version of the 2-pdr gun, a semi-automatic weapon, plus a co-axial Vickers machine gun. However, there was always an idea of interesting the War Office in these private designs, so an alternative was shown featuring a dummy War Office 2-pdr and a co-axial Besa machine gun. The War Office was uncertain how to classify it. Its armament and 16mm of armour qualified it as a cruiser tank, although a turret for only two men was reckoned to be inadequate for service use. The term Light Cruiser was considered, as it was later for the American M3 Light Tank, but in the end, under the General Staff specification A17, it was accepted as the Light Tank Mark VII and given the name 'Tetrarch', which was a Roman form of government headed by a four-man council.

The Tetrarch had two novel features. Firstly, the engine was a horizontally opposed, 12-cylinder unit, water-cooled: Henry Meadows' MAT engine of 165hp. The other unique feature was the suspension-cum-steering system which featured four large, dish-shaped road wheels on each side, working against hydro-pneumatic struts and designed in such a way that they would all turn, gently bending the track in the process and enabling the tank to negotiate a minimum 94ft-radius turn without having to revert to skid-steering. This system was the brainchild of Leslie

Vickers-Armstrongs' original prototype for the PR light tank that later became Tetrarch. Note that it is fitted with the Vickers 40mm gun and co-axial Vickers machine gun.

Little, a brilliant engineer who had taken over as Vickers-Armstrongs' chief tank designer following the sudden death of Sir John Carden in 1935. So enamoured was Mr Little with this steering system that he wanted to try it on a larger tank, although this proved impossible. It was still possible to skid-steer for tighter turns, even on the Tetrarch, using the handbrake lever as a steering stick. The wheels themselves were armoured to improve protection for the chassis of the tank. Drive from the engine passed through a five-speed gearbox into a regular differential, the rearmost wheels on each side acting as drive sprockets. It is said that the tank could run on its wheels, without the aid of tracks, like a Christie tank, but this cannot be confirmed.

The same hull from the same angle but now fitted with wooden representations of the approved War Office armament; the Ordnance Quick Firing Two-Pounder (40mm) and a co-axial 7.92mm Besa air-cooled machine gun.

OPPOSITE Another Tetrarch inside a Hamilcar.

The driver at the front had a conventional steering wheel for doing large-radius turns, but his cab was so narrow it proved impossible to hold the wheel in the normal way. Instead the driver was taught to hold the wheel at the bottom and, since steering anyway required a lot of effort, this was not always easy. The tank had a top speed on the road of 40mph. The turret was not unlike that fitted to the Daimler armoured car with a sort of 'sunshine roof' hatch at the back. It mounted the 2-pdr anti-tank gun with a Besa 7.92mm machine gun on the right. The 2-pdr could also be fitted with the 'squeeze bore' Littlejohn adaptor which increases the muzzle velocity and improved armour-piercing performance.

Perhaps because Vickers-Armstrongs was so focused upon building the Valentine tank, Tetrarch production was switched to the Metropolitan-Cammell Carriage & Wagon Company at Birmingham. Here they encountered problems with the cooling system but no sooner was that solved then the factory was bombed heavily. The production line was destroyed with only 20 out of a total of 170 tanks completed. It was some time before production could be resumed.

Twenty Tetrarchs were donated to the Russian Red Army in 1941, and were used briefly in southern Russia, where it was not so cold, but they were not a lot of use. Among the tanks landed on Madagascar in May 1942's Operation Ironclad were six Tetrarchs belonging to B Special Service Squadron, Royal Armoured Corps. At least one A17 was tested in the Middle East but the type was never used out there, and in fact the Tetrarch had to wait until the evening of D-Day for its moment of glory. Eight Tetrarchs, some equipped as close support tanks and armed with 3in howitzers, were flown across the English Channel in Hamilcar gliders, which had been specially designed to carry the 7.5-ton tanks. Serving with 6th Airborne Reconnaissance Regiment, they were to support the British airborne forces that had landed that morning, but coming down on fields already strewn with discarded parachutes many were disabled by getting parachute lines tangled around their running gear. Those that did get into action were quickly taken out by German anti-tank guns, revealing what should have been known already – that light tanks dating from 1940 had no place on a 1944 battlefield. Even so, the rumour that tanks had landed behind them worried German forces making for the coast.

A Tetrarch inside a General Aircraft Hamilcar glider is inspected by General Montgomery. Notice the line on the front for forcing the door open when it has landed.

A25 HARRY HOPKINS

Harry Hopkins was President Roosevelt's special adviser who got on very well with Winston Churchill. But why he should have a British tank named after him is not known.

A25 Harry Hopkins, or the Light Tank Mark VIII, was an improved version of the Tetrarch with which it shared the same engine (now reduced to 148hp) and the same steering system, albeit now hydraulically assisted to make steering easier. Although some sources say that it also had the same wheels, they are clearly a different pattern, except for the drive sprocket.

Although it still had a three-man crew, the hull was larger and roomier with side escape hatches for the driver and thicker armour (38mm maximum), and it weighed 8.5 tons. The turret was also a different shape, with more elbow room for the loader, but it shared the same armament. Although 99 production tanks were built by the

BELOW LEFT The prototype of Harry Hopkins, the Light Tank Mark VIII. Note the sloping rear of the turret.

BELOW A photograph taken in Cairo in 1947. The Harry Hopkins is parked up with its turret reversed and the 2-pdr gun on high elevation. The tank may have been sent out there for Middle East trials in a hot climate.

A front view of a service tank, showing the driver's position and the armament layout.

Metropolitan-Cammell Carriage & Wagon Company, none was ever issued for service use. Production was not completed until 1944, by which time the era of the light tank was virtually over. A modified version of the chassis was used for the Alecto self-propelled gun which did see service.

A33 EXCELSIOR

The version of A33 built for the Americans, with uncharacteristic British markings, on display outside Lulworth Camp.

Designs for Assault Tanks seem to have dominated the middle years of World War II; A28, A31 and A32 were all assault tank designs based on the Cromwell, and although some lasted a while, none was ever built. A33 was slightly different in that two prototypes were built, again along Cromwell lines, but up-armoured and with a new style of suspension. Indeed, it seems to have been considered as a replacement for the Churchill, which at that time had failed to display its potential and was destined for replacement, if something suitable could be found.

A33 was to be built by the English Electric Company at Stafford. Although it looked like the Cromwell it featured armour to a maximum thickness of 114mm and was powered by a Rolls-Royce Meteor engine driving through a Merritt-Brown transmission. It is reported as weighing about 45 tons, was armed with the 6-pdr (75mm) gun and had a five-man crew. The real differences were the suspension, which on Pilot A was similar to the American horizontal volute spring system, and the American-style tracks, covered by side skirting

The British version of A33 seen after the war, outside the Tank Museum, with a sign fitted over the turret. Notice that the stowage bin on the nearside rear track guard shows signs of damage.

plates that stopped below the track guards rather along the lines of the American heavy tank M6. Pilot B on the other hand had a suspension known as the RL type, a joint design by Rolls-Royce and the LMS Railway, with British-style tracks, and in this case the skirting plates covered the top run of the tracks and met the track guards.

The idea was to send Pilot A to the United States in exchange for an American Locomotive Company T14 assault tank, so that they could be compared and the better one used as an assault tank by both armies. In the end Pilot A, which mounted a 6-pdr gun, was first subjected to two 1,000-mile trial runs across country in Britain, the second of which effectively wore it out. In the end it did not matter, as the Americans lost interest in the Assault Tank project while in Britain the ultimate success of the Churchill tank rendered it unnecessary. Pilot B, which mounted the 75mm gun, was relegated to the Tank Museum along with the T14, where they can both still be seen.

A39 TORTOISE

An album in the archive of the Tank Museum contains a series of drawings of proposed AFVs, starting with AT1 on 13 May 1943 and culminating with AT16 dated 5 February 1944. Although AT seems to stand for Assault Tanks, implying a vehicle with relatively heavy armour, only AT1 appears to be fitted with a turret in the normal sense. Apart from a few with odd combinations of armament, including multiple machine guns, flamethrowers and mortars, the rest are essentially self-propelled guns – although styled as tanks which justifies their inclusion here. The album appears to have been compiled by Nuffield Mechanizations (formerly Nuffield Mechanization & Aero) so we assume all the designs are theirs.

Tortoise P1, the first prototype, not yet fitted with machine guns or smoke dischargers.

We do not even know how many of these drawings were shown to the Department of Tank Design, although since none were ever built, any that were shown were rejected. All we know is that on 23 December 1943 members of the Tank Board, having inspected a drawing of AT15A, said that such a heavy machine required a weapon larger than the 17-pdr gun shown and suggested one based on the 3.7in anti-aircraft gun; this would become AT16 which was submitted on 5 February 1944.

Nor do we know for sure who in the Nuffield Organisation was behind the project. Lord Nuffield himself is a likely candidate, although he would not have liked the Rolls-Royce Meteor engine. Most probably it was Sir Miles Thomas who was the company's interface with the Ministry of Supply. We do also know that the project was a favourite of Duncan Sandys MP, who besides being Secretary of State for War also happened to be the Prime Minister's son-in-law.

Tortoise P3 from above, before any weapons have been installed but offering a good view of the rotating machine-gun turret on top.

The 3.7in anti-aircraft gun was now being referred to as the 37-pdr in this role, although investigations soon proved that as an anti-tank gun its performance would be no better than the 17-pdr firing new ammunition. A version firing a slightly lighter round that would give improved performance was decided upon; this new weapon would be a 94mm gun with a muzzle velocity of 2,880ft/sec, and would be known as the 32-pdr. It would appear in prototype form as a towed anti-tank gun and in a self-propelled mount to be known as Tortoise. In the tank the gun was mounted at the front, passing through the front of the hull via an enormous ball mounting; elevation and traverse were accomplished in the normal way, although the ball mounting permitted traverse at any degree of elevation, or vice-versa. The gun therefore had an arc of fire of 40 degrees at the front (20 degrees either side of the centre line) and an elevation of 20 degrees above horizontal and depression of 10 degrees below. For travelling the gun barrel rested in a cradle attached to the forward part of the hull.

That Tortoise would be large was inevitable, but in fact it broke all the rules. It was too wide to travel by rail, or cross any existing Bailey Bridge. It was even too wide to pass through the bows of any existing landing craft. It was 33ft long including the gun, 12ft 10in wide and 10ft tall. This made it difficult to move by road on a transporter, and with a top speed of 12mph, long distance trips on its tracks were out of the question.

The entire front of the vehicle and the fighting compartment was formed from one enormous casting, with separate panels forming the roof and another one at the front. The casting itself was heavy and an awkward shape, although we do not know where it was cast or how it was transported. Tortoise was powered by a 650hp Rolls-Royce Meteor V engine, built under Rover Company parentage, and linked to a Merritt-Brown combined gearbox and steering unit. The machinery was all mounted under armour in the back, driving the rear sprockets.

The suspension comprised four bogies on each side, and each bogie comprised four rollers of relatively small diameter running on broad rubber tyres. Each bogie was linked to a system of twin torsion bars; even the two wheels at one end of a bogie were designed to lift independently, although why this should be necessary is not explained. Track links were 36in wide. Thick armoured side skirts were brought down to protect the suspension. The total weight of the completed vehicle was 78 tons.

Tortoise had a crew of seven, including a commander; a driver; a front machine-gunner seated to the left of the driver but ahead of the commander, who had a Besa machine gun that fired through the front of the hull to the left of the main gun; and a second machine-gunner in charge of a pair of Besa machine guns in a rotating turret situated on top of the tank, behind the driver. This is not an anti-aircraft turret as stated elsewhere, since the guns only elevated to 15 degrees, but simply for dealing with personnel and soft-skinned vehicles that came within range. The main gun was served by a gunner and two loaders. Two-piece ammunition was supplied; loading procedures would depend on whether the loaders were using the Royal Armoured Corps technique, where each loader was responsible for loading a projectile and charge, or the Royal Artillery technique where each man was responsible for loading one item only.

Production fell seriously behind schedule. The original plan was to have 25 vehicles ready for service by September 1945, but when this proved impossible the order was reduced to the point where, in the end, five prototypes were built in 1946 (not six as stated elsewhere). One of these, without a gun, was used to test heavy-duty mine-clearing equipment.

Movement by road was always difficult. Here the Tortoise proceeds slowly on a trailer hauled by a pair of Diamond T tractors – an object of curiosity, liable to hold up other traffic.

SELECT BIBLIOGRAPHY

Anon, *A Squadron Diary 7th Royal Tank Regiment* (1945)

Anon, *The Story of 79th Armoured Division* (1945)

Anon, 79th *Armoured Division Final Report* (1945)

Anon, *A Short History of the 51st Royal Tank Regiment*, C.M.F. (1946)

Anon, *Contribution to Victory*, AEC Ltd (c. 1946)

Anon, *Final Report of the Specialised Armour Establishment Royal Armoured Corps, War Office* (1951)

Courage, G., *History of the 15th/19th King's Royal Hussars 1939–1945*, Gale & Polden (1949)

Fitzroy, Olivia, *Men of Valour (VIIIth Hussars) 1929–1957*, private publication (1961)

Jones, Keith, *Sixty Four Days of a Normandy Summer*, St Edmundsbury Press (1990)

Knight, Colonel C. R. B., *Historical Record of The Buffs Royal East Kent Regiment 1919–1948*, The Medici Society (1951)

Miller, Charles, *History of the 13th/18th (Queen Mary's Own) Hussars 1927–1947*, Chrisman Bradshaw (1949)

Ness, Leland S., *Jane's World War II Tanks and Fighting Vehicles: The Complete Guide*, Harper Collins (2002)

Perrett, Bryan, *The Valentine in North Africa 1942–43*, Ian Allan (1972)

Robotham, W. A., *Silver Ghost and Silver Dawn*, Constable (1970)

Sellar, R. J. B., *The Fife and Forfar Yeomanry 1919–1956*, William Blackwood & Sons (1960)

Taylor, Daniel, *Villers-Bocage Through the Lens, After the Battle* (1999)

Townsin, Alan, *AEC*, Ian Allan (1998)

Wilson, Andrew, *Flame Thrower*, William Kimber (1956)

INDEX

References to images are in **bold**.

A

B

C

D

E

F

G

H

I

J

K

L

M

N

O

P

R

S

T

U

V